The Virtual Marshall McLuhan

The Virtual
Marshall McLuhan

DONALD F. THEALL

WITH A HISTORICAL APPENDIX
BY EDMUND CARPENTER

McGill-Queen's University Press
Montreal & Kingston · London · Ithaca

© McGill-Queen's University Press 2001
ISBN-13: 978-0-7735-2119-3   ISBN-10: 0-7735-2119-4 (cloth)
ISBN-13: 978-0-7735-3154-3   ISBN-10: 0-7735-3154-8 (paper)
Legal deposit first quarter 2001
Bibliothèque nationale du Québec

Printed in Canada on acid-free paper
First paperback edition 2006

This book was first published with the help of a
grant from the Humanities and Social Sciences
Federation of Canada, using funds provided by the
Social Sciences and Humanities Research Council
of Canada.

McGill-Queen's University Press acknowledges the
financial support of the Government of Canada
through the Book Publishing Industry Development
Program (BPIDP) for its activities. It also acknowledges the support of the Canada Council for the
Arts for its publishing program.

Canadian Cataloguing in Publication Data

Theall, Donald F., 1928–
    The virtual Marshall McLuhan

    Includes bibliographical references and index.
    ISBN-13: 978-0-7735-2119-3   ISBN-10: 0-7735-2119-4 (bnd)
    ISBN-13: 978-0-7735-3154-3   ISBN-10: 0-7735-3154-8 (pbk)
    1. McLuhan, Marshall, 1911–1980.   2. Mass media
    specialists—Canada—Biography.   I. Title.
    P92.5.M24T44 2001   302.23'092   C00-901053-X

Typeset in 10/12 Sabon by True to Type

To Three McLuhanesque Friends and Colleagues

DUŠAN MAKAVEJEV
Cinéaste Extraordinaire – Poet, Satirist,
and Master of the Human Comedy

JACQUES LANGUIRAND
Modernist Pythagorean Poet, Broadcaster,
and Multi-media Artist,

BRIAN MOREL
Master Pedagogue, Co-conspirator,
and Guide in Media Convergence

Contents

Preface and Acknowledgments

The Virtual Marshall McLuhan arose from a number of serendipitous events. First, meeting Robert Dobbs, who shared a common interest in James Joyce's later writings and in Marshall McLuhan. That meeting occurred during the time that McLuhan was again coming to attention through his adoption by the "Wired" world, beginning with Stuart Brand's *The Media Lab* in the mid 1980s. In 1992 I published a paper entitled "Beyond the Orality/Literacy Dichotomy: James Joyce and the Prehistory of Cyberspace" in *Postmodern Culture*, which clearly raised the relationship of James Joyce and McLuhan's pre-vision of digital culture. As a result of that paper I made contact with Darren Tofts, Lawrence James, Michael Groden, and others interested in Joyce and Hypermedia. In the mid-1990s two invitations to participate in conferences in New York City, one, co-sponsored by NYU and Columbia and at the invitation of Sylvere Lotringer and Sande Cohen, on "French Theory in North America" where I spoke of McLuhan as a precursor of French theory in North America; and the other, on McLuhan at Fordham University and at the invitation of Lance Strate, chair of Media Ecology, renewed and stimulated my interest in the importance of McLuhan's unique role in the final decades of the twentieth century. During the same period I met Adrienne Wortzel in New York, a generous and perceptive artist, whom I first encountered through her web page. That encounter and those meetings further increased my interest in revisiting McLuhan. These events not only rekindled a need to situate McLuhan within a context contemporary with his own development as an acute observer of the rise of digitalization, but they brought to my attention the extent to which McLuhan's canonization was deflecting attention from what was probably most important to him – the humanities, the arts, a Catholic intellectual inheritance and apocalyptic religious faith, the university wit of Britain as revised in the *New Yorker*, and the power of satire as critique. Perhaps most important was to free Marshall from being regarded as a theorist – postmodern or otherwise – since he himself contested such identification. It is possible that, if he had lived long enough, he would have been intrigued by cognitive science; but like all techno-science it would have become a target for his modernist satiric ambivalence. Added to this were attacks on my earlier work on McLuhan by an "official" biographer and allegations that I had been part of a demonization of McLuhan that led to his decline in attention from the mid 1970s until the 1990s.

Perhaps most important, though, was meeting again with Edmund ("Ted") Carpenter, the co-founder of the original Culture and Communication seminars and founder of *Explorations* during visits to New York in the mid-1990s, and then reading his recollections of McLuhan as they appear in Appendix B of this volume. We both felt that there was much to be told of the seminal period of McLuhanism, the 1950s and early 1960s, and I began to realize that an account of McLuhan involving my knowledge of him during that period would have historical value. Since I had had a close association with McLuhan, my thesis director and colleague for a crucial period from 1950 to 1965, and since he had in the 1950s been a close friend and godparent to my first son, it seemed important to put in perspective those aspects of the history and biography which had not come to light. So *The Virtual McLuhan* was created. Subsequent to my first book on McLuhan, *The Medium Is the Rear View Mirror: Understanding McLuhan,* and some articles about him in the 1980s, I never expected to write about him again after returning to my main interests in communication, the arts, and literature (particularly contemporary art and literature), but the events of the 1990s made it imperative to re-conceptualize Marshall McLuhan within the values he himself espoused and to present him as the complex, contradictory and conflictual person he was – a genius, human, warm, witty, sometimes arrogant and sometimes insecure but always perceptive and penetratingly intuitive.

In such a project the debts are manifold, since this story began over half a century ago. A particular debt is owed to Ted Carpenter. Colleagues at Toronto during the 1950s and 1960s who either in the past and/or the present have been of assistance include Patricia Bruckmann, Lawrence Dewan, Dennis Duffy, and Fred Flahiff who, as a lifelong friend, has been in a continual dialogue with me about Marshall. Many other colleagues at St Michael's College, particularly the late Very Rev. L.K. Shook, c.s.b, the late Rev. John Kelly, c.s.b., and Rev. John Madden, aided in my understanding of issues raised here. A particular thanks is owing to the late Arnold Rockman with whom I discussed and debated about McLuhan over four decades. Later colleagues at McGill and associated with the National Film Board–McGill Summer School of Media in the late 1960s and early 1970s deserve mention, particularly Mark Slade, Terry Ryan, Hugo McPherson, and Peter Ohlin, but so do the participants of those schools as well as colleagues and participants in a seminar at York University in 1965–66 on the New Media. Contacts with David Crowley, John Fekete, David Mitchell, and Paul Heyer since the 1960s have contributed substantially to my understanding of the issues of culture, technology, and communication in which McLuhan was involved.

This particular work was greatly assisted by those who read, commented, and criticized the manuscript in its early stages: Ted Carpenter, William Toye, Gregory Downing, Robert Dobbs, and Fred Flahiff. Lawrence James and Darren Tofts also added comments and encouragements. The strength of this book is owing to their gift of assistance, but the limitations are my responsibility. Special encouragement came from Virgil Duff of the University of Toronto Press. This work also received encouragement from Frank Zingrone through his sensitive awareness in reminding me of the complexity of my own relations with McLuhan.

The University of Toronto Library was extremely helpful in the preparation of this work, particularly Lari Langford of the Access and Information Department at the Robarts Library. Michael Edmunds, director of the Information Commons at the library, was also helpful and encouraging. My daughter, Margaret Theall, read the manuscript and offered suggestions and support, as did my son John Theall, in Winnipeg. My son Lawrence Theall (of the legal firm, Fernandez, Hearn and Theall) as a legal scholar provided useful discussion on a number of issues concerning publishing as it related to this manuscript. Ken Brown and the entire computer services operation at Trent University were also of important assistance during the period I was working on this project.

The Social Science and Humanities Research Council and the Aid to Scholarly Publishing Program of the Humanities and Social Science Federations of Canada supported the research and the publication of this work respectively. The staff of the McGill University Press and its director, Philip Cercone, and Joan McGilvray and Brenda Prince were most supportive and helpful.

As ever, last but far from least, the collaboration of my wife, Joan, in every stage of the conception, writing, and editing of this work is the primary factor in its coming to be. Apart from her immense direct contribution and the sustaining great food she always prepares, without her encouragement, reassurance, support, and presence, it is very likely this work might never have come to be.

Donald Theall
Peterborough, January 2000

Parts of this book have appeared in The *Canadian Journal of Communications* and in the *Canadian Journal of Social and Political Thought*. A shorter version of the chapter on French Theory will appear in a forthcoming publication of the proceedings of the NYU/Columbia University conference on French Theory in North America. *Media International Australia* will publish a shorter version of the Introduction in a forthcoming special issue on Marshall McLuhan. Edmund Carpenter has kindly allowed the publication of his historical reminiscences on McLuhan and the early 1950s as Appendix B, a truncated version of which appeared in *Canadian Notes and Queries* 46 (Spring 1992).

Introduction to the Paperback Edition

The Virtual Marshall McLuhan stresses the "poetic image" that Marshall McLuhan crafted to support his persona as an intellectual committed to a unique perceptualist poetic vision of everyday life in the post-electric, new media world. This persona – the "virtual" McLuhan – is very different from both what we might call the "real" Marshall McLuhan – a devout, dedicated, Roman Catholic academic deeply enmeshed in the humanistic and theological orientation of the classical era and the high middle ages – and the "imaginary" McLuhan created by various "McLuhanisms" and "McLuhanites."

McLuhan approached the communication, culture, and technology of the 1950s through a poetic vision, essentially a schizo-analytic perspective, that allowed him to generate the witty, comic, poetic images that permeated his work from *The Mechanical Bride* to his posthumous works, *Laws of Media* and *The Global Village*.[1] One major aspect of his schizoid approach to the contemporary post-electric, new media world was his close affinity with both Wyndham Lewis and James Joyce. His approach and his complex use of Lewis and Joyce are part of an extremely complex problem that involves aspects of his personal encounter with Lewis in Canada and the U.S. in the 1940s; religious issues; questions about tradition, modernism – particularly postmodernism – and the rapidly changing technological world; Canadian nationalism; and his personal history.

The Virtual Marshall McLuhan discusses this and also demonstrates McLuhan's commitment to the trivium and quadrivium of the liberal arts with a particular emphasis on grammar and rhetoric, as well as his commitment to the art of poetry and its relationship to techné and to the arts in general, ancient and modern. One of the major aspects of his program throughout his career was to make the history of the liberal arts, the creative arts, and their relation to techné (and hence technology) an immediate part of the reality of the present moment – relevant to the new media and the arts they were engendering. This interest provided him with the technique he used to pursue Ezra Pound's advice in a July 1952 letter: "start looking for credits rather than debts// not matter much where a man GOT what, but what he did with it (or without it) AFTER he got it."[2] McLuhan uses his understanding of the past and his immense knowledge of literature and the arts to demonstrate how those in the present, himself included, were involved with the past.

The "virtual" Marshall McLuhan first appeared in the late 1940s, just after McLuhan completed his doctoral thesis, "Thomas Nashe in the Learning of His Time," at Cambridge University and was beginning work on his first media book, *The Mechanical Bride*. The development of his poetic vision was aided by his encounter with James Joyce's *Finnegans Wake*, which was facilitated by his relationship with the major expatriate Canadian critic of high modernism, Hugh Kenner. In the early 1950s, when McLuhan began a group reading of the *Wake*, he had just discovered the work of Harold Innis, encountered the cybernetics of Norbert Wiener, and was deepening his exploration of Catholic theology (particularly Augustine and Thomas Aquinas), encouraged by personal contact with Etienne Gilson and, to a lesser extent, Jacques Maritain, as well as with their writings.

Through the *Wake* and its involvement in high modernism (W.B. Yeats, Ezra Pound, T.S. Eliot, and Wyndham Lewis) and radical modernism (the avant-garde, Cubists, Dadaists, Futurists, and Vorticists) McLuhan established the crucial links between his history of the liberal arts and poetry and the arts as well as between his theological and humanistic interests and the transformations of communication media in the emerging contemporary world. These interests had, however, been preceded by his encounters with Lewis while teaching in St Louis and later in Windsor (from 1943 to 1945). Lewis, who as part of the character of Shaun the Post is a major presence in *Finnegans Wake*, was one of Joyce's major critics. McLuhan found in Lewis's figure of the satirist as enemy who engages in "blasting and bombardiering" the middle-brows a useful base for his own approach.

It is clear that McLuhan's fundamental project in approaching mass media and everyday life in the post-electric world of new media was shaped initially by Lewis and his interpretations of early avant-garde art, since McLuhan did not become deeply involved with Joyce's major works until after he began *The Mechanical Bride*. In the 1940s McLuhan immersed himself in Lewis's writings; by the time he encountered *Finnegans Wake* in his readings with Hugh Kenner in the mid 1940s he had already absorbed most of what Lewis had written before the 1940s. Lewis's writings, particularly *Time and Western Man,* were probably the primary source of his growing interest in popular culture and media that was first expressed in *The Mechanical Bride* and in articles such as his piece in *Neurotica* on "Time, Life and Fortune."

Parallelling his personal interest in Lewis was McLuhan's complex religious attitude. Lewis, in contradistinction from Joyce, who was an apostate and a heretic, ultimately never rejected, though he seriously questioned, a belief in Christianity. His situation closely parallels McLuhan's, a Baptist converted to Catholicism and totally committed to the Church who also embraced and endorsed the ideas of the avant-garde, high modernists, and others who were a-religious, anti-religious, or agnostic. McLuhan apparently adopted Lewis's "transformed moralism," which vitiated his critiques of the contemporary world.

While it is clear that Lewis was a major early influence on McLuhan's perceptual approach to media and everyday culture, many of the key strategies McLuhan developed in the *Bride* and used throughout his writing career, such as his aphoristic style, owed a great deal to other sources as well. Pound shared Lewis's Vorticist direction in the early twentieth century and his use of aphorism influenced McLuhan directly and also through the subsequent influence that Pound had on Eliot. This interest in aphorism, though perhaps most immediately influenced by *Blast* and Vorticism, is also influenced by the headline style of the "Aeolus" section of Joyce's *Ulysses* and the frequent use of aphorisms throughout *Finnegans Wake* and is one of a number of reasons that Alexander Pope's writing, particularly *The Dunciad* and his mock-rhetoric *Peri Bathous or The Art of Sinking in Poetry,* provides a major part of the conclusion to *The Gutenberg Galaxy*.[3]

Through his interest in Joyce, Lewis, and the French *symbolistes,* McLuhan developed an interest in such figures as Duchamp, Picasso, Marinetti, Léger, Schoenberg, Antheil, and many others. All of these interests enabled him to confront the way in which, after the mid-nineteenth century and particularly in the early twentieth century, art began to become once again an important guide to understanding technology and the techno-scientific. *The Virtual Marshall McLuhan* traces the influence of the contemporary world, the early historical world, and the new technologies on McLuhan. It shows how he extended the work of major commentators on arts and technology, such as Sigfreid

Giedion and Lewis Mumford. This was particularly true of Giedion and his wife, Carola Giedion-Welcker, who were close friends of Joyce and knowledgeable participants in the new arts and media, as exemplified in their various writings.[4] It is this complex background that allowed McLuhan to construct his unique poetic persona and awareness, first demonstrated in *The Gutenberg Galaxy* and *Understanding Media*.

A major, implicit thread of *The Virtual Marshall McLuhan* is the interaction between Joyce, Lewis, and the various modernisms and the way these relations affect McLuhan's positions on tactility, the interplay of the senses (with an emphasis on "play"), and the problems of orality, literacy, and print. McLuhan was one of the few to discover that the playful satire on Lewis and on Joyce's own early role as an artist that can be found in the *Wake* is crucial to understanding contemporary problems and to revealing that the orality-literacy (or oral and written) opposition is transcended by the grounding of human communication in tactility and gesture.

McLuhan found both the importance of tactility and its relation to gesture and the Aristotlean-scholastic conception of a *sensus communis* (a common sense through which all the senses interact within the human nervous system) throughout Joyce's work. His discovery occurred in the period between 1950 and 1954 when he was writing his key articles on Joyce.[5] Tactility, he wrote, "the integral sense, the one which brings all others into relation," was "greatly enhanced" by "the new electric environment."[6] In the *Wake* Joyce had developed a complex interplay between the oral, aural, visual, tactile, and intersensory activities of the human body.[7] McLuhan grasped the tactile nature of TV from its treatment in the *Wake*, which led him to elaborate its closer affiliation with the gestural – for "tele-media" implied a projection over distances as well as, in the case of TV, a scanning of the image and its projection as light *through,* rather than light *on,* the screen.

Joyce's complex ambivalence, playing with and revealing aspects of modern media and post-electric culture, led to McLuhan's commitment to *perceptual* revelation as opposed to *conceptual*. Lewis, in spite of his artistic aspects, confronted Joyce as a conceptualist, while Joyce, in spite of his complex intellectuality, remained a "perceptualist." In his schizoid manner, McLuhan embraced Lewis's intellectual critique and moralism, while in his poetic mode he adopted (perhaps with some reservations) Joyce's playful "perceptualism." McLuhan had strong Lewisian biases and yet was attracted by the playful, intellectual complexity of Joyce. While approving of Lewis's moralism and cynicism, he was still seduced by Joyce's playful, poetically based intellectualism. McLuhan's analysis of technology was more advanced than Lewis's, although committed to Lewis's relative comfort with the period in which he lived, whereas Joyce's position was, ultimately, more advanced than McLuhan's, as shown by his success with the avant-garde in the arts such as Cage, Cunningham and Rauschenberg and his overall success: Joyce is probably the top "novelist" of the twentieth century, based on his three major works: *A Portrait of the Artist as a Young Man*, *Ulysses*, and *Finnegans Wake*.

While Joyce may have gone further than McLuhan in his vision of the paramodern, McLuhan has a unique vision of his own that manifests itself through poetic images crafted by interplay within everyday life – the conflicts generated by the world of new media and the evolving techno-cultural world of human communication. McLuhan became a juggler of the video, the verbal, the audio, the tactile, and the interplay of all the senses within the central nervous system of the everyday person. While his poetic practice may have been implicit in Joyce, McLuhan played it out for the broader audience of those whose whole life was governed by the media. He had learned from Lewis that the tribal world was re-emerging in the twentieth century and he intuited that those enmeshed in an electric age lived in an era that was "out of its mind." In this project he was not directly influenced by anyone.

His position was further complicated by the intersection between his religious beliefs and the influence of the history of humanities and humanistic activities. Here the later medieval period (the thirteenth century) was crucial and the writings of Gilson a significant influence on the way he related the scholastic philosophy of Albertus Magnus and, particularly, Thomas Aquinas to the humanistic tradition. This was complemented by his understanding of the way cathedrals represented a marriage of art and technology within the medieval vision. It is here that he discovered his contrast of light *through* as opposed to light *on*, which he then applied to the difference between film and TV, allowing him to show the latter's greater affiliation with tactility.

His knowledge of the later medieval period also allowed him to explore the technology of writing through the manuscripts of scribes. His embrace of Aquinas (which had significant echoes in Joyce, although not in Lewis) was based on his view of Aquinas as fundamentally a humanist using dialectic within a grammatic-rhetorical tradition. Joyce's complex wit was associated with Aquinas's wit as exemplified in his Latin hymnody and in his discussions of theological disputes in his Summae (*Summa Theologica* and *Summa Contra Gentiles*). Both had a major impact on the prose poetics McLuhan developed for a post-new media culture. This play with wit and aphorism continued through Renaissance figures such as Erasmus and Thomas More (who were both Catholics) as well as Rabelais and on into the seventeenth century with Blaise Pascal in his *Pensées* and then into the early eighteenth century with Alexander Pope.

The importance of these past associations and their relation to McLuhan's dedicated commitment to Catholicism as an "apocalyptic" is underlined in two of his three posthumous publications: *Laws of Media*, where the tetrads are consciously associated with "media poetics," which led him to Vico, the last great, pre-electric grammarian to influence James Joyce (and incidentally the most quoted source in *Laws of Media*), and *The Medium and the Light: Reflections on Religion*, a collection of essays and interviews on the Catholic religion and its relevance to the contemporary media world. It is this awareness of the past that makes him a schizoid visionary, for he can embrace Lewis's stance as the enemy and as a contemporary moralist while also evincing a preference for Joyce's powerful radical modernism. The playing out of this tension in the context of his classical and medieval training is the key to understanding his approach to the new media and grasping his penetrating insight that an awareness of the conversion of historic learning to its status in the present moment in time is crucial to being able to understand the ascendancy of arts in the world of modern communications technology.

McLuhan also discovered that the satirists he favoured throughout literary history all participated in modifications and transformations of a genre originally defined by the Roman poet Varro as Menippean satire, which later came to be described as Varronian satires. The great practitioners of this tradition were satiric poets and writers such as Ovid, Erasmus, Dryden, and Pope. The form, as McLuhan observed, was further transformed by Joyce, who described himself as a Menippean satirist – using the original term to acknowledge the founder of the form, Mennipus, the Greek cynic philosopher and poet, although in Joyce, and earlier in Pope and Ovid, this form had moved far from its original cynic foundations. In its modified form it is the shaping principle of McLuhan's prose poetry, particularly in his work following *Understanding Media* (e.g., *The Medium Is the Massage*, *Counterblast* (1969), and *War and Peace in the Global Village*). In these works he brought together his knowledge and understanding of traditions to illuminate the contemporary dilemma of culture and technology. In contrast, Lewis, who looks to the past and mistrusts the modern, is a true cynical post-Menippean satirist.

The Virtual Marshall McLuhan demonstrates that the arts and literature were the crucially relevant grounds from which McLuhan developed his mode of investigation of contemporary media, culture, and technology. His method of investigation provides a poetic technique through which he can create his "percepts" of contemporary culture and avoid the snares of the conceptual and the moralistic. His first experiment with with this technique was in *The Mechanical Bride*, but at the time he still took a moral stance and supplemented his poetic probes with conceptual analysis. It was during the years of *Explorations* and his early culture and communication seminars with Ted Carpenter that he liberated himself from the overtly moralistic and conceptualistic, which made possible his landmark writings, *The Gutenberg Galaxy* (1962) and *Understanding Media* (1964). *The Virtual Marshall McLuhan* elaborates on this in appendices by his lifelong friend Ted Carpenter and his first Ph.D. student, myself, who were both involved in the launching of the seminars and in the formation of McLuhan's mature vision of "understanding media," which was developed in that critical decade

The McLuhan who launched the poetic probing of communication and technology – the "virtual" McLuhan – was committed to exploring the way that contemporary arts, particularly poetry, created a rebirth of the marriage of art and technology that permeated classical poetry and poetic theory and formed the foundation of the *techné*, which permeated the history of the trivium, from Plato to Pope and Sterne, and the high modernists and radical modernists of the first half of the twentieth century. Consequently, some of our deepest understandings of what occurred as a result of the impact of electro-mechanization on contemporary culture emanate from wisdom that has existed for centuries. McLuhan and Joyce reincorporated this wisdom as a vital, living aspect of the present, enabling it to confront the future. A recognition that he had made this confrontation possible is the highest tribute McLuhan himself would have wanted, for he never felt comfortable as a figure affecting the corporate-political force nor did he feel committed to the acceptance of any contemporary political body – even the Church – which is why, although he was a "true believer," his belief was undertaken as an "apocalyptic" with a satirist's view of all power structures.

NOTES

1 The importance of the schizo-analytic approach to understanding the modern movement was articulated by Giles Deleuze in 1982 and further developed in his writings and his collaborations with Félix Guattari.

2 *Letters of Marshall McLuhan*, 232 n 1

3 It is important to note that Pope's works, particularly *The Dunciad Variorum*, are extensively referred to in the final pages of *The Gutenberg Galaxy* where McLuhan obviously shares Pope's vision of the decadence

of print culture, his aphoristic wit as a mode of critique, and his apocalyptic vision as a mode of viewing the cultural "mess." While McLuhan's
direction is most clearly in the mode of Pope, his appreciation early in his
career of the entire satiric-aphoristic (and Senecan) tradition is clearly
shown in the final footnote on page 149 of his thesis on Nashe (the original typed version in the Canadian National Archives), where he mentions
Swift and others as well (The subjects of aphorism, wit, and the tradition
are discussed extensively in my first book on McLuhan, *The Medium Is
the Rear View Mirror*). The difference between Lewis and Joyce in relation to aphorism, a form they both use, is marked by the affinity of
Joyce's play with language with the complex, multi-level wit of Pope's
couplets, which were apparently key for McLuhan in the 1950s and
1960s and certainly remained the dominant feature of his writing
throughout his career.

4 (Gideon, in his book on *Space, Time and Architecture* (explaining the
evolution of modern architecture), his discussion of everyday life as a creative form in *Mechanization Takes Command,* and his two-volume
magnum opus, *The Eternal Present* (vol. 1 *The Beginnings of Art*; vol. 2
The Beginnings of Architecture), explored the same relations between
contemporary art and technology and their grounding in the early history
of the arts as McLuhan.)

5 "Joyce, Aquinas and the Poetic Process"; "Joyce, Mallarmé and the
Press," "James Joyce: Trivial and Quadrivial."

6 Marshall McLuhan and Quentine Fiore, *War and Peace in the Global
Village*, 77.

7 In *Finnegans Wake* the characters of the twin brothers, "Shem the
penman" and "Shaun the post," are central to the action. Shem partly
represents the early literary Stephen Dedalus as Joyce – the artist as a
young man – and Shaun partly represents Lewis. Shem is committed to
the auditory and Shaun to the visual. Anna Livia Plurabelle, their mother,
and her daughter Issy are primarily "tactile." Within the dream of the
virtual dreamer, Joyce as Finnegan, they are all reconciled in the father
figure, Here Comes Everybody.

The Virtual Marshall McLuhan

Prelude: McLuhan's Basic Probes and Perceptions

The following prelude offers a brief discussion of McLuhan's contributions and their significance in the second half of the twentieth century. It is designed primarily for readers who do not have great familiarity with McLuhan and his writings. Readers who grew up after the heyday of McLuhanism (from 1965 to 1975) may also find this a useful prelude to my subsequent expositions. Other readers may choose to skip this section or, preferably, to read it as a Coda to the book following the Conclusion.

Marshall McLuhan, whose major work had been completed by 1970, died on 31 December 1980. Since then his name has become associated with a myth as much as with the life and work he really lived. Consequently, this chapter is primarily useful in providing a brief outline of the ongoing significance of his major contributions, particularly from 1954 until the early 1970s, for those who did not live through those years or are not familiar with McLuhan's contributions to the contemporary scene. It provides some insight into the reasons McLuhan acquired an international reputation among media, politicians, academics, and artists, making him a twentieth-century archetype and culminating in his having become, in the closing decade of the last century, the patron saint of the "Wired World."

At the end of World War Two, TV was in its infancy, the world of mass advertising was just becoming a controversial and dominant presence in society, and talking films were only a little over a decade old and movies in full colour were relatively recent, having first been established in commercial movie theatres in the early 1930s.[1] Computers were scarcely a presence in the mind of the average person, much less among most of the university community. McLuhan, as a Canadian from a small city in the prairies, born in 1911 and growing to adulthood between the two World Wars, was simultaneously lured by two opposing colonial empires – the British, which was just beginning its decline, and the American, which was well on its way to ascendancy. Four of the most important factors that contributed to McLuhan's development from 1930 to 1946 are his intense interest in the earliest history of the teaching of communication in Greece and Rome through the classical educational program for educating orators – the so-called "trivium" of grammar, dialectic (or logic), and rhetoric – the result of his studies for a Cambridge B.A (1936) and years later a PH.D. (1943); his histrionic capabilities as a performer, which had been encouraged by his mother's career as an actress; his conversion to Catholicism, accompanied by readings in G.K.Chesterton and the French Thomist historian of medieval philosophy, Étienne Gilson; and, finally, his life-long career teaching English literature. All of these were mediated by his being a Canadian fascinated with the new North American culture of the United States while also, as an "Anglo" of Irish descent in prewar Canada, essentially distrusting newness and thus seeking "truth" in the British and continental traditions of the Cambridge School of English and the newly emerging Continental histories of the rise of culture from Greece and Rome through the Catholic Middle Ages.

The Cambridge School of English, presided over by F.R. Leavis whose approach had been affected by the semantics and literary theory of C.K. Ogden and I.A. Richards, provided McLuhan's earliest links with literary and artistic modernity, while his Canadian fascination with the new popular culture of the United States – Hearst, Disney, Hollywood, the syndicated comics, tabloids, etc. – provided his grounding in what Gilbert Seldes in the late 1920s had labelled "The Lively Arts." The Cambridge Critics, imported into the United States through the "new criticism" and based initially in the South and at Yale University, led McLuhan to embrace a kind of pragmatic and empirical interpretation of poems, novels, and dramas that was exemplified by interpretations of Edgar Allen Poe, John Keats, Gerard Manley Hopkins, and Elizabethan drama which appeared in the then-dominant "little magazines" of the "new poetry" and the "new criticism."

As a young professor, first in the late 1930s at the University of Wisconsin and then in the early 1940s at St Louis University in St Louis, Missouri (T.S. Eliot's hometown, but in many ways the world of Mark Twain), McLuhan became frustrated trying to teach first year students in required courses how to read English poetry, and began using the technique of analysing the front page of newspapers, comic strips, ads, and the like as poems – applying the new critical techniques he had encountered in the Cambridge school as interpreted through his sense of the history of literature and rhetorical expression and expressed in a histrionic stance reinforced by his natural wit. This new approach to the study of popular culture and popular art forms led to his first major move towards new media and communication and eventually resulted in his first book, *The Mechanical Bride,* which some consider to be one of the founding documents of early cultural studies. While the *Bride* was not initially a success, it introduced one aspect of McLuhan's basic method – using poetic methods of analysis in a quasi-poetic style to analyse popular cultural phenomena – in short, assuming such cultural productions to be another type of poem. While some reviewers, such as *The New Yorker*, one of the popular cultural phenomena analyzed in *The Mechanical Bride*, frivolously rejected McLuhan's work, the prime foundation of his vision had been established. Robert Anton Wilson, author of the *The Illuminatus! Trilogy*, *Schroedinger's Cat*, and *The Masks of the Illuminati*, still considers the opening pages of the *Bride* to be one of the most significant documents of the twentieth century and worth all McLuhan's other work.

Later McLuhan's only reservation about the *Bride* had to do with what he took to be its overt moralism in which he exposed the motives of the major producers of mass culture. But the poetic strategy adapted from the new criticism as a way of dramatizing media as vortices of power was to underlie his work throughout the rest of his career. As a corollary to viewing ads, comics, newspapers, magazines, etc. as such vortices McLuhan applied the image of Poe's mariner – who saved himself by studying the action of the whirlpool and cooperating with it – placing his readers "at the centre of the revolving picture ... where [they] may observe the action that is in progress" and which may suggest to them "many individual strategies" (McLuhan 1951, v). The author's approach, like that of Poe's sailor, is "amusement born of his rational detachment as a spectator." So the *Bride* illustrated yet another aspect of the ongoing McLuhanesque approach to cultural phenomena – the satiric use of wit and the comic as a mode of "tweaking" hidden levels of meaning and complexity from material that seems to be relatively simple – *Blondie*, *Li'l Abner*, the front page of a Hearst tabloid, ads for caskets, laundry soap, or stockings. The essay that provides the book's title, "The Mechanical Bride," comments on an ad for Gotham Gold Stipe nylon stockings. The ad consists of a pair of slim, svelt, stockinged legs (no torso) displayed on a column with the text "on a pedestal." Analysis of the stocking ad immediately follows an essay entitled "Love Goddess Assembly Line" on proportioned girdles and includes an additional nod to Duchamp's famous (then still infamous) works, *Nude Descending a Staircase* and *The Large Glass, or The Bride Stripped Bare by Her Bachelors, Even*.

He expressed his wit and sense of comedy in a photographic layout, headlines and telegraphic aphorisms (one-liners), and a short, quasi-journalistic commentary of a page or so, mimicking and parodying the style of the mass "pop kulch" world he was discussing. Throughout he peppered his "jazzy" commentary with references to major academic studies and quotations from poets and writers such as T.S. Eliot, Wyndham Lewis, John DosPassos, and James Joyce. By challenging and questioning the then-normal type of "social science" discourse created a new mode of quasi-poetic, critical-intellectual satire (an early anticipation of some aspects of cultural studies), underlining a central thesis of the *Bride* that academics, particularly those who studied the new culture and modes of communication, were not themselves coping with the society around them. This anti-academic stance of McLuhan's, which persisted throughout his career, contributed to his profound impact and attracted public intellectuals, artists, and journalists outside the academy and dissidents within it.

The *Bride* also established what was to be another of the central foundations of McLuhan's strategy for understanding technology. He analysed each item he discussed – an individual ad, the front page of *The New York Times*, images from *Blondie*, or the cover of a pocketbook romance novel – as a cultural object or artefact. Using each artefact as a starting point, he treated the entire phenomenon of its production as if it were a poetic text. Working from his classical roots in Aristotle and the rhetoricians he viewed the newspaper as an artefact (a made object, a designed assemblage) which could be interpreted poetically, for a poetic text could be made in words, music, gesture (e.g., mime), etc. Although he would not have thought of it quite this way in 1950, he was treating the popular cultural phenomena of his day as both cultural productions and soft technologies.

At that time this approach offered a startling new insight and attracted a small cult following in academia and among intellectuals. This same approach, which was to last throughout his career, attracted major attention in the later 1950s and the 1960s when he turned his full attention to the media themselves. In *Understanding Media* (1964), for example, all constructed artefacts, whether buildings or clothes, poems or paintings, movies or videos, were included in media and each medium – speech, writing, clocks, roads, the press, radio, TV, automation, etc., – became an artefact susceptible of a "poetic" analysis. Each of these cultural artefacts involving electric technology became the subject of an ambivalent, somewhat satiric, "social scientific" prose poem. Over thirty years later in his posthumous *Laws of Media*, with his son, Eric as co-author, he reiterates that his approach is a "poetic science." Such a procedure permitted McLuhan's commentators a vast amount of freedom in using his material as a take-off point for discussing or criticizing or theorizing or thinking about particular phenomena. Like any poet or cultural producer (e.g., a film director) McLuhan came to mean different things – often radically different things – to those who used his work. Thus he can be embraced by technophiles and technophobes alike, such as Stuart Brand and Neil Postman, respectively, or by critics and artists alike, such as Tom Wolfe and John Cage.

In the *Bride* McLuhan had discovered an intellectual way of dealing with cultural productions, and hence technologies, in terms of their effect as percepts and affects rather than in terms of the concepts they represent. This was the beginning of what were to be famous refrains as related to his work – providing probes for understanding technologies and cultural artefacts. Although the *Bride* was not an immediate success, it did establish McLuhan as a unique analyst of popular culture and it led him to think about relating the research of his PH.D thesis on Thomas Nashe, involving grammar and rhetoric, and the poetics of "pop kulch" of the *Bride* to what was happening in communications throughout North America, as viewed from outside the U.S., for he had returned to Canada and was now teaching in Toronto. Two major publishing events in the techno-mathematical world in the late 1940s had a major impact on McLuhan and almost simultaneously on North America. In 1948 Norbert Weiner's *Cybernetics: Or Control and Communication in the Animal and the Machine* and Claude Shannon and W. Weaver's article "A Mathematical Theory of Communication" were published, underlining the rise of the digital computer and suggesting its ultimate significance for communication, culture, and technology.

By 1950 McLuhan had begun encountering colleagues and graduate students on whom the new "communication revolution" had had an impact. This led to his intuiting the important interaction that would occur between the world of "mass" communication and "popular" culture, and the long term implications of these new mathematical theories of communication and control. This awareness led McLuhan, in collaboration with his colleague Ted Carpenter, a young anthropologist, together with other colleagues from psychology, political economics, and architecture to organize an interdisciplinary seminar in Culture and Communication at the University of Toronto. This was the moment of conception for McLuhan's ultimate birth as an international figure and communication guru and for the multitude of "McLuhanism(s)" that would arise in the second half of the century, as expressed by a variety of conflicting groups who chose to advance McLuhan's perceptions or adapt his insights.

The complexity of McLuhan's poetic explorations of technology, media, and modes of communication and the variety of his disciples, interpreters, enemies, and inspired creators assured McLuhan's ultimate impact in the 1960s but made it difficult to provide an account of what he achieved, since what he contributed were not ideas, arguments, theories, or critiques, but intuitions, perceptions, wandering explorations of unexplored terrain, satiric responses, and poetic reactions. Consequently, to understand McLuhan it is necessary to become like him, a nomad wandering that terrain, and to review the high points of what he encountered and how he perceived and intuited them. Looking back from about 1975, when McLuhan's initial impact had reached a peak and his ongoing relevance could no longer be disputed, the cause of that impact and the problem of explicating it is obvious in the complex contradictions by which McLuhan's poetic drama of media, communication, and technology unfolded. His first moves into the area that was to lead to his ongoing commitment to the interdisciplinary study of culture, technology, and communication using the methods of poetry, Baconian-Viconian science, and the traditional grammarians and rhetoricians began during the three years (1950-53) between the completion of the *Bride* and the launching of the first seminar in Culture and Communication.

McLuhan started to explore a series of questions about communication theory and modern poetry and encouraged his graduate students to pursue research projects in this area. For instance, under his influence I wrote a master's thesis on *Eliot's Theory of Communication* (1951) and a doctoral thesis on *Communication Theory in Modern Poetry: Yeats, Pound, Eliot and Joyce* (1954). Using these poets, their French forerunners and contemporaries, and twentieth-century anthropologists from Fraser, Frobenius, and Malinowski to Sapir, Bateson, and Mead, McLuhan developed a view of communication as participation and transformation, which led eventually to his contrast of what he later called "hot" and "cool" (borrowing the terminology from then-current slang buzzwords) media. As he ultimately articulated it in the late 1950s, a hot medium like radio (at least as McLuhan perceived it) did not encourage participation since its signal was relatively precise or highly defined; on the other hand TV, where the signal was considerably less precise and ill defined or of low definition, required greater participation on the part of the audience to fill in the message. At the time Patrick Watson, TV producer and later president of the Canadian Broadcasting Corporation, said that it didn't matter that Marshall might be wrong about the technical details, his insight pointed toward the greater audience involvement in TV – an insight that Watson's historic, controversial weekly TV program of the 1960s, *This Hour Has Seven Days*, exploited.[2] Watson obviously recognized that McLuhan's poetic vision could not be conceptualized.

So what made McLuhan an international phenomenon? Since he did not conceptualize, it is not possible to provide a set of ideas or concepts. Instead his most significant probes – and the pressing issues of the moment that they dramatized – can be identified. When he wrote the *Bride* the power of the press was an issue, so he demonstrated that the front page was a mosaic arrangement of radically juxtaposed fragments – designed not to inform but to have an effect - an impact similar to a cubist landscape or a symbolist poem. Such an image could reflect the relatively new, growing fragmentation in U.S. society, which he later identified as the result of an age of literacy; reveal the emotional manipulation of the publicist and advertiser; and explore how mechanization had taken command of society through the power of the press. While the increasing power of the press was fairly widely discussed, the affective impact of its form and style were essentially unexplored by university researchers in postwar North America – as shown in the late writings (1948 until his death late in 1952) of the Canadian historian of political economy Harold Innis. Innis, who analysed the effects of the economic, organizational, and technological role of the press on knowledge, was not primarily intereted in the effects of the newspaper itself as an artefact or its affective and rhetorical aspects. (McLuhan had not read the works of Harold Innis before he wrote the *Bride*; but he did read them in 1951–52.)

As the 1950s unfolded, leading up to the publication of his two major works in the 1960s, McLuhan turned his rhetorico-poetic technique to issues that centred around human communication, media, and technology – sensing, but not yet saying, that these areas were rapidly moving together as an inter-related cluster. A few of the probes that were launched then and have now become relative commonplaces are orality and literacy; acoustic space and visual space; participational ("cool") and non-participational media ("hot"); the printed book and lineality; the history of communication as a history of artefactual form (media) rather than content [i.e., history as "the medium is the message]; tactility and the central nervous system; technology and the extension or "outering" of the senses; the interior landscape; the global village and the global metropolis; figure/ground; interface and pattern rather than point of view; technological artefacts as effects; writing, the alphabet, and the printing press as media involving codes; interdisciplinarity vs. specialism; electricity and the encylopedic; paradox and ambivalence.

Fundamentally, all of these probings are inter-related, since they focus on the effects of artefacts, both social and technological, human communications, or media on people. McLuhan, as an article by Carpenter in *Explorations* outlines, first saw that all media and later all technologies are languages. "Each codifies reality differently; each conceals a unique metaphysic."[4] In *The Gutenberg Galaxy* McLuhan shows how this perception of media as languages interrelates with many of the other perceptual fields with which he is dealing: "Languages being that form of technology constituted by dilation or uttering (outering) of all of our senses at once, are themselves immediately subject to the impact or intrusion of any mechanically extended sense. That is, writing affects speech directly, not only its accidence and syntax but also its enunciation and social uses" (McLuhan 1962, 35).[5] So TV as a form of technology expands, amplifies, and extends film, while being itself susceptible of being effected by other "languages," such as the World Wide Web. Just as speech and writing interact, according to McLuhan all modes of communication – in fact, all technologies – interact because they are affecting the senses and the central nervous system.

An early example of how McLuhan actually developed his probes poetically is exemplified in a short essay first published in *Explorations 4* (1955) in which he explores a large number of the probes listed above. The essay is entitled "Five Sovereign Fingers Taxed the Breath," a title taken from a then well-known poem by Dylan Thomas, "The Hand That Signed the Paper," the first quatrain of which is:

> The hand that signed the paper felled a city;
> Five sovereign fingers taxed the breath,
> Doubled the globe of dead and halved a country;
> These five kings did a king to death.

Using the second and fourth lines of this quatrain and the concluding line, McLuhan alludes to the entire poem, which refers not only to the power of the written word but to the dominion it comes to have over people both physically and socially, for:

> The mighty hand leads to a sloping shoulder,
> The finger joints are cramped with chalk;
> A goose's quill has put an end to murder
> That put an end to talk.

yet it also is:

> The hand that signed the treaty bred a fever,
> And famine grew, and locusts came;
> Great is the hand that holds dominion over
> Man by a scribbled name.

Thomas's recognition of the historical "effects" of writing as a medium dramatized a central aspect of McLuhan's perception of writing as a medium. But his use of Thomas's poem in this brief key essay has another aspect, for the essay itself is a prose poem playing poetically with Thomas's poem. In a first anticipation of the "global village," McLuhan begins by declaring "The CITY no longer exists, except as a cultural ghost," for it is, as Thomas's poem dramatizes, writing that established civil society, so now McLuhan can say "The INSTANTANEOUS global coverage of radio-tv makes the city form meaningless, functionless." His prose poem circumscribes Thomas's stanzas on the power of the written word both referring back to the pre-written era when McLuhan declares that:

SPEECH structures the abyss of mental and acoustic space, shrouding the race; it is a cosmic, invisible architecture of the human dark. Speak that I may see you.

WRITING turned a spotlight on the high, dim Sierras of speech; writing was the visualization of acoustic space. It lit up the dark.

These five kings did a king to death.

and McLuhan then also juxtaposes to the pre-written, the later move that would lead beyond writing for:

A goose's quill put an end to talk, abolished mystery, gave architecture and towns, brought roads and armies, bureaucracies. It was the basic metaphor with which the cycle of CIVILIZATION began, the step from the dark into the light of the mind. The hand that filled a paper built a city.

Then playing on Thomas's opening line "The hand that signed the paper felled the city," but in the spirit of the ambivalence of Thomas's poem, he underlines aphoristically that through writing the hand could both effect destruction and creation.

But now "The handwriting is on the celluloid walls of Hollywood; the Age of Writing has passed." Playing on his probe of old media becoming content of new media, his text has surrounded Thomas's text with the perception that we have now succeeded in "surpassing writing." He builds up to this by inventing "a NEW METAPHOR [to] restructure our thoughts and feelings." This metaphor is outlined through an epigrammatic history of mechanization taking command that moves from "The MECHANIZATION of writing [that] mechanized the visual-acoustic metaphor on which all civilization rests; [and] created the classroom and mass education, the modern press and telegraph. It was the original assembly line" through the emergence of photography, telephone, and radio to culminate with how "movies and TV complete the cycle of mechanization of the human sensorium.

With the omnipresent ear and moving eye, we have abolished writing."
By so doing "we have regained our WHOLENESS... on ... a cosmic
plane." Being back in acoustic space (but on a new level) we must seek
a new language for this technological culture and our new tribalized
world of primitive feelings, so that McLuhan's concluding line in the
essay is the concluding line of Thomas's poem: "*Hands have no tears
to flow.*"

These perceptions had considerable shock value in 1955, and in
1962 and 1964 when they were probed at length in *The Gutenberg
Galaxy* and *Understanding Media*, since until then they had been
explored only in specialized areas of the humanities – paleography,
classical studies, etc. McLuhan's view of the power of technologies that
led to his seeming to be a technological determinist corroborated a
growing panic concerning new technologies, which was highlighted by
the fact that a whole series of new modes of technology were challenging print. So there was a new public urgency to examine them, and
consequently new metaphors and new languages were needed. This is
why this particular essay is a key illustration of the connection of
McLuhan's mode of operation and the influence he came to have. It is
a popular socio-critical poem about a poem, for it is the poet who is
master of perceptions and affects who can construct the new languages
and metaphors; but, as we have seen and will see, not just the poet of
speech or writing but the poet of all media and modes of expression.
When in the same essay McLuhan declares that telephone, radio, and
phonograph are "the mechanization of postliterate acoustic space"
leading to movies and TV, which complete "the cycle of mechanization
of the human sensorium," he is demonstrating the ambivalence
involved in his probing of media. For while recognizing that movies
become the content of TV, since by the time he wrote his major works
McLuhan had articulated the perception that the content of any
medium is always another medium, he is also dramatically reiterating
his agreement with the early modernist perception of the convergence
of media by which, through the "omnipresent ear" and the "moving
eye," writing comes to an end.

This is much more the poetic language of mystery than a philosophical language. What excited readers was that, as with all such languages that structure feeling, it spoke to each of them in its own way.
By focusing on the fears and unknowns of the everyday world barraged
by TV, shocked by the undermining of the printed word, it spoke with
urgency and permitted a multitude of interpretations. This is what
attracted the attention of such diverse people as John Cage, Hubert
Humphrey, Pierre Trudeau, Yoko Ono, Stan Brakhage, Frank Zappa,
Woody Allen, and many others to his work. Aphorisms such as "the

medium is the message" could, like mystical mantras, spin off a multitude of meanings, initiating in the process a multitude of new ways of looking at, exploring, feeling about, and adapting to technological change. Yet simultaneously, in keeping with McLuhan's own ambivalent abhorrence of that change, it could encompass a comedic-satiric element, as when within an aphorism such as "the medium is the message" we arrive not only at "the medium is the massage" and "the medium is the mass age," but " the medium is also the mess age." One could explore still further all the multiplicities of meaning implicit in McLuhan's various parabolic phrases with their elements of paradox.

McLuhan himself illustrated this potentiality in what he was doing again and again by re-visiting his own ambivalent aphorisms and techno-epigrams, a strategy confirmed by the prevalence in his work of various poetic interpretations of earlier phrases such as "the medium is the message" or the "global village."[6] McLuhan's appeal is to the imagination and the ability of the individual to survive the whirlpool (vortex, maelstrom) by generating, through detached observation, her or his own strategies for understanding and coping with change. Having implied such a poetics of technology and media at the outset of his career, he copiously illustrated it in his final work by presenting his new poetic science of tetrads – essentially diagrammatic metaphorical structures that played poetically with the traditions of the logical square. These tetrads constructed, as most of his work did, mind games or mental play as aids to understanding our world of fabricated artefacts, from the classical techne of the arts of speech and writing through mechanized and electric media to our contemporary technologies which are their inheritors.

McLuhan obviously is, as he himself declared, not a philosopher, a theorist, or a traditional scientist, for he is not concerned with concepts or functions (nor the laws that govern them), but rather an artist playing with percepts and affects – particularly since he probes the subliminal effects and the counter-intuitive effects of media while stressing the contemporary need for an intuitive study of the effects, of artefacts, media, and technologies, which he claimed had never been pursued earlier in history. In his work he carried this artistic aspect even into designing or co-designing a variety of "mixed media poetic" modes of typographical and/or pictorial presentation and arrangements, such as those in *The Mechanical Bride* and continuing on in his *Counterblast* (1954) and in such works as *Explorations 8* (Verbi-Voco-Visual), the poetic "concrete essays" – *The Medium Is the Massage*, *War and Peace in the Global Village*, *Through the Vanishing Point*, and *Culture Is Our Business* – culminating in the "tetrads" of *Laws of Media*, where photographs, typographical arrangement, and colour, diagrams, paint-

ings, and the like are arranged in radical juxtapositions. Simultaneously he dabbled experimentally in TV and recording.

As an artist developing such probes, McLuhan's approach is essentially pragmatic, as he himself insisted, since he developed his perceptions without preconceptions or fixed positions. The pragmatism of
this poetic "empiricism" is not the North American pragmatism of
Dewey, James, and the Chicago school; it is closer to the semiotics and
"pragmaticisim" of C.S. Peirce as transmitted through British semoti-
cians and the "new criticism." McLuhan had read Ogden and Richards
at Cambridge. Richards's *The Principles of Literary Criticism* and particularly Ogden and Richards's seminal, *The Meaning of Meaning* had
introduced both Peirce and Malinowski to literary circles. At that time
McLuhan did not read or explore the "structuralism" of de Saussure,
whose work, although he first encountered it in the mid-1950s, he
never read until nearly a quarter of a century later (1975). But by combining the insights of *The Principles* and *The Meaning of Meaning* as
well as those of the "new criticism" with his own knowledge of the
history of the trivium he was able to restore the grammatico-rhetorico-
poetic exegesis of nature and explore the effect of people's transformation of it into a second nature – cultural productions. This had an
immediate, practical impact on McLuhan's success, since it allowed
him to design new kinds of poetic games as a way of exploring the new
post-electric world.

Take, for example, his treatment of the electric light bulb, which
he asserts is "pure information – a medium without a message"
(McLuhan 1964,10). Such an aphorism has its own transverse and
somewhat ambivalent connections with many, many other motifs that
McLuhan develops in his exploration of electricity, such as new information patterns emerging at the speed of light and the global village
being based on the reversal of mechanical forms through electricity. In
creating these motifs McLuhan is well aware of the fact that electricity
is produced mechanically and runs mechanisms – facts he is using to
invoke the shock through paradox and ambivalence that re-focuses the
"electric revolution." "In the electric age our senses and energies go
outside as a new kind of collective and corporate environment. As
such, this information environment of all-at-onceness and instant
retrieval makes it difficult for the young to accept the specialized goals
and fragmentary consciousness of nineteenth-century specialized man"
(McLuhan and Watson 1970,66).

What has been little appreciated about this type of McLuhanese is
that the verbal repetition throughout texts and between texts assists
the reader mnemonically, helping to make links between different
techno-epigrams and thus permitting her or him to widen and deepen

their contemplation of the particular complex of artefacts and/or technologies – an activity that provides pleasure and amusement as well as insight and knowledge. By the end of his career McLuhan could produce one of his tetrads on electric light in which it enhances "space as visual figure and turns it into ground," while it obscolesces "the non-visual," eliminating the limitations of night, thus reversing "blinding; outer light to inner seer" and retrieving "daytime activities: night baseball, etc." simultaneously putting "outer (sunlight) inside enabling, e.g. brain surgery" (McLuhan and McLuhan 1988,194). It is important to note that in the tetrads the aphorisms are diagrammatically arranged, creating what is almost a visually established cluster of "mobile," multivalent haiku – a strange type of typographic poem.

McLuhan produced his multi-media, rhetorical works of art as a means of dramatizing the impact of artefacts and technologies on people and environments. This is the dramatization mode of both the traditional and the modernist artist, poet and cultural producer and is how and why he had his impact. Although in his usual cryptic way he did not directly say so, McLuhan was trying to give new life to the grammatico-rhetorico-poetic – " the Shakespearean rag" – in a multitude of new media, an attempt that was a natural outgrowth of the interfacing of his traditional and modernist studies. For McLuhan as modernist artist, the poetic was a form of knowledge dedicated to human discovery, which is why he so readily adapted Pound's aphorism that the artists are the antennae of the race and, rightly or wrongly, saw himself as one of the super-radar or satellite antennae.

The major direction of most of McLuhan's work was well developed before the end of the 1950s and prior to the publication of his seminal books on *Gutenberg* and *Understanding Media*. After 1965 he used the poetic vison of those works to attain an international presence through advertising and promotion. The first three of the four laws of media that form the centerpiece of his posthumous book, were articulated before 1962 and appeared in *Understanding Media*, while the fourth, which appears in *From Cliché to Archetype*, was articulated by 1969, according to his son (Eric McLuhan 1991,27-8). The tetrads themselves were on the way to being well developed by 1960 when his report to the National Association of Educational Broadcasters was filed (McLuhan 1960). *Laws of Media* was primarily written to establish that there was a "new science" indebted to Bacon and Vico – a poetic science. While such a declaration of the epistemological value of the poetic causes considerable discomfort among most social and human scientists and philosophers, McLuhan's strategy and techniques have obviously illuminated many areas of contemporary inquiry. His percepts and probing of affects are modes of inquiry, ways of raising questions and setting research agendas, for as he always insisted, as he did in a letter to Nobel Prize winner, John Polanyi, "I have always found questions more interesting than answers, probes more exciting than products. All of my work has been experimental in the sense of studying effects rather than causes, perceptions rather than concepts."[6]

Of course, he is hedging on the word "experimental," using a Baconian sense of experiment: "A tentative procedure; a method, system of things, or course of action, adopted in uncertainty whether it will answer the purpose" (*Oxford English Dictionary*, def. 2). But he goes on to point out to Polanyi: "My motives ... are simply an intellectual enjoyment of play and discovery."[7] This, of course, is one of McLuhan's key insights – the seriousness of play as a mode leading to discovery, the close affinity of play to the poetic and the artistic, which he could trace back to Aristotle's *Poetics*. This seemingly esoteric and erudite view was immensely powerful in attracting both a general public and a community of researchers, for McLuhan not only intuited the importance of play but the renewed importance of play in a modernist world and its aftermath – a return that had been or was being theorized by Huizinga, William Stephenson, and Jean Piaget. And he understood how seductive the spirit of play could be in making his probes more compelling and vital. Moving into a post-electric society of games and playfulness, he reintegrated the traditional importance of play to knowledge with the role of the artist and the rhetorico-grammarian (the ideal of modern publicist in a responsible mode) in its development and transmission.

Through the core of his "poetic science," he restored the importance of, and created the interest in, the history of communication, media, modes of expression, and technologies. McLuhan was able to situate contemporary dilemmas in relation to history – the pre-history of writing, the unfolding history of writing and its mechanization, the history of the modes of understanding communication within the classical trivium, the history of printing and of electro-mechanization, and the history of post-electric media, and, finally, to associate this entire project with its parallels, echoes, and the like in the history of arts. Through this historical imagination he contextualized what was a growing object of concern – and to many a source of fear and panic. The scope of his project far exceeded Innis's historical account and theories, owing much more to Sigfried Giedion, Lewis Mumford and, startlingly enough, James Joyce. McLuhan launched the interest in such historical investigation through his perceptual and probing challenge led communication scholars to look at Innis, to contemplate orality/literacy, and to grasp the exciting importance of the affiliation of art and technology.

McLuhan's presentation of history is not that of an academic historian; it is not the primary material you will find in an anthology of communication history. But it was central to his project and his influence was marked by the fact that he launched his major publishing career with a key historic volume, *The Gutenberg Galaxy*. While the *Galaxy* inspired major work, such as Elizabeth Eisenstein's history of printing or Walter Ong's history of orality/literacy, McLuhan has frequently been misunderstood by heavy, sombre academics, since he played games, he used wit and satire, and he employed a strategy of decentering and fragmentation. Yet he opened up access to Innis and other historians of communication, media, and the trivium and went on to popularize and demonstrate the significance of this history by writing *Understanding Media*, which confronted satirically, comically, somewhat sardonically, playfully, yet intensely seriously, the importance of examining the rapid, short-term history of media since Gutenberg and exploring poetically the new phenomenon arising in the age of electricity and its movement through automation and computerization into a post-electric world.

McLuhan made people not only think about the new technological revolution which they were experiencing but probe their feelings about it. Simultaneously he somewhat exposed his feelings in prophetic visions of what was in the 1960s already coming to be – the new tribalism, an oral collectivity processing new information patterns at the speed of light. By the time of *Take Today*, this world becomes the world of the dropout. McLuhan, like Innis, has an oral bias and could intuit that in the post-electric age new patterns of information and data must move at the speed of light. He uses the one-liner (a kind of jokester's aphorism) as the most satisfactory mode of communication for that age, while still considering himself to be a "bookish" man. His personal orality is a post-electric transformation of the tactility of the pre-print world, not what his disciple Walter Ong has described as the "secondary orality" of the electric world. His insight into the new tribalism, in which the people imitate the participational nature of their technologies (TV and tele-computing), is ambivalent. His perspective is that of the observer of the maelstrom and the true believer in a religious salvation, who looks towards another world – of an apocalyptic, who is neither an optimist nor a pessimist. What makes McLuhan a great force in the last decades of the millennium is his ability to combine the comic, rhetorical effect, and poetic vision, turning them towards the new technoculture to simultaneously analyse its technologies, media, and society as artefacts.

Who/What Is Marshall McLuhan?

In 1951 Marshall McLuhan gave a copy of his newly published *The Mechanical Bride* to my wife and me with the inscription "To Don and Joan, From the Mechanical Bridegroom, Marshall". That inscription is a penetrating insight into the lifelong vision that shaped the writings and conversations of the man who many would consider the key observer of the last half-century of the second millennium, for Marshall, even before launching on his study of media, saw himself entrapped in the growing symbiosis between man and machine, the first gleanings of the cyborgian consciousness that was to evolve in those closing decades. While in the *Bride* he had not yet embraced the idea of technologies as extensions of each and every person, Siegfried Giedion's *Mechanization Takes Command* had revealed to him the all-pervasive takeover of mechanization – in the household, the kitchen, and the bathroom; in agriculture, including the abattoir; in human surroundings (furnishings, adornment).

The Marshall McLuhan my new bride, Joan, and I met in the Summer of 1950 when I arrived at the University of Toronto as a graduate student was a charming, good looking, witty, fun-loving, highly intelligent devotee of the world of letters and the traditional arts. Far more significant for what has come to be, he was a technophobe and a devoted Catholic. McLuhan, surprisingly enough for someone who has become the prime techno-prophet of the twentieth century, distrusted (often despised) technology. In 1950 he did not own an automobile or a vacuum cleaner, and throughout his life he avoided driving a car and usually initially resisted adopting new technologies when they first appeared. He did not type but used pen and ink and stored his notes in small boxes that had originally contained Laura Secord chocolates;[1] he beat rugs on the clothesline. Perhaps equally as significant as being a technophobe, McLuhan was a deeply committed, pious believer in the Roman Catholic Church. He attended daily mass; a group of us regularly (not quite daily) read and discussed questions with him from St Thomas Aquinas' *Summae* and avidly discussed the philosopho-theological debates of the Pontifical Institute of Medieval Studies.

These are not just gossipaceous biographical facts, for they provide a key insight into one aspect of the depth of McLuhan's schizoid approach to his world – an approach that is even more significant in typifying the split-person of the twentieth century, ensnared in a rupture of thought and feeling.[2] The split-McLuhan not only faced the division between the new technoculture and "Culture" ("high" culture) but the division between a traditional, pietistic Catholicism and a fascination with the Nietzschean abyss as well as the split between a commitment to the basically reactionary poetics of Wyndham Lewis and Ezra Pound and a transgressive attraction to the seriocomically rebellious, carniva-lesque, and "patently offensive" "pornographic" wit of James Joyce. Furthermore, as a Catholic moralist McLuhan was actively pro-life and even argued for the banning of books on sexual education for children. He nevertheless urged others to read Joyce's major works, *Ulysses* and *Finnegans Wake*, which in May 1946 (in a letter to his friend Felix Gio-vanelli) he described as demonic while noting the centrality of the Black Mass in both books (McLuhan 1987,183). Here then is a man who, although disturbed by the genuine (to borrow a "joycing" from the *Wake*) "ambiviolence" of the intellectual in the modern world, never-theless was able to understand intuitively the radical power of commu-nications technology in transforming a person's lifeworld in an era when most people were preoccupied with the atom bomb, the Cold War, and later the war in Vietnam.

Next to the discovery and dropping of the atom bomb (and perhaps even more important), new technological and empirical knowledge about the potential power of communication as an instrument of control over time, distance, information, and people was to exercise a most profound effect on the last half of the twentieth century and the conclusion of the second millennium. By the last years of this century, to speak of the decisive transformation of everyday life that resulted from the development of cybernetics (the science of communication and control in the animal and the machine) and culminated in the inte-gration of telecommunications and computers, thus revolutionizing the transmission and storage of information, has become banal. Yet since the mid-point of the century a single name, McLuhan, has brooded, ghost-like, over social and cultural understanding of the intersection of communication, computers, persuasion, and the emergence of a techno-culture. While at first glance it may seem surprising, and it certainly is rather paradoxical, that McLuhan has become the guru of the cultural impact of new technologies and the patron saint of the enthusiasts of technological change, in retrospect it is quite natural: the combination of major aspects of his biography equipped him with both interest in and yet remove from the rising technoculture in the U.S.A. immediately after World War Two. Born in Edmonton, Alberta, but brought up in the Canadian mid-Western town of Winnipeg, Manitoba, in the second decade of this century; spurred on by an intense, ambitious, intelligent mother who was an actress; lured as a colonial by the literate culture of Oxbridge and by his fascination with the late Victorian and Edwardian glorification of the "man of letters" to do graduate work in England; having first settled as an adult in the U.S. where he lived off and on over a decade (having married a charming Texan beauty, he became fascinated with American popular culture and media); and finally in 1946 moving back to Canada where he lived for over thirty years, first in Windsor for about two years and then, from the Fall of 1946, in Toronto until his death.

In 1950 Toronto was an overgrown village inhabited by three-quarters of a million people. Compared to New York, with its seven million plus inhabitants, and other densely populated major cities in the U.S., Toronto was a sedate, stuffy city where on Sundays the major department store drew curtains across its windows, stores did not sell cigarettes, and people could not have wine or other alcoholic beverages with a restaurant meal. It was not permissible for women to wear shorts in public and it was illegal to drink a glass of beer in the yard at home. The police who walked the beats were unarmed. There was no television; the only radio network, the Canadian Broadcasting Corporation (CBC), like the BBC in the United Kingdom, was government owned. The University of Toronto, Canada's largest university (second then in international prestige only to McGill University in Montreal) had less than ten thousand students. The undergraduate population of the University of Toronto was spread out over four quasi-independent colleges. These colleges were primarily representative of different theological positions, and still dedicated to the Oxbridge ideal, although unable to preserve the traditional tutorial system. Faculties other than the Faculty of Arts and Science and its Faculty of Graduate Studies were not well supported or endowed and did not have the reputation they do today – in the mid-1950s the U.S. management consultant Peter Drucker described the University of Toronto's medical school as a "slum."

McLuhan's vision was launched in this somewhat idyllic (if you did not look under the surface), still semi-colonial, marginally contemporary city. Only the Catholic college, St Michael's – to which Marshall had moved from Assumption University in Windsor, Ontario, in 1946 – had a substantial number of students from the U.S. Here is where what burgeoned as McLuhanism, lasting well into the late 1990s, began. When he arrived at St Mike's, McLuhan became the only lay member of the English Department, which primarily consisted of a handful of priests and three nuns. In 1953 I became the second lay member of this department; there were by then two or three other lay faculty in the Philosophy Department and one in languages. In this marginal and very quiet "backwater" McLuhan would meet Edmund (Ted) Carpenter, later editor of *Explorations*, and, through the support of his old friend Claude Bissell, then vice-president of the university and starting in 1957 the president who made the University of Toronto into a major international multiversity, he and Carpenter would obtain a Ford Foundation grant of $40,000 and establish an ongoing multi-disciplinary graduate seminar in culture and communications.

This was the local seedbed which started the process that resulted in over forty years of international debate as to whether McLuhan was a prophetic visionary or an academic charlatan. While biographies of McLuhan, and particularly the publication of his letters, have provided much valuable factual information although relatively little interpretation, so far neither a variety of Mcluhanisms or the institutionalization of McLuhan have done justice to the way in which the entire complex mixture of disciplinary interests that he traversed contributed to his understanding of the twentieth century. Consequently McLuhan's own particular genius and status as a historical figure still need to be fully clarified – how he bridges a variety of areas in the humanities, a range of the arts of cultural production (from music and painting to film and multi-media), and areas in the social sciences through a variety of histories (communication, education, rhetoric, technology) to develop a visionary poetic insight into technology, culture, and communication. Even today, to achieve a fuller understanding of McLuhan's significance it is necessary to return to the roots of his entire work and career. *The Virtual McLuhan* is a preliminary contribution to such a multi-faceted project in which the central goal is to establish the richness, complexity, and sometimes the contradictions and contrariness of Marshall McLuhan. From time to time the phenomena of Mcluhanisms and of the institutionalization of McLuhan will be counterpointed against this primary goal, for McLuhan predicted that Mcluhanism(s) would become a movement (movements) but said that he would never be, nor approve of someone's being, a Mcluhanite.

What was first called *McLuhanisme* in France is the hype, exploitation, and mythology that have surrounded and continue to surround the poetic pop philosophy of the guru cum prophet cum philosopher cum promoter cum popularizer cum pseudo-artist Marshall McLuhan. As I noted in 1971 in *The Medium is the Rear View Mirror*:

The strategy that McLuhan employs, like the strategy of advertisers, appeals to a variety of audiences in different ways ... he not only involves the people who find him a source of agreement or reassurance, he also involves those who hold him in considerable skepticism, if they wish to reach an audience of a more general kind in the media area. He will be quoted (even if negatively) by most individuals wishing to show an inner awareness of the complexity of the media scene. References to what he has to say turn up in work by major anthropologists and sociologists, futurists, government officials, and among executives – all of which merely intensifies the myth of McLuhanism. He therefore becomes the objective correlative of what he preaches, a fact he himself illustrates again and again in references to himself in his latest work *Culture Is Our Business* (Theall 1971, xvi).

Culture Is Our Business completes a process McLuhan began in earnest with *The Medium Is the Massage*, the process of converting himself into a mythology through conscious playing with his own previous work and his evolving public image. Yet he insisted on remaining above and beyond that very mythology whose acceleration he aided and abetted after 1965.[3]

If the local seedbed of McLuhanism was Toronto of the 1950s, its institutional seedbed was the interface after World War Two between the postwar world of everyday life and the postwar university world of North America and Western Europe. While the postwar world saw the rising dominance of popular culture, produced, reproduced, and distributed through technologies of mass media, the central non-professional, non-scientific core of the universities – history, philosophy, literature, political economy, and anthropology – largely disregarded the study of popular culture, and the professional and scientific sectors continued on the path of developing the wartime consortium between the university, government, and industry. The presumed propaganda-producing capabilities of behavioural psychology, which had proved so crucial to the war effort, were largely unexamined outside psychology itself. The rising study of communication in the United States moved primarily in a professional direction, disregarding the philosophic, historical, ethical, and semantic implications of the rise of "the lively arts," as the controversial critic Gilbert Seldes had dubbed them in the 1920s at an early stage in their emergence.[4] So when McLuhan began his explorations in the mid-1940s using the recent, highly influential semantic analyses of C.K. Ogden, I.A. Richards, and the Cambridge critics, he was pursuing a radically new area within the university and a relatively new area without (Theall 1971, 56–7, 201–4).

If one attends to the trajectory of his work, it quickly becomes an index of the ambivalence and of the dis-ease permeating life in the second half (and particularly the last three decades) of this modernist century. While many words have been written about McLuhan, relatively little has been said about him as an index to, an epitome of, and a symptom of this century's everyday perplexity and panic about technology, social change, and the emergence of the technocosm or global metropolis. Although McLuhan was a social phenomenon not an author, a pop poet not a theorist, these roles, which he occupied frequently, throw more light on our everyday world than the work of theorists, analysts, or interpreters. Ted Carpenter has noted that although McLuhan's phrases and insights came primarily from others, it was his poetry and rhetoric that converted them into universal tags such as "global village" (from Wyndham Lewis), "the print era as linear" (from Dorothy Lee), "the medium is the message" (from Ashley Montagu) and "the medium is the massage" (from Sam Zacks, a Canadian art collector).[5]

No one would doubt either McLuhan's erudition or his wide reading in popular culture. His real power, however, was in his sensitivity to his social environment, for as a popular artist he firmly believed, along with Ezra Pound, that "artists are the antennae of the race," and thus possess the empathy to register motifs that respond to those significant moments that reveal the agenda of an era, thus presumably serving society as an early warning system about its "socio-unconscious."[6] As such an empath, McLuhan, in an insecure and fearful world where many people were waiting for a prophet – obviously the real basis for the pre-millennial popularity of futurology after the 1960s – quite naturally "put on" the role of guru and quirky prophet. His early interest in using the objects of popular culture – ads, comics, newspaper layouts – to lure first-year university English students to an interest in poetry, led to his constructing his first book of concrete essays, *The Mechanical Bride* (1951). It was a brief step from these essays to the development of his subsequent lifelong strategy as revealed in his articles in *Explorations* (1954–57).[7] He invoked the Renaissance and romantic association of the poet as prophet and adapted the persuasive devices of the media and advertising world to the creation of a hybrid prose/poetry exploring the everyday technoculture of the twentieth century. But this poetry was rooted in the conjunction of his contradictory fascination with technologies and his profound fear of technological change. This schizoid split, intensified by his attraction to the Nietzschean and the transgressive on one hand and his Jansenistic-like pietism on the other, shaped the critic as a poet into a split-man. This schizoid McLuhan consisted of a sophisticated luddite dedicated to the literacy of the man of letters, who was still fascinated by the modernist, technocultural "tradition of the new" and by the potential post-literate revival through the technoculture of a "new tribalism."

Consistent with the ambivalence of the contemporary world, McLuhan was also an erudite, elitist intellectual who admired the reactionary figure of the "modernist as fascist," while simultaneously stressing the importance of a very different, radical modernism that he found in Joyce and the obscure, occult poet of French *symbolisme* Stéphan Mallarmé, figures committed to a "revolution of the word." Yet McLuhan was deeply rooted in the word: a scholar of classical theories about language and grammar, logic and rhetoric, a specialist in Elizabethan and Jacobean as well as modern literature, a student of what in the 1940s was dubbed "popular culture," a learned amateur in theology and medieval philosophy. His very love of the literate and of the word provided him the opportunity of foreseeing a future that had moved beyond the word. As a complex amalgam of fear of and fascination with the emerging technoculture and with a deep desire to preserve the values of the past through reassessing them in the "new light" that the modern moment was throwing upon them, McLuhan and the McLuhanism(s) that emerged in his wake are symptomatic indices of the problems people confront when facing the transformations of exponential technocultural change.

While McLuhan is the source of what since the 1960s has been a sequence of McLuhanisms, he is by no means coterminous with any McLuhanism or even the sum of all McLuhanisms. Whatever his weaknesses, McLuhan is complex and comprehensive, while McLuhanisms are usually more simplistic and far less comprehensive. For example, when Terrence Gordon, a recent critic and biographer of McLuhan, suggests that McLuhan does not make big demands of us he is promoting not McLuhan but a variety of a new limited McLuhanism, whose simplicity may insure its popularity but substantially distorts McLuhan's project (Gordon 1997). McLuhan emphasized again and again the importance of his readers knowing some of the things that he knew – Wyndham Lewis, Ezra Pound, James Joyce, the French symbolist poets, particularly Charles Baudelaire, Arthur Rimbaud, Jules Laforgue, and Stéphane Mallarmé, Sigfried Giedion and Lewis Mumford, Elizabethan drama, the classical tradition of language study (the "trivium"), and Thomistic philosophy. His first major book, *The Gutenberg Galaxy*, was essentially a scholar and researcher's poetic exploration within the context of the history of literature, art, and theology of the history of language from its inception in speech and gesture through writing and print to the post-print era. It was published by a university press and praised for its brilliance by other scholars, such as the Cambridge cultural critic and Marxist literary scholar Raymond Williams.[8]

McLuhan may not make big demands of us if we allow the surface of his prose/poetry to seduce us, but he does make such demands if we, as he apparently wished and as he communicated to others, attend to the sources to which he is pointing. While not a theorist or analyst, McLuhan is an allusive poet and his probes, like the work of poets from Dante to Pound, are embedded in allusion to poets, philosophers, artists, other cultural producers, and theologians. In contrast, what is often called McLuhanism is an enthusiasm based on McLuhan, either by the transformation of his non-doctrinaire probes and insights into a system and doctrine or through adopting his pithy formulae as a Yogic mantra. Obviously McLuhanism was partly encouraged by McLuhan, since his egotistic temperament with its craving for attention found it attractive to have a following with a strong and exclusive commitment to his work, while secretly despising those who undertook such a commitment without possessing the erudition on which he depended. What is fascinating about so much of the critical commentary about McLuhan as well as about the various McLuhanisms is virtually the total absence of an interest in such seriocomical modes of art and literature as parody and complex verbal play.

McLuhan was noted for his wit, word play, and sense of fun, which is epitomized in the ease with which he made a brief appearance in Woody Allen's *Annie Hall*. His work, based on his own claims, is witty and satiric and he uses comedy seriously in his presentations, notably in his concrete essays: *The Mechanical Bride*, *The Medium Is the Massage*, and *War and Peace in the Global Village* (Theall 1972, 239–42). But this is a recurrent thread throughout all of his works, from the essays in *Explorations* (1953 on) to the *Laws of Media* (published posthumously). As McLuhan's first doctoral student at the University of Toronto in the early 1950s, I can attest to his early fascination with the comic, satiric, and carnivalesque, for I collaborated with him, co-discovering the importance of the brief epic or *epyllion*, particularly the brief comic epic, and brought to his attention the significance of the tradition of Varronian and Menippean satire in Pope and Swift's poetic programs, recently elevated to a new urgency by Mikhail Bakhtin and such post-structuralists as Julia Kristeva. But the accompanying feature of such a seriocomic and satiric approach is that the writer's work necessarily becomes complex, ambivalent, and transgressive due to the seductive attractiveness of this mode. It enabled McLuhan to make his work deliberately cryptic – an aspect of his writings whose importance he reiterated on various occasions. The initially enigmatic nature of his pronouncements, such as speaking of TV as a "cool" medium or crafting phrases like "the medium is the message," were for him necessary to the nature of his "probes," which were meant to be suggestive poetic insights rather than theoretical statements, generating through their resonance still further probes. The combined effect of comically playing with his own sayings is easily exemplified in all the transformations a phrase such as "the medium is the message" might undergo throughout his writing, such as "the medium is the massage," "the medium is the mass age," or "the medium is the mess age." It was the same poetic ability that allowed him to appropriate phrases from others, such as the term linearity from Dorothy Lee, and turn them into his own multi-faceted probes or to convert Ezra Pound's aphorism "Artists are the antennae of the race" (Pound n.d., 81) into his description of the poet as an "early warning system," alluding to the then-topical Dew Line that used radar to provide early alerts of air or missile attacks.

A comic sensibility combined well with this linguistic play and both contributed to McLuhan's being able to avoid being pinned down – in fact, just like a modernist poet, he made complexity and ambivalence virtues. So there is no disingenuousness when he argues that his goal is not to articulate theories or authoritative statements, for he once wrote to one of his interpreters, William Kuhns: "I have no theories whatever about anything. I make observations by way of discovering contours, lines of force and pressures. I satirize at all times and my hyperboles are as nothing compared to the events to which they refer." He suggests that his method is that of a 'symbolist' (i.e., a French *symboliste* poet such as Baudelaire, Laforgue, or Mallarmé) and he relates his satiric stance to modernist art: "My canvasses are surrealistic and to call them "theories" is to miss my satirical intent altogether" (McLuhan 1987, 448). Describing his works as canvases is in keeping with his view that, like the French philosopher-mathematician Blaise Pascal in his essays and the symbolist poets, he was constructing paintings of the mind in action *(la peinture de la pensée* or an interior landscape). McLuhan anticipated the major French theorists who have so dominated American intellectual thought in the past three decades – from Roland Barthes and Jacques Derrida to Jean Baudrillard and Paul Virilio – primarily because he shared with them such interests as *symboliste* poetry, modernist art, and James Joyce.

McLuhan's contemporaneity was not a function of detailed technological knowledge, his grasp of which even he would admit was minimal, but a function of his knowledge of twentieth-century cultural production and its affinities for science, engineering, and technology. As I discovered in 1950, McLuhan could almost instantaneously intuit the relevance of Norbert Wiener's and C.E. Shannon and W. Weaver's ideas about cybernetics and systems theory in the light of modernist art, literature, poetics, aesthetic theory, and cultural production. In the Spring of 1950, before moving to Toronto, I had published in the *Yale Scientific Magazine* a typically undergraduate review of Wiener's *Cybernetics*, which I discussed with McLuhan when we first met that Summer. Grasping the growing significance of communication, he broadened his interest in popular culture, public relations, advertising, and media into an interest in human communication, Wiener, and cyberneticians. He quickly rejected this mathematical theory of communication, but the impact of the world examined in Wiener's *The Human Use of Human Beings* (1950) had a profound effect on McLuhan, even if Wiener himself and most other cyberneticians had a largely negative effect.

He read critically, but avidly, many other cyberneticists and also began reading about what was going on in communication studies in U.S. universities; but his main interest continued to be in contemporary poetry and art, history of art and literature, Renaissance History, and the history of the arts of language, i.e., the basic liberal arts (the trivium of grammar, logic, and rhetoric) and the history of liberal education. With his graduate students, such as Archie Malloch (now professor emeritus of English at McGill) and me, he studied Greek under the tutelage of a classicist, a tough-minded Sister of St Joseph, Sister St John. His fascination with cybernetics increased the year following our first meeting when he encountered Jurgen Reusch and Gregory Bateson's *Communication: The Social Matrix of Psychiatry*, which I had urged him to read. His immediate move was to underline the affinities between the way cubist, expressionist, or surrealistic painting worked and these new ideas about communication and to assert how much these communication theorists could learn from the poets and the artists.[9]

Just as he had discovered, in his teaching experiments that led up to *The Mechanical Bride*, the affinity between popular culture, modernist art, and the rise of electro-mechanization, so in the period that led up to the launching (with Carpenter) of his Ford Foundation–sponsored seminar in culture and communications, he explored the affinity between the new technologically inspired approaches to communication and their affinity with modernist art and literature.[10] Those Ford seminars that he taught with Ted Carpenter and three other professors were to contribute to delineating for North America the avant-garde intellectual agenda of the 1950s and early 1960s through their inter-disciplinarity, the variety of topics discussed, and the various individu-als who published in its journal *Explorations*, most of whom were to play important parts in the formation of McLuhan's own work. For example, Lawrence Frank wrote on "tactile communication," Dorothy Lee, the anthropologist, on Wintu linguistics and lineal and non-lineal codifications of reality, the British poet Robert Graves provided his cri-tique of Lee on lineality, Ray Birdwhistell wrote on kinesics, Sigfried Giedion on conceptions of space in prehistoric art, cubist painter Fernand Léger on colour, Gyorgy Kepes on art and technology, the then-famous sociologist David Riesman on the oral and the written, H.J. Chaytor on reading and writing, Gilbert Seldes, the art and media journalist, on the communications revolution, Karl Williams, the psy-chologist in McLuhan's group, on acoustic space; Tom Easterbrook, the economic historian, on Harold Innis, Ted Carpenter on Inuit lan-guage, myself on James Joyce, and a group of graduate students from the seminar on Wyndham Lewis.

This list of topics spans anthropology, linguistics, sociology, kinesi-ology, mythography, medieval studies, history, history of art and archi-tecture, literary theory and criticism, painting and sculpture, media criticism, and creative literature, making the McLuhan-Carpenter project one of the first wide interdisciplinary collaborations across the humanities, the social sciences, the arts, and engineering (technology), and one of the first projects to embrace the range of interests that were later to constitute the domain of cultural studies. Perhaps even more important, these topics, partly generated by the faculty collaborating in the project – a psychologist, an economist, a town planner, as well as McLuhan and Carpenter – actually embrace most of the major themes of McLuhan's writing, suggesting that his agenda was well formed by the mid-1950s. The over-riding emphasis on the artistic, the literary, and the humanities in that agenda is further underlined by one issue, *Explorations 8* (October 1957), entitled "Verbi-Voco-Visual," produc-tion of McLuhan's in which Carpenter did not participate.[11] It illus-trates McLuhan's affinity with the avant-garde arts for it also includes some of his first publicly published attempts at typographical essays (preceded only by the early, privately published *Counterblast* in 1954), assisted by one of his many collaborators, Canadian artist Harley Parker.[12]

Carpenter and McLuhan complemented one another in a fascinating way. The former was an ethnologist and archeologist fascinated by aboriginal and prehistoric art and the different civilizations of aborig-inal groups, and the latter a historian of early language arts (grammar, logic, rhetoric) deeply attracted to the more radical aspects of the avant-garde modernists (Joyce, Picasso, Leger) yet even more to the radical conservative aspects of modernist writing (Pound, Lewis, Eliot, Valéry, T.E. Hulme) and avant-garde art (futurism, vorticism, surrealism). McLuhan, the Ford seminars, and *Explorations* were situated in an interplay between what in those times was denominated as the "primitive" and the prehistoric, and what was considered to be the avant-garde, whose practitioners had an obsessive fascination with the differences evoked by the primitive and the Nietzschean vision. Carpenter's expertise. which centered around an interest in language, symbols, art, and cultural production of aboriginal times, supplemented by the modernist theorizing of figures such as T.E. Hulme and Malinowski, led McLuhan into his interest in the "tribal."[13]

The multiplex motifs of modern communication, modernist poetry, avant-garde anarchism, and the man of letters as media star permeate not only McLuhan's analysis of the "media world" but his ultimate desire to become one of its stars. Nevertheless he still hoped to preserve, because of his avant-garde interests, the sense of the negative, the power of the poetic, and the concept of eternal return characteristic of a modernist, post-Nietzschean world, while maintaining, because of his humanistic commitments, the stance of a committed Catholic, a quixotic neo-Thomist, and a cultural and literary historian applying a humanistic grammatico-rhetorical critique to the new era of an electro-mechanical technoculture. The combination of his intellect, his histrionic ability, his formal education, the multi-disciplinary education he gained as a professor and researcher, and his lifelong theological commitment as a Catholic intellectual equipped him to become a unique historical figure in the second half of the twentieth century and the closing years of the second millennium. Those who chose to develop McLuhan's project – the projectors of McLuhanism – were, if his contemporaries, seldom, if ever, able to replicate the complexity of his "poetic" vision and, if after him, generally unable to appreciate the contradictory complexity of the currents that produced him.

McLuhan's sources were not only rich and amazingly complex but he had a comprehensive knowledge of the works of those writers who played a major role in his own work. Working with Marshall in the early 1950s was a constant stimulation, since he could shift with ease from classical literature to contemporary film, from the history of education to the history of technology and the machine, from Shakespeare and Renaissance drama to Joyce's *Wake* and Mallarmé's *Coup de Dès*. During the same session we might talk about cybernetics and T.S. Eliot's theory of communication (on which I had written my master's thesis), patristic theology and possible sources for John Milton's conception of Satan, the "mechanical bride" and "mechanization taking command," Alfred Tennyson's landscape poetry and Giedion's theories of space in modern architecture, and Thomas Aquinas's theory of grace and the Joycean epiphany.

It has been alleged that McLuhan was too professional to allow his religion to influence his work, but this is certainly to misunderstand the mission of a Catholic intellectual revived by neo-Thomism and Christian Humanism in the 1940s and 1950s, a mission which Arthur Kroker carefully documented in his early work on McLuhan.[14] The role of the Catholic intellectual in McLuhan's work is ambiguous, partly because of his strong attraction to modernism and partly because of the conflict between his emotional pietistic tendency to fideism – which he shared with Blaise Pascal and Alexander Pope – and his intellectual commitment to scholasticism. *The Virtual McLuhan* should make it clear that a critique of this aspect of McLuhan is crucial for understanding his position in the twentieth century. McLuhanisms, on the whole, have evaded such a critique by either dismissing the relevance of his faith or by simplifying the struggle implicit in his various schizoid conflicts. In neither case have they read the texts in which writings of Pope, Pascal, Michel Montaigne, and even the Papal Magisterium are an important presence. Furthermore they have more generally shown little respect for the breadth and depth of McLuhan's poetic vision and the ambivalence and intellectual struggle from which it emerges. McLuhan could reject McLuhanism before the fact since he realized that all too frequently his work would be translated into theories and methodologies or even reduced to slogans that would rapidly become hackneyed phrases.

There are other tantalizing tensions in his work. For example, while the McLuhan who was an intellectual publicist and journalist highly aware of the new languages of media wanted to seize the impact and power of the advertising slogan, he hoped to accomplish this in a poetic manner that would ambiguate the slogan and hence avoid its becoming a reductive formula. The latter, of course, is what ultimately happens when individuals like Bill Clinton or Al Gore speak of the global village – probably largely unaware of the complexities invoked by its having arisen from McLuhan's probing its relation to margins and centers, villages and cities, tribal collectivities and democratic individualism, and from his wishing he could call it the "global metropolis," since "village" obviates much of the complexity of the multiculturalism that is a defining mark of McLuhan's Canada. The point here is not that people can and will borrow language from major rhetorical prose poetry but that in the process of borrowing McLuhanism frequently tends to use the language and reject the artistic force – the complexity – of the percepts.

There are fascinations with and commitments to McLuhan (that might be called McLuhanisms) which, while McLuhan might not embrace them, retain basic aspects of his spirit, such as his wit or his endless curiousity about the hermetic and the occult or his interest in the avant-garde. The interest that publications such as *Mondo 2000*, *21*C*, or *Wired* have shown in playing with McLuhan's work explore a central aspect of his spirit, his sense of humor and playfulness, and toy with his associations with a New Age world or a world of alternative lifestyles. *Mondo 2000* and *21*C* are more congenial to the anarchic intellectual, *Wired* to the rhetorical publicist and advisor to the board rooms and the throne rooms (e.g., Canadian Prime Minister Pierre Elliott Trudeau). While, paradoxically, McLuhan's jokes always had a substratum of anger, expressing, as Freud and G. Legman (who wrote for *Explorations*) have suggested, the joke as a way of coping with insecurity, fear, or repulsion, McLuhan was intellectually playful and had a strong streak of the gamesman in him.

All McLuhan's most significant contributions to our understanding of contemporary communication, culture, media, and technology were grounded in his work in the 1940s and 1950s. During this period he developed as a literary interpreter and historian; wrote his groundbreaking doctoral dissertation on *The Place of Nashe in the Learning of His Time*, which featured a history of education and the arts of expression and communication (the "trivium") from classical Greece to the Renaissance; immersed himself in contemporary literature and art, particularly the major Anglo-American and Irish modernists (Yeats, Pound, Eliot, Joyce), the French *symbolistes* (Baudelaire, Rimbaud, Laforgue, Mallarmé and Valéry), and Wyndham Lewis; associated himself with the New Critics and their Southern regionalism (especially Cleanth Brooks and William K. Wimsatt, Jr.); and explored his new-found faith in his conversion to Catholicism. These roots in the traditions of humanism reaching back to the Greek, Judaic, and Roman worlds produced the phenomenon of Marshall McLuhan.

In exploring such complexities my exposition will unfold in a multifaceted rather than linear fashion, in keeping with the poetic nature of the subject of McLuhan's vision, a particularly powerful combination for the digital era of the poetic, the visionary, mysticism and faith, and a fascination with technologies. It will be discovered that McLuhan was an intellectual, satirical, "social scientific" (allowing his definition of science) poet – a contemporary exponent of learned, carnivalesque anatomy of culture. Therefore the subsequent chapters will take up various aspects of the McLuhan phenomenon, beginning with an overview of its fundamentals, including a brief view of the peculiar significance of his thesis and its history of education, expression, and communication from Greece and Rome until the beginnings of the Gutenberg era. As this examination unfolds in subsequent chapters, I will look at McLuhan's published letters (Chapter 2) since it is relevant that as a correspondent he considered the epistolary style to be nearest to what I will dub the dia-{mon}-ologic conversation that characterized one of his greatest strengths and thus is most revelatory of his essential conservatism and commitment to faith and tradition. Subsequent chapters will examine McLuhan's new poetic science of the tetrad and his role as an interpreter of culture through artefacts (Chapter 3); his self-image as a publicist (Chapter 4); his fascination with power and its intellectual and instrumental roles in his project (Chapter 5); his fascination with the gnostic, the alchemical, and traditions of secret knowledge and their persistence in occult and hermetic traditions that played a central and important role in his work (Chapter 6); his relation to and situation as a prepostmodernist anticipating French theory and consequently partly preconditioning the arts environment for its insurgence into North America (Chapter 7); his view of art and magic, of himself as a shaman, trickster, and artist, and his affiliation with other arts and artists (Chapter 8); his particular fascination with Joyce as a technologically oriented poet who anticipated the rise of digiculture, the emergence of the wired world, and of virtual reality, thus providing one possible pre-history of cyberculture (Chapter 9); his seduction by and critique of radical avant garde modernism (Chapter 10); his exploration of the traditions of learned carnivalesque (i.e. Menippean or Varronian) satire climaxing in his becoming a contemporary satirist of media, technology, and culture (Chapter 11); and concluding with a bringing together of the various moments of his career to reveal the consistency of his vision and provide a critical assessment of the success and failures of his project and what it, as a pre-history of cyberculture, implies for the future of research and higher education in the digital era (Chapter 12).

In the process, since the structure is multi-faceted, these motifs will overlap and intersect with other motifs that run throughout the work. Some brief personal moments describing my experience of working and virtually living with McLuhan in the early 1950s until 1956 and being his colleague in a small collegiate unit within the University of Toronto for another nine years as well as events after I left Toronto are interjected to provide a context for his development and the basis of my understanding of and divergencies from his work. Other significant motifs which such an examination must consider are the extent to which his history of communication should be considered as primarily Innisian; the importance of his studies in literary history and the history of expression and education on his vision of the contemporary cosmos of global communication; the schizoid nature of the fideistic Catholic and the post-Nietzschean verbivocovisual artist; and his essentially conservative, technophobic position as the "last Victorian."

My analysis reveals that McLuhan had a consistent and coherent project that he began developing in the late 1930s and 1940s when he was working on his doctoral thesis, *The Place of Thomas Nashe in the Learning of His Time*, and which is confirmed in one of his two final posthumously published works, *The Laws of Media*. I will show how McLuhan's claim that he was not a theorist but was interested in probes, percepts, and affects was grounded in his commitment to the traditions of classical learning as they evolved through the Middle Ages and the Renaissance and that he shocked the academic, artistic, corporate, and journalistic worlds by adapting ancient modes of exegesis and argument to understanding the newly emerging world of post-electric technologies, thus making him implicitly one of the leading twentieth-century promoters of a presumably "posthuman" transformation of the foundation of the liberal arts, particularly those aspects associated with the "trivium" (grammar, dialectic, and rhetoric), into a prepost-modern semiotic for the global village.

As a supplementary appendix, to further illustrate Marshall's vitality and the excitement he created among those with whom he worked in the 1950s, I am including an article by Ted Carpenter, since it should be made more widely available. One of the other important reasons for writing this book is to establish Ted's important role as McLuhan's colleague in the original Culture and Communication seminars and as the founding editor of *Explorations*, in which McLuhan honed his enigmatic, suggestive, prophetic, and apocalyptic style and from which he derived much of the material that was later to become a key to his work. The lasting aspects of Marshall's project are deeply indebted to Ted, as to a large extent is his having survived a serious brain tumor in the late 1960s (see Appendix B).

In another appendix I will raise the issue of my relations with Marshall over the years to place this work and my other writings about him in a social, psychological, and human context. Since the two biographies published so far have both briefly alluded to either McLuhan's disapproval of my doctoral thesis or my book length study of his work, *The Medium Is the Rear View Mirror*, this is discussed in detail in the biographical essay on my years with him and on the problems that arose. To the extent necessary to defend my interpretation of that story, I quote documents misleadingly, prejudicially, and selectively quoted or suppressed by Terrence Gordon in his biography. Marshall initially endorsed some aspects of my book and complimented my efforts, while sharply criticizing other aspects, but subsequently, as the evidence suggests, he was misled by others into an unintellectual attack on freedom of expression in order to suppress its publication. Although for over twenty-five years I have never written or commented publicly in detail on this incident, if I wish to revisit the subject of Marshall McLuhan, Professor Gordon's book has put me in the position of having to present the full story.

The biographical appendix and the reminiscences in the main text will, I trust, show that I had great respect for Marshall but that I also felt that one should be free to disagree and dissent. I hope that my differences from McLuhan, as well as my respect for him, will become clear. In the process a portrait should emerge of a remarkable intellectual and preposthumanist whose own vision is rich, conflictual, and respectful of the incredible complexity of our contemporary "chaosmos" – a contemporary, learned trickster who was able to envision the drive and thrust toward the close of the second millennium and who was also a symptom of the emergence of the new global city that is rapidly moving beyond media.

1 The Techno-Prophet as Poet and Trickster

In 1965 the cult of McLuhan – which quickly came to be known as McLuhanism – was born. Its conception began in 1950 as Marshall McLuhan was seeking for new projects on the eve of the publication of his first book, *The Mechanical Bride*.[1] It went into a quiescent state in the 1970s, as the spirit of the sixties came to a close, but was reborn in the 1990s when, subsequent to the posthumous publication of *Laws and Media* in 1988, *Wired* magazine, the mouthpiece of the new computer revolution, declared McLuhan its patron saint and the equally successful alternative lifestyles mag *Mondo 2000* reconstructed him as a transformed New Age vision of the sixties and critically explored his quirkier sides.[2]

Phenomena such as virtual reality (VR), the Net, the Web, and the pentium powered, multi-media personal computer spared the rebirth, because McLuhan's basic vision since the early 1950s had always included an ever-accelerating convergence of media in a world of the intersensory (the synaesthetic), where a total orchestration of the media would be achieved (the coenaesthetic).[3] The media analyst and critic of newpapers, magazines, radio, film, popular fiction and romance, advertising, and comic books in *The Mechanical Bride* was to become the prophet of technology's absorption of people and their real world into cyborgs and artificial realities. In 1950–51, when McLuhan shifted his examination from media products to the actual processes of communication themselves and their implication as technologies, he was breaking still newer ground. This had come about through his turning the new interest in cybernetics into a series of queries about poetry, art, technology, and communication coupled to a new awareness of some of the interests in communication of ethnolinguists such as Edward Sapir and Benjamin Lee Whorf.[4] Marshall's consciousness of his mission at the time, prior to the beginnings of the Ford Seminar, led to his producing a fluid-duplicated, usually one page, news sheet, *Network*, which he circulated by mail to his friends and handed out to his associates. Often he would come to our apartment to produce the ideas that were to form the handout, a precursor of such later items as "The Sheet" and the newsletter aimed at the corporate sector, *The Dew Line*.

His growing interest in studies of language and art by anthropologists eventually lead to my inviting him and his wife, Corinne, to spend an evening with Carpenter and his first wife at our apartment where they could come to know one another better. Cybernetics and ethnolinguistics confronting his commitment to literature and criticism were the goads that started McLuhan down the path to his famous Culture and Communications seminars – an exploration into what Carpenter and he dubbed the "new languages."[5] To say that such a direction was foreign to the university atmosphere of Toronto in the early 1950s (and for that matter to much of the academic world in the U.S.) would be an understatement, since it and its successors were met with a hostility that existed at the university (and elsewhere) throughout McLuhan's career.

That hostility has been noted by others, such as Philip Marchand, and William Toye in the apparatus to the *Letters*. But it is difficult to reconstruct its intensity in the 1950s and early 1960s, particularly in the English Department and the humanities. In the fall of 1950 I had been warned against working with McLuhan by the director of Graduate Studies. During my fifteen years of association with the department, the antagonism towards McLuhan and his reciprocal dislike of many of his colleagues was extremely obvious. While McLuhan was not an easy colleague, like many extremely intelligent and highly individualistic professors, the hostility he experienced was not only personal but was directed towards the credibility of his literary scholarship and, more particularly, his multidisicplinary studies. His position was protected primarily by his friendship with Claude Bissell, (vice-president of the University of Toronto 1952–56 and then president 1958–71), and by his affiliation with the Catholic college, whose senior administration, particularly Very Rev. Lawrence Shook, CSB (chair of English, superior of the local Basilian order, and later president of the Pontifical Institute of Medieval Studies in St Michael's College), strongly defended him.

McLuhan's intellect, individualism, uniqueness, audacity, and arrogance guaranteed that he would never be a Mcluhanite, as attested by his own denial – although he certainly must accept responsibility for its paternity. McLuhan was a new kind of artist, whose existence was made possible by the simultaneous emergence of modernism and mass media. He cannot be categorized as a theorist, since he denied that he dealt with concepts and theory; his thrust was to deal with percepts and affects in a manner that opened up connections between the commercial media, the arts, and academia in such a way as to legitimize the intellectuality of the media and enable willing academics and intellectuals to become media stars – the type of figures that he and later Neil Postman or Camille Paglia imitating him have become. But McLuhan was different from such imitative media stars. He insisted on having it both ways: being an intellectual, avant-garde, anarchistic poet, and simultaneously a media star, outstripping even the Tom Wolfes of his period.

McLuhan, who as a young graduate student in the 1930s had been impressed by the Renaissance Thomas Nashe, the Edwardian G.K. Chesterton, the Victorian Thomas Babbington Macaulay, and the Neo-Augustan Joseph Addison's *Spectator*, certainly demonstrated an interest in such literary journalists as possible models – models he saw transformed in the 1940s into the forerunners of the pundits of the *New Yorker* and *Harper's*. Furthermore, such models could not help but suggest the power that such journalism would eventually attain in our new era of technological production, reproduction, and dissemination through the newer modes of communication. The potential of a modern equivalent to the informed, educated, essayistic commentary of such authors combined in McLuhan's development with a modernist literary "fix" on the news (reflected in the opening pages of *The Mechanical Bride*) and an intellectual classicist's penchant for the poetic and the satiric. Pound had pontificated that "literature is news that STAYS news"; Joyce had incorporated the newspaper and its headlines into the seventh episode of *Ulysses*; in *U.S.A.* John Dos Passos intensifies the stories of his fictional characters with a sense of real history through the use of "newsreels," interspersed and artfully selected montages of actual newspaper headlines and popular songs of the day; the French symboliste Stéphan Mallarmé wrote a major poem based on headlines.

The real danger, which McLuhan may well have grasped in his remarks about how he could never be a Mcluhanite, is that one aspect of this mix – which involved the media star and media guru histrionically probing the new media technoculture – might be imitated by later media theorists who disregarded the importance of McLuhan's involvement with the entire spectrum of the arts and humanities and his understanding that he was trying to produce "news that stays news" – i.e., a poetic production whose value is not in what it says but what it is: the modernist principle that "a poem should not mean but be."[6] His particular strategy was to adopt the role of a learned human-istic satirist who, through poetic assemblages, could expose by means of probing and manifesting, without evaluating and articulating. For him this was not a cynical stance, as some seem to have suggested, but his realization of what he considered to be a contemporary recon-struction of Christian humanism.

McLuhan practised satiric writing since he believed that the tradition of learned satire permitted the poet to goad others into making value judgments, even if she or he was deliberately trying to hold his or her own evaluation in abeyance in the poem. This is the basis for McLuhan's oft-stated view that his work did not make value-judge-ments, even though he argued that it was satiric. He thus recorded and transmitted perceptions in ambivalent and paradoxical assemblages shielded from closure by his poetic involvement with percepts and affects. Gilles Deleuze and Felix Guattari, in a 1991 philosophical analysis of the relation of the philosopher, the scientist, and the artist (poet), have distinguished the role of the philosopher, with his com-mitment to the construction of concepts, from that of the artist, whose constructions with their emphases on sensation are concerned with percepts and affects.[7] Since in his writing McLuhan frequently stresses the importance of "affects" and "percepts" in the structure of his probes as they deal with sense processes and the intersensory, there clearly is an affinity between what McLuhan does in playing with arti-facts and the activity of those persons whom Deleuze and Guattari identify as poets and artists.

While McLuhan, by his own insistence, is neither a theorist nor a philosopher, he is a complex maker of poetic assemblages. Some pro-ponents of Mcluhanism, however, insist that he is primarily a media theorist or a media philosopher, even to the extent of denigrating his extensive literary and artistic interests, his role as a literary critic, or his continually avowed interest in modernist writing and art and in the history of literature.

One of his most oft-recurring complaints to his critics was their lack of knowledge of the contemporary artistic tradition, since there has always been a reluctance within the mainstream of North American communication studies to accept the poetic as a mode of discovery. A simple enumeration of specific references in McLuhan's major works indicates the dominant presence of the humanistic, literary, and artis-tic. While there are seventeen references to Harold Innis (his presumed mentor) in *The Gutenberg Galaxy* (only one less than the eighteen to the U.S. cultural historian Louis Mumford), there are thirty-two references to James Joyce and thirty-five to Sir Francis Bacon. In the subsequent *Understanding Media* there are twenty-three references to Joyce and only one to Innis. Perhaps not surprisingly, his *Cliché to Archetype* has no references to Innis; it has thirty-one to Joyce and thirty-two to T.S. Eliot. The posthumous *Laws of Media* has fifteen references to Giambattista Vico (who provided the framework for Joyce's *Wake*), nine to Bacon, six to Eliot and only two to Innis. Only in the posthumous *The Global Village*, which has a large section on Canada, are there more Innis references than those to Joyce – five for Innis and three for Joyce – but there are five to Eliot and four to Wyndham Lewis.[8]

The references to Bacon and Joyce, whose *Wake* as a history of the world is Viconian, underline McLuhan"s *Gutenberg Galaxy* as producing a "poetic history," just as the later *Understanding Media* is a "poetic analysis" of modern media. The subsequent publication of *The Vanishing Point* and *From Cliché to Archetype* further reinforce the artistic stance from which McLuhan wished to operate. While one cannot deny that Innis's history is an aspect of McLuhan, another history more central for McLuhan is in his hopefully soon to be published doctoral dissertation, *The Place of Thomas Nashe in the Learning of His Time*, which is a history of the trivium: a history of a conflict between differing modes of education in speaking and writing, and between the builders of concepts (the logicians and dialecticians) and the constructors of affects (the rhetoricians and poets). This interest in the trivium persists for over fifty years: the final references to it appear in *The Laws of Media*, where a page in the tetrads section entitled "The Trivium" contains three tetrads: the rhetorical tetrad shows that advertising is one aspect of the retrieval of oratory; the grammatical shows that the scriptural is one aspect of the retrieval of literature and tradition. The third tetrad, dialectic, McLuhan relegates to philosophy, retrieving the logos as a means for restoring the process of abstraction of "the word in the mind." The first two tetrads demonstrate again the co-existence of McLuhan the guru and publicist with McLuhan the poet as interpreter of nature and aesthetic who is also a believer in scripture.

McLuhan played a rather significant role in the road from the "New Criticism" to Cultural Studies, which is partly reflected by Raymond Williams's (1964) initial praise of *The Galaxy*. John Fekete in his *The Critical Twilight* (1977), while sharply critical of McLuhan, clearly shows that not only was McLuhan's insight into poetics more penetrating than that of the earlier new critics (including Northrop Frye) but that he had many intimations of the ways in which literature and the arts would illuminate a broader project in cultural theory.[9] Later,

in a more positive assessment of McLuhan, Fekete (1982) demonstrates that much of McLuhan's work anticipates that of Derrida.
Despite the fact that McLuhan did not study de Saussure until 1975,
certain directions within the "new criticism," as they culminated in
McLuhan's broadened vision of techne and the cultural artifact, anticipated some aspects of poststructuralism and postmodernism.[10] As a
spin-off, Fekete's article shows why the postmodernism of Derrida is
implicit in the movement of "new criticism" and why Yale became one
of the main focal points for that postmodernism.

Some time ago Tom Wolfe asked the question "What if he's right?"
But the more penetrating question might be "What if McLuhan,
accepting his vision of the millennial return of tribalism and its relation to Vico and Joyce, had decided that poetic history and poetic
prophecy must become a "new science," replacing social scientific
history and statistical prediction?" This decision surely accounts for
his radicalism, particularly when he places all new technologies on the
same basis as other artefacts. Such a poetic history permeates
McLuhan's early writings after the mid-1940s, both in literary journals and in *Explorations*, providing the foundation from which he
focused on the theme of the "new languages" in the initial Culture
and Communication seminars. McLuhan's writings steered studies of
communication, culture, and technology into becoming explorations
of the new languages of the emerging world of new media, from TV in
the 1940s (the early 1950s in Canada) to hypertext, the Internet, and
virtual reality in the 1990s.

His study of the avant-garde arts had encouraged McLuhan in this
project, for he avidly read such works as Gyorgy Kepes's *Language of
Vision: Painting, Photography, Advertising-Design* (1951) with a
preface by Sigfried Giedion, and Laszlo Moholy-Nagy's *Vision in
Motion* (1947), which specifically linked the new Joycean language of
the *Wake* with the new arts of vision and motion. These readings were
supplemented by Sergei Eisenstein, who in his *Film Form* (1949), like
Pound in discussing the imagist image, used a theory of the ideogram
as a means of understanding montage and film form (an anticipation
perhaps of the media as message). Eisenstein's writings about "film language" and its syntax, and his theories about synaesthesia and the
orchestration of the arts were to provide important insights and motifs
for McLuhan's later explorations of media convergence. Such insights
and motifs were reinforced from a multitude of other quarters, since
they are the earmarks of both the radical and conservative high modernist movements in the latter half of the nineteenth and the first half
of the twentieth century. For example, the McLuhanesque stress on
synaesthesia – a prime key to discussions of media convergence – is

also grounded in the earlier writings of Baudelaire and Rimbaud as well as other painters and writers.

That these were the prime directions that McLuhan was then pursuing can be seen by examining the contents of *Explorations*, Carpenter's brilliant publishing coup, which was one of the most unique, avant-garde, and earliest of multidisciplinary journals of the 1950s. Allowing for the avant-garde and interdisciplinary nature of the journal, which makes clear classification difficult, it is safe to say that about three-fourths of each issue was predominantly a mixture of the new anthropology, sociology, and ethnolinguistics as well as McLuhan's historical, artistic, literary, rhetorical, and humanistic interests. The last issue with which McLuhan was associated, *Explorations 8: Verbi-Voco-Visual* was a collaboration with a visual artist and designer, Harley Parker. In *Verbi-Voco-Visual* (a title borrowed from Joyce's *Wake*) McLuhan, with Parker's assistance, composed over half the material; of the other half, virtually two-thirds of the material written by others was on art or literature.[11] The main influence on McLuhan's thought from the social sciences during this period was Ted Carpenter, his prime collaborator, who opened up for McLuhan the contemporary world of anthropology, archeology, and sociology: Dorothy Lee, Edward Sapir, Clyde Kluckohn, David Reisman, Gregory Bateson, Margaret Mead, Benjamin Lee Whorf, and Edward T. Hall.

It is interesting to note that nearly forty years later when his last work, *Laws of Media*, was published some of the same scholars from the social sciences are still dominant influences and Carpenter's impact is still present. The contribution of the Culture and Communications seminars and of *Explorations* to McLuhan's development as a "thinker" reveals his real gift – the gift of a poet or artist; the ability to appropriate a wide spectrum of diverse materials "stolen" from various individuals and juxtaposed in such a way as to magnify the differences which frequently go unobserved by others. "Immature poets imitate; mature poets steal; bad poets deface what they take, and good poets make it into something better, or at least something different. The good poet welds his theft into a whole of feeling which is unique, utterly different from that from which it was torn; the bad poet throws it into something which has no cohesion" (Eliot 1932, 182).

One of McLuhan's fundamental refrains, that artists are the control tower in the electric society, clearly reveals that he saw his work as artistic; that is, poetic. But he is the seriocomic trickster as poet – a contemporary shaman – participating in one aspect of an age-old tradition of learned, carnivalesque satire, by which he plays on and plays with his readers.

He was fully aware of his role as a trickster as demonstrated, first, by research he carried out on this satiric tradition in 1951–52,[12] and in which I collaborated. Second, he admired Wyndham Lewis, perhaps the modernist master of the role of the trickster. Third, the concluding sections of *The Gutenberg Galaxy* are about Pope's *The Dunciad*, a masterpiece of such satire (which, incidentally, had influenced Lewis). Fourth, he encouraged his son to pursue doctoral research on Joyce and Menippean satire; or what his son, perhaps following McLuhan, called "cynic'" satire in his book, *The Role of Thunder in "Finnegans Wake."*[13] While the trickster is only one aspect of the poetic voice in this satiric tradition, it is clearly the one which McLuhan, with his radical conservative orientation and his proclivity for Lewis's tyros and tricksters, identified and found congenial. It is this element of the trickster that allows McLuhan to be comfortable with the confusion he deliberately creates for most of his readers, a strategy that has invited strong reactions to his work.

Some basic principles that he articulated and which function well in justifying his stance as a trickster are the idea that his work should be cryptic; his principle that he never wrote about anything that he did not dislike – a principle somewhat, but as will be seen later, not totally hyperbolic; and his willingness to appear to be writing theory while denying that he is a theorist and insisting that he is an observer dealing with percepts, not concepts. But McLuhan's predilection for the trickster stance was reinforced by a number of things: his conviction that the post-electric era would return to a tribalism where the shaman-trickster has a peculiarly important role to play (a position he found support for in anthropological research through Carpenter, Lee, Bateson, and others); the simultaneous affinity of the trickster with aspects of the medieval and Renaissance traditions in which he had done his early research; the extent to which contemporary advertising, which he saw as a type of poetry (perhaps a *poésie manqué*), was itself the product of tricksters.

The younger McLuhan of the early 1950s – playful, transgressive, subversive, and complexly disingenuous – was fascinated by figures such as the confidence man, the anti-establishment anarchist (e.g., Gershorn Legman, editor-publisher of *Neurotica*, who on two occasions published in *Explorations*, the second of which led to conflict with the administration of the University of Toronto; see Appendix B) and, most particularly, the "bad boy" of British modernism, Wyndham Lewis. Such fascination, when added to his early ambition of being a Victorian man of letters on the Roman Catholic model of G. K. Chesterton, shaped a multi-schizoid McLuhan who could apparently contradictorily appeal to both the post-Marxist left and the libertarian right, to orthodox literary figures such as Tom Wolfe or Hugh Kenner and to the new avant-garde such as John Cage, Merce Cunningham, and Robert Rauschenberg. For whatever impact or influence *Explorations* may have had on their formation early in their careers, according to Ted Carpenter in Appendix B in the 1950s Roland Barthes, Jacques Derrida, Claude Lévi- Strauss, and Susan Sontag were all subscribers. Trickster or not, McLuhan's agenda and the agenda of *Explorations* before the 1960s identified some of the major areas of discourse for the second half of the century.

McLuhan was a learned clown or trickster, a "reasonable" role for someone who had, by his own admission, moralistically explored the worlds of journalism, advertising, mass publishing (science fiction, romance, comic books, etc.) and commercial propaganda in *The Mechanical Bride* and then a few years later shifted to acting as an amoral observer of the emerging contemporary technoculture.[14] This was a role which "fit" more easily into a world where the directors and managers of the enterprises that McLuhan had explored in the *Bride* were assuming control, manipulating society as unprincipled tricksters and con-men, and whose agendas were shaping the true governing power of the emerging techno-culture. If others emphasized the atom bomb as the threatening and problematic invention of World War Two, McLuhan, like his Toronto colleague and Canadian compatriot Harold Innis, a historian of political economy and dean of the Graduate School at the University of Toronto, saw the less-immediately dramatic but perhaps over a number of decades equally critical threat as coming from the transformation of the behaviouristically oriented U.S. military propagandists into commercial hucksters (the subject of Frederic Wakeman's best-seller, *The Huckster* (1946), which portrayed the advertising, media, and entertainment world). But since McLuhan wanted to achieve the celebrity status of success, fame, and power as well as the satisfaction of revealing the implications of the technoculture, the seriocomic aspect of amoral satirist as trickster provided a traditionally poetically grounded mask that still allowed him to be part of both scenes, the media and the university research community.

Within the limits of his partially conflicting desires for media fame and high intellectual stature, McLuhan demonstrated a poetic sensibility that allowed him to intuit the transformation that had begun in the postwar late 1940s with cybernetics, the unleashing of television, the acceleration of the communications industry, and the behaviouristically and empirically oriented control of media and audiences. But to a large extent that poetic sensibility was shaped by key modernist artists and writers, a fact McLuhan always admitted but which his various masks deliberately and substantially concealed from much of

his audience and from critics who did not wish to confront the difficulties implicit in his true challenge. Artists and writers had been
exploring the early history or pre-history of the digital era since the
inception of electromechanization and electrochemistry, providing
insights McLuhan combined with the predictions in Norbert Wiener's
Cybernetics and *The Human Use of Human Beings* and the social
applications of cybernetics and system theory in Bateson, Ruesch, and
Karl Deutsch to anticipate the broad motifs of the emergence of cyberspace, virtual reality, and the telecosm.[15] It was a question of the poetic
juxtaposition of percepts, but it was accompanied by all the ambivalence implicit in such strategic structuring.

Ambivalence is the ideal environment for the trickster and ambivalence is the very nature of the hidden ground of a figure in McLuhan's
distinction between figure and ground. The ground that affects you
may encompass a multiplicity of perceptions, so that the medium (the
ground) can not only embrace a multitude of figures, but can also be,
for example, the massage, the mass age, and the mess age.[16] Even when
McLuhan appears deceptively open, explaining his position as in the
1969 *Playboy* interview, ambivalence is at the heart of the exercise. As
Philip Marchand has noted, a large aspect of this interview is a "put-
on" – McLuhan putting on the approach of his intended audience,
while satirically putting on the audience through the duplicity of his
observations. "Indeed, the entire *Playboy* interview has the flavor of an
extended put-on, as when he put on the mask of the academic futurist
to assure *Playboy* readers that, 'projecting current trends, the love
machine would appear a natural development in the near future – not
just the computerized datefinder, but a machine whereby ultimate
orgasm is achieved by direct mechanical stimulation of the pleasure cir-
cuits of the brain'" (Marchand 1989, 206).

There are additional examples, such as his response to questions
about marijuana, drugs, the hallucinogenic quality of his own writing,
and his fear of the extermination of Negros and Indians.[17] The
absences in such an exercise are as significant as what is present, for
many of his usual references are suppressed, although he initially
covers himself by insisting on the primacy of the poet and artist and
repeatedly reminding his interviewer that he merely observes. A further
ambivalent complexity is introduced in that presumably the interview
was edited and substantially rewritten by either the interviewer or
others at *Playboy*.

Ambivalence encourages simultaneous contradictory or paradoxical
approaches to the same material. For example, consider an analysis to
which we will return later: McLuhan's descriptions of human communication differ markedly depending on whether they involve dyadic or

triadic relations – the one being logocentric, emphasizing the privileged status of the Word; the other being sensuously embodied like a Deleuzean "body without organs," emphasizing tactility, the central nervous system (CNS), and gesture. Both are seminal, yet their co-presence can "beg many questions." One type of emphasis on orality and literacy, which tries to subsume tactility under the category of a secondary orality, is oriented to the theological and philosophical traditions of the Logos, particularly the theological status of the Word, as Ong's work suggests. The other type of emphasis is embedded in the sensory and the bodily, more directly affiliated with the transformed or reborn primitivism or tribalism arising at the end of the millennium (the *fin de siècle* of the twentieth century). When critics like Ong subsume the second account into the first, they are consciously theologizing and sanitizing the Nietzschean birth of radical modernism more extensively than McLuhan does.

McLuhan is a comic poetic historian writing the history of humanity as a history of the ways in which people communicate. The history of orality and literacy and the history of gesture and the sensory system are both relevant to his project, which gave major impetus to the subsequent growth in importance of the history of communication. His *Gutenberg Galaxy*, followed by *Beyond the Vanishing Point, From Cliche to Archetype*, and particularly the posthumously published *Laws of Media*, make this historical project clear, even though in most of his writings it is concealed behind the primarily synchronic treatment of contemporary technoculture that predominates in *Understanding Media* and most of his other works. McLuhan's historical contribution is of major importance, but he obscures it by mischievously attributing most of his insights to Innis. This has led communication scholars to forefront the strictly politico-economic aspects of communication history without providing the vital, complementary grounding in the poetic and artistic on which McLuhan insisted.

While Innis's presence at the University of Toronto introduced a different type of research interest that traversed some of the same terrain as McLuhan, Innis, who had a more social scientific, political economy oriented conception of history than McLuhan, was primarily interested in communications as a major aspect of the history of nations ("empires") and their political economy. Like McLuhan in *The Mechanical Bride*, he was coping with the post–World War Two expansion of the American empire, particularly through its cultural production, but unlike McLuhan he was not interested in the history of the arts, of techniques of rhetoric or modes of languages, nor did he exhibit a substantial interest in everyday or popular culture. While

Innis's style was often dense and discontinuous, he was not writing "poetic histories" in the tradition of Vico as McLuhan did. McLuhan first read Innis in 1951, some three years after the initial publication of *Empire and Communication*, and it will become clear that McLuhan was necessarily ambivalent towards Innis.

One can speak loosely of the existence in the late 1940s (in spirit, if not in fact) of a "Toronto School of Communication"[18] – since Eric Havelock (who was beginning his studies of orality and literacy), as well as Innis and McLuhan were all at Toronto. However, there was little actual contact between Havelock, Innis, and McLuhan, even though they were aware of one another's work. The spirit that generated this interest in communications existed, primarily because of the still-persistent importance of classics and humanism at the university in the 1940s and 1950s – the same spirit that produced Northrop Frye, McLuhan's alter-ego, who was one of the dominant forces in North American literary theory in the late 1950s and 1960s. That spirit surfaces in the initial commitment of McLuhan's seminar to the "new languages" – a focal point that joined the classic-humanist tradition in which McLuhan, Frye, and Havelock were all actively engaged – and which Innis admired – and the contemporary arts and cultural productions of the first half of the century with the new anthropological interest in language(s) and culture.[19]

Yet as Carpenter asserts in Appendix B: "I remain unconvinced of his allegiance to Innis ... [who] ... was never Marshall's mentor, not really. Marshall followed no one. Only poetry and scripture escaped contention." From my personal contact with McLuhan, which began three years prior to the seminar, I learned that he had already developed the historical fascination for communication in his own doctoral work on the history of the trivium; that he was not personally close to Innis – which was clearly confirmed on two or three occasions at which I was present when Marshall conversed with Innis; and that he was genuinely disappointed with Innis's lack of a foundation in literature and the arts. McLuhan's strategic use of Innis as a forerunner was an absolutely essential defensive strategy, protecting his interests in the relatively hostile context of the University of Toronto as well as adapting to a growing Canadian nationalism in Ontario and Canada. Yet it further contributed to the confusion about the nature of communication history and the relevance of the arts, poetry, literature, and the humanities to his project. The later revival of Innis, while perhaps intensified by McLuhanism, had more to do with the congeniality of Innis's politico- economic emphasis to the "spirit of the times" during and after the post-Marxism and renewed Canadian sense of national identity of the 1960s.

McLuhan had a superb and penetrating mind – but it was directed, as he himself insisted, to the poetic and artistic, to the grammatic and rhetorical (etymology and exegesis), and to the macro-historical, an aspect of the discipline which has become complexly problematic in the latter half of the twentieth century (McLuhan and McLuhan 1988, 128). These may strike one at first as strange tools with which to approach the complexities of our technoculture, particularly with the emergence of global digitalization and the resulting telecosm. But McLuhan's over-riding theme was that one can understand artefacts – the products of technologies or of art – only if it is understood that they are a new kind of language, a point underlined in *The Laws of Media*. And it is his claim that this language is interpretable only through a poetic transformation of the logical square of opposition.[20] In developing such strategies, primarily as a tactic like that of Poe's mariner in "The Maelstrom," McLuhan reveals where we are going in order to provide a shield against our fear of technology and to reorient us to the strength of tradition, despite the contemporary chaos of exponential change. McLuhan was an ambiguous patron saint for the glossy, computer generation mag *Wired* at its inception in 1993, particularly since its motto is "Change is good." McLuhan moved into exploring technology and culture because of his commitment to preserving a world in which a man of letters could assume authority through authoring essays and books that demonstrate "Change is dangerous and threatening." In pursuing the real relevance of McLuhan to the digital millennium, it is necessary to keep in mind his multi-schizoid orientation with its dislike of technology and change, its Nietzschean underside, its Catholic pietism, and its penetrating understanding of how the traditional domain of the artist and the humanities (in contradistinction to the humanist) was the crucial guide to understanding technoculture.

2 McLuhan the Correspondent: His Writings as Probes, Percepts, and Affects

When I first met Marshall McLuhan, in the summer of 1950, he was thirty-nine and on the verge of publishing his first book, *The Mechanical Bride*. In his mind that book was partly a "defence of poetry" – a strategy for leading young students from their immersion in popular culture to an understanding of poetry, the arts, and culture. Culture, in the sense in which it was used in discussions of the tradition in British and American poetics at mid-century, was always a central concern for McLuhan. McLuhan's culture then was that of a graduate of the Cambridge tripos – the culture of a cultivated man of letters. Marshall was a superbly inspiring teacher and an inveterate intellectual, critical of "middlebrows" and "lowbrows." Although later he was to abandon evaluation for a presumably detached objectivity, in his thirties Marshall was a satirist dedicated to exposing the weaknesses of the new world of advertising, the tabloid press, mass media, and popular culture. That this concern never disappeared from his personality is reflected in the endless letters he wrote. While only a portion of those letters have been published, the published collection is a valuable guide to someone who wishes to understand McLuhan's ideas, his sources, and his situation. The collection might well have been subtitled (playing on the title of a critical book by T.S. Eliot) "Notes Towards the Understanding of Culture."

In one of these posthumously published letters, a key to how he wished to be regarded, McLuhan chidingly disagrees with a writer who had failed to understand his works, primarily, McLuhan explained, because the writer had not previously studied Joyce or

Baudelaire: "I have no *theories* whatever about anything. I make observations by way of discovering contours, lines of force and pressures. I satirize at all times, and my hyperboles are as nothing compared to the events to which they refer. If you study symbolism you will discover that it is a technique of rip-off by which *figures* are deliberately deprived of their *ground*. You do not seem to have grasped that the message, as it relates to the medium, is never the content, but the corporate *effects* of the medium as an environment of service and disservice."[1] By implication, McLuhan reveals what he makes very explicit elsewhere in his correspondence: his own writings are dramatic, comic, and satiric, utilizing such satiric tactics as hyperbole, analogy, and metaphor, so that (as he suggests) he ought not be described as a framer of theories but as a creative communicator – an essayist and poet.

Such a statement raises problems for most critiques of McLuhan, which usually regard him, in one way or another, as a theorist; but he did not regard the writing of theoretical works as creative and for him creative activity was the prime means of understanding the processes of the new electric age. Writing in 1959 to an editor of *Marketing* he reveals that this creative instinct is becoming more and more extended throughout society, for he declared that "The citizen of the Electronic Age is a do-it-yourself man," which implies that such a citizen is "increasingly creative and playful." "In our Arts, we have seen the pattern shaping up for a long time. A hundred years ago, the painters abandoned pictorial space ... in favor of what they call "automorphic" space, a space in which each person, each thing, makes its own world. This is the kind of world that the Beatniks are struggling towards; they spurn consumer goods, they crave the do-it-yourself-world, even though it is a shabby and from a consumer point-of-view, fourth rate kind of world – because they insist on assuming the producer role in all matters and at all costs."[2] His insistence on the importance of the creative stance for everyone as a potential cultural producer permeates all of his work.

A number of these published letters discuss Innis's writings, including one written in 1971 to Claude Bissell, then president of the University of Toronto, announcing what he calls the biggest "discovery of my life" – a discovery which he points out Innis never made. McLuhan claims (being a little disingenuous, seeing that he had said the same things in the 1950s) that he didn't make this discovery until 1971. He claims that what Innis had not realized "Put in a word ... [is that] for 3500 years the philosophies of the Western world have excluded all technology from the matter-form entelechy treatment." In what seems like an anticipation of his later explanation of the foundation of his tetrads in *The Laws of Media* he explains this by suggesting in the same letter that: "Entelechy or energeia is the recognition of the new actuation of power brought about by any arrangement of components whether in the atom or the plant or the intellect. Pens and swords and ships and sealing wax which actuate human potential, creating specific new patterns of energy and form of action – these along with all technologies whatever .... were *written off*. That is, the Greeks and their followers to the present time have never seen fit to study the entelechies generated by the human arts."[3] He suggests that this happened because: "only natural and living forms are classified as hylomorphic" so that in considering the life of forms expressed by Aristotle in the terms *energia* (act) and *entelechia* (perfection) the human arts had by definition been excluded. In this corollary of his treatment of media in his works in the 1960s, McLuhan dramatizes how in the history of Western thought the natural and living forms are privileged in opposition to the products of the human arts.

Without pursuing at this point the complicated discussion that would be required to cope with the technical and historical problems posed by these statements, they do demonstrate the extremely high value that McLuhan placed on the relationship between the fine arts and *tekhné* in the shaping of human society. Accordingly, McLuhan finds Innis's work deficient in two ways: first, for having missed the importance of the relative downgrading of technology in the history of forms of human culture; second, in his general ignorance of the arts for, as McLuhan clarifies in another letter, "Harold Innis (incidentally, he was baptized Herald Innis very prophetically by a mother who was devoted to the *Family Herald*!) had no training whatever in the arts, and this was his gross defect." McLuhan contrasts Innis's ignorance of the arts with his own "surrealist" canvases, observing that: "As you will find in my literary essays, I can write the ordinary kind of rationalistic prose any time I choose to do so".[4]

Such a conscious counterpointing of his work with Innis's, which did not appear in his previously published writings, shows that he was quite conscious of having made advances beyond Innis and, in fact, that his building on Innis was partially a strategy for gaining appropriate response for his own work in Canada and particularly at the University of Toronto. Such awareness on McLuhan's part might well lead to a re-examination and critique of James Carey's aphoristic summation of how the development of Canadian communication theory ought to have taken place: "Despite the simplification, it is possible to describe Canadian communication theory by an arc running from Harold Innis to Marshall McLuhan. 'It would be more impressive,' as Oscar Wilde said staring up at Niagara Falls, 'if it ran the other way'"

(Carey 1975, 27). While McLuhan's letters do not achieve the miracle that Carey or Wilde were looking for, they clearly make a claim by McLuhan that he believed his work to be an advance, critique of, and extension of Innis's work, which Carey laments that it is not. If McLuhan's claims to his correspondents are correct, his approach ultimately reveals more facets of the actual situation of human communication in the electro-technical era than Innis and he also regards that era far more critically than Innis did.

While in 1964, in his "Introduction" to Innis's *The Bias of Communication*, McLuhan praises Innis for his insight as the discoverer of a strategy for understanding the role of technology in culture and communication and as a discoverer and teacher, even suggesting that: "I am pleased to think of my own book *The Gutenberg Galaxy* ... as a footnote to the observations on the subject of the psychic and social consequences, first of writing, then of printing," there are a number of reserved qualifications made throughout the article. For example, "[Innis] expects the reader to make discovery after discovery that he himself has missed"; [he] "sometimes mistook the interplay of the written and oral form"; [he] "manifests technological blindness" when through being "hypnotized by his respect for the pervasive conventional view" he associates radio with the centralizing tendencies of visual culture rather than the decentralizing ones of the new orality; and he has "managed to misread Wyndham Lewis radically," failing to realize "electric technology is instant and omnipresent and creates multiple centres-without-margins" (McLuhan 1964B, ix, x, xii, xiii).

Counterbalancing the Innis influence, his remarks in a letter to Ezra Pound underline the importance of Sigfried Giedion, the historian of art and architecture who in 1940, along with his wife Carola Giedion Welcker, a modernist art critic, arranged to have James Joyce and his family flee from France to Switzerland during the Nazi occupation, in his project: "My object is to learn the grammar and general language of 20 major fields in order to help on an orchestra among arts, cf. S. Giedion's *Mecahnization Takes Command* [1948] as a sample of how I should like to set up a school of literary studies. Basic modes of cogntion on this continent not linguistic but technological. Artistic experience comes to the young only via that channel. Must work with that *at first*."[5] On another occasion McLuhan observed that "Giedion influenced me profoundly. *Space, Time and Architecture* was one of the great events of my lifetime. Giedion gave us a language for tackling the structural world of architecture and artifacts of many kinds in the ordinary environment."[6] Even in 1953 when McLuhan first wrote in "The Later Innis" about his discovery of Innis's later works, he notes that: "It is quite evident that Innis was not prepared for all this. No individual can ever be adequate to grappling with the vision of what Siegfried Giedion calls 'anonymous history'. That is to say, the vision of the significance of the multitude of personal acts and artefacts which consitute the total social process which is human communication or participation. For in this kind of awareness 'commerce' or 'technology' are tools of extremely limited usefulness in discussion." He further notes that "The patient, watchful analysis of intricate modes of social experience, such as Sigfried Giedion brings to anonymous history, was lacking in Innis" (McLuhan 1953c, 386).

The importance of the arts, including literature, to his project becomes clear in this critique of Innis and still further in his telling Bissell that Innis's work was inhibited by the fact that he did not notice that "our philosophy systematically excludes *tekhné* from its meditations," (*tekhné* is the Greek term for art}.[7] The only extant letter, written twenty years earlier, to Innis clearly establishes how erroneous it is to consider Innis one of the most significant, if not *the* most significant, influence on Mcluhan's writings. This letter is an extended lecture on the arts in which McLuhan explains to Innis that what he is trying to do is to link "a variety of specialized fields by what might be called a method of aesthetic analysis of their common features." Confirming what is indicated above, he attributes this method to his friend Sigfried Giedion. Giedion's *Space, Time and Architecture* and *Mechanization Takes Command* were central to McLuhan's project, since both books present a specific parallel use of the arts, particularly architecture, as an aesthetic method for examining not only the history of art and architecture since 1850 but also the anonymous history of everyday objects and the rise of electro-mechanization.

In this same long letter to Innis, McLuhan criticizes an article by Karl Deutsch, a political scientist who was applying cybernetic concepts to his discipline. McLuhan points out that a prime fallacy in Norbert Wiener's work as well as in Deutsch's is "a failure to understand the techniques and functions of the traditional arts as the essential type of all human communication." He further charges that cybernetics is dialectical since it is derived from technology.[8] William Toye, in a footnote to this 14 March 1951 letter, observes that: "The manuscript of this letter is headed in the upper-left corner: 'Rewrite of letter for mimeograph HMM'. The original letter ... was acknowledged by Innis on February 26 (with apologies for not doing so earlier). Innis said he had been 'very much interested' in McLuhan's letter and that he would like to have it typed and 'circulated to one or two mutual friends', adding that he wished to receive the 'mimeographed sheet' referred to. Innis wrote over the body of the letter: 'Memorandum on humanities' (McLuhan 1987, 220).

Nearly thirty years later, McLuhan identifies the Shannon-Weaver theory – and therefore Wiener's theories as well as all other techno-scientific theories of communication – as "left-hemisphere" rationalism, against which he poses the understanding of communication by cubism which explored the grammar of "right-hemisphere" intuitionalism freed from a fixed point of view. While McLuhan's becoming aware of new discoveries concerning the bicameral brain allows him to further elaborate this insight, he still maintains that contemporary artists as discoverers of a multiplexity of points of view and critics of lineality are the "antennae of the race" (McLuhan and McLuhan 1988, 76, 86–90).

In this same letter to Innis he suggests that it is the artist-critic Wyndham Lewis who, having written *The Art of Being Ruled*, is the best diagnostician of those who, like Deutsch, are "technicians of power uninterested in social effect." Nearly thirty years later McLuhan features Lewis in unveiling his "laws of media" as a "poetics of media" by stating, in a subhead, that: "THE ARTIST IS THE PERSON WHO INVENTS THE MEANS TO BRIDGE BETWEEN BIOLOGICAL INHERITANCE AND THE ENVIRONMENTS CREATED BY TECHNOLOGICAL INNOVATION" (McLuhan and McLuhan 1988, 98).

The *Letters* reveal many other aspects of his work that were not as openly expressed in his books. For example, in 1978 he wrote to Robert Fulford, one of the editors of the *Toronto Star*, after Fulford described Roland Barthes as France's Marshall McLuhan, saying that "the article was very flattering: he placed me in the company of Roland Barthes who once asked me to collaborate with him on a book."[9] By then the subject of Barthes and McLuhan was quite topical, since McLuhan had met Barthes in Paris. In the fall of 1975 Barthes and McLuhan were the subject of a seminar series that I presented to students in the Communication and Canadian Studies programs at the Université de Bordeaux. Prior to that their work had been a continuing theme in seminars in Montreal where the bicultural development of communication studies made it a natural topic for discussion. In writing about Barthes McLuhan differentiates his work from Barthes's by saying that Barthes studies patterns as a phenomenologist, while McLuhan prefers "to study pattern minus the theory." Although the writings of Jacques Derrida are not mentioned in McLuhan's correspondence, the *Letters* also provide grounds for a comparison with Derrida.

Even though Derrida appears not to have taken serious note of McLuhan's work, since he mentions him only once in his various books and essays, there are a suprising number of similar themes (Derrida 1972, 329). These are the very themes that McLuhan reiterates again and again in the *Letters*: the fundamental opposition between speech and writing as well as such associated themes as logocentrism, writing, phonetic transcription, dissemination, plurivocity, synaesthesia, and a mutual fascination with the writings of Mallarmé and Joyce, to mention only a few (Fekete 1982, 50–67). Perhaps the most significant factor, though, is that both Derrida and McLuhan reiterate again and again how important Joyce was to their work. (I will return to discussions of McLuhan and post-modernism, including Barthes and Derrida, which form an important aspect of any revaluation of McLuhan or any critique of the introduction of structuralist and post-structuralist theory into current discussions of communication theory.)

One important question is why from the 1950s to the 1970s did such parallel interests as those of Barthes and McLuhan evolve in Canada and France (without any consciousness on the part of thinkers in either country of the interests of the other) much earlier than they appeared in the United States or England? McLuhan, following Innis, suggests that it has to do with the distinctness of vision provided by being from a marginal culture, for McLuhan says: "Today with electronics we have discovered that we live in a global village, and the job is to create a global *city*, as center for the village margins. With electronics any marginal area can become center, and marginal experiences can be had at any center."[10] Since in an electronic society the margins can become the center, it was clear to McLuhan, writing in the 1950s in the relatively village-like atmosphere of Toronto, that he should naturally be able to understand the changing patterns of American society more readily than those directly involved in the process. McLuhan regarded this as similar to the way that thirty years earlier the achievement of getting English poetry into the mainline European intellectual currents could not be done by the English but could be by Yeats and Joyce (two Irishmen) and by Pound and Eliot (two Americans) – from countries then at the margins of the British Empire and Europe.

As McLuhan often observed, Canada provided a DEW line (an early warning system) for the States, intellectually as well as militarily. In his *Letters* we see a McLuhan so dedicated to the DEW line concept that he writes to Ann Landers, whom he had met in Puerto Rico at a meeting of the Young Presidents Association, trying to sell her a subscription to the executive suite platinum card publication, the monthly *McLuhan Dew-Line Newsletter*, and inviting her to a conference of "Dew Liners" on Grand Bahama Island at which there would be "lots of Bucky Fullers and such sitting around chatting." In this 1969 letter he tells her of the inclusion of a bonus in the most recent issue – a new deck of playing cards for playing management games! He describes it as working by triggering off creative thought through startling associations, for he tells her "On each card there is an outrageous aphorism such as "Thanks for the 'mammaries'." and the directive is "Relate this aphorism to your top hang-up." But he also lectures "Dear Ann," (while inviting her to a Dew Line conference in the Grand Bahamas for executives on the future of management) on her privileged position to "make a creative contribution in this troubled area of identity image," by "eliciting anecdotes from twins via your column."[11]

While it is interesting in the *Letters* to see McLuhan playing with or playing up to the great names of his generation – Pierre Elliott Trudeau, Hubert Humphrey, Jimmy Carter, William Jovanovich, Ashley Montagu, Jacques Maritain, Ezra Pound, Wyndham Lewis, John Wain (the English novelist), John Cage, and many others – it is more significant that his *Letters* reveal a perpetually curious, rather perverse, yet dedicated intellectual confronting the collective socio-political phenomena of his time. Further, it is the conversational frankness of the *Letters*, which complement his other writings, that underline just how far McLuhan's poetic insights into the age of communication were developed to protect a set of biases which were *conversational* as well as conservative. Rightfully, McLuhan can now be called "the last Victorian," for these messages to family, friends, and colleagues clearly document his lifelong commitment to being a later twentieth century man of letters, a contemporary equivalent of his youthful hero G.K. Chesterton. He repeatedly suggests his bias is for print; his preferences, for the life of Oxford and Cambridge between the two wars; his motivation, the dislike of the new tribal world and its corporate activities.

The *Letters* also further confirm the claims that Arthur Kroker (1984) and I (1971) made concerning the importance of McLuhan's Catholicism by suggesting that his thought was metaphysical; that he was primarily a Thomist (though hardly one accepted by Thomist orthodoxy); and that, in spite of the stupidities of its bureaucracy, he believed that one can only live reasonably within the Roman Catholic Church, whose spiritual mission is triumphant. Consequently he expresses in his personal correspondence moral views that may appear contradictory when related to his writings: his condemnations of abortion, of pornography, and of frank, illustrated texts on sexual education for young children. From the outset of his career, agreeing with the Vatican, he was critical of Marx and Marxism, considering them as largely irrelevant to serious thought.

These aspects of his *Letters* hardly present the ultra-modern, futuristic, sometimes left-wing idol who dominated the media for nearly a decade in the 1960s and early 1970s as the prophet of the communication society. But the *Letters* also underline that split intellect that is central to understanding why McLuhan achieved what he did and made some of the most central contributions to dialogue concerning communication in our time. Balancing his Thomism is McLuhan's continuing use of Joyce's work, even though early in his career he had concluded that Joyce's work was demonic. In the *Letters* he says of the last page of *Finnegans Wake* and the opening of *Ulysses*: "Looking at Joyce recently. A bit startled to note that last page of Finnegan is a rendering of the last part of the Mass. Remembered that the opening of Ulysses is from 1st words of the Mass. The whole thing an intellectual Black Mass. The portion which Joyce read for recording concludes with an imitation of the damnation of Faust. As he reads it (I heard it in Toronto for 1st time) it is horrible. Casual, eerie. Speaking of Existenz and the hatred of language—what about Finnegan?"[12] In 1953 he tells a former student and colleague, Father Walter Ong, that the church has it all wrong with respect to Nietzsche: "God is dead" (Nietzsche) equals: God has abandoned the work of grace in creation? Prelude to incarnation as understood in pagan cults? At least, so I hear from the inside boys. Catholic view of Neech [sic!] would seem to be a bit off the beam there."[13]

The whole of his achievement – in fact, even his interest in communication – he attributes to Baudelaire, Mallarmé, Valéry and other French Symbolists, but even more particularly to their English modernist and post-modernist successors, Yeats, Pound, Eliot, and Joyce. Symbolists, modernists, Nietzsche, the avant-garde, diabolists – these provide the counterweight to McLuhan's love of print, his literary humanism, and his Thomism. Intellectually, McLuhan inhabits the world of Walter Benjamin, Georges Bataille, and Roland Barthes; emotionally, he seeks refuge in the comfort of the traditional academy, in personal romanticism, in a pietistic Catholicism and a romantic reconstruction of medieval universalism. The resulting tension and paradoxes between faith (emotionally based) and knowledge (intellectually based) reflects a prime modern dilemma, whatever the emotional or intellectual poles may be. McLuhan is himself representative of Havelock's " crucifixion of intellectual man" that permeates the philosophy and literature of the twentieth century. Yet from this tension, often nearing the edge of schizoid dimensions, there arise penetrating elucidations of what he considers to be modernity's prime concerns: culture, communication, and technology. To understand what he contributes to such a discussion it is necessary to confront a problem that it appears until quite recently the mainstream of Anglo-American communication studies has found nearly impossible to confront: the role of the arts and the artist in furthering understanding of communication. For the major, though by no means exclusive, influences on McLuhan's work are artistic, literary, or poetic.

This ought not to be surprising, since many other very important contributors to discussions concerning communication either have been writers or have been strongly influenced by contemporary and near-contemporary literature and the arts: the post-modern French (Barthes, Derrida, Deleuze, Lévi-Strauss), Italian (Umberto Eco), a British Marxist (Raymond Williams), the great Irish and American writers of the early contemporary period (Yeats, Joyce, Pound and Eliot) and Marcel Proust.[14] For McLuhan, as his *Letters* reiterate, literature, especially poetry, is essential for understanding the modern world. The other arts – film, the visual arts, sculpture, and dance – are also very important, but they clearly occupy a secondary role compared to that of the poet. He relates the creative processes of poetry and other arts to the creative act as he understands it to be described in Thomistic philosophy.

McLuhan believed he was developing a Thomistic-derived account of communication that differed from those classic and romantic theories that considered art and poetry to be involved with the "communication of thoughts and feelings" as a process of transmission from poet to audience through the medium of the poem. McLuhan's view of the Thomistic doctrine of participation involved the audience, through participation in the poem, retracing the poet's process of cognition and experiencing the percepts and affects involved through the labyrinth of the senses (essentially the Aristotlean-Thomistic *sensus communis* or the contemporary conception of a central nervous system). While he does not specifically explain it in this way to Innis, he was simultaneously writing his essay on "Joyce, Aquinas and the Poetic Process" (originally published in *Renascence* in the Autumn of 1951). In his letter of 14 March 1951 to Innis he distinguished his theory of communication as participation from those of Wiener, Deutsch, and Weaver and Shannon, whose theories were transmissional: "The fallacy in the Deutsch-Weiner approach is the failure to understand the techniques and functions of the traditional arts as the essential type of all human communication."[15]

If participation is essential and it occurs through interaction, then McLuhan is speaking of a communicative action similar to Kenneth Burke's concept of symbolic action in which all of the participants are co-creators. Such a bias towards participation, by which McLuhan characterizes modernity, is the basis of the drama of human communication. For McLuhan associates this communicative action with the activity of making sense, which he relates to the Thomistic conception of the agent intellect. "Knowing is making," he asserts and for him the poetic activity is every bit as rational as other forms of cognition. This, he claims, concerns the process of recognition and *re*-cognition, retracing and thus remaking the product of the labyrinthine human consciousness. His view of communication as a shared process of human making – of producing and reproducing cultural works (one of the leading forms being conversation) – recognizes the collective aspect of social communication.

McLuhan again and again stresses that he is reading the collective unconscious of the drama of society, even though he uses other signs to symbolize this. Gregory Bateson's writings (which McLuhan certainly read) should prepare us to understand this position, since Bateson has argued that the most important aspects of what we ought to consider the unconscious are only revealed by turning Freud upside down .[17] When McLuhan repeatedly refers to Joyce's "His producers are they not his consumers?" (FW 497.1–2), he is asserting that only through reading the social text produced by the participants in society can the poet or any artist produce his or her own text. For its producers, that social text is primarily unconscious. The artist transforms it by making sense of the producers' work, which they then consume, literally devouring it. About this, McLuhan says in a letter to the Canadian poet Wilfred Watson, his collaborator in writing *From Cliché to Archetype*,

Redoing old things. Remember the phrase in the mass?
Mirabiliter condidisti
Mirabilous[sic!] reformasti[18]
[Miraculously founded / Still more miraculously re-formed][18]

It is the difference between matching and making, between spectatorship and total dramatic participation. Through the drama of the mouth, we participate daily in the total re-creation of the world as a process.

For McLuhan, conversation or speech constitute the ideal mode of communication. Music, he argues, is always based on some mode of speech so that there are substantial ethnic differences in the production of music. To Wyndham Lewis in 1955 he wrote, "I find myself somewhat lacking in pride of authorship. I prefer conversation."[19] The "drama of the mouth" in the context of the quotation from the opening of the Offertory of the Mass strongly suggests how McLuhan understood the nature of the dramatic dialogue of communicative interaction to be communion-like.

In his stress on communicative interaction, as in the high valuation he places on creativity and participation, McLuhan's work is not deterministic. In fact, his stress on the importance of conversation as interactive and participatory is contrary to a deterministic position. McLuhan is, however, susceptible to the charge of using a pseudo-deterministic terminology as the surface for his satiric constructions. All the modes of technological reproduction and distribution (which McLuhan includes with all other artefacts as "media") are discussed in one or another of his letters. The various remarks concerning TV are typical. In what might seem paradoxical in view of the "deterministic" orientation of his surface, McLuhan does not argue that TV achieves its effects exclusively through a technically realized system of projection and distribution. He believes TV also has a "metaphysical" form which, while including its technological aspects, arises from the way in which TV functions as a social institution both in terms of its socio-economic practice and of its particular use of signifiers, which is a result of the biases implicit in the nature of this particular medium .

Reading through the letters brings attention to all the varied ways McLuhan approaches television and how many of them are not related specifically to hardware. Naturally he takes notice of the effects of the technology. In 1952 he wrote to Pound noting that radio and the telephone were the mechanization of speed, while cinema and TV were characterized by the mechanization of total human gesture.[20] While this division does not specifically distinguish television from cinema, it is implicit that only television as a medium of transmission combines the mechanization of speed with that of total human gesture. When with respect to TV he speaks of the "intensely dramatic character of this image," and that people are introverted (i.e., driven inward) by the screen,[21] McLuhan extends his analysis to social aspects of TV as well. The image is more dramatic and more "introverted" because of the social situations in which TV is experienced – in the home or in small groups and in a setting where members of the audience are potentially visible to one another (not in darkness).

Since McLuhan considered TV to be very, very polluting, he could write in 1977 to Clare Booth Luce declaring that media ecology programs must promote the restriction of its use, since it is "as radioactive as radium" and contains within its form a paradoxically hot and aggressive reflection of its social reality, advertising.[22] TV's intimacy, manipulation, and persuasiveness are partly implicit in the technology that responds to a world which is itself sensuously responsive, as reflected, for example, in its slang, which McLuhan described to the editor of U.S. Catholic as "tactile, haptic, proprioceptive, and acoustic."[23] That the sensuously responsive generation of the 1960s, shaped by this electric age of television, agreed in their attitudes and actions with such an analysis is apparent both through their commitment to the romance of the "hippie" and to the social criticisms implicit in student radicalism. That they also agreed in their ways of "feelfully" thinking is only too clear from their having initially uncritically embraced Marcuse as well as McLuhan as hero figures in the later 1960s. When McLuhan speaks of the "form" of TV, it encompasses all of these. McLuhan's familiar aphorisms present elements that are like the components of a mosaic, a form which he associates with TV but which clearly reflects his understanding of how to communicate in the electric age.

His strategy (which he compares to Joyce) is vivisective: a presentation of the living community of people in action. It is, therefore, itself a practico-poetic activity, not theorizing in the sense we would understand today. This provides it with a strength that no theorizing can achieve, for while he is not producing a theory and never claimed to be, he is thinking and elucidating the way communication works in much the way a psychoanalyst engages in a process of elucidation with and about the one being analyzed. His *Letters* clearly reflect that practice and provide the basis for a renewed perspective on his work informed by a much deeper understanding.

A concept of sensuous, dramatic action is central to McLuhan's feeling his way through the process of thinking reflectively about communication. It underlies his conception of the iconic form that is characteristic of the electric media and of his own mode of communicating. He suggests that the satiric genre, within which he believes his reflections must be realized, is associated with such iconic form.

Such a poetic technique permits him to merge figure and ground to study their interplay in communication and to involve his audience in participating actively in the process of understanding. If, as he tells Barbara Ward, he saw TV presenting "an X-ray icon which penetrates our entire organism," he also saw his own poetically crafted essays as presenting the interior landscape of the community's drama with equal penetration, thus justifying the description of it as vivisective.[24] But the mosaic method also provided a distancing that permitted him to see his activity as formally and generically comic and satiric. He writes to Michael Hornyansky (a Canadian poet and English professor) that: "Those people who think that I am an enemy of the book simply have not read my work, nor thought about the problem. Most of my writing is Menippean satire, presenting the actual surface of the world we live in as a ludicrous image." [25]

This genre of learned satire, discussed in detail later, provided a somewhat unusual yet stylistically appropriate genre for McLuhan's comic critique of contemporary communication. He speaks frequently in the *Letters* of one of his favorite examples of this genre, Pope's *Dunciad*, which is also one of the earliest critiques of the new potential for mass production of printed literature. McLuhan asserts to another correspondent that this work sums up the liquidation of traditional learning (the trivium and quadrivium) by the mass production of print. To illustrate, he quotes from *The Dunciad*: "Art after art goes out and all is night."[26] McLuhan sees this satire as one example of the "more ludicrous extremes of mechanism perceived by Swift and Pope. *The Dunciad* is a dismissal of the crushing impact of an excess of printed matter on the human intellect."[27] This "exposure to seas of ink" produced "the illusion of separate and private individuality" and of "inner light."[28] The strategy of this learned satire is especially well adapted to situations involving communication and society, since the development and dissemination of knowledge is so intricately interlaced with the networks of communication.

For McLuhan works of learned satire present dramatic cross-sections of the actual process of communication in the production of knowledge and of the means by which distorted communication impedes that process. Consequently, the sense of humor that permeates the letters is an equally essential aspect of his writings. "Humor as an institution," he tells Jonathan Miller, "can be seen as an anti-environment for grievances, whether it is Hamlet's 'antic disposition' or Steve Allen's theory 'the funny man is a man with a grievance.' What a light that sheds on the medieval clown, and King Lear!"[29] In an unusual letter to a prison inmate who had been free only about ninety days in the previous thirty years, McLuhan wrote stressing the importance of play and humor: "Perhaps it is the ability to *play*, the good humor needed to enter into fun and games, which is the final mark of sanity. When people become too intense, too serious, they will have trouble in relating to any sort of social game or norm. Perhaps this is why jokes are so important. On one hand, they tell us where the troubles and grievances are, and, at the same time, they provide the means of enduring these grievances by laughing at the troubles."[30]

McLuhan is aware that jokes and humor, like anecdotes and clichés, have an essential role in how serious communication takes place in business, diplomatic, and political circles. Such strategies provide an allusive means of communicating about critical issues, so in his *Letters* he periodically shares jokes and humorous anecdotes with his friend Bissell as a way of equipping him with an arsenal for making speeches on critical issues. His own mnemonic method for remembering jokes and anecdotes was based on hints and suggestions, for as he explains to Ernest Sirluck (then president of the University of Manitoba),who had requested a file of these conversational gems for use in his speeches: "Apropos the joke file – alas! My stories exist as one-line reminders, on backs of various sheets and envelopes and are not in narrative form."[31] In fact, those who knew him well were familiar with the 3x5 cards (which he kept in Laura Secord candy-boxes) that contained notes for his books, his anecdotes, and his teaching as well as the joke file.

This idea file continually nourished his conversational style. "Conversation has more vitality than books, more fun, more drama," he said in a *Life* interview in 1966.[32] The vitality of laughter as a conversational mode is essential to dealing artistically and satirically with the relation between communication and knowledge, which McLuhan had analysed as essential as early as *The Gutenberg Galaxy* (1962). From a post-Nietzschean perspective, his pursuing such an aim is understandable when viewed in light of what he said about Nietzsche. It also explains that strange combination of Aquinas and Nietzsche that he discovered in Joyce's writings. Aquinas's *Philosophy of Being* provided a justification for poetic knowledge and Nietzsche's negation of value opened a way to utilizing satire in exploring knowledge. McLuhan saw himself, like Lewis, as an artist who is "engaged in writing a detailed history of the future because he is the only person who lives in the present."[33] Ultimately, whether such a perspective can teach us something about communication awaits an extended discussion oriented towards the understanding of McLuhan that was not achieved during the first period in which his name stood for an international fad and which still seems not yet to have been achieved despite his revival in the early 1990s.

His complex analysis of the problems of communication, knowledge, and the arts has yet to be fully confronted. First, like Innis, McLuhan's work on communication is rooted in the importance of the concept of the university. The *Letters* bear ample evidence of his deep interest in the history of the university, just as Innis's *Idea File* (1980) does. The double theme of communication and knowledge has been central to the establishment and growth of the university as a social institution. McLuhan and Innis saw the university as itself an instrument of communication and as the institution by which the teaching of the modes of communication has been nurtured. McLuhan's interest in the trivium shows not only an interest in rhetoric but also an interest in the the history of education, both as they relate to art and communication. This major theme concerning higher education, which pervades his writings to Bissell and other university colleagues, complements the many sharp criticisms he made of academics and the academy.

The incredible complexity and ambiguity of McLuhan's interest is reflected in a rather surprising feature of the *Letters*: they reveal not only an interest in the history of occult knowledge that has characterized many contemporary artists and thinkers but an immediate concern with the ongoing operation of occult knowledge through "secret societies." While the latter reflects part of his own darker side, inclining to delusions of persecution, the former is surprisingly important to understanding the arts which he sees as so central to communication.[34] In his *Letters* he praises the work of Frances Yates, especially her *Art of Memory*. Describing this "marvelous book," McLuhan is obviously remembering the value of her work in showing the intrinsic connection between the growth of modern knowledge, the development of post-medieval literature and drama, and the importance of the "occult tradition" in the Renaissance.[35] Throughout his work, as he alludes to the importance of the "secret societies" in the shaping of modern art, he plays with what is the core ambiguity of his thought: the way the value of the new electric age and its demonic aspects are intertwined, if not inseparable (an issue that will be revisited in a fuller discussion of the significance of occultism and hermeticism for McLuhan). "Electricity scrapped industrialism and retrieved the occult," he writes to a former student, and we may rest assured that the individual who wrote to Pound of his disillusionment with the modern arts (shortly after the discovery of what he considered to be the importance of esoteric knowledge), seriously considered the vast potential within esotericism, which Morris Berman (1984) has associated with part of the "re-enchantment of the modern world" – McLuhan's "electric eco-land."[36]

But while the university as institution and the hidden "University of Being" as they relate to the themes of communication and knowledge are only two aspects of McLuhan's thought which are illuminated by his *Letters*, his contemporary conception of the mystical "University of Being," where intellect was regarded as the foundation of Being (not Being of intellect) stresses the centrality of the intellect in the "information society." In such an environment, understanding the process of intellection becomes the central product in the sciences and the arts and "the increasing volume of information flow substitutes for products in the sense of becoming the major product."[37] From his insistence on his role as poet, satirist, "pattern watcher," and sci-fi predictor of the future (because of his living in the present and loving the past) capable of major contributions to our understanding of the information society, a new figure of McLuhan emerges which demands his revaluation as a twentieth-century poet and satirist concerned with probing rather than theorizing about communication, culture, and technology in the emerging technoculture.[38]

3 From the Trivium to the Tetrad: Media as Artefact and Language

In late 1960 I was hired by the Canadian Broadcasting System (CBC) as a consultant to "translate" Marshall McLuhan's mimeographed report to the National Association of Educational Broadcasters (NAEB), *Report on Project in Understanding Media* (June 1960), the forerunner of *Understanding Media*. One day, while I was working in my office, Marshall accosted me and pointed out something I already knew – that mystery was of the essence of his writing. I replied that all I was doing was trying to explain to others how they might use his insights in their practical work, so I was *not* therefore trying to demystify the poetics of his work by translating it. As Ted Carpenter always pointed out (echoing Archibald MacLeish), "Marshall's work does not mean, it is." McLuhan's writing is not the work of a linguist, a theorist or a semiotician, but an inspiration and guide for linguists, theorists, and semioticians. McLuhan's correspondence confirms this, for he repeatedly explains that he is not a theorist but a satirist and artist. In the letter to a critic, mentioned earlier, in which he stresses the importance of symbolist poets to his work, McLuhan specifically indicates that he is consciously writing in an obscure and cryptic style: "I would be grateful to you if you could give me examples where I Have *mis-stated* any fact whatever. My canvasses are surrealist, and to call them theories is to miss my satirical intent altogether. As you will find in my literary essays, I can write the ordinary kind of prose any time I choose to do so. You are in great need of some intense training in perception in the arts." The problem McLuhan's work presents is that, while he shared knowledge of his "poetic" method with his colleagues and correspondents, he did not actively discourage – in fact, often encouraged – his public image as a communication expert and guru of media analysis.

The power of ambiguity to imply more than can be said and the power of juxtaposing items without comment to intensify observation are two strategies McLuhan had learned from Pound, Eliot, F.R. Leavis and his early association with the southern American New Criticism. These confirmed and supplemented lessons he had learned at Cambridge during his extensive study of the history of grammar, rhetoric, and the trivium. As well, his knowledge of the obscurity of surrealism, modernist *symbolisme*, and high modernist post-symbolism (Eliot, Pound, etc.) reinforced and radicalized lessons he had learned earlier from Francis Bacon's observations about the advantages of a deliberately obscure parabolical style – what Bacon called *crypsis* – which McLuhan saw as similar to Mallarmé's formula that a poem should be a "labyrinth sealed at both ends."[2] While talking about poetics may seem to be far removed from exploring contemporary technoculture with its machines for processing communication and information, the poetics of science fiction, as represented in works such as William Gibson's or Bruce Sterling's cyberpunk novels, provide some of our most powerful insights into the implications of contemporary technoculture, a fact widely recognized by the instant popularity of Gibson's term "cyberspace,"coined in his intensely poetic prose.

What have come to be known as McLuhanisms, which have frequently invited the ire and exasperation of McLuhan's more severe critics, are actually, as he insisted, "poetic probes" not scientific principles – percepts rather than concepts. To speak of TV as a cool medium or technologies as extensions of man is to speak in a deliberately allusive, suggestive manner. The value of speaking in such a way is indisputable in view of how frequently McLuhan's aphorisms have appeared in discussions and debates about culture, communication, and technology in the past forty years. To examine a specific example, a phrase such as "global village" takes on its peculiar resonance by having appositionally related two nouns that had not previously been brought together. While it is now often used as a stock phrase, when McLuhan launched it, there was shock at the association and partial equation of the globe with a village. McLuhan demonstrated how to build on such poetic phraseology by developing further percepts, such as post-electric tribal man – a phrase whose value is primarily in what it suggests rather than what it specifies. Generating such clusters of new terminology as global village, post-electric, and new tribalism has illuminated and highlighted contemporary social problems. This McLuhanesque strategy, derived from modernist poetics, is illustrated in its most complicated and potent form in such complex, multiplex Joyceanism's as "Television kills telephony in brothers' broil. Our eyes demand their turn. Let them be seen!" (FW 52.18–19), a phrase that McLuhan cites when commenting on TV as fostering the extreme and pervasive tactility of the electric environment (Mcluhan and Fiore 1968, 76-7).

In passages such as the following one about reading, Joyce plays with complex, multiple combinations of four-part structures consisting of eye-I-aye; ear-ere; code-decode; cord-chord to delineate the complexity of reading that is itself a complex interplay of reading, writing, and raiding.

The prouts who will invent a writing there ultimately is the poeta, still more learned, who discovered the raiding there originally. That's the point of eschatology our book of kills reaches for now in soandso many counterpoint words. What can't be coded can be decorded if an ear aye sieze what no eye ere grieved for (FW, 482.31–6).

Poetic strategies such as these multiple quadruple interactions articulated by Joyce guided McLuhan's exploring and probing of communication, culture, and the emerging technoculture from 1950 for over thirty years. The pages of *The Mechanical Bride* (1951) were an early use of a four-part structure, which was to persist into the "tetrads" of his late works. Each of his brief essays in the *Bride* is a "cultural object" – a newspaper page, an ad, a comic book cover, a frame or frames from a comic strip – embedded in a four-part structure where each of the visual illustrations is juxtaposed to a parodic headline; a sequence of short, pithy, witty, often comic questions; and a text shaped on the principles of a Baconian essay, using its fundamental technique of *pro et contra* by counterposing the positive and negative intellectual, social, and/or moral effects of the particular object under study.

The four parts operate in a kind of counter-point, implying more than is said. Using an advertisement for *Time* magazine as an example, McLuhan probes "The Ballet Luce," posing questions like "Is the newspaper world a cheap suburb of the artists' bohemia?" or "Where did you see that bug-eyed romantic of action before? Was it in a Hemingway novel?" Exhibiting the "poetic" art of this ad provides a counterpoint to the probing of its sources – the manipulation of communication and control by the Luce empire – through presenting a "cynical omniscience and detachment," the strategies of which are derived from the romantic and early modernist artists and writers (McLuhan 1951, 9–11). The *Bride*'s style and structure were more closely affiliated with the poetics of cubism and dadaism than with the pre-post-modernism of Joyce's *Wake,* since only after beginning *Explorations* did he abandon the overt moralism of the *Bride* for what he considered the stance of objectivity of a "scientific" or empirical observer.

Four part structures have always attracted interest, since they readily shape themselves into diagrams that can contain horizontal, vertical and diagonal lines, assuming the shape of a parallelogram, rectangle, or square. McLuhan's fascination with a four-part structure arises from three sources: its deep roots in mystical, mythological, and esoteric traditions; its persistence in the literary tradition with respect to both macro-structure (e.g.,Spenser's *Four Hymns,* Pope's *Moral Essays,* Eliot's *Four Quarterts*); mythopoetics (Blake's *Four Zoas,* the four elements, the four bodily humours); micropoetics (quatrains, the four part heroic couplet); the authority of the logical square of opposition in the history of the trivium (the basic liberal arts); and literary theory (the Jungian emphasis on quarternary developed by McLuhan's colleague Northrop Frye in his *Anatomy of Criticism*). The contemporary application of the term "tetrad" in biological science (e.g., cell meiosis) joined with the historic relation of the term to the Pythagoreans probably eventually led to his calling his four part structures tetrads. Yet in emphasizing the importance of four parts he wished primarily to establish that his project was producing a quarternary structured Viconian, poetic, "history of the world."

McLuhan first introduces the term tetrad in his posthumously published *Laws of Media* (co-authored with his son, Eric) to describe his basic technique for explaining artefacts (or media). In *Laws of Media* he explains that his tetrads are presented in an "appositional" poetic form ["*Appositio*: apposition; two juxtaposed nouns, the second elaborating the first" (Lanham 1991, 20), which presumably distinguishes his tetrads from the linear squares of opposition of classical logic that depend on the triadic structure of the syllogism: thesis, antithesis, synthesis. He associates the tetrad with the analogy of proportionality (A is to B as C is to D), but, unlike the traditionally analogical, McLuhan is intrigued by its dramatizing elements of difference rather than its use of similarity. In *Laws of Media* McLuhan returns to material he was working on in the 1950s, revealing far more clearly than ever before that his earlier work has its roots in the "new sciences" of Bacon and Vico as well as in the more conservative aspects of high modernist literature and art of the twentieth century. *The Laws* also illuminates the significance of his project for understanding the post cyberfied global metropolis (McLuhan 1987, 278) that will arise from "transformations in world life and media in the 21st century."[3]

In the McLuhanesque vision – since he develops a poetic strategy of considering all artefacts (material, intellectual, or imaginative objects) as media – Renaissance philosophers like Bacon or Vico are as relevant today as modernist artists for exploring the transformations of technoculture. An examination of the list of media in *The Laws of Media* reveals that media involve everything from chairs and refrigerators to metaphor and symbolist poetry to VCRs and computers. While the principle that all artefacts are media constituted McLuhan's fundamental poetic discovery in the 1950s, and provided the foundation for *Understanding Media*, this principle was finally only fully and clearly articulated nearly a decade after his death.[4] Although in *Understanding Media*, which established his international reputation, McLuhan's analysis is structured on the principle that the term "medium" is synonymous with the term "artefact" so that artefacts or media can be "tangible," he never overtly or specifically says so in this work.

But fifteen years later, written shortly before he died (31 December 1980), the very first words of *Laws of Media* (not published until 1988) are, "One fundamental discovery upon which this essay rests is that each of man's artefacts is in fact a kind of word, a metaphor that translates experience from one form into another" (McLuhan 1988, 3). The *Laws* proceed to illustrate how everything from booze, a brothel, a cigarette, or a refrigerator to cubism, a computer, electric light, Aristotelian causality, or the Copernican Revolution is an artefact or medium. Today cyberspace, the Internet, or a product of genetic engineering can be considered as such an artefact. This, of course, is the specific power of McLuhan as a sociological poet: he applies a traditional interpretative (hermeneutic) approach to "media" (i.e., cultural objects or human artefacts). The tetrad, which McLuhan makes the center of *Laws* and *The Global Village*, is a poetic aid to memory (a mnemopoetic device) that schematizes a "reading" of an artefact as if it were a text.

So McLuhan says that his tetrad is a poetic square of apposition (rhetorically playing it off against what he considers the linear-oriented logical square of opposition) that poses four questions: what does an artefact or media (1) enhance, (2) obsolesce, (3) reverse, (4) retrieve? So a tetradic exploration of the introduction of the computer, according to McLuhan, dramatically displays how the computer speeds up calculation and data retrieval (an enhancement), how in the process it presumably reduces anarchy by further empowering bureaucracy (a reversal), how it provides a more nearly perfect, comprehensive, and precise memory (a retrieval), and, finally, how it renders less valuable a variety of factors such as approximation or perception as well as a variety of hardwares (obsolesces) (McLuhan 1988, 188-9). Towards the end of his life McLuhan consciously links the tetrads of his two posthumously published books to the technique of exegesis of *Understanding Media*. In *The Global Village* he suggests that at the end of the 1970s Bruce Powers and he are looking into the now-immediate future of the twenty-first century just as his books in the 1960s looked at the future of the late 1960s and 1970s.

The value of the poetic method that he embraces is that it allows for its extension by others and it allows for additional supplementary or complementary exhibits, so that today we might design a tetrad for the ARPA-net (the creation of the Defence Advanced Research Projects Agency [DARPA]) developed, rhizomic Internet as follows:

(A) it enhances a universal global theatre where all participants can interact
(B) it obsolesces mass media and partially interactive technologies such as the telephone
(C) it retrieves anarchy and personal freedom
(D) it reverses bureaucratic control

and it also allows for alternative analyses, as McLuhan illustrates with other artefacts in *The Laws*, so that the Internet under governmental and/or corporate control:

(A) enhances universal accessibility of every one to every one else
(B) obsolesces individualism and the privacy of the home
(C) retrieves the panopticon (universal surveillance)
(D) reverses privacy and personal freedom from scrutiny

The value of McLuhan's prose poetic essays for discovery or invention (heuristics) and interpretation (hermeneutics) should be indisputable since his success and influence as a mass media guru – a cultural icon – who shaped the languages through which we speak about communication and control technologies has proved it to be forcefully effective.

McLuhan started playing with his square diagrams (the embryo of his tetrads) as early as the late 1950s. In the earlier 1950s he had been fascinated by William K. Wimsatt's explication of how Pope's heroic couplet, by playing with 'hateful contraries' (which Joyce in the *Wake* describes as a 'zeroic' couplet), could contain a complex poetic play with and on the logician's square of opposition.[5] This was reinforced by the fact that he considered a four-part structure a characteristic of metaphor and of proportional analogies. Under such literary and philosophical influences, and with his proclivity for rhetoric, he continued to play with various juxtapositions of four elements as a means of explaining media. Through his reading of and research on Pound and other high modernist poets and artists, McLuhan had discovered the power of radical apposition (essentially juxtaposing in surprising combinations terms for or associated with cultural objects, usually nouns) to trigger a rich, ambivalent environment that generates numerous potential insights.[6] A first intimation of a tetrad appears in his 1960 mimeographed report to the NAEB (which was not published for sale in the 1960s)[7] where he utilized what he considered to be the interplay between four aspects of all media: High Definition, Low Definition, Structural Impact, and Subjective Completion. (While he later used these concepts in *Understanding Media*, he did not show them as arranged appositionally in a square as he had in the mimeographed report.)

While there is no suggestion that these "four aspects of all media" are precisely the same as those in the later *Laws of Media*, it is apparent that McLuhan is already thinking about notions such as enhancement, obsolescence, retrieval, and reversal; about four governing principles of media; and about the conflicting interactions within any medium. If TV's four-part structure in the NAEB report places "do-it-yourselfness" in high definition, since "you are the screen" and "you are the scalpel," then "introversion, cool[ness] ... impersonality" are placed in low definition. But this is like saying that TV enhances "do-it-yourselfness" and obsolesces "introversion" and "impersonality." If in the NAEB report, TV's subjective completion is "maximal participation via all senses" and its structural impact in low definition is "visual-kine" as opposed to an "acoustic resonance via sculptural form," then it could be said that this is like TV's reversing the specialization of the senses and retrieving through the "visual-kine" the maximal participation of all the senses (McLuhan 1960, 137).

This not only has some interesting similarities to, but is nearly identical with, the tetrad for TV in the *Laws,* where McLuhan has TV enhancing the "multisensuous using the eye as hand and ear" described as a "do-it-yourselfness" where "you are the screen" and "you are the scalpel" and obsolescing "radio, movie, point of view" (associated elsewhere by him with introversion and impersonality).[8] Similarly in retrieving the "occult"[9] it does so by routing one sense through another – ear and hand through the eye, and reverses "the inner trip" through "the maximum participation of all the senses." The play with tetrads also involves McLuhan's assertion that one media technology becomes the content of a newer one, as film becomes the content of televison, with its implications of reversal and retrieval. Both the retrieval and the reversal aspects of the tetrad involve metamorphosis. The tired cliché, movies, became available as an art form when TV replaced them as the entertainment surround (McLuhan 1988, 105-6).

Another factor that McLuhan attributed from time to time to the elements of such transformations is the distinction between media which invite participation (TV as a cool medium) and those which do not (film as a hot medium). In the case of TV and film, he related this to the way light was projected to create the images. Film projects light on the screen; TV projected light through the tube. TV then could be compared to stained glass where the window is illuminated by the light coming through it (Theall 1971,143). While the phrases "hot" and "cool" were more characteristic of the writings of the 1960s, the underlying distinction between participation and non-participation persisted.

Whether we now accept McLuhan's entire discussion of cinema becoming an art form (since there is a relative revival of the local film theatre in the shopping malls), or his discussion of participation (hot and cool media), his development of the likeness or analogy between film and TV and then his dramatization of their differences provide crucial factors for understanding them. Whether the technical details of his analysis work or not, its poetic overtones open up a series of illuminating synchronic and diachronic interpretations of the "televisible". This is precisely the point of his tetrads in *Laws*, which he uses as proportional poetic presentations to dramatize differences. One of the advantages of using the tetrad as a poetic device is the possibilities it offers for generating multiple interpretations that intersect and partially overlap, but which are distinct, complementary, and supplementary. This permits McLuhan to play a double game – to be the scholastic metaphysician-dialectician which, on one side he claims not to be and, on the other, to be the humanistic grammarian-rhetorician he claims to support – the two opposing sides in McLuhan's history of the trivium in his Nashe thesis.

Early on in his work he appears to have abandoned what he once considered to be the Thomistic balance of Aquinas, although apparently he never overtly recognized that he did so, for by following the modernists, particularly Joyce, he moved towards the monism of Scotus while believing, or at least asserting, that he was dedicated to the authorized neo-scholasticism of Aquinas.[10] While the Aristotlean-oriented Aquinas grounded his philosophy in dialectic, logic, and rationality, McLuhan's tetrad, as a post-structuralist parody of the traditional square of logic, is based on appositional rather than oppositional principles. Belief and faith in Catholicism and a commitment to what he considered Thomism led Mcluhan to a strategy of sanitizing the Nietzschean aftermath and to his concealing the affinities that he might share with Baudrillard or Deleuze (like Joyce, a Catholic apostate).

That this is the thrust of McLuhan from *Explorations* of the early 1950s to its fruition in *The Gutenberg Galaxy* (1964) is only too apparent in the way that *Laws of Media* actually represents a return to the 1950s – in fact, even earlier to his Cambridge thesis and his various critical writings of the 1940s that were influenced by Leavis and the New Criticism. But *Laws* and the subsequent *Global Village* have a significant difference in that reference to Joyce becomes relatively minor and muted. Still, even the central emphasis on Vico in *Laws*, – whose "poetic history" of *The New Science* McLuhan mentioned as early as his introduction to Kenner's *Paradox in G.K.Chesterton* (1947) – and on Bacon, whose writings were significant to McLuhan's research into rhetoric and style at Cambridge, were clearly present in his critical writings of the 1940s and 1950s in *Explorations* and his seminars in Culture and Communications.[11] All the basic ingredients of McLuhan's intensely poetic vision, which was to have such an impact on the anti-poetic direction of "official" communication and media studies from mid-century into the new millennium, were present in this earlier work.

The *Laws* also correspond to an aspect of McLuhan's program which recognizes that the ideas of media convergence and synaesthesia ("the perception by one sense of a stimulus to another") were interrelated with some modernist theories that recognized the tendency of the newer technologies and modes of cultural production to move "beyond media."[12] McLuhan's ability to intuit the significance of this tendency is deeply grounded in his historic interest in rhetorical and poetic theory – particularly the awareness of the association between the Aristotelian conception of art as *techné*;[13] its subsequent role in the scholasticism of the age of Aquinas; its potential relevance for the initial era of technological producibility, reproducibility, and dissemination; and its transformation in the post-structuralist era of Joycean poetic "machines" and Guattarian "machinics." In the *Laws*, McLuhan clearly articulates this historic connection of poetic and technics which, throughout his work from the 1940s, linked art and technology as common manifestations of the "second" nature that people make – a theme common in the history of Renaissance poetics in formulations such as Philip Sidney's "Apologia for Poetry" where he speaks of the poet making a golden world.[14] As such the entire doctrine of making (mimesis) rather than matching (copying as imitation) that predominates in McLuhan's thought is also related to the importance of art as *techné*, a constructive process such as weaving (perhaps the root meaning of *-teks from which text, technology, tectonic, and architect are all derived).

As he indicates in the *Laws* when electric information media obsolesce the "first nature": "Made discarnate by our electric information media, the West is furiously at work retrieving its obsolesced organic first nature in a spectrum of new aesthetic modes from feminism to phenomenology. As our second nature consists entirely in our artefacts and extensions and the grounds and narcoses they impose, their etymologies are to be found in first nature, the wild body. They have no hierarchy or orderly sequence; they subsume, obsolesce, retrieve, extend each other . Burrow on each other, hybridize and miscegenate endlessly" (McLuhan and McLuhan 1988, 116). It is technologies (media, artefacts) as extensions of people that create these effects, so he is speaking of mechanical forms extending limbs and organs as the telescope extends the eye, and of electric technologies as extending the central nervous system as a satellite extends the whole culture. But it must be remembered that these are poetic percepts and so they do not have identical meanings as you move from artefact to artefact. While Benjaminian and then Joycean modes of European radical modernism may be non-Aristotlean, their reassertion of a new affiliation of art and technology cannot help but reassert the affiliation of art and techné, for while admittedly techné is usually not regarded as precisely synonymous with technology, it does prefigure new relationships between cultural production and technologies.

The association of the title of McLuhan's first book, *The Mechanical Bride*, with Marcel Duchamp's fascination with mechanism expressed in *Nude Descending a Staircase, no. 2* and massively developed in his *The Large Glass or The Bride Stripped Bare by Her Bachelors, Even*, has been frequently identified by now.[13] This opens up the wider affinity of McLuhan with the mechanical and techno-scientific interests of modernists such as Le Corbusier, Fernand Léger, Paul Klee, Walter Gropius, Alexander Calder, Moholy-Nagy, and others, who were productive in the first third of this century, and focuses on how their creative activities relate critically to the popular cultural production of advertising, the press, publicists, Hollywood, and the embryonic TV of the 1930s and 1940s – the harbinger of infotainment. The very concept of the "mechanical bride," and far more startlingly the anticipation of the "cyborgian person," results from cultural producers bridging the avant-garde fascination with the new techno-science and their absorption in a society where popular culture is becoming manipulated by advertisers, promoters, publicists, and financiers of entertainment.

The very concept of a "mechanical bride" is anticipated by these artists and was explored a little later by art and architectural historians, such as Ozenfant and Sigfried Giedion, one of Joyce's close friends. McLuhan derived his analysis of electro- mechanization from Giedion's discussions of the mechanized household and mechanized kitchen in *Mechanization Takes Command* (1948) and from the way all the various cultural producers working in the first half of this century – film directors, composers, visual artists, poets, cartoonists, etc., – frequently comically or satirically dramatized their world's fascination with the newly emerging technoculture and the everyday implications of the rapid rise of the new technologies. In exploring the technoculture emerging in the second half of the century, McLuhan borrowed from modernist artists and writers such techniques as his use of analogy, which emphasized differences; his fondness for collage, montage, and radical juxtapositions; his verbal play and puns (e.g., the duplicity of his use of "cool"); and his anti-dialectical hermeneutics which are characteristic of the ways in which Lewis Carroll and Joyce play with logic and mathematics in their writings (Deleuze 1969, 39, 56, 260–4). It should be noted that such tactics are themselves machinic or mechanical, well adapted to the exploration of a world where electro-mechanization is taking command.

The mechanical, or better the electro-mechanical, occupies a central position in McLuhan's final works, for he distinguishes the dominance of the abstract, dialectical, analytic capabilities of the left brain – an activity which he names, harking back to the early 1950s, "angelism" – from the dominance of the intuitive capabilities of the right brain, which he, apparently somewhat quixotically, names "robotism." Robotism does not, according to McLuhan, indicate the activities of a rigid, impercipient automaton, but rather those of a person in which the "conscious 'observer-self' or the conscience" is suppressed "to remove all fear and circumspection, all encumbrances to ideal performance (McLuhan and Powers 1989, 67). The interesting aspect of this move is that he chooses to denominate what he considers the "mechanical"-like thought of the dialectician, logician, and academic as "angelic" while denominating the mystically detached, value free, objective stance of the modern grammarian-rhetorician as "machinic."

For McLuhan angelism is characteristic of the Euroamerican world, with its historic emphasis on Cartesianism, while robotism is characteristic of the Afroasian and aboriginal worlds where detachment and meditation are valued. The robotic provides the means of maximizing the result of being an embodied mind, the fate of being human. The selection and opposition of these particular terms might initially seem curious, but for McLuhan it is precise: angelism, a relatively rare word borrowed from humanistic theology, had a short period of vogue among Catholics in the 1950s when the French Catholic philosopher Jacques Maritain introduced it in a critique of Descartes and the Cartesian aftermath in his discussions about poetic and creative intuition. It also appeared in the early 1950s in the title of a critical discussion about the French avant-garde poet Rimbaud with which McLuhan was familiar, but it was attractive to him since it partly mirrors, in a more contemporary mode, Aquinas's explanation of the difference between the cognitive activity of angels and that of humans, whose knowledge is always mediated by the nature of being embodied.

The selection of the term robotism may initially seem even more curious since it is a deliberate revising of Karel Čapek's coinage of this term in his play *R.U.R* (Rossum's Universal Robots) in 1923 (not 1938 as mentioned in *The Global Village)* from a Czech word meaning "forced-labor." McLuhan's revision, which he appears to make the contrary of the robotic in Čapek's sense and thus closer to contemporary discussions of cyborgian bodies as potentially liberating, relates the robotic to what he considers the Japanese emphasis in Confucianism, *chu*, a concept of loyalty to the sovereign as a sign of the collective. [15] There are two interesting aspects to McLuhan's interpretation – first, it dismisses the individualism associated with the Enlightenment; second, it approximates cyberpunk and pro-cyborgian accounts of the experience of disembodiment in cyberspace. The association of the "robotic" with the Eastern world fits well with McLuhan's modernist commitments as exemplified in such opposite exemplars as Pound and Joyce as well as Sergei Eisenstein and W.B. Yeats's. Pound's and Eisenstein's interest in the ideograms to which McLuhan frequently refers; Pound's further interest in Confucianism and early Chinese poetry; Yeats's interest in the Noh drama; and Joyce in a phrase from *Finnegans Wake* often quoted by McLuhan as to how in the awakening "The west shall shake the east awake. Walk while ye have the night for morn" (FW, 473.22–3), as well as in the oriental motifs of the conclusion of the *Wake* in the closing debate between the Archdruid and St Patrick on the nature of light and the rising of the sun which, in one aspect, is oriented to Chinese and Japanese motifs.

This robotic interpretation of the human person, reversing the Cartesian angelizing he attributes to academia and modern science, indicates why the tetrads of his *Laws of Media*, which are hermeneutic and rhetorical, are thus poetic, not a logical or dialectical, construct. It illuminates the apparently mechanical surface of the ambivalent play throughout his work with twos, threes, and fours: the dyads of contradictions and contraries; Hegelian and Piercean triads; and Viconian-Joycean, mythopoetic quarternaries. In his writing of the 1960s in *The Gutenberg Galaxy* he establishes the dyad of speech and alphabetic writing (as well as the dyad of script and print), both of which are placed in new relationship in the triad of language as gestural – which is itself further absorbed into his conception of touch and tactile space or the central nervous system[16] as the common sense and its implications for technologies as cyborgian extensions. McLuhan insists that the absorption of dyads and triads into quarternaries results from his poetic method being grammatical and rhetorical in contradistinction to the dialectical, logical, or postivistic (and perhaps even the scholastic, since it is interesting to note that the analogy of proper proportionality, as McLuhan uses it, is itself a quarternary).

This strategy becomes even more complex and quasi-mathematical when McLuhan supplements it with Joyce's and Carroll's verbal play, characteristic of the grammarian, rhetorician, and the counter-dialectician. Word play has a natural affinity with McLuhan's roots in modernist poetry and modernist criticism, but most particularly with Joyce, Elizabethan and Neo-Augustan literature, and Carroll's nonsense language. McLuhan translates Joyce's use of the pun and verbal play with portmanteaus and figures of speech into the foundation of a science of discovery – a way of generating "fluid concepts and creative analogies" (to borrow the title of Richard Hofstadter's book on fuzziness in artificial intelligence and cognitive science), for McLuhan argues for a contemporary science of discovery – a mnemonic, Baconian, Viconian science. This way of speaking about McLuhan is not meant to be mischievous or misleading, for McLuhan, preceded by Walter Benjamin, anticipates – as Baudrillard argues – the "human science" of French post-modernist and post-structuralist theory by his poetic critique of social science, which I would argue is partly why Jacques Derrida, Jacques Lacan, Julia Kristeva, Jean-François Lyotard, Gilles Deleuze and Félix Guattari share with McLuhan a fascination for Joyce, and that Joyce provides the crucial guide to going beyond McLuhan by implementing McLuhan's method.

Going beyond McLuhanisms means also going beyond McLuhan by being prepared to advance his method, while critiquing his inconsistencies and the prejudices implicit in such distinctions as robotism and angelism. His method, as we have seen, is directed towards exploring the post-literate world of the hyper-sensory, the new technological artefactual cosmopolis where synaesthesia and coenesthesia produce a more inclusive, tactile space resulting from a digitilization – which in some ways would have been anathema to McLuhan, who early on condemned structural linguistics for its emphasis on the binary. The implicit pessimism, the apparent preference for the age of literacy, the near-reactionary political stance nevertheless are contradicted by his anti-dialectical hermeneutics and Joycean playfulness, by his adoption of the stance of a learned, yet anarchistic, satirist of the contemporary "chaosmos," by his early willingness to see human communication as enmeshed in a complex dynamic system. His method of probes, of interpreting artefacts as components of a complex system, and of writing of an imaginative, poetic history of the evolution of the telecosm can be reinterpreted and reapplied. For example, recognizing that modernism and its aftermath constitute a pre-history of cyberspace suggests how McLuhan intuited the transformation of the book into a synaesthetic hypermedia and a language composite of the entire sensory system. It is a lesson he learned and that we can further advance by recognizing its basis in Joyce and his contemporaries, rooted in the long march from Egypt and Athens to Paris, New York, and Toronto, and by using McLuhan's method to revise McLuhan's vision. But before tracing that path further it is important to look at aspects of McLuhan's project emanating from his early study of Nashe and the days of *Explorations*. In successive chapters the contemporary impact of McLuhan's early fascination with journalism will be examined; then his understanding of the historic roles in terms of power exercised by some of the literary satirists and poetic grammarians such as Pietro Aretino, Joseph Addison, and Francis Bacon; and then his specific interest in the spiritual and political power of the hermetic and the occult, reflected in the ambivalences of angelism and robotism as they relate to what McLuhan apparently regarded as the esoteric and potentially diabolic aspect of a techno-scientific modernity.

4 The Professor and the Publicist: Tom Wolfe, the Firehouse Boys, and Marshall

The 1940's were as much the age of the newspaper, the pictorial magazine, and the advertising agency as they were the age of radio or film. *Citizen Kane* (1941) focuses on the importance of William Randolph Hearst, head of of the chain of Hearst newspapers; Henry Luce's *Life* and *Time* dominated public and private life; and ad agencies became the Madison Avenue byword of business success, as exemplified in the massive international successs of J.Walter Thompson. Coming to Toronto from Yale in 1950, I found it fascinating to encounter the differences in a society where the "yellow journalism" of Hearst had not risen to any prominence (although the pictorial magazine everyone read was *Life*, just as in the U.S.) and where ad agencies were just beginning to sense their importance. But it was also refreshing to encounter a highly erudite and intelligent English professor who spoke with ease about the cultural importance of such topics as journalism, Henry Luce, or Madison Avenue, virtually non-existent as serious topics in the humanities courses at Yale. As McLuhan himself always noted, it was his presence in the then marginal world of Canada – living in Toronto and having grown up in Winnipeg – that enabled him to see what eluded virtually all of the Americans.

It would be difficult today to fathom the intellectual excitement McLuhan generated in class and in discussions out of class about the intrinsic importance of such commercial productions of popular culture as newspaper headlines, the advertising business, and Joyce; the importance of the notion of news in Pound's literary theory; jazz, film, and the urban landscape in T.S. Eliot; and advertising style in e.e.cummings to the poetry, literature, and art of the twentieth century. McLuhan communicated to his students both the ambivalence of the poet to her or his world and the value of using the artefacts of popular culture to teach the modes of interpreting the cultural productions of poetry and art. As early as the 1950s, he was fascinated with the power of those who produced the exhibits from mass media he examined in *The Mechanical Bride*, so that early in his career he was convinced to ghost-write editorials for and make contributions to Canadian *Liberty* for Jack Kent Cooke, its publisher, as well as for a group of Canadian newspapers . While obviously forced to do this – given the dismal academic salaries at St Michael's in the early 1950s (around $6000 CDN for full professors), on which he had to support his wife and six children – Marshall initially expressed pleasure in the work and the power to which it might lead.

Although *The Mechanical Bride*, published in 1951, was not a smashing success, in spite of some coverage in *The New Yorker*, in many ways most of the tools that would shape McLuhan's general rhetoric, and those interests that would lead to his ultimate success and his most problematic aspects, were already present. These included his interest in headlines, aphorisms, advertising copy, photography and graphic presentation, juxtapositions of pictures, headers, and text, and his particular use of wit and humour. The *Bride* exemplified his use of wit and humour and his concern with communication, with poetry and the arts, with the liberal arts and its history, with mass media and mass culture, with technology, particularly mechanization, and with an interdisciplinary approach. But implicit in the *Bride* was also a fascination with the power and effectiveness of the forces of commercial culture and the artificially generated sophistication of Fifth Avenue and Madison Avenue. Only *The Gutenberg Galaxy*, McLuhan's next book, widely considered to be his best, would add any further intellectual dimensions to his lifelong exploration of culture and technology, the primary of which were: the history of language, media and technology.

Implicit in the way McLuhan wrote in *The Mechanical Bride* was his capacity, which would be revealed in the 1960s, to become a new kind of enigmatic, pop poetic journalist. The *Bride* was the first book to demonstrate successfully that advertising agencies in the 1920s, 1930s, and 1940s had created a new kind of pop poetry and pop art and was, as has often been noted, an extension of McLuhan's work with the Cambridge school led by F.R. Leavis and his enthusiastic encounter with Wyndham Lewis's major polemical writings, from *The Art of Being Ruled* (1926) and *Time and Western Man* (1927) to *Men Without Art* (1934). McLuhan intuitively grasped the political implications of all poetic activity, although overtly relegating this to a matter of secondary importance under the influence of the theories of new critics such as Cleanth Brooks, John Crowe Ransom, and Alan Tate, who held that "a poem should not mean but be," i.e., a poem is something (an artefact), not about something – a position that allows the differentiation of a poem from a persuasive argument and/or seductive inducement, which presumably was the nature of advertising and many media productions. In *The Mechanical Bride* McLuhan took a "moralistic" stance towards the production of popular artefacts, showing them to be pseudo-poems, with their creators merely aping artists, as Lewis had suggested in his writings.

In 1968, at the peak of McLuhan's rise to international prominence, Toronto professor of sociology and freelance journalist Arnold Rockman listed the image-maker journalists and critics – "highbrow and middlebrow alike" – who in 1967 had recognized McLuhan as "an international intellectual hero": Benjamin De Mott, Tom Wolfe, Dwight Macdonald, Leslie Fiedler, and Frank Kermode. Rockman pointed out that McLuhan was "seen as a legitimator by all those who feel that their activities are not quite legitimate when judged by standards appropriate to the traditional academic enterprise". This ability had been aided and abetted by the media, who by 1967 had created an aura about him such that when "a writer describes something as having been influenced by McLuhan's thinking, the subject written about seems more significant, no matter how trivial it may have seemed to us before." Rockman (1968) argued that McLuhan, as a revolutionary prophet, had had to exaggerate the force and application of his vision in order to persuade his audience that it would re-order their experience and provide it with new significance.

The phenomenon of his success was associated with the peculiar role of the university in North America in the 1950s and 1960s, which functioned both as a substitute for "the church," providing legitimacy to all activity that was in any way associated with the intellect, and as a new ally (eventually to become a partner) for the financial-industrial-governmental complex, providing not only basic research to industry and intellectual credibility to business and governmental policy initiatives but also further legitimizing the role of the complex as the leading social force in society. McLuhan's ability to accept the business community, as the evolving multiversities of the 1960s were doing, provided him with powerful affiliations. His position as an Oxbridge-oriented academic – though still somewhat an outsider, being Catholic and Canadian – and an intellectual who lacked the then-usual university antagonisms to popular culture, business, media, and the new technologically oriented avant garde arts provided him with a set of often conflicting and contradictory power bases. It is the same mix that has supported his revival in the 1990s through Stuart Brand's 1987 discussion of his importance to the MIT Media Lab and *Wired*'s adoption of him to legitimize the corporate, media-oriented, and artistic aspects of cyberculture. Since his biographers, advocates, and critics have frequently traversed this territory, I will only examine one specific promotional program and one major advocate which, in 1965, accelerated this potent mix: his associations with promoters Howard Gossage and his partner Dr Gerald Feigen and Tom Wolfe's description of him.

During the years of the Ford Seminar and his co-editing of *Explorations* with Ted Carpenter, McLuhan, through his developing realization of the hegemony of commercial communication, gradually abandoned moralistic criticism for what he described as objective recording of factual observation. He obviously believed this objective stance permitted him to use strategies of implication and allusion to maintain his Lewisian critique and satire of the unfolding world of high culture, academia, and everyday pop, while still advancing an apparently objective empirical analysis of the technoculture. Freedom from the taint of moralism and of intellectualism thus enabled him to serve as an advisor and consultant to the financial and political elite – an obvious contemporary transformation of the Renaissance artist or intellectual serving and being supported by his patrons. This stance of disinterested objectivism was to contribute to the way in which he was promoted as well as the way in which he promoted himself.

In his essay on McLuhan "What If He's Right?" in *The Pump House Gang*, Tom Wolfe notes the importance of McLuhans's meeting with Howard Gossage and Dr Gerald Feigen of Freeman, Mander and Gossage, a San Francisco advertising agency which at that time was one of the most celebrated in the U.S. The firm was housed in an old San Francisco firehouse, which further enhanced its uniqueness. Gossage was the then well known maverick PR and advertising executive who, while a persuasive promoter, simultaneously criticized the industry for a variety of questionable ethical practices. While he became noted for a "soft sell" style of advertising that countered the central trends of the business at that time, Ted Carpenter, who was at the meeting with McLuhan, Gossage and Feigen explains, their approach was for him and others quite questionable: "In 1965 I was invited to join Marshall at the offices of a PR firm in San Francisco. Gossage & Feigen held forth in a former firehouse. What I witnessed there is today so commonplace, so accepted, it dates me to say how much it disturbed me. Howard "Luck" Gossage and Gerald Feigen pioneered in creating news for clients. News costs little to invent, nothing to broadcast. A network of journalists cooperated. Gossage invented the icon T-shirt, backed *Ramparts* magazine, converted a ski resort into a year-round operation, mixed marketing and news, design and promotion, PR and journalism, etc., etc. The house became an 'in' scene, heady with power, the ultimate in Innis' 'fact faking factories.' Journalistic ethics weren't high on the agenda. Some day a biographer may detail the personal tragedies that followed. In the meantime, we have Tom Wolfe's *The Pump House Gang*. Tom was there. His account left out a lot" (see Appendix B). While the title "the pump house gang" referred to a group of surfers who gathered near a pump house on the beach, Wolfe's book, associating surfers and other subjects he analyzes with status and influence in San Francisco, led some commentators on McLuhan to metaphorically associate the PR men and their Fire House with the "Pump House Gang" and their modish, Pacific coast world.

The year after Gossage's death in 1969, another of his partners, the president of the firm Jerry Mander, resigned. He went on to write a major condemnation of TV. Later he wrote books on technology in general as well as media technology and was head of a think tank dedicated to the environmental critique of technology. Mander's critical attitude in the polemical *Four Arguments for the Termination of Television* (1977) clearly invokes what he considers to be McLuhan's erroneous analysis of TV as giving aid and support to the enemy – technological commercialism. Yet in *Ramparts* in 1966 Gossage had written a moderately intellectual, promotional article on McLuhan that presents him favourably as one of "The World's Great Experts."

This aspect of McLuhan as simultaneously advisor and consultant to business, industry, and government and also "patron saint" of most mixed-media artists and many young underground moviemakers confirmed his instrumental success with the world of power and finance, while still preserving his integrity as a pop poet. Tom Wolfe's famous (or infamous) articles, published under the banner "What If He's Right?", particularly the version published in *The Pump House Gang* (1968, 118), clearly describe this phenomenon, while celebrating McLuhan's conscious transformation of himself into a PR celebrity – "a person who is well-known for his well-knowness." McLuhan as the enigmatic, pop poetic journalist provided Wolfe with a superb complement to his own writing, which many reviewers regarded as the greatest American journalism of the "sixties era" by a writer who also had some of the qualities of a "genuine poet." Yet McLuhan – ambivalent, allusive, aphoristic, enigmatic – was more the poet than Wolfe, who became the journalistic equivalent of an academic interpreter of literature, which is somewhat ironic since in the McLuhan piece he puts down the *littérateurs* and praises McLuhan for being "the savager of literary intellectuals" (Wolfe 1968, 126).

Wolfe's article is so important because it establishes what was to become McLuhanism, fostered by McLuhan's own ability to be a PR chameleon. Wolfe's ongoing relationship with members of the McLuhan family, particularly the editing, with Stephanie McLuhan, of a series of video-tapes of McLuhan, attests to Wolfe's endorsement by McLuhan during his life and shows him as an ongoing voice of McLuhanism (McLuhan 1958). The association of his original 1965 article on McLuhan with the promotion of McLuhan by Feigen and Gossage confirms that he is positioning the already well known McLuhan to become a jetset celebrity and international media guru. Not only is the title of the article, "What If He's Right?" both ambiguous and uncommitted, Wolfe presents McLuhan as a somewhat comic, somewhat pathetic, idiot-as-genius. While he appropriately attributes to McLuhan all the literary credentials of a major professor, he also describes the world of "EngLit academia" as inconsequentially "redolent of nothing" and portrays the two "contradictory, incongruous" McLuhan's he met in 1965:

One moment he would look like merely the English teacher with the Pree-Tide tie on, naïve, given to bad puns derived from his studies of *Finnegans Wake* and worse jokes from god knows where, a somewhat dishevelled man, kindly, disorganised – the very picture of the absent-minded professor. The next moment he would look like what he has, in fact, become: the super-savant, the Freud of our times, the omniscient *philosophe*, the unshakable dialectician . That was whenever the subject was Theory, which it usually was. On those occasions the monologue began. (Wolfe 1968, 110)

Leaving aside the Wolfean hype and misleading simplifications – e.g., McLuhan, by his own admission, from the 1950s to his death did not consider himself a dialectician or *philosopher* (though, in Wolfe's defence, in terms of his actual practice he was somewhat disingenuous about the claim), this description basically confirms one of the multiple schizophrenic splits that existed in this remarkable man. But it didn't work as neatly as Wolfe suggests, for the Marshall I knew as a mentor for five or six years and a colleague for sixteen years used monologues in his EngLit role when exegeting texts, just as he did in his guru role when pontificating about whatever might strike his fancy. Both the public McLuhan, whether teaching, participating in meetings, or speaking publicly, and often even the private McLuhan, one-on-one in your dining or living room, could dia-mono-logize" (appear to converse with one or very few people, while actually carrying on a monologue). But the monologues were virtually never directed towards Theory (which

McLuhan claimed to despise); they were the conversation of an ancient grammarian and filled with the stuff of rhetoric and poetry. McLuhan's response to Wolfe's essay in a letter in 1965 demonstrates his own ambivalence to the portrait, for while expressing that he was "very happy" with it, he notes that "sitters are not supposed to enjoy their portraits." Claiming to recognize Wolfe's essay's "power and fidelity" and complimenting him on its very considerable success in elucidating his approaches to various problems, he still suggests that it creates "a considerable mood of disillusionment that is both deserved and salutary." The bottom line, however is that "It is sure to prove a major asset to McLuhan, Inc." and its only serious disadvantage is that it might cause the internal revenue to demand a bank statement.[1]

Wolfe clearly provided a platform for launching McLuhan, Inc. and that platform not only transformed McLuhan into the public media image of a universal guru but created a new place for iconoclastic academics lured by power to join the ranks of media celebrities and contribute to the global mediaverse's ecstasy of communication – its world of enigmatic, new age virtual information as knowledge: "Perfect! Delphic! Cryptic! Aphoristic! Epigrammatic!" as Wolfe sound-blasted. Wolfe positioned McLuhan as the contemporary Freud – who also experienced a meteoric rise to universal prominence after a visit to the U.S. – but by so doing gave him a new spin, since McLuhan's rise was through conscious manipulation of the very instruments and strategies that he, by his own admission, had moralistically criticized in *The Mechanical Bride*. Yet Wolfe could paradoxically claim that the man whom he argued was "the savager of the literary intellectuals" adopted a style seductive to literary types, for "Both McLuhan and Freud present scientific theories, but in an ancient, priestly, aristocratic idiom that literary and artistic souls find alluring" (Wolfe 1969, 124).

Wolfe shaped McLuhan like a pop Pygmalion sculpting his statue, creating an image he and his sophisticated, hip, well-heeled, and well-educated audience of the mid-1960s could love. That image was and was not McLuhan, for McLuhan would not have agreed with Wolfe's way of reading Joyce's language in the *Wake* as bad puns, any more than he would have assented to Wolfe's presentation of his view of the artists's early warning system as "a rather retrograde performance" in which the "avant-garde" is always one technology behind. McLuhan was fond of quoting Lewis that "The artist is engaged in writing a detailed history of the future because he is the only person who lives in the present."[2] In the Introduction to the second edition of *Understanding Media*, subsequent to Wolfe's essay, McLuhan noted:

The power of the arts to anticipate future social and technological developments, by a generation and more, has long been recognized. In this century Ezra Pound called the artist "the antennae of the race." Art as radar acts as "an early alarm system," as it were, enabling us to discover social and psychic targets in lots of time to prepare to cope with them. This concept of the arts as prophetic, contrasts with the popular idea of them as mere self-expression. If art is an "early warning system," to use the phrase from World War II, when radar was new, art has the utmost relevance not only to media study but to the development of media controls. (McLuhan 1964B, xi)

McLuhan as pop poet mastering percepts and affects obviously intuited that the dream of Joyce's *Wake* was a premonition of cyberspace.

Howard Gossage, the Pump House Gang style co-conspirator with Feigen in promoting McLuhan, overtly recognizes the importance of the centrality of Joyce in McLuhan. Unlike Wolfe, he does not see McLuhan as a distributor of bad puns based on the Joycean model. He reflects McLuhan's view that the pun and verbal play in general is a "breakdown as breakthrough":

A major key to McLuhan's prose style and his outlook is to be found in his undoubted status as a Joyce scholar, which is where he started out while working on his doctorate at Cambridge. He regards *Finnegans Wake* as the most important book of our era and the one that has done the most to chart his own explorations. His immense Joycean joy at snuffling and roiling about in the double-bed of language is evident throughout his work; as is his delight in elaborate puns, some of which are pointed and pregnant (which is to say I get them), while others are so obscurantist as to demand a "Key to McLuhan's Wake." (Stearn 1967, 8)

McLuhan's own public response to Wolfe's article appears in *Culture Is Our Business*, with his comments juxtaposed to an ad for Wolfe's *Pump House Gang* and *The Electric Kool-Aid Acid Test* and introduced by the headline SHEEP IN WOLFE'S CLOTHING next to an ad in which the mod dressed Wolfe is pictured with his books. McLuhan comments: "At the beginning of his very flattering essay on myself ... Tom Wolfe has a drawing of me which at once suggests another title for his essay ... namely, "I'd Rather Be Wrong." At the end of his essay he confronts me with a waitress in a topless restaurant to whom I uttered the assurance, "The topless waitress is the thin edge of a trial balloon." (I.e., the silicone bust) (McLuhan 1970, 212–13).

Wolfe is indicative of what McLuhanism was to become, since he creates a virtual McLuhan, who will be re-created again and again, a situation McLuhan invites because, a pop poet, he is also crafting Marshall McLuhan as the pop poem. While others who follow may produce differing McLuhan's, in a way they will all be different, as most of the varying exegeses of a modernist poem differ. Wolfe's particular McLuhan is shaped to Wolfe's particular brand of that New York City cynicism, that arose in the 1960s and 1970s. McLuhan becomes the symbol of Wolfe's newly emerging world with its despisal of academics and early contemporary poetry and art, its introduction and justification of the postmodern journalism that has now become practically the exclusive practice of modern cultural and entertainment media. McLuhan permitted this image and most of the other images that established him as a celebrity, a force, and a foreseer of the future. Wolfe took advantage of McLuhan's willingness to let others construct images of him with which he did not necessarily agree. Consequently, Wolfe makes McLuhan a symptom as well as a seer – a symptom Baudrillard foresaw – of a world becoming lost in an ecstasy of communication where everything becomes virtual.

Examining Wolfe's problems in understanding McLuhan (or, perhaps better, in deliberately misunderstanding McLuhan and making him a Wolfean image) clearly establishes the beginnings of McLuhanism as myths about McLuhan partly encouraged by McLuhan himself. Wolfe, for example, asserts that Innis and Bergson are McLuhan's major influences. As indicated earlier, the extent of Innis's importance to McLuhan is certainly open to question. Furthermore, Innis, who condemned any association between the world of academia and the world of consulting with business and government, would (even though today it might seem a hopeless cause) have categorically condemned the concept of McLuhan, Inc. With regard to Bergson, McLuhan apparently shared Lewis's view of Bergson as an uncritical "time-mind."[3] In 1969 he wrote to a correspondent, "I think of Jasper, Bergson and Buber as very inferior conceptualist types, quite out of touch with the immediate analogical awareness that begins in the senses and is derailed by concepts or ideas."[4] In his published writings, McLuhan considered Bergson's theory of laughter to be mechanistic and his philosophical orientation to be suspect. Wolfe wants to posit McLuhan as a Theorist but not a "communication theorist," rather an intuitive "cognitive scientist" interested in the sensory system (what McLuhan talks about as the ratio between the senses) and the effects of communication technology on the sensorium, who in the process studies a kind of neurology, for Wolfe notes that "It is all quite literary, this neurology" (Wolfe 1969, 124–5).

Wolfe's situating McLuhan as a cognitive scientist in the mid-1960s is parallel to McLuhan's having situtated himself as an expert in media and communication in the 1950s and McLuhanism's situation of him in the

1990s as an early prophet of digital culture. The chameleon-like quality of a witty pop poetry grounded in the powerful insights of the arts in the first three-quarters of this century provided McLuhan with a form in which to exhibit his intuitive awareness of the percepts and affects that underlay the rapidly changing technoculture. And his complex schizoid pronouncements – multiplex and perplexing – produce this wittiness. Behind Wolfe's portrait and, in fact, behind McLuhan's own conception of the role he had to play, there is a recognition of the centrality of schizophrenia in modernity and capitalism. In *The Gutenberg Galaxy* McLuhan had declared literate man to be a schizophrenic – the "split man" of Lewis's writings. Wolfe reduces this "split man" theme to the split between McLuhan the stereotypical "don" from "EngLit academic life" and McLuhan the visionary, Nietzschean prophet teasing and pontificating to the world of power. Wolfe evades the still deeper splits in McLuhan, such as the one between the converted Baptist become Catholic pietist yet quirky neo-Thomist intellectual and the post-Nietzschean pre-post-modernist revealed in productions within which McLuhan adopted the conflicting visions of Lewis, the poet as fascist, and Joyce, the poet-apostate as socio-anarchist.

Wolfe's simplification is necessary to protect his argument, not only for journalistic effect but because McLuhan's splits, which bridge his simultaneously being both a reactionary intellectual like Lewis and a North American anti-intellectual in the rural American evangelical tradition, would partly undermine the anti-intellectualism that is the focus of Wolfe's argument. The tensions arising from the ambiguities generated by all the conflicting elements in McLuhan's works dramatically reflect the essential tension of the era within which his vision unfolded. McLuhan, as a dedicated, later closet, intellectual assumes the importance he does as an index and a symptom of the closing decades of the second millenium and the twentieth century because of his schizophrenic and paranoid streaks, since they connect his sensibility with the very nature of the capitalist global metropolis within which he wanted to exert power while simultaneously carrying out a quasi-anarchistic revolt against its hegemony. McLuhan's perceptual and affective grasp of his world, which made him, at least temporarily, the patron saint of avant-garde artists and film-makers, also provided the insight that enabled him to recognize the means of seducing the powerful. His pietistic Catholicism provided a spiritual combination of the evangelical and the intellectual within which he could justify his activities, while his modernist (and post-modernist) academicism provided a shield behind which he could seek privacy and even isolation – a situation attested to by the purposefully cryptic, enigmatic, Zen-like nature of his work. These qualities were to make him attractive to both religious conservatives and many new age personalities. McLuhan has persisted, resurfacing in the 1990s, because in the 1960s he had become a virtual summation of the conflicting currents of Euroamerican culture as it moved towards the new millenium.

Wolfe's presentation of McLuhan dramatizes the crux of the problem of McLuhanism and how it is symptomatic of contemporary conflicts, for McLuhan actually invited the Wolfean presentation of his work and Wolfe still occupies a significant position in presenting McLuhan to the public. Wolfe attempts, unopposed and in fact probably encouraged by McLuhan, to reduce McLuhan's insight of the contradictions of global, multi-national life to that of a renegade academic turned prophetic, pseudo-journalistic guru. He associates McLuhan with nonsense: "cryptic, Delphic, Oriental ... He was like a serious faced Lewis. Nobody knew what he was saying" (Wolfe 1969, 130). In a way, he even "beclowns" McLuhan without McLuhan apparently having been fully conscious of it, since he makes McLuhan a cynical robot – an image McLuhan, in a different sense, was to develop and endorse in his later years, as seen primarily in his posthumous writings with their emphasis on the virtues of "robotism." Wolfe's portrait, illustrating a McLuhan being managed by Feigen and Gossage, shows McLuhan as endorsing the very PR hype that the *Bride* and moments during the *Explorations* period had exposed and which McLuhan's cynical type of Menippean satire continued to expose throughout his writings.

Wolfe's argument that McLuhan was a cognitive science theorist who had been interested in communication only in the period when he was writing *The Mechanical Bride* exemplifies the type of interpretation that produces the worst of McLuhanism while perverting the nature of McLuhan's multiple interests. Even Wolfe implicitly acknowledges some interest on McLuhan's part in communication, since he believes that Innis, a historian of communication, was a major influence on McLuhan. *The Gutenberg Galaxy* is primarily a work on communication history and his final book, *Laws of Media*, is still structuring those laws historically.

But popular McLuhanism – being interested in a quick fix on media analysis – wants, as far as possible, to dehistoricize McLuhan. The route of cognitive science theory taken by some can be used as a move in achieving this end. Of course McLuhan was interested in neurological problems and technology; but that interest co-existed with the historical and was not independent of it. As Wolfe himself implies, McLuhan's neurology, like Freud's psychoanalysis, was primarily literary, so that McLuhan would have found the same problems with "hard" cognitive science that he did with logic, dialectics, and mathematics. But in his final book, *The Laws of Media*, McLuhan reiterates the key to the foundation of his work – the study of the history and nature of artefacts. He reiterates his earlier interpretation of the trivium as a history of communication. McLuhan had even alerted Wolfe to the importance of his work on the trivium and his Nashe thesis in a letter in October 1965 written prior to Wolfe's article in *New York*.[5]

My point here is not to limit McLuhan's range of interest by suggesting he theorized about some particular area but to insist on the breadth of his intellectual concerns: communication, culture, technology, and their history; sensory processes; the nature of artefacts; and many others. But when he undertook to utilize these concerns in his encounter with the vast field of the transformations of the electric age, this plenitude could only be encompassed within the intuition of a poet involved with percepts and affects, not through systematic theory. McLuhan's complexity is McLuhan's strength, whether or not he credits all of his sources or falls short of some of them. The value of that complexity is a poetic value tied to McLuhan's insight that a "linguistic of flow" is the language of capitalism and of the modernisms, postmodernisms, and post-structuralisms which critique it. Unfortunately McLuhan's appeal ultimately has to lead in the direction of simplification, since a popular audience is necessarily grasping for opinions rather than ambivalent insights.

McLuhan's association with postmodernism and poststructuralism will be examined in greater breadth in Chapter 6. But his position as a virtual summation of the conflicting currents of contemporary culture is one reason why, although Jacques Derrida appears to have summarily rejected McLuhan, that Derrida credits Joyce as a major influence on his work. Deleuze and Guattari, apparently recognizing the importance of the conflicting strains of schizophrenic revolt and paranoiac hierarchicalism in McLuhan, acknowledge the importance of his announcing the collapse of the "Gutenberg Galaxy" and his apparent understanding of the "linguistic of flows" instead of the "linguistics of signifiers":

the significance of McLuhan's analyses [is] to have shown what a language of decoded flows is, as opposed to a signifier that strangles and overcodes the flows. In the first place, for nonsignifying language anything will do: whether it be phonic, graphic, gestural, etc., no flow is privileged in this language, which remains indifferent to its substance or its support, inasmuch as the latter is an amorphous continuum. The electric flow can be considered as the realization of such a flow that is indeterminate as such. But a substance is said to be formed when a flow enters into a relationship with another flow, such that the first defines a content and the second, an expression. (Deleuze and Guattari 1972, 240-1)

They even annotate this passage with a reference to McLuhan's having declared that "the electric light is pure information ... a medium without a message" which characterizes the "content of any medium [as] always another medium. The content of writing is speech, just as the written word is the content of print, and print the content of the telegraph" (McLuhan 1964, 23). McLuhan thus becomes the prophet of electric language, which as we have seen is the goal of the synaesthetic and coenaesthetic achieved in digitalization, for "the computer is a machine for instantaneous and generalized decoding" (Deleuze and Guattari 1972, 241). For McLuhan, a motif from the *Wake* is probably playing in the background, for of the *Wake*, Joyce says, "That's the point of eschatology our book of kills reaches for now in soandso many counterpoint words. What can't be coded can be decorded if an ear aye sieze what no eye ere grieved for" (FW 482.33-6).

Elsewhere Deleuze and Guattari affirm McLuhan's primary role in asserting the presence of the anarchic, for they posit two copresent directions in the contemporary world: "worldwide ecumenical machines" (e.g., "commercial organizations of the "multinational type" or industrial complexes, or even religious formations like Christianity, Islam, certain prophetic or messianic movements") and "a neo-primitivism, a new tribal society as described by Marshall McLuhan" (Deleuze and Guattari 1980, 360). Nevertheless, these are the two directions to which as split man McLuhan simultaneously responds – on one hand, the ecumenical machines of multinationalism and of the Vatican, and, on the other hand, the neoprimitivism of modernist art. Yet McLuhan's dilemma is that of a feeling and thinking person in our contemporary world, of which he, as an intelligent explorer of percepts and affects, necessarily possesses a supersensitive awareness.

McLuhan as celebrity is a very interesting figure, since McLuhan used the role of celebrity as a mask through which to advance his intellectual program. The difficulty with this strategy is that he had to offer his audience "news that stays news" – aphoristic headlines that could take on a wide variety of functions, such as the term global village. He therefore donned the mask of an intellectual journalist, but one who marketed the delphic, the enigmati. Yet, essentially, he believed himself to be a cynical satirist and a propagator of a new science – like Vico's, a poetic science. He had to declare his inconsistency to be a basic principle of his probing and exploring, for this permitted him to be all things to all people since he, like the poet, could not be pinned down to a point of view – one possible strategy of a master entertainer (Stearn 1967, xiii). Ultimately, however, he had a strong view of his own direction and despised those who attempted to simplify his positions.

In a penetrating biographical and autobiographical reminescence, Ted Carpenter reveals the quixotic, talented, intuitive individual who could borrow phrases and ideas from virtually anywhere and convert them into brilliant and illuminating rhetoric. Carpenter's portrait is not of a thinker but of a magus, a shaman, a ritualistic artist – someone, as he himself suggests, who arises from the anthropological worlds that he studied. Carpenter notes that McLuhan had already crossed over into the world of manna and magic – which he had discovered in modernist literature and read about in such sources as Malinowski's appendix to Ogden and Richards' *Meaning of Meaning* – the domain of phatic communion. Such a McLuhan becomes far more significant than a McLuhan used to authorize academic programs in culture and technology, media studies, cognitive studies, or what you will. The latter activity, while not unjustified, is much more trivial than that of the somewhat mystifying and mystical image that both foresaw the years of the closing of the second millennium and stood as a dramatic symbol of that very process. It is this latter figure that ultimately gained the respect and recognition of John Cage, Woody Allen, Stan van der Beek, Robert Rauschenberg, Dušan Makavéjev, Jacques Languirand, and many, many other artists. What remains relatively unlearned from that figure, with its strengths and weaknesses as a pop poet bridging modernism and postmodernism, is the vital importance of the arts and literature and their history to the understanding of technology, culture, communication, artefacts and the processes of human perception. What he took to be most important was seldom perceived with the depth of understanding he would have wished. This is particularly true of the importance of arts and literature and the quintessential position he attributed to them as foreseeing the future.

5 McLuhanesque Ambivalence: Power and Cultural Production

One day in the early fifties when Marshall was having lunch with my wife and me in our small apartment about half a block from the St Michael's College campus, he began speaking about personal power and his desire to achieve it. At the time he had begun writing a series of columns for the Canadian media entrepreneur Jack Kent Cook and I believe he intuited that this was part of the road to becoming a media guru on which he had embarked with the writing of *The Mechanical Bride*. *The Bride* was a book before its time. It had encountered opposition from the advertising and media world, which even put pressure on his publisher to keep him from discussing certain ads and other popular media exhibits. At the time, I believe, power was not a mere ego satisfaction for Marshall but a genuine way to promote his mission. Revealing the implications of the world of electric media could only be accomplished through the influence of a journalistic observer backed by corporate power, rather than through conventional academic publishing.

Consequently, he gradually developed a conscious program through which he aimed to become a power-exercising wordsmith (a contemporary rhetorician). This became his goal partly because he was fully aware that power and fame would attract followers and, if he was as successful as some of those he used as models, he would become the object of a movement. In his later years, when this was precisely what had occurred with the emergence of "McLuhanism" (or in the French *macluhanisme*), he could, in his sardonic, satiric, witty manner, sincerely say that, consistent with the individualism his position represented, "Temperamentally I'm a stodgy conservative ... If there are going to be McLuhanites, you can be sure I'm not going to be one of them." In his introductory material for McLuhan's *Letters*, William Toye notes that while McLuhan enjoyed his fame and responded favorably to it, he still treated it lightly and never let it put his ceaseless intellectual probings in second place, nor prevented him from sharing with others, perhaps more amply, the results and implications of those explorations (McLuhan 1987, 179).

The roots which led him to assume this role are to be found in his early studies of the history of the arts of language and in his life-long fascination with late nineteenth- and twentieth-century art and literature. Through his study of grammar and rhetoric he learned of the importance in the history of education and rhetoric of academic publicists, who appeared at specific moments in history – often at moments which McLuhan was later to associate with important moments of transition in the history of communication media. McLuhan apparently conceived of himself as a similar type of figure. His willingness to allow Feigen and Gossage to promote his work and his welcome and encouragement of Tom Wolfe's early essays on his work clearly rose out of his own PR consciousness, the theoretical understanding of which had already clearly surfaced in *The Gutenberg Galaxy* (1962), with its specific references to satirists and rhetoricians of the early Renaissance, the Elizabethan era, and the early Enlightenment.

The *Galaxy* specifically examines the PR context of the sixteenth-century Pietro Aretino, "the scourge of princes" – a scathing satirist and a backroom boy for a Borgian pope; Sir Francis Bacon, Elizabethan courtier and philosopher; and Joseph Addison, author of the *Spectator Papers*. For example, in the headline style title for one of the individual sections of the *Galaxy*, McLuhan announces: "Francis Bacon, PR voice of the moderni had both feet in the Middle Ages." Bacon, although not widely mentioned in discussions of "McLuhanism," was obviously quite important to McLuhan for, as noted earlier, references to him appear almost as frequently in the *Galaxy* as those to James Joyce or Wyndham Lewis and almost two decades later McLuhan again refers to him a number of times in the *Laws of Media*.[1] McLuhan's positioning of himself in the closing decades of the second millennium seems to have been conceived on a parallel with Bacon, since he could also be described as adopting the role of PR voice for contemporary poets and artists (particularly the symbolists and high modernists) while keeping both feet in the Middle Ages. (Ironically, as McLuhan certainly appreciated, contemporary modernists were not *moderni* in Bacon's sense but were consciously returning to the ancients, transforming, while transcending, the classical tradition.)

As a contemporary grammarian-rhetorician, McLuhan's historical studies seem to have given him a strong justification for becoming a conscious PR practitioner. This was further reinforced by the way that Ezra Pound had acted as a promoter of poetry, and painter-writer Lewis had deliberately sought controversy to attract attention to his critique of contemporary art, culture, and society. The example of Lewis, a contemporary artist who thought all great art was satire, complemented by his knowledge of a figure such as Aretino (who McLuhan compared, somewhat problematically, with Cervantes and Rabelais) encouraged McLuhan to conceive of himself as the modern traditional grammarian-rhetorician transformed into a publicist and a satirist. Thus he attempted to pursue a satiric practice (which will be examined more extensively later) – a satire of learning like that of Rabelais, Jonathan Swift's *Tale of a Tub*, Pope's *Dunciad*, Laurence Sterne's *Tristram Shandy*, Lewis's *Apes of God* and the trilogy of *The Human Age*, and Joyce's *Finnegans Wake*.[2] Such an attempt fits well with the role which McLuhan was developing: to be, like Aretino, a scourge of the establishment, yet a key influence on some of the prime movers of his age; to pursue a long-standing Chestertonian mission, yet be a post-Nietzschean modernist in his grammatical-rhetorical practice; to defend and promote the values of the history of Western thought, particularly the importance of contemporary art and litera-ture, yet to maintain the populist appeal of a media star; to maintain a strong ethical commitment to critiquing the contemporary world, yet simultaneously assuming the stance of an *objective* observer or "spectator."

This exposes the very complexity of McLuhan, lost in battles about "who and what is McLuhan" – battles that also involve sharp divisions such as McLuhan, pro or con, and McLuhan, hot or cool, in which, to his supporters, any criticism becomes demonization and, to his critics, any support or approval becomes adulation or enthusiasm. McLuhan had well understood, as he argues Aretino did, that intellectual impact must be based on using the newest technological tools to gain as much power and patronage as far as possible. Quoting Samuel Putnam's introduction to his translation of Aretino's works, McLuhan points out: "If Aretino, at this time, was probably the most powerful man in Italy, perhaps in the world, the reason is to be found in the new force which he had discovered, *that force which we today would call 'the power of the press'*" [italics mine] (McLuhan 1962, 194–5). McLuhan had realized as early as 1950 in *The Mechanical Bride* that in an extended sense these technological tools had become "the power of the media," which included advertising, PR, the tabloids, radio, TV, and whatever else furthered dissemination of information. His tactical problem was how could he, a lifelong avowed intellectual, preserve the integrity of the complexity of differences that constituted his lifeworld while maintaining his impact. The very nature of the kind of art and poetry whose history and criticism McLuhan had "professed" throughout the first thirty years of his career, when integrated with the particular stance of the informed satirist of learning that he tried to present, provided the strategies and tactics through which he would seek a solution. In so doing he would develop, partly unconsciously, the very pattern of public, apocalyptic discourse about mania and panic that would increasingly appear in public discourse as the millennium moved to completion.

In the poetics of the New Criticism and the aesthetics of the new art the buzz word of the 1940s and early 1950s had been "ambiguity," closely linked to "paradox" which McLuhan's association with the Southern–agrarian dominated movement of "New Criticism" had led him to adopt as well. Seeing that the prime exempla of "ambiguity" were poets such as T.S. Eliot and Pound, ambivalence and paradox naturally became central aspects of McLuhan's writings, especially since he had early recognized the importance of paradox in his study on Nashe where he observed that the Stoics privileged this rhetorical device – which actually is no mere figure of rhetoric. It is a figure of thought based on antilogy (often called *dissoi logi*), two opposing arguments expressed by a single speaker within the same complex argument – thus, the foundation of dialectics.[3] In the key work *From Cliché to Archetype* he cites Rosalie Colie's encyclopedic work on paradox and notes how it illuminates the "duplicity" of his use of cliché as probe: "It is even more complicated than Mr. Eliot's tactic of standing on both sides of a mirror simultaneously. Miss Colie also notes: '... paradox equivocates. It lies, and it doesn't. It tells the truth, and it doesn't ... The one meaning must always be taken with respect to the other – so that the Liar paradox is, literally, speculative, its meanings infinitely mirrored, infinitely reflected, in each other.' In cliché-archetype terms, the paradox is a major form of cliché-probe dependent upon an encyclopedic retrieval of older clichés for its exercise" (McLuhan and Watson 1970, 162).

The Medium Is the Rear View Mirror: Understanding McLuhan discusses at length the role of paradox in McLuhan and its relation to the "new critical" movement and to high modernism in literature and the arts. Paradox and ambiguity are core strategies for McLuhan, related both to his historic studies and his studies of contemporary literature and art, and which, therefore, identify a major aspect of his fundamental commitment to poetry, the arts, and literary writing. It might be argued that ambiguity or paradox is the essential element in effec-

tive poetry, as the "new critics" did when they established its pre-
eminent and primary role in poetry and other literary theory by not
taking into account either the author's intention or the social context
within which the work would be read. The early McLuhan, as represented by essays such as those included in *Interior Landscape: The Literary Criticism of Marshall McLuhan*, clearly embraced the new critical stance towards the nature of poetry.

On the modernist side, McLuhan associates paradox with Lewis
and Joyce's interest in the machine. Discussing Lewis's aesthetic of
the vortex he quotes Lewis speaking about how "you must talk with
two tongues, if you do not wish to cause confusion" and to achieve
this how you must "become mechanical by fundamental dual repetition."[4] Respecting Joyce he asserts that the whole of the *Wake* is
paradox and that Joyce, in saying he was an "engine driver" and
"one of the greatest engineers" making an engine with only one
wheel and at that a wheel that was all square, simultaneously discovered the mirror as wheel, i.e., the mirror, in taking in and feeding
back the same image as in "Viconian" cycles, can ultimately retrieve
all history of experience and events. McLuhan declares this to be an
extreme instance of the "paradox" as "a major form of cliché-probe"
dependent upon an encylopedic retrieval of older clichés (McLuhan
and Watson 1970, 162).

When he turned his attention to media as artefacts susceptible of
being analysed or read as a poem, and when he later extended that to
human technologies, he not only identified the paradox with the
probe but he was able to poeticize about these artefacts paradoxically
while concurrently, as artefacts, the very nature of what he was poeticizing was itself paradoxical – a fact that later enables him to build
his various tetrads with their attention to divisions, differences, contraries, and contradictories. The problem this presents is that if
McLuhan's method is that of a satiric poet, and if such a poet plays
with ambiguities and paradoxes that may not be explicated or
explained with relation to attention or affect, McLuhan's work as a
presumed path to understanding the artefact may well be subject to
interminable interpretation. Given this situation, McLuhan is free to
construct his paradoxical probes, so that they may have multiple,
often contradictory meanings. While there is nothing wrong with such
an approach as long as it is advanced and accepted as a rhetorico-
poetic strategy, it can become a means of mystification when it is
interpreted, either by the author or his commentators, in some nar-
rowly or univocally authoritative way.

If McLuhan explores or probes using percepts rather than concepts,
sense-datum rather than notions or ideas, and if, as he contends, his

approach is both that of an observer and a pragmatist, then he is himself creating insightful artefacts, which trigger his audience's or readers's own creative understanding of the objects that he is discussing. This has been his great strength – to be the first historically grounded poet of the rapidly changing artefacts of the new technoculture. The potential weakness appears when his rhetorico-poetic project becomes fact or formula rather than insight and intuition. If he has sparked the writing of communication/history, far more than Innis did, it is because of his poetic genius. If he has a proclivity for Joyce, and through Joyce for Vico, it is because Vico's *New Science* is a poetic, and ultimately phenomenological, science and Joyce's major works are poetic visions of the encounter of every(wo)man with the transformations of contemporary technoculture. McLuhan repeatedly stresses this, but he also always does so while being tempted by the lure of the media marketing of his image.

McLuhan's very use of science in subtitling *The Laws of Media "The New Science"* involves paradoxical play, for his "new science" is, on one hand, Bacon's and Vico's new sciences in the sixteenth and eighteenth centuries respectively. On the other, it is also rooted – like Bacon's and Vico's science – in the "sciences" of the patristic and medieval periods that McLuhan explores in his Nashe thesis, which include the sense of theology as the "queen of sciences." In his thesis he had become aware of traditions that considered poetry, music, and grammar as empiric sciences, so that he could make a leap from his interests in Bacon and Vico to a contemporary sense of human science. Yet his "new science" allows him to bridge poetically the power claims of the contemporary techno-scientific, while simultaneously grounding his science in a patristic tradition – rhetorico-grammatical and theological. From this perspective he satirically critiqued the new sciences of cybernetics and communication.

As the 1950s unfolded and McLuhan started his Culture and Communication seminar, early library acquisitions for that seminar included Norbert Wiener's *The Human Use of Human Beings: Cybernetics and Society*, Reusch and Gregory Bateson's *Communications: The Social Matrix of Psychiatry*, Karl Deutsch's *The Nerves of Government*, and William Stephenson's writings on the theory of play. Ted Carpenter's partnership added a complement to the cyberneticians and communicators in the anthropologists who had shaped Bateson's communications work, particularly Edward Tylor, Edward Sapir, Edward Hall, and Franz Boas. The post–World War Two rise of the International Communicaton Association in the U.S. and Innis's three books published between 1948 and 1951 rounded out a cluster of communication- and culture-oriented approaches, which McLuhan rapidly complemented by looking at communication in modern poetry and art. In 1951, at his urging I wrote a master's thesis on T.S. Eliot's theory of communication rounded out by a doctoral thesis in 1954 on communication theory and modern poetry with specific reference to the poetic theories of Yeats, Eliot, Pound and Joyce, which coincided with the launching of the seminar.

A few years later communication would disappear as one of the poles of emphasis in the seminar, giving way to technology, since the concept of *techné*, which McLuhan used to relate works of art, other artefacts, media, and modes of communication, enabled him to interrelate culture with the then more power-oriented analysis of communication technology. It is easy to trace the interlacing of what are seen as the foci of power to McLuhan's emerging interests, from the power of mass culture in the *Bride* through the power of the new communications in the early days of *Explorations* to the gradual transformation of his seminar's interest towards technologies as extensions of man. This path increased the relevance of McLuhan's project, but it also permitted him to make direct entrée into the seats of power, culminating in his 1965 launching by Gossage and Feigen.

His poetic ultimately came to be based on an ambivalent satire of the sources of power through the use of rhetorical strategies allied to such power. Intimations of these strategies had begun with his play with headlines, page layout, advertising slogans and images, and other such devices in the *Bride*. It continued during the *Explorations* period with the private publication of *Counterblast* (modelled on the typographical experimentation of Wyndham Lewis's *Blast*) and with his editing of *Explorations 8* in which there is elaborate play with typography, colour typography, page design (layout), and some limited imagery. The *Galaxy* (except for the introductory headline introducing each section) and *Understanding Media* are more conventional books – in the former he first seeks an academic and intellectual audience; in the latter, a broader media-oriented audience. Immediately following *Understanding Media* he produced the most full blown of his concrete essays, *The Medium Is the Massage*. His satire of the media uses the very devices of the commercial media themselves, as he yearns for the advantages of the genuine media power of TV and film, particularly of the conversational interview – conversation being an oral mode in which he functioned most easily.

While McLuhan, as he attests, could never become a McLuhanite, the nature of his technique encourages McLuhanism(s), for it not only appeals both to those who wish to critique the power of the media and those who are working with or within the media but also artists and cultural producers who wish to use the new media in distinct ways (such as John Cage) to continue the traditions of modernism that are the primary source of McLuhan's force and insight. As Robert Anton Wilson suggested in *Mondo 2000*, "perhaps the most important idea that Marshall McLuhan ever uttered is in the opening chapter of his very early work *The Mechanical Bride*," where he shows the first page of a typical edition of the *New York Times* indicating that it is a collage of what later he would dub our "global village"and "then shows what this Everyday Pop Art has in common with such avant-garde works as Pound's *Cantos*, Cubist painting and *Finnegan's [sic] Wake*" (Rucker et al. 1992, 166). Today this "nonlinear communication" is hardly exceptional, but it provided the bridge between what was then called high art and everyday pop art that launched McLuhan to fame. "McLuhanisms" naturally arose from all interested parties – artists, media practitioners, art and media critics, and even the more with-it public at large who were already living in this "brave new world."

Yet while McLuhan's rhetorical pose invited and encouraged McLuhanites, his satiric, perhaps cynical satiric, distancing permitted him the luxury of continuing in the line of modernist poetry. The threat was that the public McLuhan, not being a theorist or philosospher in the usual sense, would become a collage of McLuhanisms, which, of course, is what happened. Pursuing a strategy utilizing insights of the French symbolists, Joyce, and Nietzsche, in which closure should be anathema, while continuing to stress simultaneously that he was a true believer seeking the integrity of a renewed medieval universalism and that professionally he was an objective, "scientific" observer and recorder of facts, he attracted groups that would stress his pragmatic approach to modern media mania; groups that would promote his essentially Catholic image; groups that would see him as the epitome of the avant-garde looking to the future; and groups that would condemn him as the maverick of a serious pursuit of the study of com-munication and its history. And he delighted in the very ambivalence that he created!

Such a stance, which is closer to that of the poet as cultural producer than the thinker or the researcher, also shows a streak of the journalist on the part of McLuhan – his particular, unique way of applying Pound's modernist adage that he was fond of quoting, "Literature is news that STAYS news" (Pound n.d., 29). Ironically, McLuhan was to become a source of one-liners for educated or informed journalists who wrote about or commented on the emerging technopanic in the late 1960s and early 1970s, even more after his return to power as patron saint of *Wired* and through discussions in *Mondo* and *21*C* in the 1990s. While there were informed and balanced critics such as

Gary Wolf and Mark Dery, McLuhanism still occupied a major position in discussions of the new interactive digital technologies, both in the creation of artificial or virtual realities and in the understanding of the Internet with its World Wide Web. McLuhan's visions from the 1950s and early 1960s had intuited the significance of the modernist arts to understanding the historical emergence of the unfolding technoculture and had gleaned from it the need to craft new languages (verbal and non-verbal) to explore how people would re-orient themselves to the new social realities.

As we have seen in earlier chapters, McLuhan did not discover the phrases and concepts himself, but he did raise them to their "first intensity," situating them as permanent contributions to the technocultural dialogue.[5] Not only items such as the regularly invoked "the medium is the message" or "the Global Village", but "the new orality" and the accompanying "orality/literacy" opposition; the return to a new tribalism, the "rear view mirror"; technologies as "extensions of man"; print and vision as linear; acoustic space; and a host of other phrases. The editors of *Mondo 2000* (Rudy Rucker, R.U. Sirius, and Queen Mu) note that "Reading Marshall McLuhan is kind of like reading Shakespeare – you keep stumbling on phrases that you thought were clichés ONLY HE MADE THEM UP" (Rucker et al. 1992, 166). While he did not precisely make them up, as we have seen, he did make them memorable – a primary function of the poet and the rhetorician. Their constant repetition in print and audio-visual media attests to his having crafted a language which is "news that STAYS news!"

The editors of *Mondo 2000 Users' Guide* also show how McLuhan's poetic vision could lead him to anticipate the 1990s when discussing automation nearly thirty years earlier. If you substitute computer for automation in the final paragraph of *Understanding Media* it describes a circumstance remarkably like that of the 1990s: "Persons grouped around a fire or candle for warmth or light are less able to pursue independent thoughts, or even tasks, than people supplied with electric light. In the same way, the social and educational patterns latent in [computers] are those of self-employment and artistic autonomy. Panic about [computers] as a threat of uniformity on a world scale is the projection into the future of mechanical standardization and specialism, which are now past" (McLuhan 1964, 359). These words, written in 1964 as the conclusion of *Understanding Media*, constitute a poetic vision, but not really a futuristic prophecy, since by this point in the development of computers it had already become apparent to the leading edge that the creation of artificial realities was possible and that the amassing of complex databases and their availability throughout the world was imminent.

McLuhan's linking of automation and autonomy is partly prompted by verbal play, but by 1964 McLuhan – well grounded in the foundations of the marriage of art and technology in the writings of Sigfried Giedion, Gyorgy Kepes, László Moholy-Nagy, Amédée Ozenfant, and others – could appreciate the significance of the beginnings of a linkage between the TV screen (a precursor or forerunner of the computer monitor) and the computer. His 1964 writings were to inspire both researchers at MIT's *Media Lab* and the various affiliations of art and technology, such as Robert Rauschenberg's association with Billy Kluver in E.A.T. Victor Papanek, in his essay in *Explorations 8*, which includes references to a wide range of artistic activities from 1900 to the 1950s, responds to a question raised by Giedion in an earlier issue of *Explorations*: "What is it separates us from other periods?" In *Explorations 8* Papanek offers the answer, in which he concurs with McLuhan's theme in the issue, that "after thousands of years of written processing of human experience, the instantaneous omnipresence of electronically processed information has hoicked us out of these age-old patterns into an auditory world" (Papenek 1957, 5).[6]

If McLuhan's transformation of the phrases and concepts of others into memorable aphorisms was guided by a hypermodernist poetic, his perceptualization of the emerging technoculture was filtered through the modern arts and architecture and their affiliation with technology. When he returns to the theme, he reiterates, in a note to his posthumous *The Global Village*, his consistent relationship of the computer to electricity, citing *Understanding Media*. Creating a tetrad somewhat different from the one used in *The Laws of Media*, he stresses how digitalization retrieves tactility and how by "reversing into simultaneous pattern recognition ... it brings back the Pythagorean occult embodied in the idea 'numbers are all'" (McLuhan 1989, 103–4, 176, 192n.9).

That return to Pythagoreanism is also in a way a return to the world of art and technology in the twentieth century, for the Pythagorean motif runs through the history of contemporary art in its fascination with numbers, geometrical form, and technology. Joined to the contemporary implications of Pythagoreanism were the obvious significance of Pythagoreanism in the Renaissance and its affiliations with hermeticism and the occult philosophy as well as Leonardo's fascination with "divine proportions" and the "golden section."

Once again the McLuhan fix on electrification, the computer, and automation has affiliations with the artistic, the poetic, and the intuitive nature of mysticism, although it should be noted that if he considers himself to be a "print man," committed to the rationalism of modern mathematics (i.e., as of Leibnitz and the calculus), his relation to the Pythagorean and the contemporary necessarily situates his attitude toward digitalization as ambiguous. If the computer is providing a freedom and autonomy, a potential thrust toward decentralization as opposed to an acceptance of hierarchy, and is replacing the rationalism of the mathematics of modernity with the irrationalism of neo-Pythagorean digitalism, then the stance of the conservative "man of letters" who is not a McLuhanite (since he is Marshall McLuhan) is necessarily to be a critic of the "brave new world." However the Marshall McLuhan among the avant-garde poets and artists is fascinated with modernist neo-Pythagoreanism. His early fascination with LeCorbusier, Paul Klee, Paul Kandinsky, Kepes, Moholy-Nagy, René Duchamp, and the Cubists invoked an interest in modularity, in mathematical proportion, and in contemporary fascinations with modularity, golden sections, and Pythagorean triangles.

McLuhan's early interests in the American and Irish modernists stressed the importance of T.E. Hulme's *Speculations*, echoing Lewis's own stress on Hulme. Hulme's argument for the Egyptian-Byzantine rather than the classical-Renaissance grounding of modernist art privileged the geometrico-mathematical orientation of the Pythagorean tradition. McLuhan associates his view with that of Lewis's critique of the modernist bias towards the Bergsonian emphasis on space-time, which Hulme's theories certainly support (McLuhan 1953A, 77–88). It is probably important to keep in mind that in Nietzsche's *The Will to Power*, Nietzsche links the anti-Hellenic stance of the post-Socratic philosophers to a value judgment favouring the Egyptian, the Semitic, and the Pythagorean ("the subterranean cults, silence, terrorism with a beyond, mathematics"); the religious valuation ("priestly, ascetic, transcendental"); and the dialectic ("a repellent and pedantic concept splitting already in Plato"). Nietzsche summarized by suggesting that: "Two decadence movements and extremes run side by side : (a) sensual, charmingly wicked decadence, loving art and show; and (b) gloomy religio-moral pathos, Stoic self-hardening, Platonic slander of the senses, preparation of the soil for christianity" (Nietzsche 1968, sec. 427, 232). This neatly summarizes the schizoid dilemma of McLuhan, which he apparently recognized when he wrote to Walter Ong that "the Catholic view of Neech would seem to be off the beam" (McLuhan 1987, 234).

From the perspective of his having both attracted some of those lured by the new world of technology while simultaneously preserving the conservative traditions of church and state, the particular mixture that this ambivalence generated permitted him to have a simultaneous appeal to seemingly opposed interests, whether the youth and radicals of the "sixties," power figures of the media business and politics, agnostic avant-garde artists and thinkers, or conservative defenders of the Catholic Church. This appears to have been partly conscious, but primarily a function of his schizoid dilemma, which so dramatically provides an oblique reflection of the schizoid nature of an era dominated by the emergence of digitalization and international technoculture. Arthur Kroker, who wrote one of the first insightful analyses of McLuhan in relation to his compatriots Harold Innis and George Grant, later responded to the McLuhanesque vision when he explored the modern age under the motif of an era of panic, for McLuhan himself expressed the very essence of that panic in his personna as well as his intellectual and artistic stance.

In his work McLuhan preserved this precarious, ambivalent, somewhat hysteric stance reflective of his age by adapting the medieval and early Renaissance role of the wise fool – a role he characteristically declared he occupied and simultaneously denied. In 1971, when I discussed his work in terms of this complex Renaissance understanding of folly, well documented in his own work and quite consistent with the traditions of the learned satire that he was trying to compose, he suggested that I had "beclowned" him, again reflecting the depth of his schizoid dilemma, since he seemed to want to appear to be a serious academic theorist and analyst (although always insisting he was dealing with observations and percepts not concepts) while simultaneously condemning such academic seriousness as theory and analysis in the name of the power of comedy and satire. Essentially, however, he was a highly trained medieval and Renaissance scholar who well understood the importance of the figure of the wise fool or learned clown as well as the importance of wearing the mask of a clown or fool. Such a stance fits well with the figures of Erasmus, Rabelais, and others praised in his Nashe thesis; with the rhetorical tradition of the paradoxical encomium, as McLuhan first points out in his thesis and later in *From Cliché to Archetype*; and with the Christian tradition of the holy fool. McLuhan's willingness to play with the role but to attack others who suggest that a major aspect of his ambivalent work is a continuation of the "praise of folly" further suggests the schizoid streak in which he wishes to be regarded as serious, while using the lack of seriousness to protect himself against criticism.

This complexity of stance is part of what makes him as powerful a figure as he is, but it also means that, in trying to be attractive to everybody, his basic vision is diminished and dissipated. The "new age" figures that are the subject of *Mondo* are probably closer to McLuhan's vision than those various groups who have begun to promote him, while adopting only part of his complex project. Some of his sharper critics, such as Wolf, Dery, Jean Baudrillard, or Kroker show a greater appreciation of the depth of his real worth than those who promote him as part of an agenda, for what gave McLuhan his original power was the paradoxical foundations of his project – a project that weds the patristic, medieval, and Renaissance to the modernist and can simultaneously combine the technological with the hermetic and the occult within the ambivalence of learned folly. This is part of the significance of *The Gutenberg Galaxy* opening with *King Lear* and closing with Pope's *The Dunciad*. Let us turn to look at the response of McLuhan to the re-emergence of the occult and hermetic in the new technoculture.

6 McLuhan and the Cults: Gnosticism, Hermeticism, and Modernism

While studying under Marshall, in the fall of 1951 I began extensive research into Alexander Pope's satires, especially *The Dunciad Variorum*. This led to a series of questions about why Pope had satirized Rosicrucians in his *Rape of the Lock* and Freemasonry in the final version of *The Dunciad*. This led us both into an extensive examination of the role of Freemasonry in neo-Augustan England, particularly in the first half of the eighteenth century.[1] In the process Marshall increased his already deep interest, and I became involved in the history of gnosticism and related movements. While working on gnosticism together, I remember Marshall's reaction of scandal at the "hidden knowledge" in contemporary poetry, art, and scholarship. This interest, well documented in his correspondence and elsewhere, persisted well into the 1970s, as reflected in his letters.[2]

Besides this fascination with "the secret societies," which surfaced around the same time, he also began his active interest in attaining power and influence, which was in one sense research into what he believed to be complementary concentrations of power that brought together political, fiscal, and mystical or magical power. McLuhan's schizoid paranoia led him to stress only indirectly and allusively the contemporary power of what he regarded as Gnostic conspiracies and this eventually contributed directly to his own participation in producing the growing sense of technocultural panic that developed subsequent to the Second World War. It eventually vitiated the obsession that he had developed with secret societies after 1952, as expressed in his letter to Pound, 3 December 1952.

As a Renaissance scholar, McLuhan was naturally deeply interested in magic, alchemy, occult belief, and mystery religions. These interests went back at least into the 1940s as reflected in his discussions of alchemy, astrology, and magic in his Nashe thesis with its discussions of grammatical and allegorical exegesis. He was also aware of the important role physics had in the allegorical and tropological interpretation of texts from the time of Varro in Rome (McLuhan 1943, 26, 215–17). He notes in his discussion that alchemy found its basis in the relation of classical and medieval physics to exegesis (i.e., what he calls "grammatical physics"), so that behind Boyle's alchemy or Newton's occult interests he finds a continuing tradition going back to Alexandria and the early fathers of the Church (McLuhan 1943, 307). It is thus not surprising that Newton, who came out of a continuous tradition of biblical interpretation that interrelated the two books of Nature and of Scripture, devoted a large part of his life to his commentary on the apocalyptic Book of Daniel. McLuhan's criticism of Newton was that his rationalism, like Descartes's, was a result of the great divorce between rhetoric and logic that had been effected by "left wing scholastics" anticipating Ramus, such as Roger Bacon, William Ockham, and the gnostic-oriented Giordano Bruno, who plays a major role in Joyce's *Finnegans Wake*.

But McLuhan's interest in esotericism and occultism went further, since he firmly believed that the "secret" tradition with which they were associated had an immediate and important historical impact.[3] His interest in the occult traditions and its importance in his work of the 1950s and 1960s was well recognized in Canada, particularly in Quebec. In 1972 a Quebec author, media artist, and radio and TV personality wrote a book about McLuhan whose cover displayed a bust of Pythagoras wearing a Montreal Canadien's hockey uniform. The author, Jacques Languirand, a well-known Radio Canada broadcaster and new age personality and one of the creators of the multimedia exhibits in "Man in the Community Pavilion" at Expo 67 (part of the theme complex "Man and his World" for which McLuhan's writings provided inspiration while his aphorisms were used as guiding quotations), entitled his book on magic and communication *De McLuhan à Pythagore* (*From McLuhan to Pythagoras*) (Languirand 1972). From his Québecois perspective, Languirand had no difficulty reconciling the McLuhan who was a fideist Catholic entranced by technology, with the McLuhan who was at the same time fascinated with the esoteric thought associated with magic, secret cults, alchemy, and mystery religions.

Like McLuhan's *The Medium Is the Massage*, *De McLuhan à Pythagore* is a multi-media medley of illustration, typography, and aphoristic text – an *essai concrète*.[4] Languirand explores McLuhan's relation to hermetic and occult wisdom, discussing relationships between contemporary modernist and postmodernist art and occult knowledge, tracing the tradition from Pythagoras to McLuhan. To traverse the same ground in a more prosaic and analytic way requires a confrontation with one of the main roots of all the cryptic and complex statements that are found in McLuhan and that contributed to making him so memorable and quotable – medieval and modern Catholic theology and philosophy. To pursue this important element in McLuhan's work, which he felt permeated extensive areas of modernist literature (e.g., W.B. Yeats, Wyndham Lewis's presentation of Bloomsbury's fascination with magic and other secret knowledge, Charles Williams's novels, Arthur Rimbaud's angelism, etc.), it is necessary to probe the relations between engineering and esoteric thought, gnosticism and *The Gutenberg Galaxy*, Catholicism and modern science. In so doing we have to confront the importance of theology to McLuhan's project and its role as a source of many of his strengths and some of the worst of his weaknesses.

For McLuhan, as for Lewis, the artist is in some ways "an ape of god." If the poet's own knowledge is in part esoteric (quite a legitimate interpretation of the role of the poet or artist in many cultures), then the function she or he performs in understanding the future of her or his culture is in itself enmeshed in the occult and hermetic. This is similar to what the alchemists hoped to achieve in their quest: the poet-artist believes that nature delivers a brazen world, but she or he will transform it into a golden one.[5] McLuhan had early encountered the significance of the alchemical and hermetic in his Nashe thesis and had noted the connection of these early "sciences" with the Renaissance motif of the poet creating a second nature (McLuhan 1943, 319). In an extension of McLuhan's own thought, using many of the same sources as McLuhan – the work of modern artists and their preoccupation with such concepts as the "golden number" – Languirand sees the artist as a kind of modern magus.

Languirand's concerns and that he found McLuhan's work relevant are not surprising, for modernist art by which Languirand was influenced, as was McLuhan, has been permeated by an interest in engineering, which in early modernism had its own fascination, particularly when joined to architecture, with the creation of a second nature. Yeats, Eliot, Pound, and Joyce, who were then the undisputed major English-speaking poets of the earlier twentieth century, provided a framework for McLuhan in which an interest in esoteric beliefs, a commitment to the study of technique, and an interest in the theoretical aspects of the creative process were allied. Paul Valéry's writings provide typical examples, for he utilized the occultism of Mallarmé, while still considering the poet and artist to be an engineer. He explained that the "golden number" and Pythagoreanism contained basic aesthetic as well as scientific insights. In his critical writings Valéry argues that Leonardo da Vinci's works address our contemporary audience with a very special immediacy. This was a pronouncement to which McLuhan was only too pleased to listen and which was consistent with the theories of architecture, art, and music in which McLuhan was most interested.[6]

On one hand, McLuhan, having started university life believing he would be an engineer, had a lifelong attraction to technology, even though he had virtually no practical mastery over any technological device he encountered or employed at home, work, or leisure. He was fascinated by those Utopian and counter-Utopian thinkers who were themselves concerned with technology: i.e., Buckminster Fuller, Sigfried Giedion, and Lewis Mumford. On the other hand, his poetic and religious interests led him into a study of esoteric symbolism and associated beliefs. The ascendancy of William Blake and Carl Jung as sources of symbols for contemporary writers in the English-speaking world had led most major artists to an interest in various occult doctrines such as gnosticism, hermeticism, alchemy, astrology, the Tarot, ancient mystery cults, and esoteric Buddhism. [7] This vision of the modern artist truly involved an awareness of the modern tendency (partly inspired by ecology) towards the "reenchantment of the world" (Berman 1981, passim). In fact, McLuhan found literary models for such a vision among cubists, surrealists, symbolists (the French and their followers) and, most particularly, in James Joyce.

McLuhan's view of the poet, derived from the same combination of theological, poetic, neo-Platonic, esoteric, and alchemical sources, was that the poet was a prophet, even a privileged "natural prophet" in the sense in which St Thomas Aquinas spoke of natural prophecy in contradistinction from the work of divine prophets. McLuhan's entire approach depended on a conviction that an artist is an individual who has special insight into the future directions of his culture. Edgar Allen Poe's conception of the poet contemplating the maelstrom of change, one of McLuhan's favorite images, presents the poet using his knowledge to control his own fate within the changing world around him (McLuhan 1967, 144). McLuhan again and again reiterated that his poetics were meant to communicate insights for becoming, like Poe's mariner (or poet), the still point of the turning world – protected against the rapid technocultural change by having become an observer. In the process McLuhan becomes a kind of poetic futurologist, an extension of the role of "poetic engineer." As has subsequently become clear, the futurologist, our hopes for information technology, and the technocultural community participate in a mystical technognosticism, which McLuhan feared, yet which fascinated him and which much of his work anticipated while still satirizing it.

From the beginnings of the Renaissance until the eighteenth century many intellectuals, writers, painters, musicians, and architects had recognized the close relationships between alchemy, Rosicrucianism, mysticism, and other esoteric doctrines. Muriel Bradbrook (McLuhan's thesis director) and Frances Yates, whose writings McLuhan cited in his thesis well before her recognition as a major scholar concerned with Renaissance thought, had both investigated aspects of the significance of these relationships. In a series of fundamental studies on art and philosophy in the Renaissance and the Enlightenment in Europe and the British Isles, Yates subsequently clearly established the connections between the arts, various sixteenth- and seventeenth-century occult philosophies, esoteric dogma, and contemporary politics.[12] McLuhan, initially a scholar of Renaissance drama, was ideally prepared to realize that the moderns were returning to old traditions and that from the time of the Renaissance Platonists right through the neo-Augustan Age of Pope – in fact, in Pope's poetry and Swift's prose – and beyond in Blake, the Romantics, Tennyson, and others these elements were present. But up to the time of Pope there was a strong, mainline, patristic-oriented critique of the more enthusiastic mysticisms and of Ramism and rationalism, though subsequently such critique weakened exponentially. Once again, from a new perspective, it is possible to see that McLuhan's perceptive analysis of Pope's *Dunciad* in the conclusion of his *Gutenberg Galaxy* rises out of the development of his esoteric as well as his historical themes.[13]

In various writings on the subject of Bruno and the Rosicrucian Enlightenment Yates confirms that the occult sciences had a role in the growth of the enlightenment and in the evolution of scientific knowledge. She traces the relationship between the magus and the scientist-engineer in such figures as John Dee, an influential personality in the court of Queen Elizabeth I, and shows how his magical knowledge found its way into the works of Edmund Spenser and George Chapman and the architecture of the designers of Renaissance theater.[14] Such a vision casts a new perspective on Joyce's use of the kabbalah and alchemy in *Finnegans Wake*, as well as his claim that he was the greatest engineer. [15] It also partly explains McLuhan's increasingly extensive use of Joyce as a counterplot in his mid-career writings, such as *War and Peace in the Global Village*.[16] With his fascination for engineering, technique, know-how, and the effects of technologies, it ought not to be surprising that in places McLuhan appears to be on the side of the experimentalists who in the everyday world are the engineers and technologists and in the history of theology are represented by the alchemists, the magicians, and the hermetic thinkers.

The occult and esoteric entered McLuhan's thought mainly through their provision of a natural poetic theology within which the panoply of mechanized nature – the technological world – could be contemplated.[17] The study of technology, culture, and communications provided him with a natural route into the labyrinth of the technological world. It also permitted him to use the world of the occult as an analogical mirror of technology, for the technique implicit in magic, mystery religions, and alchemy had profound implications for the interaction of people with one another and with the natural universe.[18] One of McLuhan's strengths arose from his discovering these implications and realizing how many theological and philosophical disputes were more concerned with human understanding of the interrelationships within a society at a specific time and place than with abstract relations with the Deity. This meant that gnostic and hermetic currents of thought could be viewed in part as discussions of how humans communicate with one another, with nature, and with the Deity.

Furthermore, given the particular historical moment at which McLuhan emerged, this insight into the social construction of knowledge also provided him with a way to explore the most powerful aspects of the social effects of technology. Communication, as McLuhan developed this concept, bridged a world of technology and a Neo-Thomistic world of faith that is based on reason, going beyond the usual sense of communication to include the concept of communication as phatic communion.[19] McLuhan had a lifelong fascination with the concept of a poetic-oriented natural theology as relevant to the understanding of the creative. Therefore an orthodox rational theology, such as Thomism, occupied a place of key importance alongside (and to the extent that Thomas shared the alchemical interest of his mentor, Albertus Magnus) an equally compelling interest in the esoteric theologies of gnosticism, the hermetic-alchemical tradition, and the complex poetics conceived by avant-garde modernists and artists such as Marcel Duchamp, Paul Klee, Stéphane Mallarmé, and Joyce.

McLuhan's Thomism, while possibly a deviation from the neo-Thomist orthodoxy of mid-century as represented by the Pontifical Insitute of Studies in the University of St Michael's College at the University of Toronto and the writings of McLuhan's colleague Étienne Gilson, initially arose from his interests in the Renaissance and his early reading of Gilson's works in relation to his study of patristic humanism.[20] For many in the Renaissance the roots of Thomism were affiliated with alchemy through the alchemical interests of Albertus

Magnus and, quite typically, Thomas Nashe shared the alchemical interests of substantial numbers of his colleagues. Early Renaissance philosophical figures such as Tomasso Campanella had developed humanistic readings of Aquinas, in Campanella's case encompassing his own metaphysics directed towards reading the signs in the Book of Nature. Such interpretations certainly fascinated McLuhan, who was also intensely interested in Francis Bacon, who had some sympathy with and knowledge of aspects of alchemy. Such an orientation probably predisposed McLuhan to the interest that he was to develop in alchemistry and occult science and the concern that this would create for him when he was confronted with its gnostic and Masonic associations. His pursuit of these problems would have been further reinforced by the appearance in the 1960s of Frances Yates's seminal works on Giordano Bruno, on the arts of memory, and on the history of science and the human science with their importance for the study of Joyce as well as Renaissance studies: *Giordano Bruno and the Hermetic Tradition*, *The Art of Memory*, *The Rosicrucian Enlightenment* and *The Occult Philosophy in the Elizabethan Age*.

Turning to the role of the occult traditions in McLuhan's thought, it is necessary to keep in mind that, as in other areas, his interest was eclectic, his method of assembling information unsystematic, and his interpretations radical and individualistic. Thus coupled with the usual tortuous complexity of the history of underground beliefs, one finds all the usual characteristics of other areas of McLuhan's thought. For this reason alone it would be unwise to expect any consistency in the way such material manifests itself in McLuhan's writings. Furthermore, McLuhan seldom overtly admitted the importance of these preoccupations in his overall discussions of technology and culture. A further complication is, as his correspondence demonstrates, that he not only found the ideas of the occult tradition important, he (perhaps unfortunately) also believed the occult to be an important socio-political force in the modern world. In letters that he wrote to Ezra Pound and Walter Ong, he laments the fact that he had been kept out of the secret structure that was the fabric of the contemporary arts and contemporary intellectual life (McLuhan 1987, 233, 235, 283). Put simply, he believed in a conspiracy theory of current history in which secret societies, possessing a hidden knowledge of secret doctrines, manipulated the intellectual and political life of the world. When he first read Eric Voeglin's *The New Science of Politics* on the influence of gnostic intellectual currents on Western political and philosophical thought (Voegelin 1952, passim), he translated Voeglin's thesis into a much stronger form in which the reason for the persistence of the gnostic tradition in thought was the presence of hidden groups of socially influential individuals who preserved and transmitted that tradition.

In one of McLuhan's favorite satiric novels about Bohemian Blooms-bury, *The Apes of God*, Lewis introduces the figure of a society magus, Horace Zagreus,(whose name is supposed to remind the reader of the Egyptian god Horus and the deity of the Eleusinian mysteries Zagreus). He is the mentor of the anti-hero of *Apes*, Daniel Boleyn. Zagreus (modelled on figures such as Aleister Crowley) is an expositor of the way the Bloomsbury literary coterie works, describing it as part of "a freemasonry of the arts" (a notion borrowed from Pope and Swift). Lewis as narrator uses the phrase in relation to the "apes" who inhabit this pseudo-Bohemian world, which parodies the world of creative ac-tivity. Lewis, who frequently echoes Pope in the *Apes of God*, struc-tures the novel on a principle similar to Pope's *Dunciad* with its satire of Cartesian rationalism, enthusiastic religions, and gnostic groups (e.g., the Masons, the Rosicrucians), and its view of artistic creation as an initiation ritual into a mystery religion.[21] McLuhan's corres-pondence and his interpretation of Voeglin demonstrate that he inter-preted Lewis' "freemasonry of the arts" quite literally as being a direct allegorical symbol suggesting there were important social groups directly guided by magi, such as the contemporary magus Aleister Crowley. In an essay on Lewis, McLuhan writes:

"His attacks on the romancers of Progress and romancers of the Past have this single aim, to deliver us from the bondage of primitive reli-gion with its obsession with recurrence, and the way of destruction as the way of rebirth. And it has been this sense of equal menace pre-sented to any living present by the cultist of East and West that has pro-cured his exclusion from the public attention which they control" (McLuhan 1969).

McLuhan's concern with the "menace presented" by the "cultists of East and West" was pressing, as his correspondence demonstrates. Yet its main function was to further encourage his studies into the her-metic, gnostic, cabalistic, and mystical. It expanded his command of the modern arts and provided a rich heuristic source for his analyses of culture and technology, which were based on a poetic-metaphoric method rather than on a coherent theoretical position. Nevertheless, holding the belief as firmly as he did also led to further complexity, obscurity, and occasionally distortions of his thought, resulting in many paradoxes and contradictions. In the early 1950s McLuhan turned as naturally to these subjects as he did to subjects like cyber-netics, systems theory, mass communications, and popular culture. His approach to communication, culture, and technology was rooted in knowledge provided by the practice of artists, for McLuhan believed artists to be at the leading edge of the modes of practice that their societies would evolve to solve technological and cultural problems.

As a would-be engineer turned literary scholar and later cultural analyst, McLuhan respected technical know-how and could see how the aspirations of an alchemist like Paracelsus and the twentieth-century designer of a computer were involved in the same desire to control their environment by the manipulation of materials. Rightly or wrongly, McLuhan saw the artist as involved in a similar process but attracted to understanding the full range of implications of how such manipulation is applied and how it has operated both within the contemporary world and throughout history. It was natural, therefore, for him to be interested in the ways that the wisdom of Pythagoras or Paracelsus exist in the modern world, just as it was natural to be interested in the images of engineering and mass culture. In McLuhan, as Languirand's writing suggests, one can retrace the Pythagorean-hermetic visions of classical occultism. But why is this background important for understanding McLuhan's writings about culture and technology? His whole sense of technique or know-how as it related to technology was modelled on poetic knowledge, which he had always seen as a *techné*. The very root of his conceptual apparatus for dealing with technology is to be found in his knowledge of literature, the arts, and theology. Essential to understanding poetry, the arts, and theology is a knowledge of the occult tradition: a corollary is that such knowledge is also essential to understanding culture and technology – the transformation of nature and the transformation of man.

When we turn with this in mind to McLuhan's readings of media, popular culture, and technology, the effect of each of these areas, particularly the poetic and the occult, is central. If the modern world is preoccupied with such oppositions as those of East and West, print and electronic media, Russia and China, Europe and the United States, McLuhan sees these oppositions as a world-wide reflection of the tensions existing between differing forms of theology and envisions their eventual reconciliation in a post-modern, post-industrial, electric world. Emphases or biases in favour of the ear or the eye will be shown to be associated with similar biases in the domain of human affairs, so the ear and the eye are associated in *The Gutenberg Galaxy* with differing philosophical and theological perspectives and then somehow reconciled and transcended in the synthetic (and synesthetic) operation of tactility. These motifs obviously echo idealistic philosophers; they also relate to the way the doctrine of unity in multiplicity unfolds in esoteric thought.

To understand how these opposites work within the global world, McLuhan employs the heuristic potential of the major poetic traditions and of esoteric knowledge in developing a "poetic" understanding of the function of technology. Strategies of analogical thinking derived from these areas are used in his various analyses of media (e.g., his concepts of vertical and horizontal, of the labyrinth of cognition, and of East and West). One could further explore the structure of the ear, the shape of the labyrinth of cognition, and the spherical nature of acoustic space as forming part of a cluster of imagery with which McLuhan approaches the concept of acoustic space. The labyrinth, the sphere, the act of hearing the word, all enter into the structure of mystery religion and the liturgies with which these images in part are associated. Yet he also finds they can assist in interpreting the analysis of acoustic media and the shifts from ear to eye and eye to ear. Besides, the media and the senses that they extend become in their own right analogies revealing the effect of technology – a position McLuhan develops – yet also revealing the shaping effect of politico-economic society on technology, which he suppresses.

To select another example, McLuhan's use of "hot" and "cool," deriving (as Languirand observes) from Far Eastern religions' use of yin and yang, is a striking example of how esoteric or occult thought permeated his analysis (Languirand 1972, 169ff). Such strategies link McLuhan's approach, in spite of his protestations to the contrary, with the same intellectual milieu that produced Jung's interest in universal myths and Northrop Frye's in archetypes. "Cool," which for McLuhan carries the sense of involvement or participation, echoes not only a Catholic interest in communion but the interest of esoteric cults in mystical participation of the initiates. "Cool" is a horizontal notion; "hot," a vertical one. Such a range of semantic sensitivity in words is reminiscent of symbolist writers and artists and presents a very ambivalent vision of contemporary technologies, even if McLuhan himself seems to insist on his statements literally saying what they mean. The sense of ambiguity, tension, analogy, and difference in his statements produces a more profound affect than his statements about them would allow us to believe.

None of his divisions are absolutes. His is essentially a world in flux and in that very process the nature of the opposites themselves is perpetually changing; just as in the alchemical aspects of Joyce's world in *Finnegans Wake*; opposites separate, then coalesce, undergo metamorphosis and re-emerge, often at the diametrically opposite pole. The intellectuality of the Western perspective can merge with the mysticism of the East and re-emerge as a distinguishing characteristic of the East itself.[22] According to McLuhan, as the East awakes, the tactile and the primitive come into prominence. This is realized in the movement from the Gutenberg stage of visual, vertical, and "hot" media to the electric stage of the transistor and computer. With the prediction of the rebirth of primitive man that will result from the tactility of the electric age, an apocalyptic tone of rebirth and reintegration enters McLuhan's work, intertwining motifs of traditional Catholicism with motifs of esoteric beliefs. The hermetic and gnostic overtones implicit in Catholic tradition interpenetrate his metaphoric structure.

McLuhan's "hot" and "cool" describe the effect of media technology, not spiritual states or modes. For McLuhan, however, technologies are extensions of man and as such reflect the human person of which they are an extension. Consequently, they could give rise to the development of the metaphor – a "rear view mirror." But media also can effect human actions, increasing participation or creating distance. Television as a "cool" medium increases participation and hence can achieve that *participation mystique* that is the goal of mystical initiation and phatic communion.

McLuhan does not favor television over the book. He sees television as achieving a vision that transforms man's values but which in its turn will be transformed by solid state electric circuitry predominant in computers. When considering electricity as the mark of the new world, McLuhan first stressed the importance of the electric light bulb, whose medium is its message. The theological overtones of light overcoming darkness clearly play throughout this conception, which nearly equates the electric light to a Deity whose essence is his existence. But a little later electric circuitry itself becomes an obvious replacement for the light bulb, for the function of electricity can be seen as reflecting the formula borrowed from theology concerning the God (equivalent in McLuhan to acoustic space) whose center is everywhere and whose circumference is nowhere. The "hidden god" and the all-pervasive Christian Deity interplay in the vision of the new electric age.

In McLuhan's metamorphic writing, the electric world appears to be some sort of plateau humanity has reached, some region of the absolute. Just as light holds a special place in the various worlds of esoteric wisdom, McLuhan sees the *electric*, not the *electronic*, world as symbolizing a type of integration into wholeness which is strikingly like the integration of the "fallen" man into the godhead of gnosticism and hermeticism. It might seem surprising that similar formulae dominate the occult discussions of redemption through reintegration and transcendence and McLuhan's account of the effect of electric technology on the society of humans. However it should not be surprising considering that, for him, electric circuitry is an extension of the human central nervous system.[23]

In fact, much of McLuhan's symbolic value system seems to echo aspects of occult lore. The basic theme of his major writings – that, through an electronic apocalypse, the newer media are transforming man into a new totally integrated human person, occupant of a "global village" and possessor of a sense of sensory wholeness – reflects hermetic and gnostic accounts of a redemption of man by freeing him from the world of fragmented material existence. The ethereal quality of electricity replaces the hardware orientation of Gutenberg-era mechanized print. The theme continues in McLuhan's preference in his later works for "software" over "hardware" (McLuhan and Nevitt 1972, 86–123). Fragmentation based on specialization is transcended in a reintegration achieved through participation in the "cool" mosaic styles of knowledge. Yet the whole is justified and reconciled with his Catholic orientation as a sacramentalizing of the material world, not an etherealizing of it through some movement into a transcendent spirituality.

McLuhan counterpoints the materials of the "secret" tradition and the modern arts with the world of reality and a Catholic sense of the material world, so there comes to be a dialectical opposition of the theology of the Catholic Church in one direction and the strategy of rationalization intrinsic in the principles of the contemporary technological world in the other; thus developing a complex ironic texture to his poetic prose. Beneath McLuhan's attempt to provide an appearance of empirical rationality, there lay a much more complex mode of Catholic, or more accurately his peculiar, confused version of neo-Thomist, rationality with which he confronted tradition and contemporary existence in the framework of a tension between the Church and the cults. The extent to which this rationality was closely tied to his conversion from Protestantism to Catholicism and reflective of a basic tension in Canadian society and throughout Canadian intellectual life provided a distinctively Canadian perspective from which to view a distinctively American phenomenon – the world of mass culture and technology. Naturally Northrop Frye, as an exponent of a Protestant and gnostic-like intellectual system (which McLuhan considered to be Puritan), provided the obvious foil for McLuhan within the Canadian university and literary world.

McLuhan found scholarly and historical justification for associating the introduction of Gutenberg technology with the ascendancy of Protestantism, especially Puritanism, and simultaneously with the open emergence of interest in various forms of occultism, such as Rosicrucianism and Freemasonry. He found "bookish" men like Frye to be strongly oriented towards the visual, print-structured world of privacy and interior spirituality. While there could be a "magical" aspect in the world of electric technology, where it existed it was an "orientalizing" influence that would contribute to undercutting the Westernized world of book culture and privacy. Yet in the mixture, according to his analysis, the orientalizing influence of the more "magical" and hermetic world of the East created a society that developed a technology favouring the auditory and the tactile.

In 1954 McLuhan made a key set of observations on Catholic humanism and modern letters, whose centrality to his thought had been demonstrated in the 1960s by Arthur Kroker. In his essay McLuhan observed that "the drama of ordinary human perception seen as the poetic process is the prime analogate, the magic casement opening on the secrets of created being" (McLuhan 1954, 78). He sees Catholicism engaged on the side of reason in a struggle with irrationality in the contemporary world (Kroker 1984, 64). The irrationality of the hermetic-gnostic tradition realizing itself in modern technological society is counterpointed by the redeeming activity of the artistic epiphany, the product of the poetic (i.e., the "artistic) process. He could view each of the forms of technology (e.g. comics, games, television) as "magical," whose magic could be transcended by the activity of the "miracle" of the *nous poietikos*, which he defined as the agent intellect, equating that transcendence with the poetic process (McLuhan 1962B, 251–4).

Consequently, when McLuhan wrote on various occasions in 1953 and 1954 to Pound and Ong stating that Eliot, Lewis, Pound himself, and Joyce had used the rituals and liturgies of the secret societies and that all important living artists and critics were participating in playing this game, he was invoking what had become a complex part of his own thought. While he protested that he found this disgusting and a source of lies and misdirections (such as the Puritan doctrine of the Inner Light), we must remember that as a fiction (which McLuhan elsewhere equates with lies) esotericism had been a fecund source of his analogical insights.[24] Remembering that in the mid 1950s McLuhan embarked on the program that led to his major works, one way of regarding these works, in light of his preoccupation with the secret wisdom, is to see them as establishing means for redeeming the everyday world by using the strategy of the arts and Catholic humanism; the effects of the sacramental work transcending and transforming the activities of magic and mysticism.

Allowing for this, it ought to be possible to see some continuity between Yates' demonstrations of the important impact of such thought on the "enlightenment" and the growth of science and technology in the Renaissance and its effect in modern times, where once again these doctrines have become for poets, artists, and, through McLuhan, for all of us, ways of understanding the modern world. In that process Joyce plays a particular role, since his work consciously embraces the task of transforming the communicative codes of the everyday world of the twentieth century into a poetry of luminous intelligibility through the strategy of epiphany, which elevates and hence intensifies everyday language, verbal and non-verbal, raising its level of intelligibility.[25] In his manifesto on modern Catholic humanism, McLuhan observed that: "What Joyce did was to bring the great developments of symbolist art into the focus of a Thomist philosophy. He created a great new cultural window, metaphor or synthesis. It was Aquinas who enabled Joyce to surpass all the pre-Raphaelites. It was the Thomist awareness of analogy derived from sense perception that gave Joyce the means of digesting all the ideas of all his contemporaries without relying on any of them as a prop or a frame of reference" (McLuhan 1954, 85–6).

Since Joyce is central to McLuhan's writings on culture, technology, and communication, it is necessary to confront the fact that McLuhan saw Joyce as directly engaged in those theological wars which he felt he had uncovered in the early 1950s:

For it was Joyce who first abandoned vertical or horizontal symbolism for horizontal symbolism. He lived amidst the orgy of Swedenborgian, Gnostic and neo-Platonic symbolism which still envelopes us. And he never ceased to have fun with its pagan confusion ... Now for the Platonist as for the Gnostic a symbol or poem is simply a sign linking Heaven and Hell. Art and beauty point from this world to another world from which we have all fallen. In the ancient pagan view, so predominant today, man is a fallen angel ... So that granted the pagan premise that man is simply a fallen angel, the ideal of modern industrial humanism is quite consistent. Let us doll up this fallen angel and let us put it in ever more powerful machines until the whole world looks like Marilyn Monroe in a Cadillac convertible. (McLuhan 1962B, 34)

From such an intellectual stance, art today does not have to do with analogy or incarnation but with lifting us "out of our human condition" and restoring us "to the divine world from which we fell at birth." As the Nietzschean superman, the artist becomes engaged in remaking reality, carrying on a kind of social engineering. In a passage reminiscent of the perspective of Lewis' *Apes of God*, McLuhan suggests that the secular mind that always suspects Manichean booby-traps: "has always approached art and esthetics as religion and magic. So it does today. Hence the quarrels and exclusive coteries of the art world. Art and poetry are regarded as private religions, secret escape hatches from the sunken submarine or unguided missile of existence. The Catholic alone can laugh at these antics. He alone need not be deceived by such qualms or pretensions. *And what the esoteric cultist proffers as magic* he can accept as simple shaping of experience" (McLuhan 1954, 74) underlining mine. Ultimately, McLuhan sees this as the battleground between Catholic humanism and modern industrial angelism, whose theology is that of the gnostic-Manichean vertically oriented superman. "Knowledge of the creative process shows us either the way to the earthly paradise or complete madness. It is either to be the top of Mount Purgatory or the abyss," McLuhan pontificates (McLuhan 1954, 75).

Such speculations and the analogies they suggest form an intrinsic part of the backdrop of *Understanding Media*. In the earlier draft version prepared as a report for the NAEB and the U.S. Office of Education, McLuhan develops thoroughly the tension between vertical and horizontal symbolisms, a theme which also entered into his work in *Explorations*. This concept of the horizontal and the vertical provided him with one of his primary analogies for resolving the problem of the oppositions of eye and ear, verbal and visual, East and West, and the like. Eastern thought is predominantly horizontal; Western thought, vertical. Incarnation and sacrament transcend the division denying the exclusively transmundane, hidden god. Joyce, as McLuhan's loose phrasing suggests, would seem to have discovered a new mode of horizontality, reconciling rather than opposing through the sacramental operation of the word. Presumably, a Christian humanist can transmute the cultic into truth. Yet the crux of the matter is whether the resolution of which McLuhan speaks, a potentially important human resolution, is achieved by Joyce through Catholicism within the religious sphere or through artistic practice within the sphere of man's creative activity. Is it necessary to posit the operation of cults and to create a theological war in which only Catholics can play a significant role, to achieve the shift from "magic" to "the shaping of experience"? Technology, like art as McLuhan recognized, is after all a shaping of experience which is another civilized substitute for magic. It is vital that we not separate the roots between magic and the creative activity of making, while not necessarily binding that to the fact that we all must become supermen.

The ways in which McLuhan uses Joyce in his later writings is crucial. Since Joyce was of special artistic and theological importance for McLuhan, a brief consideration of some of these aspects of Joyce in McLuhan's writing, which will be examined in greater detail later, provides the most appropriate conclusion to this consideration of the role of the esoteric in McLuhan's thought. His interpretation of Joyce's artistic theory, his treatment of the hermetic-alchemical-cabalistic ideas and theological orientation in representing the contemporary world in his poetic prose, provides the very ground that he chose as being crucial to an understanding of the post-modern world (a statement with which many post-modernists would agree, while differing sharply from McLuhan with respect to the details of such an interpretation). Joyce differed from McLuhan in some very profound ways: First, he could tolerate vast ambivalence within his creative works, producing work that has similarities with Jacques Derrida's deconstruction and a philosophical vision closer to that of Giles Deleuze and Félix Guattari than McLuhan. Second, he could cope with the genuine importance of sensuousity and sexuality, which McLuhan always found to be problematic. Third, he embraced the world of the occult, hermetic, and cabalistic without positing a conspiratorial theory of history or creating an absolute conflict between the sacramental and the occult. Fourth, while profoundly ambivalent in his vision, he could accept the value of the human senses, the human person, and the body. Fifth, he could embrace a sense of drama as the root of human communication and creative expression as realized in all ritual and liturgy. McLuhan suggests that Joyce was probably not an ideal Catholic. The fact is that Joyce was a profoundly knowledgeable critic of Catholicism, which, although he had formally rejected it, remained a lifelong influence. Yet Joyce was consciously heretical, as both his socialism and his brother Stanislaus's description of his artistic vision as a sacrament of sexual communion suggests.[26]

McLuhan, on the other hand, as his manifesto on Christian humanism suggests, is a fully committed believer. An important and characteristic example of this fact occurs when McLuhan tries to provide an interpretation of Joyce's doctrine of the epiphany and to reconcile it with a Catholic perspective. In "Joyce, Aquinas and the Poetic Process," McLuhan relates the epiphany to the *nous poietikos*, insisting that his interpretation, like Joyce's, is Thomist, Aristotlean, and Catholic. He explains that the *nous poietikos* is the agent intellect and thus he reconciles Samuel Coleridge's doctrine of the imagination with Joyce's epiphany (McLuhan 1962, 250). Behind the conception he is playing with the notion of the agent intellect as "making" concepts. But there are fundamental difficulties. Catholic philosophers would generally agree that McLuhan's interpretation of Aristotle's *nous poietikos* is essentially neo-Platonic, merging more comfortably with alchemical thought derived from neo-Platonism than with Catholic sacramentalism. (Joyce's own analysis is actually closer to being Scotistic). Joyce, in his own conception of the epiphany, was consciously expanding the permissible range of sacramental transformation in a highly ambivalent image – a secularization of the very notion of incarnation. Nevertheless, McLuhan's insight into Joyce and his application of it in his work is one of the more powerful aspects of this rather complex history, for he ultimately uses it as a justification for the use and transformation of the hermetic and alchemical.

Not surprisingly, McLuhan, in studies such as *War and Peace in the Global Village*, tries to make Joyce less ambivalent, as I demonstrated in *The Medium Is the Rear View Mirror*. But first and foremost he introduces a fundamental ambiguity about the material world that is virtually triggered by his reaction to the very hermetic materials he found so useful. Besides, it led him to see Marx and Hegel as manifestations of gnosticism and to reject on that insight the economic and social insights of Marx, even though they might in part have been consistent with his Catholicism. At the heart of his work there is a basic paradox that vitiates the whole: if he believed Joyce and others developed their artistic vision from the insights provided by the cults and that this must be transcended, he placed himself in a double-bind that could only unfold in a reactionary stance towards the world.

There is a need to counterbalance such a critique with the positive aspects of what has been achieved in McLuhan's vision. By focusing on technique, he was led to contemplate such images as the voice, the book, the nature of silence, social rhythms and the rhythm of invention, and the symbolic influence of new environments, to mention only a few of the issues that surface concerning culture and technology . While with one voice he sounds reactionary and a critic of the world of sense, with another voice he seems to speak with premonitions of the work of Baudrillard, Derrida, and Deleuze, of the new understandings of psychoanalysis, and the new ecological vision of human communications. In the latter area, he still remains a poet and "theologue" (if that term is appropriate in the current secular world) who can illuminate through his challenge to the minds and senses of his readers. In that process, the richness of the hermetic tradition, joining the richness of Catholicism and the arts, provided an important set of early insights into communication, culture, and technology with which we still must come to terms. This may come about through the more recent and more sophisticated work of Derrida and Deleuze, but the tribute to McLuhan's genius is, that impeded by the contemporary paranoia of society and ensnared in a paranoid belief in the dominance of secret cults, he could use all of these traditions in as rich and productive and unforgettable way as he did.

7 McLuhan as Prepostmodernist and Forerunner of French Theory

In 1966 I was invited by McGill University in Montreal to become chair of their English Department and to launch Canada's first doctoral program in communications. My wife and I met Marshall and Corinne again at a reception in his honour during one of his visits to Expo 67 (the 1967 International Exposition in Montreal – "Man and His World" – celebrating Canada's hundredth anniversary). Montreal, with its Québecois spirit, had a special affinity for Marshall's work and for his playful and charming style and this World's Fair, with its many multi-media and other kino-environmental pavilions, seemed to bespeak the beginnings of a McLuhanesque era. That summer at Expo I was directing a research project together with an architect, Werner Aellen, and a team of researchers, photographers, film experts, and special effects engineers to develop a documental archive of all the multi-media and environmental exhibitions at the fair for the National Film Board of Canada, four other government departments, and the National Archives of Canada.

Marshall was warm and friendly, although he did not seem particularly well – only much later did I learn he was already suffering from the massive brain tumor that he had surgically removed in a dramatic and lengthy operation later that year while he was teaching at Fordham University in New York City. On that warm summer evening on a rooftop patio in Moishe Shafdie's "Habitat" overlooking the fair, Montreal's harbour, and the backdrop of the city, we spoke about Toronto, St Michael's College, his success, my project on the Exposition, and the graduate program in communications that I was to launch at McGill. In that summer of 1967, particularly Montreal, Canada, and the United States, in fact the world, seemed to be on the verge of the great new adventure about which McLuhan was writing. Marshall was about to assume the Schweitzer chair at Fordham, accompanied for the first time in over a decade by Ted Carpenter as well as his artist-designer collaborator Harley Parker. Within a year the Expo spirit of optimism and the unqualified enthusiasm for McLuhan, a pessimist, or as he preferred an apocalyptic who was neither a pessimist nor an optimist (although celebrated by artists, activists and youths as an optimist) were to begin a steady decline from which not until two decades later would McLuhan, paradoxical apocalyptic prophet of techno-optimism, emerge once again.

Three cultural objects associated with commercial expositions such as Expo 67 and with France, the United States, and Canada respectively haunt the encounter between McLuhanism and the rise of French theory in North America: the Eiffel Tower (built for the Paris Exposition of 1889), the Trilon and Perisphere (created for the New York World's Fair, which opened just before World War II), and the postmodern theme pavilions and the Fuller Dome of Expo 67 in Montreal. As the Tower has fascinated everyone from René Duchamp and James Joyce to Roland Barthes, and the Trilon and Perisphere domesticized European modernism for the U.S., so Expo 67 was the utopian mediazation of the postmodern moment. Why begin by juxtaposing these objects of excess? Partly because of McLuhan's fascination with architecture and with popular culture; the heavy influence on his writings of architectural historians Louis Mumford and Sigfried Giedion; his impact as the prophet of the new emerging technoculture; and his interests in art, architecture, and popular culture. Expo 67 became McLuhan's Fair, a fact openly acknowledged by the extent to which the theme pavilions of "Man and His World," whose design blended Canadian history and culture, were based on McLuhan's writings, which were liberally quoted on plaques throughout the pavilions. McLuhan's Fair marked a special moment in time: a year before Paris '68, on the threshold of the popular movements in Québec, and at the moment when French theory was coming into its own in North America.

A little chronology: McLuhan wrote *The Gutenberg Galaxy* in 1962 and *Understanding Media* in 1964, taking off as international media guru by 1965; Johns Hopkins held its conference on the structuralist controversy in the U.S. during 1966; the same year Paul de Man met Derrida.[1] It is striking and significant that the French translation of *The Gutenberg Galaxy* was launched less than a year later at Expo 67 – a translation which was to mark the opening of the major debates on "macluhanisme" in France. In 1967 McLuhan had virtually no knowledge of contemporary French theory. In 1959, in a previously mentioned conversation I had participated in between him and two structural linguists at the University of Toronto, he had flatly and summarily rejected structuralism and Ferdinand de Saussure as relevant to his project. He met Roland Barthes in France in 1972, but it was not until 1974 that he finally read Saussure.

Before continuing to explore further McLuhan's role in relation to French theory in North America, it is important to note how, as a Canadian professor of English literature who founded the first graduate communication seminar at the University of Toronto, he related to the officially recognized discipline of communication studies in the United States in the 1950s and 1960s. From 1953, when his Ford-sponsored communication seminar started until virtually the end of his career in the late 1970s, McLuhan's relationship with the major debates on communication in the U.S. was quite complex. From the outset, when under the urging of the anthropologist E.S. Carpenter and with support of the university's vice-president, Claude Bissell, he established those Ford-sponsored seminars in culture and communication at the University of Toronto and began the seminal interdisciplinary journal *Explorations*, he was aware of the major scholars who had worked in the newly emerging discipline of communication in the U.S. in the 1940s and 1950s. However, he professed not to regard the work of the trail blazers as very significant in shaping the discipline. His major reservations, which caused his relative indifference to their work, were related to the then-dominant statistical, empiricist, and behaviourist emphases in mainline communication studies. In contradistinction, McLuhan's approach was historical and interpretative (i.e., hermeneutic, although he would not normally have used the term at that time). While after 1950 he had also been affected by the new cybernetic theories of communication being developed in the States and England (Norbert Wiener, Gregory Bateson, and the figures involved in the Macy conferences), he also criticized them for being logico- mathematic rather than rhetorico-grammatical.

There was little contact between McLuhan and main stream communication studies until late in his life and his writings had relatively little impact on the academic study of communication in the U.S. until after he was embraced by French theorists in the late 1960s and early 1970s, although from 1964, with the publication of *Understanding Media*, he began to have a wide impact in areas inside and outside the academy. His impact partly paved the way for French theory's emergence shortly afterwards as a major factor within American academia. Other differences between U.S. approaches to communication and those in Canada were a result of the then-dominant affiliations of Canadian universities with England or France. Early in the 1950s McLuhan showed an interest in the work of Raymond Williams (with whom he shared a Cambridge undergraduate education as well as a Cambridge doctorate). Even more than McLuhan, Williams had a considerable impact on the early development of communication studies in Canada in the 1960s. At the same time, francophone universities in Quebec and Ontario were being affected by the early beginnings of communication theory in France as represented in the work of Roland Barthes and the journal *Communications*.

Since McLuhan was consciously suppressed by large segments of academia, it is not overtly recognized that his writings first raised the issues that concerned postmodernism and poststructuralism for a majority of North American scholars, particularly in communication, sociological theory, film and media studies, and cultural studies. Emerging during the final stages of the prominence of the "New Criticism," McLuhan, one of its last major exponents, was well situated to mark those moments that epiphanized the rise of poststructuralism and postmodern theory. His significance at the culmination of the "New Criticism" should remind us why deconstructive criticism and French theory first arose at institutions where the "New Criticism" had been entrenched, such as Yale, particularly among scholars who, as students, had encountered figures such as W.K. Wimsatt, Cleanth Brooks, and Robert Penn Warren. Through the immense popularity of McLuhan's books and his comments as a successful media personality pontificating about media and everyday culture, he contributed to establishing the groundwork in the late 1960s and 1970s in North America that in the later stages of the introduction of French theory partially created the climate in which enthusiasm for Gilles Deleuze, Felix Guattari, Paul Virilio, and Jean Baudrillard would exponentially increase.

It was not his initial affinities with Richards, Leavis, and the Southern critics of the *Sewanee Review* that enabled him to occupy this role but instead what he identified in his correspondence – already noted as the key to his work – that to have a serious interest in his work it was essential to know all the works of James Joyce and the French symbolists.[2] Another letter suggests why he believed his work might be regarded as "structuralist" (actually poststructuralist): "The reason that I am admired in Paris and some of the Latin countries is that my approach is rightly regarded as 'structuralist.' I have acquired the approach through Joyce and Eliot and the Symbolists, and used it in *The Mechanical Bride*. Nobody except myself in the media field has ventured to use the structuralist or 'existentialist' approach."[3] For interested, informed audiences within and without the university – frequently without their full realization of what was happening, leaving aside momentarily his problematic equation of the structuralist with the existentialist or the phenomenological – he popularized insights, strategies, and styles of the *symbolistes*, the Anglo-American high modernists, Wyndham Lewis, and Joyce, particularly *Finnegans Wake*, some of whom had considerable impact on Deleuze, Derrida, and others.

North America in the 1950s and 1960s, with its rising postwar consciousness of media – the pervasiveness of advertising, the power of TV, the maturing of film, and the recording industry, which made Elvis Presley a mythical media demi-god – is the context in which McLuhan, first intellectually and academically in 1962 with the *Galaxy*, then mass-mediafied and popularized in 1964 with *Understanding Media* and continuing into the 1970s, built his vision. It was a vision, partly demonic and partly utopian, of the future impact of the "electric" revolution, beginning after the Second World War, derived from an unholy modernist medley of symbolists, Joyce, Lewis, and European modernism in architecture and art. Part of McLuhan's shock tactics was the sudden dissemination of strategies and concepts derived from literature and art through his practice and his explications: Joycean ambivalence rather than symbolist ambiguity; proto-semiotic signs rather than symbols; a use of analogy where difference rather than similarity is dominant; a transformation of the empiric and pragmatic *explication du texte* of the new critics into an intuitively satiric, semioanalytic (proto-semioclastic) reading of cultural phenomena; the grammar and rhetoric of the trivium, freed from logic by a poetic dialectic, becoming instruments of cultural analysis; and Edmund Burke's sublime of the natural landscape applied to the techno-instrumental sublime of the interior landscape of modernism.[4]

There had been strong intimations in the 1950s in articles in *Explorations* and from the 1960s in his books that his work would come to be regarded as paleo-Barthesian, paleo-Derridean, paleo-Lyotardian, and paleo-Baudrillardian . The 1960s were a moment when the "New Criticism," subsequent to what Northrop Frye claimed as his "scientific" revision of literary criticism, underwent a still further, more profound revision by McLuhan – a reversal which he later capsulated in the title of a book, *From Cliché to Archetype*, but which in a more profound way was akin to asserting the materialist and anarchistic nature of the poetic, somewhat in anticipation of Baudrillard's analysis of Saussure's anagrams and of Freud's *Witz*. If Frye insisted on the "New Criticism" becoming a "science of poetry," McLuhan insisted on the "New Criticism's" empiricism and the poetic itself becoming instruments of unmasking. Concurrently, deconstruction was being imported from France, first to John Hopkins, and then more dramatically to Yale, the home base of what was by then the ancient "new criticism" of Brooks, John Crowe Ransom, and Warren.

As Baudrillard, agreeing with McLuhan's own statements, has always insisted, McLuhan was not a theorist; his approach was empiric. As a satiric poet *manqué*, McLuhan wished simultaneously to conceal his poetry behind an alleged instrumental purpose of assisting the public "to observe consciously the drama which is intended to operate upon it unconsciously," while generating the "light" to offset the "heat" of manipulating, controlling, and exploiting minds through "the prolonged mental rutting" of media, ads, and entertainment.[5] Deliberately employing techniques of crypsis to conceal that purpose behind an unfathomable ambivalence, McLuhan's writings and interviews, like a ritual jester or a participant in the medieval carnival, features pointed jokes, teasing deceptions, and devastating *Witz*. Within this empiric, satiric poetry *manqué*, designed for a social scientific era, the topoi generating the problems and paradoxes of French theories characteristic of postmodernism, poststructuralism, and beyond first began circulating through North America.

The wave of *m(a)cluhanisme* that hit Paris after 1967, just when Joyce was being promoted by *Tel Quel*, Phillipe Sollers, and Julia Kristeva as a major object for cultural commentary, attests to the French theoretical interest in McLuhan, with his affinity for Joyce. In North America, however, McLuhan haunted cultural debates from the 1970s to the 1990s as a primarily unspoken presence although it was his work that had provided the language used in media, in policymaking, among researchers in human interface technology, and especially in the discussions and writings of the social sciences and social theory in the academy. The debate in France in the early 1970s as to who deserved to be denominated the French McLuhan, reveals the significance of McLuhan's ghost. Barthes and Baudrillard were the leading contenders.

There are striking similarities in McLuhan's and Barthes's interests and in the evolution of their work. Both were scholars carrying out their respective work on the high classical moment of English and French drama respectively. Both exhibited an early concern with the history of classical rhetoric and allied disciplines – McLuhan's in his unpublished but widely cited Cambridge doctoral thesis on the Harvey-Nashe controversy and Barthes's in his seminars on classical rhetoric which were published in *Communications* under the title *L'Ancien Rhétorique: une aide mémoire*. Both men began their important publishing with their first major books about everyday culture – McLuhan's *The Mechanical*

Bride and Barthes's *Mythologies* – which show striking similarities in their consideration of objects and events of popular culture: ads, products, spectacles, newspapers, magazines, fashions, photography, visual images, mass myth, even the new orality. Both wrote reflexive, ironic self-examinations of their projects and their activities as myth later in their careers – McLuhan in *Culture Is Our Business* and Barthes in *Barthes par Barthes*. Both were literary critics and intrigued by the new interest in communications. Both were essayists and admirers of the tradition of Montaigne and Pascal; both were literary critics and prose poets. Barthes was a structuralist with a left wing political orientation; McLuhan was a Catholic with a right wing political orientation. While Barthes was initially attracted to Saussurean structuralism, McLuhan was initially fascinated by C.K. Ogden's and I.A. Richard's semantic theories.[6] While McLuhan rejected the semiology characteristic of the early Barthes, he shared an interest in the "sign" that was to become the central concern of the later hermeneutic, poststructuralist Barthes. And while he overtly rejected Barthes's social critique, McLuhan's analyses were semioclastic.

Derrida had far less claim than Barthes to be the "French McLuhan" and apparently wanted none, as indicated in his single reference to McLuhan in a paper delivered at a conference in Montreal: "We are not witnessing an end of writing which, to follow McLuhan's ideological representation, would restore a transparency or immediacy of social relations; but indeed a more and more powerful historical unfolding of a general writing of which the system of speech, consciousness, meaning, presence, truth, etc., would only be an effect, to be analyzed as such. It is this questioned effect that I have elsewhere called logocentrism" (Derrida, 1972, 329). Yet as John Fekete has pointed out, "Derrida takes up again and again, without reference to McLuhan, the same themes McLuhan develops throughout the 1960s [and, I would add, throughout the 1950s]: logocentrism, phonocentrism, the eye, the ear, technic as [exemplified by]: the impact of the phonetic alphabet, abstraction, writing, linearity as the repression of pluri-dimensional thought, simultaneity, synaesthesia, etc." (Fekete 1982, 50–67). Although not mentioned, it is significant that Derrida and McLuhan, the philosopher-theorist and the publicist poet-*manqué*, shared a fascination with Joyce, for Joyce explored much earlier and more extensively the very same themes that Fekete says Derrida shared with McLuhan.

There is one aspect of Derrida's writing that apparently echoes a very specific genre, mode, or "tone" of writing which McLuhan had developed in the 1960s from Joyce's transformation of the work of practitioners of learned satire – from Lucian, Seneca, Petronius, and

Apuleius to Aretino, Rabelais, Swift, Sterne, Pope, and Carlyle.[7] It is this "tone" or genre with which Derrida associates *La Carte Postale* and which, following an *envoi* of 13 August, he also relates to Joyce's *Wake* with its "Babelian implications" and their apocalyptic affiliations. Only two *envois* later (on 18 August) Derrida says that his "anatomy" of the "post card" of Plato standing behind the seated Socrates identifies this "tone": "If you want to understand what an 'anatomy' of the post card might be, think of the *Anatomy of Melancholy* (this is a genre that is not unrelated to Menippean satire: Frye recalls the influence of the Last Supper and of the Symposium on this genre, interminable banquets, encylopedic farrago, the satiric critique of the *philosophus gloriosus*, etc.)Be Stoic, it will be our expyrosus: the end of the world by fire" (Derrida 1980, 240–5).

In 1975 McLuhan had also told his readers that his writings and his presentations were Mennipean satires (although rather lesser ones compared to Joyce). In his practice of this poetic satiric technique he predisposed audiences to a tolerance for the "anatomy" as well as other modes of Menippean discourse. It should also be noted that Joyce's *Wake* is affiliated with *La Carte Postale* through Shaun (a twin son of Anna Livia) who, as post, is delivering a note which, Shem, the other twin, (a perversely diabolic poet) had written for ALP, his mother. Derrida obviously relates his own use of the "post" to Joyce's, just as McLuhan does, when *The Post Card* plays on the post-electric technological role of the postal service, such as telegrams, in order to situate electric media as a central aspect of his exploration of technology. Thus McLuhan's project, influenced by Joyce, partly contributed to preconditioning and predisposing the reception of Derrida's complex anatomical play with post, telecommunications, and digital technologies. McLuhan, in associating Joyce's post with communication and telecommunications, traces the affiliation of the post with human speech that was recognized in the sixteenth century by Julius Scaliger, who in the opening lines of his *Ars Poetica* (1564) declares: "Our speech is, as it were, the postman of the mind, through the services of whom civil gatherings are announced, the arts are cultivated, and the claims of wisdom interceded with men for man" (McLuhan 1953, 68). Joyce appears to have known or rediscovered Scaliger's analogy, expanding it to writing and postelectric communication, a rediscovery that jointly inspires some of McLuhan's and Derrida's thought, although it should be noted that while McLuhan gives it an oral stress, Derrida associates it with his grammatological interpretation of "writing."

While not exactly candidates for being "the French McLuhan," Gilles Deleuze and Félix Guattari spoke more positively than Derrida of McLuhan and shared a variety of perspectives with him or, through Joyce, with his project. In *Anti-Oedipus*, they note McLuhan's significance in showing "what a language of decoded flows is, as opposed to a signifier that strangles and overcodes the flows" (Deleuze and Guattari 1977, 240-1). In noting McLuhan's intuitions about a language – whether phonic, graphic, gestural or audio-visual – in which no flow is privileged, they specifically recognize the significance of McLuhan's describing the electric light as "pure information," a medium without a message, for they note that "the electric flow can be considered a realization of such a flow" – indeterminate and amorphous, though a continuum. It should not be surprising then that in discussing their concept of nomadology in *A Thousand Plateaus* Deleuze and Guattari associate that process with McLuhan's description of a new neoprimitivism. They juxtapose McLuhan's notion of a global village inhabited by a new tribal society with their notion of "worldwide ecumenical machines" producing a global society of "war machines."

It is not exclusively their citing McLuhan directly that might make an aspect of their work that of "a French McLuhan" but the central body of knowledge derived from *symbolisme*, modernism, and particularly the work of James Joyce that they as French theorists share with McLuhan, who had encountered it a decade or more earlier than they. For example, Deleuze's discussion in *The Logic of Sense* has McLuhanesque aspects, for McLuhan spoke frequently of the significance of Lewis Carroll, whom he saw as a precursor of Joyce, in the critique of logic and had, since his early research into the grammatico-rhetorical traditions of exegesis and the trivium, intuited the connection of Carroll and Joyce with Stoic logicians. The entire Joycean spectrum, which meant a great deal to Derrida and which Deleuze recognized in his earlier works, *Proust and Signs* (originally published in 1964), *Différence and Repetition* (originally published in 1968) and *The Logic of Sense* (originally published in 1970), bore on motifs of fragmentation, transverse communication, dissemination, polysemy, polyvocity, writing, rhizomic structure, etc. It was these motifs that McLuhan would emblazon and broadcast throughout North America in the late 1950s, particularly after 1965. And as exasperating and imprecise as that combined poetic and promotional PR exercise may have been, it implanted in the artistic community and the avant-garde and radical elements of the academic community a predilection for the discourse of French theory.

Before probing more deeply the role of Joyce, who was neither French nor North American – although he lived a substantial portion of his life in France and opens the *Wake* by punningly referring in the fifth line to Tristan and Isolde's "North Armorica" – verbal play that

links France, North America, and Ireland – I should briefly note that
the third and perhaps prime candidate to be the French McLuhan was
Jean Baudrillard, the only figure who repeatedly cited McLuhan's work
in his own. And ultimately Baudrillard's nomination, as Gary Genosko
attests, proves to be the most revealing for understanding the role
McLuhan played in North America, since it owes as much to the striking differences between them as to the numerous similarities (Genosko
1999). The sharp difference between Baudrillard's vision of contemporaneity in the *Transparency of Evil* and McLuhan's humanistic, somewhat quietistic but, more specifically, Jansenistic Catholicism is particularly revealing, for while the schizoid McLuhan shared a fascination
and substantial involvement with the post-Nietzschean world, he was
a fully committed, pietistic believer in a very traditional Catholicism.
Any explanation of McLuhan's role in preconditioning North America
to French theory must take into account his neo-Catholic revisionist
attempt to sanitize radical high modernist theory.

Joyce is at the crux of the story, since his writings, as a valuable
resource to be exploited, fascinated the North American scholarly
industry, while his avant-garde stance fascinated Parisian and Swiss
intellectuals, so an interest in Joyce provides a link between many
French theoretical interests and McLuhan's empirical, pseudo-poetic
unmasking of the culture industry. Against McLuhan's schizo-
Jansenism, Joyce's own poetic, closer to Georges Bataille, is clearly a
true poetic of excess dedicated, if I may borrow from Baudrillard, to
the extermination of the name of God. For in the *Wake* Joyce's deity
"is vrayedevraye Blankdeblank, god of all machineries and tomestone
of Barnstaple" (253.33–6) and his poet is "a skipgod, expulled for
looking at churches from behind" (488.22–3). Similar to Baudrillard's
analysis of Saussure's anagram and of anathema, the *Wake* grounds the
word and, beyond the word, the media, within the interactive virtuality of his dream of the post-electric world. Finnegans' fatal fall initiates
a symbolic exchange and death within a design in which Joyce plays
games with political economy, contemporary science and math, and
the ritualistic use of analysis.

In 1946, the fideistic McLuhan, in a letter to a friend, noted the darkness of Joyce's poetic in *Ulysses* and the *Wake* as "consituting an intellectual 'Black Mass'". On the other hand, the schizoid McLuhan disseminated a poetry of excess, for the presumed purpose (unless we take
him to be one of the greatest cynics of this century) of undoing and
exposing through empiric observation the workings of Joyce's rebellion
– that carnivalesque resurrection, which is in reality a revolution, an
insurrection, a phallic erection, and the resurrection of Nietzsche's
superman. McLuhan correctly sensed the Nietzschean depth of Joyce's

poetic, for what Nietzsche describes as "poetic violence which replaces the order of all the atoms of the phrase"[8] becomes in Joyce's *Wake*, "the abnihilisation of the etym" (353.22). This is why McLuhan's most extensive use of Joyce's *Wake* occurs in *War and Peace in the Global Village* (1968) – the title ironically echoing that of a later essay by Derrida in which he analyses two *Wakean* words, "he war" (Derrida 1984, 145–59). But intuiting, then reproducing and exposing those Nietzschean depths as an empiric observer to defend the Catholic *logos* against the Joycean "letter" as "litter," while preparing a ground for radical French theory in North America, is oddly enough a paradoxical move worthy of the witty apologetics of McLuhan's early role model, the Edwardian Catholic, G.K. Chesterton. To perform these empiric, poetic acrobatics, McLuhan produced penetrating aphoristic insights for late radical modernity and poststructuralism, such as "The Medium is the message, the massage (tactility), and the mass age (the abyss of the crowd)," events whose importance Baudrillard identifies in unveiling the implications of "symbolic exchange" – the simulacra, ecstasy, transparency.

McLuhan, who believed there is too much communication in the modern world (perhaps similar to Joyce's treatment of Silence), communicated about communication primarily to detour, delay, conceal, and eradicate it. From the outset McLuhan had intuited the cosmos to be the Joycean "chaosmos" (a term Deleuze and Guattari apparently borrowed from the *Wake*) – a "chaosmos" of a *deus absconditus*, a hidden god. In the 1940s, he had used Edgar Allen Poe's "The Maelstrom" to explain symbolically the nature of the whodunit as the tension between a world moving toward chaos and a sailor who, while paralyzed with horror, discovers the "power of detached observation," thus taking a "scientific"' interest in the action of the storm. In 1951 in the *Mechanical Bride*, whose working title had been "The Guide to Chaos," McLuhan used the same image to explain his new empiric method (Wilmott 1996, 51, 159). In 1970, in *From Cliché to Archetype*, schizo-McLuhan – committed to both his Roman Catholic faith and to Joyce's Chaosmos – still declares that chaos is the devil's world – and that such chaos is produced by the very type of cyclical reversal that Baudrillard considers characteristic of the simulacra, resulting in the ecstasy of communication, but also characteristic of Joyce's Viconianism.

While Joyce's chaosmos is the comic, carnivalesque domain of an earth goddess whose "redtangles are all abscissan for limitsing this tendency ... to expense her selfs as sphere as possible, paradismic perimutter ... [while] the infinisissimalls of her facets [are] becoming manier and manier as ... her umdescribables ... shrinks from schurtiness " (FW298.25–30), McLuhan's naturalistic chaosmos has affinities with his acoustic space, the return to the oral, tribalized society. Developing and adopting this notion from Edmund Carpenter's (1959 and 1973) analysis of pre-literate Inuit culture to the postelectric world, McLuhan explained that "Acoustic space has no center. It consists of boundless random resonations" (McLuhan 1989, 133). His description of this approximates the twelfth-century Augustinian theological poet Alain of Lille's description of God, in which "God is an intelligible sphere, whose center is everywhere, and whose circumference is nowhere" (Borges 1968, 6-9). This situates McLuhan's hidden or absent god as a deity beyond nature, like that of Blaise Pascal's *deus absconditus*, for both hold that nature, not God, is an intelligible sphere. For Pascal, as Jorges Luis Borges notes, absolute space becomes the abyss, for he: "hated the universe and yearned to adore God. But God was less real to him than the hated universe. He was sorry the firmament could not speak; he compared our lives to those of shipwrecked men on a desert island. He felt the incessant weight of the physical world; he felt confused, afraid and alone; and he expressed his feelings like this: "It [Nature] is an infinite sphere, the center of which is everywhere, the circumference nowhere" (Borges 1968, 6–9). Borges also notes that, according to the manuscript version, Pascal first wrote frightful (*effroyable*) rather than infinite, reminding us of McLuhan, who also fears the postliterate death of the book and insists on the *logos* as a primal writing – for his God is absent from the media world. Consequently his vision disseminated a sense of panic to North American intellectual discourse as it assimilated French theorists – first Derrida, who had rejected McLuhan, and ultimately, Deleuze, Guattari, and particularly Baudrillad, who was the most appreciative of McLuhan's ambivalent awareness of the transparency of evil and the awareness of fatal strategies and cool memories. Even though personally committed to the Vatican and its defence through a pseudo-Thomism – yet actually a schizo-fideism – McLuhan chose to be of what Blake, describing Milton's Satan as Jehovah, called the devil's party; simultaneously becoming the prophet for the global, transnational electronic entrepreneurs, while intensifying and accelerating the hysteric broad reception of the insights of French theory.

If Virilio and Baudrillard, and to a lesser extent Deleuze and Guattari, appear to have a greater affinity with McLuhan than Barthes, Derrida, and Jean-François Lyotard, McLuhanism has played a role in their rise to prominence in North America because the schizoid McLuhan's demonic side, let loose in his empiric poetry, provides familiarity with the issues that Baudrillard and Virilio – not being encumbered by McLuhan's hidden fideist agenda – reveal as the transformation of reality into virtuality. Through his immersion in the symbolists, particularly Joyce, which released his demonic side, McLuhan's work has for over four decades disseminated intimations of retribalization, becoming-object, rhizomic nomadism, seduction, simulacra, ecstasy, exponentially accelerating speed, the aesthetics of disappearance, and the new "chaosmology" of the chaosmos, familiarizing an increasingly less naive North America with the Continental visions of excess but always with the intent of inverting the reversal implied in that project by turning Joyce and French theory upside down and inside out. For that reason, remembering how in the eighteenth century the middlebrow popularism of Joseph Addison had essentially tried to stem the insurgence of the French thought of Michel Montaigne, François Fenélon and Pascal, embraced by Pope and Swift, into England, Pope's aphoristic closing to his satire on Addison seems more apt than ever when applied to the "pseudo-socio-anarchist," man for all seasons, Marshall McLuhan and his project:

Who would not laugh, if such a man there be
Who would not weep, if *McLuhan* were he!

8 McLuhan as Trickster:
The Poetry of Cliché

In 1950 new vistas of interpretation and understanding were opened up by my introduction to what McLuhan understood as his pedagogic strategies, for example, his method of juxtaposing the percepts and affects of contemporary art with everyday cultural forms. Through such examples as his comparison of the front page and page layout of a major daily newspaper with Picasso's cubist landscapes he could demonstrate how art could both illuminate and critique the everyday modes of mass communication. The poets and contemporary literary theorists I had studied at Yale with Cleanth Brooks and W.K. Wimsatt took on a deeper and wider significance as the relevance of Ezra Pound's or Sergei Eisenstein's ideographic method of illuminating any cultural artefact revealed the social unconscious latent in comic strips, films, popular romances, and, most particularly, advertising. To work with McLuhan then was to live in a continuity of poetry, novel, painting, sculpture, classical music, advertising, science fiction, comics, radio, jazz, and other such forms a decade or more before the birth of "cultural studies."

The McLuhan I met at that time had only a few years earlier had had a close relationship with Wyndham Lewis, the British vorticist painter, novelist, satirist and critic, whose visit to North America he had strongly encouraged. McLuhan, reinforcing the insights that his own studies of T.S. Eliot, Pound, James Joyce, and other modernist writers and poets, learned from Lewis the relevance of seeing all of what we now call cultural production as a continuum in which the more intense forms of cultural production could illuminate and critique other forms of everyday life as well as illuminating and critiquing one another, for this, of course, is what Lewis had done in *Time and Western Man* and *The Art of Being Ruled*. In the preceding chapters we have seen how McLuhan early understood his role to be that of an artist who, as Deleuze and Guattari have explained, thinks through "affects and percepts" – in contradistinction to the philosopher who thinks through concepts (Deleuze and Guattari 1994, 66, 163-99). Throughout his writings, lectures, and conversations McLuhan repeats the refrain that he does not deal with concepts but with percepts, by which he creates probes to explore and illuminate.

He makes clear the importance of the arts, including literature, to his project in a critique of Harold Innis in his correspondence late in 1971. Earlier in the same year he had told Claude Bissell that Innis's work was inhibited by the fact that he did not notice "our philosophy systematically excludes *techné* from its meditations."[1] In his only extant letter to Innis, written twenty years earlier McLuhan delivers an extended lecture on the arts in which he explains that what he is trying to do is to link "a variety of specialized fields by what might be called a method of aesthetic analysis of their common features."[2] For McLuhan the writings of James Joyce's friend, Sigfried Giedion exemplify this method of aesthetic analysis. Giedion's books, *Space, Time and Architecture* and *Mechanization Takes Command* and later *The Eternal Present*, were central to McLuhan's project, since they present a specific parallel use of the arts, particularly architecture, as an aesthetic method, not only in examining the history of art and architecture since 1850 and the remote beginnings of art and architecture in Egypt and the Near East but also in explaining the anonymous history of everyday objects and the rise of electro-mechanization.

In this same long letter to Innis, McLuhan criticizes a recent article by Karl Deutsch, a political scientist who was applying cybernetic concepts to his discipline, and points out that a prime fallacy in Norbert Wiener's work as well as in Deutsch's is "a failure to understand the techniques and functions of the traditional arts as the essential type of all human communication."[3] He further charges that cybernetics is dialectical since it is derived from technology. Nearly thirty years later he identifies the Shannon-Weaver theory, and therefore Wiener's theories as well as all other techno-scientific theories of communication, as "left-hemisphere" rationalism, against which he poses the cubist's understanding of communication that arises from the grammar of "right-hemisphere" intuitionalism that frees one from a fixed point of view (McLuhan and McLuhan 1988, 76, 86–90). While McLuhan's becoming aware of new discoveries concerning the bicameral brain allowed him to further elaborate this insight, he still maintained that the contemporary artist as "antennae of the race" is a discoverer of multiplexity of points of view and critic of lineality.

In this same letter to Innis he suggests that it is the artist-critic Wyndham Lewis who, having written *The Art of Being Ruled*, is the best diagnostician of those who like Deutsch are "technicians of power uninterested in social effect." Once again nearly thirty years later McLuhan features Lewis in unveiling his "laws of media" as a "poetics of media" by establishing that:

The artist is the person who invents the means to bridge between biological inheritance and the environments created by technological innovation.
(McLuhan and McLuhan 1988, 98)

The dominance of literature and the arts for McLuhan is further underlined by the fact that two of his four original collaborators in the Ford sponsored Culture and Communication seminars had a substantial interest in the arts, including architecture (I.e., the anthropologist, Edmund Carpenter, who was deeply interested in Inuit, Pacific Coast, and other aboriginal art forms, and the town planner and architect Jacqueline Tyrhwitt, a student and colleague of Giedion's).[4]

In 1960 McLuhan and Carpenter published an anthology of articles from *Explorations*, slightly over half of which was devoted to the arts and literature, including articles by Fernand Léger, Robert Graves, Sigfried Giedion, Northrop Frye, and a BBC interview with Carola Giedion-Welcker and Paul Léon's wife on Joyce's death in Zurich and its repercussions in Nazi-occupied Paris (Carpenter and McLuhan 1960). This concern to keep the arts central to his project continued into the 1960s, in that his first major book, *The Gutenberg Galaxy*, opens with *King Lear* and concludes with Pope's *The Dunciad*, a prime exemplum of the learned or Menippean satire that McLuhan claims he tried to emulate. The opening of *Galaxy* is preceded by a prologue that discusses Albert Lord and Milman Parry's theories of oral poetry and its conclusion is followed by an epilogue in which William Blake, Edgar Allan Poe, John Ruskin, Joseph Addison and James Joyce are central figures.

The *Galaxy* is a history of communication through a history of the interface of art, literature, and education in the arts of expression. Because this book further advances the centrality of the main McLuhanesque thrust of art and literature supported by the traditional learning of grammar and rhetoric, as essential to an understanding of communication and everyday culture, it received unqualified acclaim from Cambridge English professor Raymond Williams, the founder of "cultural studies," even though he subsequently turned against McLuhan's later work.[5] Following the success of *Understanding Media* in 1964 and his subsequent successful promotion as *the* media guru from 1965, McLuhan felt the need to balance his growing reputation as a media expert by emphasizing his interests in art and literature in *Through the Vanishing Point* (1968), followed by a work on literary theory as it relates to communication and culture in *From Cliché to Archetype* (1970).

Throughout his career McLuhan frequently collaborated on his various projects and writings with artists, writers, and critics, his collaborations with the anthropologist Ted Carpenter and later Barrington Nevitt, a consultant in international engineering, marketing, and management, being the prime exceptions. The "Verbi-Voco-Visual" issue of *Explorations*, which preceded any of his major books, exemplifies this interest in visual art and design as complementing the poetic and literary, since it pervades his substantial opening contribution of twenty-four short presentations that constitute about the first half of this issue of the journal, concluding with "item 24" entitled "No Upside Down in Eskimo Art." This is immediately followed by an article by Victor Papanek, who was then teaching at the Ontario College of Art. Papaneck later became an internationally recognized author on design and environment. This article, "A Bridge in Time," presents a detailed agenda of what were to be life-long points of reference in McLuhan's work to the visual arts and dance. Papanek's article provides a supplementary, expansive answer to a question originally posed by Giedion which McLuhan presented and answered rather briefly in the conclusion of his section of "Verbi-Voco-Visual": "What is it that separates us from other periods? What is it that ... is now reappearing in the imagination of contemporary artists?" In his title of his reply Papanek adopts the metaphor of "the bridge" (*die Brücke*) – a title borrowed from the early founding period of German Expressionism – and argues that "the most revolutionary subject affecting European designer-artists since the early part of the century was machine technology" (Papanek 1957, 1). The bridge of which he speaks is the necessary "highly oral, myth-generating mechanism, ...[a]... poetic bridge to ease understanding of technological constructs."

Papanek's survey, which I will discuss in some detail since it is so close to McLuhan's own interests in the arts, retraces Giedion's path and outlines the artistic aspect of the agenda of McLuhan's ongoing interest in technoculture, beginning with the fascination of the Futur-

ists with the machine's dynamism as declared in their Manifestos of
1909 and 1910, also one of the central concerns of Wyndham Lewis's
critique of contemporary arts in *Blast* and his other early vorticist writings.[6] Papanek then goes on to note the substantial interest of the other
modernist groups in the abstract design of the machine, beginning with
the cubists and constructivists. An early version of what becomes the
McLuhanesque concept of "acoustic space" is cited from Naum Gabo
in *The Second Constructivist Manifesto* (Berlin, 1924):

> "SPACE CANNOT BE SEEN BY THE EYE. IT IS ALL
> AROUND US LIKE A GLOBE STRETCHING INTO
> ETERNITY. SCULPTURE IS TO BE *HEARD* LIKE MUSIC."
>
> (Papanek 1957, 2)

Next the notion of a machine age demanding a non-Euclidean painting is illustrated from Apollinaire's *Les Peintres Cubistes* (1913). The
central emphasis is given to Dadaism, with its pre-cybernetic insight
into the cyborg and to surrealism with its panic at people being con-
sumed by machines. Specific reference is made to Eugene Jolas's *transition* (1927–38), which, incidentally was the major conduit for
introducing Joyce's *Finnegans Wake* through the publication of a
series of his early fragments as "Work in Progress" from 1927 to
1938. Parallels in architecture are noted from Le Corbusier's "Le
machine à habiter," from Frank Lloyd Wright, and from Buckminster
Fuller's *Geodesic Domes,* noting the dome's propinquity to "auditory
space."

To develop how the avant-garde, European artists avoided noun-
painting, Papanek quotes Picasso commenting on his Guernica: "THE
ONLY WAY TO SEE THE 'GUERNICA' IS TO FEEL ONESELF INTO ITS
CENTER!" Picasso:"Poemas y Declaraciones," Mexico 1945 (Papanek
1957, 5). He argues that by reacting on a "mutli-valent feeling level"
the avant-garde European artists avoided noun-painting by responding
"haptically." He cites Louis Danz, who said that in speaking of Pablo
Picasso this way, "one also speaks of others: Joan Miro, Marc Chagall,
Piet Mondrian, Constantin Brancusi, Georges Braque, Wassily Kandinsky and Paul Klee – all of whom were of great interest to the early
McLuhan. To Danz's list Papanek adds Laszlo Moholy-Nagy and his
experiments at what he calls onomatopoetic typography – an attempt
to abolish the linear book-tradition; attempts in other media that
include George Antheil's "Ballet Mécanique" (an artist whom Pound's
writings had brought to McLuhan's attention); and Oskar Schlemmer's
"Triadic Ballet" of which Moholy-Nagy writes, reminiscent of similar
passages about cinema in Sergei Eisenstein's writings:

"TURN THE DANCERS INTO PISTONS AND COG-
WHEELS, TO SUBORDINATE THE INDIVIDUAL
DANCER TO THE POETICS OF THE ALL-ENFOLDING
MACHINE, AND TO COMMUNICATE SIMULTANE-
OUSLY AND ON ALL LEVELS WITH THE WILD CACOPHONY
OF AUTO, SKYSCRAPER-CITY AND JAZZ."

Oskar Schlemmer and L. Moholy-Nagy,
"Die Buehne im Bauhaus" (Papanek 1957, 7)

As a way of leading into a conclusion in which he discusses non-Euclidean concepts and quantum physics, Papanek ends his survey with a brief mention of the radically idealistic *De Stijl* movement headed by Mondrian. One of the striking aspects of Papanek's article is that it recognizes the central role of contemporary mathematics and science in modernism and consequently its presence in McLuhan's project. This is central to Joyce's techno-poetics and that of many of the artistic avant-garde such as Marcel Duchamp, members of the Bauhaus, and LeCorbusier [Charles Edouard Jeanneret] to whom McLuhan refers.

From the beginnings of *Explorations* to the completion of his work with his posthumous publications, McLuhan espoused a poetic science as the primary and most powerful way to explore the world of people's artefacts and their technologies. But have his commentators and critics been reading his work as a new type of poetry created in the aftermath of the emergence of the media revolution of the 1940s and 1950s? Writing about his work in 1971 I called McLuhan a *"poète manqué"* (in an anglicised form, poet manqué) primarily because, while he was producing a "social scientific poetry" based on his media poetics, the conflicting poses he presented to the public in his quest for recognition deflected most people's attention away from regarding his work as essentially poetic, even though he always indicated that that is precisely what he was creating. Not only the affiliation of his work with the arts, poetry, and literature but his conception of himself as one of the "antennae of the race" becomes clear when one examines the poetic sources he exploited and played upon – sources that complement and supplement those insights and phrases he actually borrows from individuals (such as those which Carpenter and others have identified and which have been noted earlier).

Clear evidence that McLuhan sees himself in the role of a poet of the post- industrial, media world can be found in *Through The Vanishing Point*. That book is set up in a series of exhibits of counterposed poems and paintings with comments by McLuhan and Parker juxtaposed on alternate pages . The first page of the second of the forty-nine exhibits that form the main body of the book consists of Ezra Pound's *In a Station of the Metro* embedded in a series of three Joycean-based poetic aphorisms – presumably by McLuhan and not Parker, in view of the use of Joyce and Pound. Given the rules of the game maintained in all the other exhibits that constitute the central section of the book, "A Spatial Dialogue" (consisting of a poem juxtaposed with a page of aphorisms and followed on the next page by an art work juxtaposed with another page of aphorisms) then the entirety of page 36, the first page of Exhibit 2, and not just Pound's adaptation of a haiku, is the poem being presented:

Like the higher apes, the alphabetic cultures knew how to
let go.
allforabit = alphabet

Consider the reversal of the cultural gradient by the poetry
that goes *allforabyte*

"*Mythos*" is a Greek word for "word." All words originally revealed complex processes and were called "momentary deities" or epiphanies.

The apparition of these faces in the crowd;
Petals on a wet, black bough.

– Ezra Pound

"Allforabit" is a Joycean pun (FW, 19.2) and "*allforabyte*" is a playful McLuhanesque 'joycing' to dramatize the problem of the alphabet in the computer era where presumably the "byte" (which is, incidentally, composed of bits) creates a reversal of alphabet culture (but a reversal that is ambivalent in its direction). This "allforabyte" marks the epiphany of this myth, so that, like the Poundian haiku, it creates a one image poem of the alphabet ("allforabit") that projects a complex percept for "getting out" of the affects (emotion) of the post-industrial era, as Pound's haiku does of the industrial. This whole assemblage plays on a "word" becoming digitally a pattern, the beginning of a new language, as McLuhan's juxtaposed commentary from Pound on the facing page underlines. The "painting" (or rather icon) related to the poem is a Chinese character, an ideograph, and therefore presumably a non-phonetic verbal unit (a "word"). The remarks on the facing page link the ideograph back to the first exhibit where the "painting" is an Altamira cave-drawing, so that we move from the cave drawing – "a prayer" – to the ideograph – "a probe" – and later to the alphabet – "a package" to be reversed by the "eternal return" of the "allforabyte." This is clearly the complex language of poetry – not language as a theory but as an assemblage of aphoristic probes presenting percepts, which imply more than they actually say.

McLuhan's treatment of acoustic space is a good starting point to examine how he plays poetically with the words and phrases delineating his key percepts, for the terminology was first brought to his attention early in the 1950s by one of his colleagues and co-directors in the early Culture and Communication seminars, Carleton Williams. Williams's observations, initially based on empirical psychology concerning auditory space, obviously led McLuhan to re-examine a whole cluster of associations from his previous research: on the traditional arts, including the arts of the trivium – grammar, dialectic, and rhetoric – and on contemporary arts and poetics and their relationship with science and technology.[7] On one hand, as we have seen, the concept of acoustic space resonates with the occult and with philosophical associations with Pascal's sphere and their probable grounding in Pythagoreanism; on the other hand, the McLuhanesque "percept" of "sphericity" and its "affects" also has specific relations to the contemporary arts and sciences. A very direct statement about this "percept," nearly contemporaneous with Williams's discovery of it, can be found in a letter that McLuhan wrote in December 1954 to his mentor, Wyndham Lewis: "Acoustic space is spherical. It is without bounds or vanishing points. It is structured by pitch separation and kinesthesia. It is not a container. It is not hollowed out. It is the space in which men live before the invention of writing – that translation of the acoustic into the visual. With writing men began to trust their eyes and to structure space visually. Pre-literate man does not trust his eyes very much. The magic is in sound for him, with its powers to evoke the absent."[8]

These themes were later expanded on in an essay Williams wrote in *Explorations* on "Acoustic Space" (1954), and they were later republished in a slightly emended fashion in *Explorations in Communication* where the authorship is attributed to McLuhan and Carpenter. Still later the term resurfaces in *The Gutenberg Galaxy* in references to acoustical space, auditory space, and non-Euclidean space. Having occurred in McLuhan's writing over a period of nearly thirty years, these themes make their final appearances in a multitude of references in the posthumously published *The Global Village* as well as being the subject of a "more elaborate" tetrad in *The Laws of Media*, a book in which "tactile space" appears as a 'simpler' tetrad. These tetrads, it should be remembered, since they are grammatico-rhetorical and poetic, are themselves a variant on concrete poetry. Although it is complex and somewhat dense, it is important in understanding Mcluhan's poetry to set out the structure of this tetrad.

This more complex tetrad presents "acoustic space" as enhancing "the simultaneous, resonant and multilocational"; advancing the "multisensory", the "tribal," and the "Protean or transformational"; reversing into the "flat mosaic" and "tactility" and therefore dealing with "all the senses at once"; and finally retrieving another complex key set of McLuhan "percepts." These are the "resonant interval between figure and ground"; the restoration of "the mode of mimesis" (i.e., making, not matching, in McLuhanesque terminology); "goalless[ness]" of the Hippies; and finally a return to a primitive world, which in a borrowing from Joyce's *Wake* is described as "astoneaged" (FW 18.15) (as astonished and of the stone age). This last retrieval presumably occurs because when in the *Wake* Joyce presents two comic-strip style Neanderthals conversing – Mutt and Jute (cf. the *Mutt and Jeff* comic strip) – the "thonthorstrok" (i.e., thunderstruck + stroke + a worshiper of the Norse god of thunder, Thor) and "astonaged" Jute, in the *Wake*, like those tuned to "acoustic space" are analphabetic – "abcedminded" (FW 18.17). (Many, if not most, of these motifs are present in a less poetic but therefore less intense and suggestive mode in McLuhan's 1954 letter to Lewis.) For McLuhan "acoustic space" is the primitive originary world that T.S. Eliot had described as "the auditory imagination."[9]

Such a way of describing the "percept' of "acoustic space" and attaching it to "affects" presents a complex multi-level poem involving allusive inter-textuality such as the references to Joyce, Eliot, Ovidian metamorphosis, the "sixties," conflicts in the history of philosophy, Jacques Lusseyran's book on blindness, and the impact of rock music. It places opposing qualities in tension – e.g., the detached *civis*, which is "obsolesced" as opposed to the "tribal," which is enhanced. McLuhan's tetrads are assemblages (or concrete poems) that deliberate using the typographical arrangement of fragmented language as a means of undermining the lineality of language – an extension of the experimentation McLuhan had begun with his *Counterblast* in the mid-1950s and extended into his poetic *essais concrètes* of the late 1960s. The initial phrase "acoustic space," probed and played with through three decades, becomes itself an artefact (or "medium"), suggestively exploring the metamorphoses achieved through the transformations affected by electric technologies of production, reproduction, and dissemination on the pre-electric technologies of print and visual prints, writing, and visual art.

It would be possible to trace the transformations of the perception of acoustic (or auditory space) throughout McLuhan's works and to situate it in different parameters with tactile space, non-Euclidean space, and other related notions. Just as in the unfolding of any poetic vocabulary, each stage would add incremental depth and resonance (note the use of McLuhanesque terms) to the perceiver's understanding of the nature of "acoustic space." Other McLuhanesque "percepts" (and it is important not to confuse them with concepts) could be treated in the same manner, such as "interval of resonance," the "medium is message" and its variants, "figure-ground" and even "tetrad" (or "quaternion" or "tetratkys") itself, since McLuhan by his own avowal was trying to maximize the evocativeness of these terms, which actually designated perceptive and affective complexes. This activity, although perhaps not easily accepted as "scientific," still pursues McLuhan's goal of attempting to construct a "new science" for the postelectric world.

The importance to McLuhan that his project of constructing a new science ultimately be recognized as poetic should become undisputedly clear when looking at the publications immediately following the attention-getting *Understanding Media*, including the more publicity oriented *The Medium Is the Massage*. Two of the works that immediately followed these publications, though, were co-authored with a Canadian poet and a Canadian painter: *From Cliché to Archetype* (with the Canadian poet and English professor Wilfred Watson, who incidentally was the husband of one of McLuhan's doctoral students in the mid-1960s, the Canadian novelist and perceptive commentator on McLuhan and Lewis Shelia Watson) and *The Vanishing Point* (with the Canadian painter and designer Harley Parker, a long-time collaborator – from the mid-1950s until the 1970s). *From Cliché to Archetype* is deeply grounded in McLuhan's involvement with literary theory and criticism; *The Vanishing Point* in McLuhan's interest in the relationship between poetry and painting (i.e., the visual arts). Together they complement his previous work by placing it firmly within the artistic, literary, and rhetorical world that he had always insisted was the foundation of his entire project.

"Acoustic space" naturally plays a role in each of these books as well, which provide McLuhan with a poetic and artistic mode of supplementing their semantic aura. The literary oriented *From Cliché to Archetype* underlines the 'occult' overtones of acoustic space, while redeeming it as a 'mystical' concept. The process allows McLuhan to criticize quantum physics for its failure to understand the spherical physical properties of its "new paradigm of resonance" and thus to continue "to make efforts to visualize the non-visual." For McLuhan the corrective if somewhat ideologically and dogmatically stated, is the poetic of modernism: "Symbolism is the art of the missing link, as the word implies: _sym-ballein_, to throw together. It is the art of syncopation. It is the basis of electricity and quantum mechanics, as Lewis Carroll understood via Lobachevski, and non-Euclidean geometries. The chemical bond, as understood by Heisenberg and Linus Pauling, is RESONANCE. Echoland. The world of acoustic space whose center is everywhere and whose margin is nowhere, like the pun. Art and Nature alike begin to involve the entire public, whether via jazz or the mystery story" (Mcluhan and Watson 1970, 39). Here McLuhan's poetic effect is further enriched by intertextual allusions for, in the context of quanta, electricity, Lewis Carroll, and puns, "Echoland," in addition to alluding to ecology and the environment, is a clear allusion to dream as a mode of acoustic space in the Joycean dream of the "eternal return":

> Behove this
> sound of Irish sense. Really? Here English might be seen.
> Royally? One sovereign punned to petery pence. Regally? The
> silence speaks the scene. Fake!
> So This Is Dyoublong?
> Hush! Caution ! Echoland !
> How charmingly exquisite! It reminds you of the outwashed
> engravure that we used to be blurring on the blotchwall of his
> innkempt house
>
> (FW 12.36–13.8).

Complementing his literary study, *Cliché*, McLuhan's and Parker's *essai concrète* on painting and poetry (the classical and humanistic, rhetorico-poetic *ut pictura poesis*, i.e., the poem is a speaking picture; the painting a silent poem) expands the rhizomic network of association to include aphoristic comments on William Blake's "The Tiger" and the poet's engraving of that poem. For McLuhan Blake's poem is:

> Resonating acoustic space.
> A vast echo chamber for reader participation.
>
> (McLuhan and Parker 1968, 139)

Against the pussy-cat like reproduction of a tiger and the text of the original engraved page, the comment appears as "Visual sensory fragmentation scorned./ Iconic sensory unity used as exploratory thrust into new age" (McLuhan and Parker 1968, 141). McLuhan further revealingly quips that Blake today might have "preferred the comic book to the photograph," which leads back to McLuhan's having noted in *Understanding Media* with respect to comics that "The pictorial consumer age is dead. The iconic age is upon us" (McLuhan 1964, 167). Relating Blake to "acoustic space" and iconicity grounds his argument in his percepts of "tactility" and "the interplay of the senses," for he assigns Blake a pivotal historical position as the beginning of the reversal of the Cartesian-Newtonian visual bias.

Supplementing and complementing *Cliché* and *The Vanishing Point* – works overtly directed toward the arts – he published *War and Peace in the Global Village*, another *essai concrète* , as a sequel to *The Medium Is the Massage*. Throughout it he uses quotes from Joyce's *Finnegans Wake* as marginalia to comment on and interplay with the text.[10]

McLuhan's exploration of the centrality of war and peace within Joyce's comic epic, *Finnegans Wake*, situates his project directly within the context of Nietzsche's eternal return and the radical, post-Nietzschean aspect of modernist art and poetry, which could be oriented to the ideological right or left. This Nietzchian emphasis partly accounts for some of his apparent affinities with Walter Benjamin's treatment of the new technologies of artistic production, reproduction, and dissemination (Benjamin 1968).

War and Peace is of particular interest since, almost simultaneously with *Through the Vanishing Point* and *From Chiché to Archetype*, the two books more specifically oriented to poetry and the arts, it still builds on the bias towards the arts in *The Gutenberg Galaxy* and *Understanding Media*. In this work, in which Joyce is a primary figure from the first page until the last and which concludes with a discussion of Blake, McLuhan uses a strange mixture of Joyce and bits of history to examine the thesis that peace could come about through art's function as a means of adjustment to the environment and that this function is implicit in the action of technology. According to McLuhan in *War and Peace*, the artist is the only person not to shrink from adapting to the global village, for the artist "glories in the invention of new identities" (McLuhan and Fiore 1968, 12). Pain as the discovery of modern art becomes a focus in *War and Peace* because modern artists, in trying to force their audience's attention to the coming new media and these new "extensions of man," create a kind of "referred pain" (McLuhan and Fiore 1968,13-16). McLuhan points out that we must learn to savour the pleasure and pain of the newer aspects of our world as an "art of being in the world." This is to behave like a Taoist or Oriental according to McLuhan for "the Oriental world is a world that was never dedicated to fragmented or specialist stress on the visual sense.

Art has been considered the primary mode of adjustment to the environment." All this further sup[ports McLuhan's aphorism that "Adjustment is Art."

The "nearest analogue to art in the Oriental sense," McLuhan argues, is fashion. In a "tribal or oral world" there are no fashions, for "all clothing and all technology is part of a ritual that is desperately sought to be kept stabilized and permanent." This is a stability far beyond that possible in the civilized and fragmented Western world, for "the oral and auditory are structured by a total and simultaneous field of relations describable as acoustic space" (McLuhan and Fiore 1968, 20–3). Acoustic space is now directly associated with the theme of the integrated lifestyle of the tribal and Oriental as transcending the diversity of Euroamerican civilization, so that acoustic space is counterpointed against the fragmentation and aggression resulting from the development of visual space. In addition to Joyce, Blake, and modernist and symbolist poets, there is a very evident Nietzschean sub-plot involved in McLuhan's argument for, as he moves towards a conclusion, the eternal return – which is an aspect, although with a difference, of cyclical (or more specifically helical) history in Vico and Joyce – is stressed in relation to the *I Ching* as an alternation of construction and destruction that has affinities with Nietzsche: "One of the peculiarities of an electric technology is that it speeds up this process of transformation. Instant and total rehearsal of all pasts and all processes enables us to perceive the function of such perpetual returns as one of purgation and purification, translating the entire world into a work of art" (McLuhan and Fiore 1968, 183).

In moving from this towards his conclusion, McLuhan sees associations between Vico, Blake, and Joyce and speaks, as Joyce does throughout the *Wake*, of the contemporary era as a period that wants to put back together the fragmented Humpty Dumpty, thus restoring "the sense of myth" as part of reality and truth. For the pre-literate, and, therefore, for the postelectric, man, the fable or myth is a scientific truth – the basis for what would become for McLuhan, following Vico, "the laws of media."

The world of acoustic space is a world of multi-sensory participation where integral vision is achieved "and the entire scope of the new environments as macroscopic enlargements of our own self-amputations can today provide the beginnings of a new science of man and technology" (McLuhan and Fiore 1967B, 186). McLuhan locates this in what he argues is a Blakean treatment of the eye as providing an integral, mosaic vision and hence a vison of acoustic space, quoting a section from Blake's *Milton:*

First Milton saw Albion upon the Rock of Ages,
Deadly pale outstretch'd and snowy cold, storm cover'd:
A Giant form of perfect beauty outstretch'd on the rock
In solemn death: the Sea of Time & Space thunder'd aloud
Against the rock, which was inwrapped with the weeds of death
Hovering over the cold bosom, in its vortex Milton bent down
To the bosom of death, what was underneath soon seem'd above.
A cloudy heaven mingled with stormy seas in loudest ruin;
But as a wintry globe descends precipitant thro' Beulah bursting,
With thunders loud and terrible, so Milton's shadow fell,
Precipitant, loud thund'ring into the Sea of Time & Space.

(Blake 1927, 392–3)

Giving this selection a somewhat different twist than Blake and using "vortex" to allude to Lewis and Pound, through it McLuhan weaves vortex, time, space, and thunders into the Blakean view that "the eye recognizes everything; and so all directions enter the eye: they are at home and its vortex is truly encompassed." Such an integral eye, is in McLuhan's terms, is "tactile," achieving a "mosaic vision" characteristic of acoustic rather than visual space. Placed by McLuhan in the context of a "message to the fish," a notion derived from the naturalist Louis Agassiz by way of Ezra Pound, which suggests that the one thing fish know nothing about is water, it suggests the human myopia to the technological environment in which technologies as extensions of the person become "self-amputations." The point to be made about the McLuhanesque 'poetic' is that it is precisely the grammatico-rhetorical method of discovery he early explored in investigating the historical background of the "learning" of Thomas Nashe and the sixteenth century which in his more forthright moments declares it to be.

The problem which "McLuhanism" presents, since it attends to the mystifications of the maestro, is twofold (or perhaps threefold): first, it does not read McLuhan as intertextually as his work invites, and thus with a full understanding of Joyce, of contemporary art, and poetry (after 1850), of literary and rhetorical history, and of the history of education as a process of discovery; second, it often does not read McLuhan's complex verbal complexes as poetic images of which his tetrads are a major exemplum, and hence it cannot accept the poetic laws of the laws of media as a contemporary "new science." Yet what McLuhan does with a percept (and affect) such as auditory space is, through visiting and re-visiting it, to seduce the reader into a probing, rhizomic reading that traverses the entire McLuhanesque poetic world. So acoustic space, a term he uses beginning in the 1950s after a contribution by a colleague in the seminars, is gradually inter-related with such other percepts as the visual mosaic, tactility, right-hemisphere brain activity, communication as participation, the West becoming Eastern as the East becomes Western, iconicism, verbal play, and the resonant interval as major characteristic of the new "resonant paradigm."

The question then becomes how to read these complex, multiplex, semiotic constructions. Essentially there are two ways to read (and for that matter to construct) a tetrad as well as any McLuhanesque percept and/or affect: first, reading (or constructing) it as a poetic construct, permitting it to have all the necessary ambivalence in the interactions of the four components, including in each tetrad all of its complementary and supplementary quotes and comments; second, imitating ("matching" its structure) by merely inserting relatively flat single-directed, or at best dual-directed elements into each of its positions as many who imitate the tetrads do. The latter readings move the tetrad away from being the rhetorico-grammatic device McLuhan suggests they should be, turning them into what he would have labelled a dialectical device – a trivialized logical square. McLuhan's weakness, which he shares with most of his commentators and most commentators on media, is that his suppleness, dexterity, and complexity is more restricted and restrained than that of a poet like Joyce or theoreticians such as Walter Benjamin or Gilles Deleuze. But in his case part of the restriction and restraint is generated by his desire to please, to seduce, an audience, placing his poetic somewhere between that of Joyce and that of a highly poetic advertisement. Even so, McLuhan's verbal trickery requires an intense and penetrating play with words, which, as they become archetypes in the Mcluhanesque sense, become less restrictive and rich until they are converted into a cliché, so that "acoustic space" or "global village," as the cliché's he constructed, must now be played with in such a way as to implode them into new poetic cliché's rather than the fillers of journalistic comments or political speeches they have become.

9 McLuhan, Joyce, and the Evolution of Cyberculture

In 1951, shortly after I received my M.A. degree, Marshall urged me to write a doctoral thesis on W.B. Yeats, Ezra Pound, T.S. Eliot, James Joyce, and Wyndham Lewis. Finally, with the enthusiasm and arrogance of youth which believes it can conquer all, I agreed to do the thesis, with the reservation that I exclude Wyndham Lewis, whose prose output, added to the works of Yeats, Pound, Eliot, and Joyce, would have been too formidable – moreover, I would have been unable to view most of Lewis's important art works . My thesis, *Communication Theory in Yeats, Pound, Eliot and Joyce*, was completed in 1954, without any chapter on Lewis.[1] I regretted the omission, since I believed Lewis to be an important factor in the discussion. Lewis's writing was powerful and penetrating, even though I rejected his extreme conservatism and, of course, it was apparent that Lewis, along with Pound, was the modernist Marshall preferred, and in the 1940s he regarded Lewis as a friend.

In the late 1940s, partly through the guidance of his then-collaborator, Hugh Kenner – who, probably under Marshall's encouragement, had written an M.A. thesis on G.K. Chesterton – Joyce's *Wake* joined *Ulysses*, Pound, and Lewis in the McLuhanesque pantheon, even though McLuhan at the time regarded these later works of Joyce as especially demonic.[2]

After reading through his correspondence in order to do a review of his *Letters*, it struck me that, while he and I were together for large amounts of time every day for over four years and were colleagues in the same small ten member collegial unit at the University of Toronto for nearly fifteen years, he seldom directly suggested to me the extremity of his views about the demonic aspects of Joyce's writings. His only indirect suggestions had to do with his general concerns about the gnostic aspects of contemporary poetry in England, Europe, and America. From 1950 on he refers very frequently to Joyce but always seems more comfortable when speaking about Pound (who never recognized any value in *Finnegans Wake*), and even more so when speaking about Joyce's arch-critic (but still admirer), Lewis. Acknowledging the difference between Joycean laughter and McLuhanesque wit is important to understanding the insights of and limitations to McLuhan's extensive use of Joyce throughout his writings from 1951 on (although, interestingly, the references markedly decrease subsequent to 1970). McLuhan regularly comments on Joyce's work, but evades taking into account Joyce's overt commitment to socialism and anarchism as well as his critique of the Roman Catholic Church and of the politics of contemporary Europe and the British Isles. McLuhan's earliest opinions about *Ulysses* being a powerful and demonic "intellectual Black Mass" appeared in his correspondence of 1946 (and it is quite interesting that this reference is immediately followed by his discussion of a paper on "Develop.[ment] of Methods of Using Atomic Energy for Military Purposes" which McLuhan says reads "like a Walpurgis Nacht transposed into the lingo of the newspaper").[3] His earliest published views on the *Wake*, quoting Pound's remarks on *Ulysses*, regard it as an extended cleansing of the Augean stables, a satire about the thrust toward international centralization of power following World War One. In 1951 in *The Mechanical Bride* McLuhan links Joyce's work to Superman and Clark Kent as an illustration of how the centralization of power suppresses human nature. He claims that Joyce, like him, rejects this nightmare of power as a conscious conspiracy, for Finnegan's waking represents "the nightmare [moving] to its unwelcome dramatic peak, the sleeper stirs and writhes ... [from] ... the pain of this collective dream and waking consciousness will come as a relief" (McLuhan 1951, 128). For McLuhan these dark aspects, although an ever present aspect of Joyce's project, were overshadowed, since "although [the *Wake* is] compact of every mood and state of mind, [it] is mainly a world of uproarious fun. No more joyous or funny book was ever conceived or executed."

McLuhan and Joyce shared roles as satirists, but McLuhan's satire is closer to Lewis's and vitiated by his extremely conservative social analysis.

Joyce's laughter is predominantly the joyful, open, festive, anarchic, affirmative laughter of the carnival or the village wake; McLuhan's wit is predominantly closed, largely negative, and cynical. McLuhan clearly appreciated and understood Joyce's range of laughters, but his predominantly festive laughter is not as frequently a part of McLuhan's stylistic repertoire. Laughter is a central issue, as McLuhan makes clear in *From Cliché to Archetype* in his section on "jokes," characteristically titled "Funferall at Finnegans Wake" (McLuhan and Watson 1970,132–3). Jokes were vital in McLuhan's method of probing the technoculture. Yet while McLuhan could admire Joyce's joking repertoire – "The man who said that there are only five basic forms of joke was obviously unaware of the *Wake*" (ibid.) – it is Joyce's alter-ego Lewis who, to a greater extent, shapes McLuhan's discussion of laughter: 'Laughter,' said Wyndham Lewis, "is an explosion of nervous energy attacking the muscles of the face.' In every sense it is a cultural and psychological face. It is inevitable that the funny man be 'a man with grievance' .... Social anger and sensitivity sharpen the awareness of the funny man so that his 'jokes' are stabs or probes into the cultural matrix that plagues him" (McLuhan and Watson 1970, 132).

This stands in sharp contrast to Joyce's Rabelaisian, festive comedy, exemplified in phrases such as "Loud, heap miseries upon us yet entwine our arts with laughters low !" (FW, 259.07). This difference is crucial to the way Joyce and other avant-garde artists with a similar commitment to parody, satire, and comedy explicate aspects of the technoculture and contrasts it with the way that McLuhan used his probes and, more particularly, to the way that mcluhanites in their discussions develop McLuhan's probes. Consistent with his schizoid stance, on occasion McLuhan would protest his being "be-clowned" by critics, yet on other occasions he readily embraced the role of the court jester or clown, for "the clown [is] indispensable as audience-tester and as checker on the moods of the ruling figure. Again without his clown the emperor has no means of contact with the public" (McLuhan and Watson 1970, 133). This is in significant contrast with Joyce who, like Fellini or Borges, distanced himself from the clown, while still understanding the power of the clown, as frequently representing the colonized way of playing up to the colonizer or the colonizers' way of playing with the colonized.

McLuhan often equated the "joke" with the probe or aphorism, usually emphasizing, as Freud did, the elements of grievance and suppression that jokes contain. In his lexicon of key rhetoric, poetic, and literary terms, *From Cliché to Archetype*, McLuhan discusses jokes and satirists partly in relation to Joyce, but the discussion does not raise any of the positive aspects of Joycean transgressive comedy. Instead, while McLuhan's humour is both stern, as Joyce implied Swift was, and swift, as he implied Sterne, was, yet Joyce's own comedic range is more complex than McLuhan's quipping analysis of Swift and Sterne, including within its range the differing values and sensibilities of Aristophanes, Horace, Apuleius, Petronius, the medieval carnival, Erasmus, Rabelais, Cervantes, Pope, and Byron. Joyce's festive satire is associated with the traditions of the old Greek comedy and the Roman saturnalia; McLuhan's cynical satire is associated with the blasting, bombardiering soldier of humour stance of Lewis, inheritor of Lucian, Juvenal, and the more sardonic aspects of Swift. [4]

McLuhan was fascinated by the *Wake*'s paradoxical techniques and their interface with a world that was rapidly and inevitably changing.

The first of his three early essays on Joyce – "Joyce, Aquinas and the Poetic Process" (1962B) – dealt with Joyce's poetic theory." In spite of McLuhan's claim that Joyce was a Thomist, the foundation of Joyce's poetic theory is closer to Duns Scotus and thus the Hopkinesque[5] Jesuit-influenced basis of his esthetic doctrine in *Stephen Hero*. His real affinity with Joyce, and his immense capabilities for understanding and misunderstanding him, is only demonstrated in his later essays and books about media, culture, and technology, from the experimental journal *Explorations* to *Culture Is Our Business*. At one stage or another McLuhan's working title for both the *Gutenberg Galaxy* and *Understanding Media* was "The Road to Finnegans Wake." McLuhan intended "The Road" to be a history of writing. "Joyce," he says, "is making his own Altamira cave drawings of the entire history of the human mind, in terms of its basic gestures and postures during all phases of human culture and technology. As his title indicates, he sees the wake of human progress can disappear again into the night of sacral or auditory man" (McLuhan 1962, 75) .

Installments of McLuhan's study of the history of communication and technology as a history of writing, launched primarily through his reading of Joyce's *Wake,* began appearing at least a decade before Derrida's *Grammatologie* (1967). Since only one-third of the history of the book has involved typography, McLuhan follows Joyce by being "abcedminded" and studying the emergence of the "allforabit" from the earliest stages of writing – hieroglyphs, ogam, and runes – through the phonetic alphabet, for, following Vico, Joyce "stresses that all ancient fables and tales are really records of moments of technical breakthrough ... and that the effects of such breakthroughs were recorded in the new wrunes – w-r-u-n-e-s joining ruins as preserved in "museyrooms" with implications of rules and wrongs" (McLuhan 1962, 74). Taking a cue from the fifth episode of the first part of the *Wake* – an involved discussion of a letter pecked up by a hen in a mud-mound – McLuhan uses Joyce's poetic exploration of the alphabet and letters to illustrate how manuscript culture is a significant stage in the evolution of writing and to explore how Joyce's technique in the *Wake* dramatically illustrates the differences between reading aloud and reading with the eye. He relates oral reading to tactility and synaes-thesia, quoting the first of the Wake's hundred-lettered thunderwords: "bababadalgharaghtakamminarronnkonnbronntonnerronntuon-nthunntrovarrhounawnskawntoohoohoordenenthurnuk!" (FW3.15–7) – the thunderwords being likened to manuscript reading, since they contain no spaces between verbal units (McLuhan 1962, 83). But the essential moments in McLuhan's romantic history of the evolution of language and technology are the discoveries of phonetic writing, of print, and of electromechanical and electrochemical media.

McLuhan's history of writing derived from his interpretation of Joyce continues in *Understanding Media*, where he examines the late stages of print culture marked by the rise of electromechanical, elec-trochemical, and electronic media, and then cybernation and mixed media. While Joyce's interest in the newer technological instruments of production, reproduction, and dissemination is now well recognized, it startled many in the 1960s when McLuhan declared that he first found in Joyce his idea of one media subsuming and transforming previous media as well as his concept of technologies as the extension of the nervous system. Briefly, McLuhan argues that Joyce regarded photog-raphy, and particularly film, "that allnights newsery reel," as leading to the "abnihilisation of the etym," and that "television kills tele-phony" as well. McLuhan further argues that the *Wake* "could not have [been] conceived ... in any other age than the one that produced the phonograph and radio"(McLuhan 1964, 249). Joyce's "abced-mindedness" (FW 64.25–6) merges the print world with film, which itself "merges the mechanical and organic in a world of undulating forms" (McLuhan 1964, 249). While it is easily demonstrated that Joyce's treatment of these issues is more complex than McLuhan's,[6] nevertheless, by going this far in applying his grammatic and rhetori-cal knowledge to an interpretation of Joyce, McLuhan inspired the contemporary study of the history of communication as it relates to shifts from speech to writing to print and electric media that has sub-squently been utilized by such writers on communication as Elizabeth Eisenstein, Carolyn Marvin, Walter Ong, David Crowley, Paul Heyer, and Brian Stock.

Complementing this analysis of the "history of writing," McLuhan first revealed the importance for him of the excrementitious and trivial as a critique of the grand narrative. This leads him to adapt Joyce's quip: "But O felicitous culpability, sweet bad cess to you for an archetypt!" (FW 263.30), for the title of his work in which he quite frequently quotes and analyses Joyce, *From Cliché to Arche-*

type. Here McLuhan turns our usual valuation of cliché and archetype upside down by invoking various aspects of Joyce's poetic practice – his interest in the banal, trash, dung, junk, and debris – to reveal the philosophic importance of cliché. In *Cliché* McLuhan notes that Joyce enables the reader to exult and triumph over trivia by letting him in on the very process by which trivia dramatizes and "floods the entire news-making situation with an intelligibility that provides a catharsis for the accumulated effects of the stereotypes in our lives" (McLuhan and Watson 1970, 176). This interprets Joyce's *Wake* as exemplifying the pattern of "one world burrowing on another" – "Toborrow and toburrow and tobarrow!" (FW 455.11-13). This reinforces Joyce's own remarks in his letters about composing the *Wake* as a tunneling process. "In the meantime I am preparing for it by trying to learn a page of the *Sirens* for the record and by pulling down more earthwork. The gangs are now hammering on all sides. It is a bewildering business. I want to do as much as I can before the execution. Complications to right of me, complications to left of me, complex on the page before me, perplex in the pen beside me, duplex in the meandering eyes of me, stuplex on the face that reads me. And from time to time I lie back and listen to my hair growing white."[7] References to museums, magazine walls, and dung heaps in the *Wake* link burrowing and tunneling to debris and ruins as modes of writing – further emphasized by the association of ruins with runes.

These references by Joyce to burrowing, tunnelling, debris, and ruins reflect his involvement with fragmentation and reassembling – deconstruction and reconstruction. McLuhan certainly shared this interest with him. It is one aspect of this process that he explores in examining the interplay between cliché and archetype and its foundation in paradox. Joyce's use of the Humpty Dumpty figure, following Lewis Carroll, is partly associated with verbal fragmentation and reassemblage. It is by relating these processes through his analysis of trivia (and, of course, the trivium) in *Ulysses* and the *Wake* that McLuhan is able to associate their epic styles more closely with the Alexandrian tradition of the so-called "little epic" or epyllion.[8] An analysis of the play with contrariety, contradictoriness, and paradox as modes of doubleness or even doubled doubleness arises from the interplay of techniques of logic and rhetoric associated with comic epic, so he asserts "The whole of *Finnegans Wake*, including the title, is paradox; based on what Joyce considered man's greatest invention-the mirror of language, the "magazine wall" of memory and all human residue" (McLuhan and Watson 1970, 163). In the 1950s and 1960s McLuhan emphasized many aspects of Joyce that surfaced as major concerns of research only after McLuhan's death in 1980. These insights figure large in the books that have led to his recent re-emergence as a major guru figure for the telecosmic nature of cyberspace.

But what he overlooked or suppressed must also be noted. In choosing a cover word for Joyce's elaborate play with trivia McLuhan selects cliché (a word which does not appear in the *Wake*) because he can relate it to the mechanics of printing.[9] Joyce, on the other hand, plays – as McLuhan recognizes – with the more comprehensive "bits," the writing of the "allforabit." (FW 19.02) McLuhan also, occasionally without informing his reader, innovates on the text of the *Wake*. He claims to cite from the *Wake* with, "There's no police like Holmes," and "the theme of mass-man, whether pre-literate or post-literate" is alluded to many times via "the mush of porter pease" – phrases which, in fact, do not occur at all in the *Wake*. Further, quotes often seem to be used in a such a way as to fit McLuhan's prose poetic meditations, for example, when he uses the opening of the tale of the Mookse and the Gripes "Eins within a space and a wearywide space it was" (FW 158.02), to argue that "eins within a space" signifies that the non-literate modes are implicit, simultaneous and discontinuous, whether in the primitive past or the electric present. Yet, with all these flaws and faults, McLuhan intuited today's cybernetic, hypermedia Joyce, as his section on automation as cybernation in *Understanding Media* illustrates.

What makes examining and re-valuating McLuhan as a Joycean so interesting is how what he excluded in discussing Joyce illuminates some major weaknesses in his own writings on culture and technology. First, he excludes some major discussions of semiotic and structuralist elements, as exemplified, first, by his omitting references to Joyce's remarkable pre-cybernetic passage about his "vicociclometer" that introduces the final version of Anna's letter; second, he gives little attention to the way that math, physics, and other sciences complement technologies and mechanization in the *Wake* – for example, while he wrote a major article in the mid-1950s on the grammatical and rhetorical aspects of the Triv and Quad episode (the second episode of book 2), it gives scant attention to the algebraic and geometrical aspects. Within his discussions of rhetoric he hardly examines Joyce's play with "toptypsical" relations between types, topes, tropes, and tips. Furthermore, McLuhan does not share the *Wake*'s structuralist fascination with codes (e.g. "the farmer, his son and their homely codes" (FW 614.31–2)). His primary thrust is towards communication media rather than towards modes of writing. Finally, he deliberately avoids confronting Joyce's play with religion and the deity, e.g., "Blankdeblank, the god of all machineries" (FW 253.33).

An even more major exclusion is the absence of a consideration of the human element within the *Wake*. While McLuhan appreciates the fun and the humour, he does not deal with the erotic sexuality, or the intertwining of the bodily and the mechanical, even though he suggests that Joyce shares his view that technologies are extensions of the body. Consequently, the kinky in Joyce is absent in McLuhan, even though the excrementitious and somewhat restricted sense of carnival are there. The literal narrative level vision of the *Wake* as about an inkeeper, his family, and their neighbors is also absent . Strangely enough, the Joyce of McLuhan's colleague and alter-ego Northrop Frye, whose critical writings McLuhan so powerfully critiques, also seems to lack these human elements, since in his anagogic vision humanity becomes rather abstract. While McLuhan can reveal the problematic of Frye's grand narrative, situate Joyce as one of the modern precursors of contemporary histories of writing and communication, and ground Joyce's writing in the most elemental bits and particularities, he still falls prey, as Frye did, to not recognizing Joyce's sacralization of the secular through a postreligious performative anthropology. The inclusions and exclusions tell the tale – in a strange way the Joyce of the Black Mass remains a spirit haunting McLuhan, since his conservative, literary, anti-technological, and pietistically religious persona found Joyce too fascinated with engineering, with the secularization of the sacred, with the rich perversity of human encounter, and with socialist anarchism. A deeper, broader knowledge of Joyce among those intrigued by McLuhan's analysis of technology and culture should lead to a richer, more complex understanding of the emerging fusion of people and their technologies – an assessment that will be simultaneously more critical and more understanding.

As we approach the beginning of the third millennium, Joyce's pre-millennial vision for the emergence of a unique technoculture, from which McLuhan's visions began, will come to be better understood. In much the same way that the speculation of science fiction writers and film-makers introduced pre-millennial motifs into the broader everyday culture, and as early as 1920 W.B. Yeats's "The Second Coming" introduced them into mainline modernist poetry, Joyce extrapolated from the changing sociocultural environment surrounding the cultural producer to anticipate entirely new, all-encompassing modes of cultural production. Joyce adapted ideas from Giambattista Vico's *Scienza Nuova* (3rd ed. 1744) to probe this technoculture and its relation to the end of a millennium. In addition to providing Joyce with a pre-modernist theory of culture, Vico provided him with a more intellectually rigorous counter-text for speculating about the coming of this new era of cyberculture than the more familiar theosophy, gnosticism, and occultism of Yeats's *A Vision*, or the cruder Spenglerian philosophy of history.

Combining Vico with Nietzsche's declamation of the era of the "over-man," supplemented by socio-anarchistic thought, psychoanalytic discourse, and a transformation of modern thought by scientific theory, established a grounding for a new poetic theorization of cultural production. Joyce critically integrates the results of nearly a century of encounter between artists, writers, and cultural producers with the new technologies and with the newer "lively arts" (Seldes 1924). Yet apart from the writings of a few artists (e.g., Beckett, Borges, Cage, and Moholy-Nagy), or some dedicated, chimerical Joyceans (e.g., Robert Anton Wilson), Joyce's insights and their aftermath are widely known only in derivative, occasionally distorted, and intentionally enigmatic versions disseminated through the writings of McLuhan to business, media, the arts, and pockets of academia.[10] One aspect of this study of McLuhan and McLuhanism, complementing various arguments that have been made about Joyce and cyberspace, is to explore how McLuhan's becoming the guru of cyberculture has inhibited or prevented many theorists and practitioners from realizing the full, vital importance of Joyce as one of the key, if not *the* key figure, in anticipating the emergence of a phenomena that would culminate in our contemporary cyberculture.

Joyce in the 1920s and 1930s, through his knowledge of the *symbolistes*, early English modernists, and European avant-garde artists and writers, discovered major practico-theoretical concepts well before McLuhan. Beginning with the so-called problematic of the death of the book in the 1960s and 1970s, McLuhan responded to earlier considerations of the book's changing role – from Alphonse Marie Louis de Lamartine's observations about the newspaper in 1831, through Stéphan Mallarmé to Sergei Eisenstein – by exploring how Joyce crafted an extremely complex "artificial language" to respond to the challenge of the syncretistic and synaesthetic tendencies of the emerging modes of communicative and expressional technology.

McLuhan's scouting of "the road to *Finnegans Wake*" established him as the first major popularizer and adaptor of Joycean insights to a media, technology, and culture discourse that has become the unacknowledged basis for our thinking about technoculture, just as the ubiquitous McLuhanesque vocabulary has become a part, often an unconscious one, of our verbal heritage for speaking about culture, technology and communication. In constructing this language, McLuhan, who raided the *symbolistes*, Eliot, Pound and Lewis as well as Joyce, popularized, yet failed to acknowledge, some of the Joycean insights that have become central and dominant in McLuhanese and the McLuhanisms that are encountered on a daily basis. The centrality of the modern city and its representations in *Ulysses* and the *Wake* are vitally important for McLuhan, as indicated by the quotes he uses from the *Wake* to provide a running marginal commentary in *War and Peace in the Global Village*.[10] In the *Wake* Joyce implicitly treats Dublin as interchangeable with an imaginary "Healiopolis" (FW 24.18) which is a "heliotropolis" (FW 594.8) [metropolis] , so that consequently our "urb" which "orbs" is a global metropolis (which McLuhan makes into a "global village").[13]

Speaking of Pythagoreanism in a tetrad on the computer, several years before William Gibson wrote about cyberspace (a term he coined) as "unthinkable complexity. Lines of light ranged in the non-space of the mind, clusters and constellations of data. Like city lights receding" (Gibson 1984, 51), McLuhan wrote that the computer restores Pythagoreanism and advancing decentralization: "When applied to new forms of electronic-messaging, such as teletext and videotext, it quickly converts sequential alphanumeric texts into multi-level signs and aphorisms, encouraging ideographic summation, like hieroglyphs."[15] Here McLuhan's particular use of hieroglyphs derives primarily from Joyce and Vico. One aspect of the *Wake* is Joyce's association of his work with "engined egyptians' whose hieroglyphs he associated with runes and ogham and used to craft the "idioglossary he invented" (FW 423.09) to produce a "nichtian glossery" that was "nat language in any sinse of the world" (FW 83.12).

It is particularly important to assess and situate McLuhan's role in the pre-history of cyberspace in that many recognized writers on the subject of hypertext and/or virtual reality – such as Michael Heim, George Landow, Richard Lanham, Stuart Moulthrop, Jay Bolter, Michael Benedikt, and Howard Rheingold – specifically include McLuhan as one of the important anticipators of the contemporary cyberculture although Joyce's role is seldom acknowledged, even though he presents a powerful, if less immediately accessible, pre-vision of the coming of cyberculture and cyberspace.[16] For instance Arthur and Marilouise Kroker's writings on cyberculture in works such as *Hacking the Future* began with Arthur's early book *Innis/McLuhan/Grant*. Even Baudrillard, who acknowledges McLuhan to have been one of the influences on his work, which culminates in his extensive critique of cyberculture in *Ecstasy of Communication*, *Simulacra*, and *Simultations*, unlike Derrida, Sollers, or even LeFebvre, does not allude to Joyce.

That McLuhan is regarded as an important prophet of cyberspace is clear in the voice of the cyberculture of the digital generations's *Wired* claiming on its masthead: "Patron Saint: Marshall McLuhan." The crucial issue is whether in the process of popularization of modernisms McLuhan obstructed others from realizing that Joyce not McLuhan, should be considered the precursor or forerunner of cyberculture, if the complexity of cyberculture is to be fully appreciated and an appropriate satiric critique provide a balanced understanding of it. To see this, consider McLuhan's and Joyce's respective ways of exploring the pre-history of cyberculture. McLuhan's approach to the emerging digital era is schizo-manic, low comic, yet conservative; while Joyce's is schizoid, satiric, tragico-comic, and radical. McLuhan is the *poète manqué* as author; Joyce is the poet as cultural producer. McLuhan articulates Joycean, symbolist, and avant-garde poetic and artistic theories aphoristically, using condensation whenever convenient to obscure or ambiguate, sometimes in a deliberately misleading direction. Primarily, McLuhan used all these sources to explore the emerging multimedia culture – for even TV, which includes elements of film and radio broadcasting, is multimedia, just as silent film had been earlier with its merging of photography and the moving, gesturing image of drama, or as talkies had become with the addition of sound.

McLuhan stresses a set of themes directly attributable to modernist and avant-garde artists and/or to Joyce, often with a specific pseudo-Joycean spin: media production and dream, space-time and the arts, external landscape and the urban landscape, interior landscape, or *la peinture de la pensée*; language and other sign systems as code, the recognition of the book as a medium, orality/literacy and tactility, synaesthesia and the intrasensory, syncretism and the orchestration of the arts, and the artwork as machine. In spite of the Joycean spin, McLuhan filters these concepts primarily through the conservative modernist perspectives of Lewis, Pound, and Eliot. If Joyce is the most frequently cited and quoted author in his writings from *Explorations* (1953–59) until *War and Peace in the Global Village* (1968), his only published work whose title makes a specific attribution to a modernist author is *Counterblast* (1969) which pays homage (even if slightly ambiguous) to Lewis's seminal publication *Blast* (1914). Moreover, his major posthumous work, *The Laws of Media: The New Science*, while alluding to the fact that Joyce uses Vico's *Scienza Nuova* as the structural book for *Finnegans Wake* (as he had done with the *Odyssey* in *Ulysses*) and opening with two epigraphs from Joyce as well as citing Joyce a few more times, alludes much more extensively to Bacon and Vico.

It has been established earlier that McLuhan first developed his technique of the "essai concrète" – of which *Blast* as well as his *Counterblast* are examples – in *Explorations*. The title of the special issue of that journal in 1957 was derived from a phrase in the *Wake*: "verbivocovisual presentement" (FW341.19). This issue of *Explorations* celebrated the place of orality, tactility, simultaneity, and synesthesia in the new technologies of cultural production. While there are innumerable citations of Joyce, the actual text is presented in typographical arrangements similar to those of Lewis's *Blast*, Mallarmé's "*Coup de Dès*," and avant-garde, Dadaist, and Futurist manifestos. As the use of this type of experimentation with typography, layout, and illustration evolves in McLuhan's later work, it leads to the typographical and pictorial styles that were used in other examples of the "essai concrète" – e.g., *The Medium Is the Massage*, *War and Peace in the Global Village*, *Counterblast*, and *The Vanishing Point* – which apparently inspired in part the "new age" style of *Wired* magazine as a non-electronic correspondent to cyberculture, particularly virtual reality, web pages, and cyberspace.

Such radical typographical exploration is not present in Joyce, although he does use devices such as the "headline style" of the "Aeolus" episode in *Ulysses* or the marginalia and foot-notes in the "Triv and Quad" section of the *Wake*. Not surprisingly, each of these sections provides the subject for one of McLuhan's few critical essays about Joyce – "Joyce, Mallarmé and the Press" and "James Joyce: Trivial and Quadrivial".[17] The first of these two articles is one of McLuhan's earliest forays into the problematic of the book in the era of technological reproducibility. He had never proposed that the book was dead or even dying. He used the book and its growth during the Renaissance as a bench mark of the effects of the appearance of any new technology acting as a teaching machine. In *The Gutenberg Galaxy* he asserted that "Far from wishing to belittle Gutenberg mechanical culture, it seems to me that we must now work very hard to retain its achieved values" (McLuhan 1962, 135). In 1966, commenting on a *Life* magazine close-up about himself called "Oracle of the Electric Age," he wrote a letter to the editor that clearly articulates his awareness of the transformation of the book in the computer era: "Not "obsolete," but "obsolescent" is the term that applies in my analysis of the present status of the printed book. Obsolescence often precedes an extraordinary development in technology. The arrival of electric xerography certainly does not mean the end of the book, but rather a great enlargement of its scope and function. Earlier, photo-engraving and also photography had transformed the world of typography and book production."[18]

Elsewhere in *The Gutenberg Galaxy* McLuhan had pointed out that "only one third of the history of the book in the Western world has been typographic," so it was simple for him to conceive of various metamorphoses of the book, thus anticipating the emergence of phenomena such as hypertext and hypermedia (McLuhan 1962, 74). McLuhan continually declared that Joyce and the *symbolistes* had provided him with such an awareness, and his analysis of the role of the book in the era of technological reproducibility was primarily precipitated by his readings of Joyce's *Ulysses* and *Finnegans Wake*, complemented by Mallarmé's prose writings in *Crise de Vers* and *Quant au Livre* and by his knowledge of the history of the book and the implications of medieval and renaissance commonplaces about books, the book of revelation, and the book of nature. McLuhan argues that the crisis facing the book was becoming apparent by the end of the third decade of the nineteenth century when Alphonse de Lamartine could proclaim that "The only possible book from today is a newspaper" (McLuhan 1969, 5). In a world pressured by the success of journalism and confronting the introduction of newspaper photography, Mallarmé had to envision the book in terms of music and dream. For *symbolisme* and the avant-garde the turn away from visual detail and external landscape (for they sensed that photography and, shortly afterward, film could treat them more effectively) toward the interior landscape (*la peinture de la pensée*) was a response to the emerging new media being better able to handle various traditional techniques and strategies used in the construction of novels.

In the 1920s Sergei Eisenstein, the film director and theorist, paralleled Charles Dickens to D.W. Griffith in a lengthy essay, particularly noting Dickens's use of parallel action as an anticipation of montage and his ability to deal with visual detail (Eisenstein 1949, 195–255). Film, as Joyce was aware, permits the instantaneous presentation of pages of written description, as well as being able, by using montage, to make the landscape's relation to the action and its characters more complex. While each novel and film has its own potential, the filmic version of the opening of *Great Expectations* has often been cited as exemplifying this relationship of increased complexity between film and novel. The impact of film's potential was a significant factor on the abandonment by the avant-garde of direct narration and external landscape in the early twentieth century. The full import of Mallarmé's opening statement in "*Le Livre, Instrument Spirituel*" – "*que tout, au monde, existe pour aboutir à un livre*" ["all earthly existence must ultimately be contained in a book"] (Mallarmé 1945, 378) – not only clearly articulated the problem Joyce explored in *Ulysses* and the *Wake* but also, perhaps somewhat ironically, anticipated an era in which the book would break the bonds of the printed page and the bound volume.

The newspaper had already provided an alternative form ("*La sympathie irait au journal place à l'abri de ce traitement*"), but a form that was irritating to a poet, because columns confined the headlines and texts, problems with which Mallarmé's "*Coup de Dès*" grappled – a poem that David Hayman has conclusively demonstrated had a significant impact on James Joyce (Hayman 1956, 2:149-83). The Mallarméan critique of the book and its subsequent impact on poetry and painting is also clearly a response to the stresses resulting from the propensity of the new electromechanical and electrochemical processes of production and reproduction to produce ever new mergers of poetic techniques. This has most recently led to the new technologies of informatics, virtual reality, and hypermedia constructing the cyberculture of cyberspace. So, if in the 1830s Lamartine was able to make his observation about the newspaper being the only possible book, the only possible book after the 1930s was a syncretistic and synaesthetic, kinoaudiovisual, multimedia production, and, after the 1990s, a medley of the powers of production, reproduction, and dissemination of computerized artificial reality – i.e., hypermedia in cyberspace.

It is widely recognized that Joyce's unique contribution to the problematic of the book, just at the beginning moments of late modernism (or postmodernism), lay in his invention of an artificial, polysemic language. It is perhaps less well recognized, although Eisenstein was aware of it in the 1920s and 1930, that in so doing Joyce was designing a way for language to cope with the problems presented by new technological possibilities for synaesthetic and coenaesthetic modes of communication and expression. Eisenstein had noted that Joyce wanted, first through the interior monologue of *Ulysses* and then in the language of the *Wake*, to use speech and print to achieve the nearest approximation to the inclusive, syncretistic character of film, including color and sound, that epitomized the most recent stage in the orchestration of the then-existing arts. Eisenstein also believed that Joyce's project could not succeed. Joyce, on the other hand, fascinated by film and intrigued by Eisenstein, realized that the intensities and complexities of the poetry of the verbal arts must become part of any such future orchestration and that for this to occur verbal language must undergo a transformation. Furthermore, he realized – as Derrida's project has confirmed – that the verbal arts must also contribute to designing a theoretical language for the critique of late modernity and the emerging cyberculture.

The overt recognition of the importance of synaesthesia and the convergence of media to the further development of extensions of cinema and other media – intermedia – was well developed by Expo '67 in Montreal, many of whose theme exhibits and audio-visual and multi-media exhibits made specific reference to being influenced by McLuhan (Theall 1969). By the beginning of the 1970s Gene Youngblood, a film theorist, could speak of the emergence of what he called "expanded cinema" as integrated technologies working together to "expand consciousness," technologies which were to develop into Virtual Reality.[19] In *Expanded Cinema* Gene Youngblood openly notes his indebtedness to McLuhan, argues that "expanded cinema" is synaesthetic and syncretistic and further asserts that this new synaes- thetic and syncretistic expansion of film will increasingly involve com- puters and other forms of telecommunication.

In *The Gutenberg Galaxy* McLuhan had associated Joyce's project in the *Wake* with a return to the orality of a manuscript culture noting that "Joyce never tired of explaining how in *Finnegans Wake* 'the words the reader sees are not the words that he will hear.' As with [Gerard Manley] Hopkins, the language of Joyce only comes alive when read aloud, creating a synaesthesia or interplay of the senses."[20] For McLuhan, reading aloud meant reversing the effect of print by restoring what had been lost in a world of silent reading: "The stripping of the senses and the interruption of their interplay in tactile synaesthesia may well have been one of the effects of the Gutenberg technology" (McLuhan 1962, 17). By the beginning of the 1960s, under the influence of Joyce, the *symbolistes* and the avant- garde, McLuhan had expanded his sense of what constituted the synaesthetic. In *Understanding Media* he asserts that "the TV image has exerted a unifying synaesthetic force on the sense-life" making it a "unified sense and imaginative life" finally attainable to fulfill what "had long seemed an unattainable dream to Western poets, painters and artists in general" (McLuhan 1964, 315). In *The Global Village* he suggests that the marriage of computers and telecommunication, which would later produce cyberspace, will intensify the synaesthetic and the syncretistic: "As man succeeds in translating his central nervous system into electronic circuitry, he stands on the threshold of outering his consciousness into the computer. Consciousness ... may be thought of as a projection to the outside of an inner synaesthesia, corresponding generally with that ancient definition of common sense ... The computer moving information at a speed somewhat below the barrier of light might end thousands of years of man frag- menting himself (McLuhan and Powers 1989, 94). When the world wide matrix of cyberspace finally emerges, McLuhan suggests that our "collective consciousness" will be "lifted off the planet's surface into a dense electronic symphony" where everybody " will "live in a clutch of spontaneous synesthesia, painfully aware of the triumphs and wounds of one another" (McLuhan and Powers 1989, 95); that is, in a globalized technology – a "global village" of "totality and inclusiveness."

Joyce's globe, unlike McLuhan's, could only be regarded as total and inclusive within the ambivalence of the artificial reality of a world of dream, hallucination, or inebriation. Early in the opening section of the *Wake*, the corpus or corpse of the fallen Finn is described as being laid "brawdawn alanglast bed" with "a bockalips of finisky" [whiskey], and "a barrowload of guenesis" [stout], so that it may be said: "Tee the tootal of the fluid hang the twoddle of the fuddled, O! Hurrah, there is but young gleve for the owl globe wheels in view which is tautaulogically the same thing" (FW6.27–30). This globe is only related to totality as an inebriated antithesis to "teetotal," i.e., abstinence, which is the "toot + all," that is the "twoddle of the fuddled" (It should also be noted that this line refers to the song, "Phil, the Fluter's Ball" – "With the toot of the flute and the twiddle of the fiddle."[21]); so the *Wake* with its tips and types and topes and tropes consequently is "typtoptypsical". Or, as it is put in the *Wake*'s concluding episode (FW IV), all artificial realities (eddas, epics, holy books – e.g., the book of the Dead – and tales such as *A Thousand and One Nights*) render forth: "The untireties of livesliving being the one substance of a streamsbecoming. Totalled in toldteld and teldtold in tittle-tell tattle" (FW 597.7–9). The total is only an imaginary moment in a medley of flows and discontinuites which constitute the Wakean "chaosmos of Alle" (FW 118.21) – "teldtold" in the flux of exposé and rumor.

If for McLuhan TV is the early synaesthetic precursor of what will become an unearthly "dense electronic symphony" characterized by "totality and inclusiveness," for Joyce, although complex and luxuriant, TV is the electronic assemblage of artificial realities – "the charge of a light barricade," a charge that consists of flows – "down the photoslope in syncopanc pulses," yet also of discontinuities – "with bitts betwugg their teffs" carrying "the missledhropes, glitteraglatteraglutt, borne by their carnier walve" (FW 349.11–13). Joyce's technical description of television – "the bairdboard bombardment screen" (since John Logie Baird was its inventor) – grounds it in a materiality, an intelligibility and a technology that is absent from McLuhan's abstractions. Joyce's "bitts," for example, playing on the relation between talking and eating – a theme which Deleuze has identified in Lewis Carroll – also anticipates communication being an assemblage of bits (Deleuze 1969). Codes composed of contrasting bits, as he implies elsewhere in his "book of Morses," underlie all mediated transmission. For if "you have just beamed listening through (a ham pig)" (FW 359.21) to a sentimental drama and then "diffusing among our lovers of this sequence ... the dewfolded song of the naughtingels," this is transmitted by pulses or signals reducible to dots and dashes – "swift sanctuary seeking, after Sunsink gang (Oiboe! Hitherzither! Almost dotty! I must dash!") (FW 359.30–360.01).

By the time of his writing the *Wake* Joyce had shifted to exploring the very codified nature of printed phonetic, alphabetic language – the "all-forabit" of the "abcedminded" – and the limits of its malleability for imaginarily exploring and critiquing a world moving beyond the word to an integration and orchestration of the arts within new modes of cultural production, reproduction, and dissemination. But throughout his analysis he is more complex than McLuhan. For while McLuhan somewhat erroneously asserts that: "Structuralism in art and criticism stemmed, like non-Euclidean geometries, from Russia. Structuralism as a term does not much convey its idea of inclusive synaesthesia, an interplay of many levels and facets in a two-dimensional mosaic" (McLuhan 1962, 230), Joyce builds an anticipatory radical modernist hyperstructuralism on a post-Saussurean sense of structure in a multidimensional world of hyperspheres and tesseracts. In *Ulysses* and the *Wake* Joyce applied and extended Mallarmé's understanding of the book and the printed text by designing books for a post-print era. This involved a radical reassessment, first of style and structure, and then of language itself, the latter occurring primarily in *Finnegans Wake*.

10 Joyce, Light, and the Road to Digiculture

When I entered the University of Toronto Graduate School in the fall of 1950, the then director of Graduate Studies of the English Department tried to warn me against doing a doctoral degree with Marshall McLuhan. The ruling establishment of the English Department at that time was not very congenial towards studies in contemporary English literature and was particularly hostile towards McLuhan's rather avant-garde, unorthodox, and, according to them, irresponsible approach towards it. Nor did they approve of his close affiliations with professors interested in the new criticism – particularly those "New Critics" from Yale such as Cleanth Brooks and W.K. Wimsatt, Jr – since they regarded the "New Criticism" as anti-historical. In fact, in December 1950 the chair of the Graduate English Department at Toronto, A.S. P. Woodhouse, an eminent Canadian Miltonist and literary historian, had participated in a major debate on the subject of history and criticism with Cleanth Brooks, one of the leading exponents of the New Criticism, at the annual meeting of the Modern Language Association.

McLuhan, however, combined his interests in contemporary literature and the new criticism with a strong knowledge of and commitment to literary history, which is why I stayed at Toronto rather than returning to Yale to pursue my doctoral studies. I felt that between the historically oriented University of Toronto Department of English and the avant-garde McLuhan I was obtaining a badly needed awareness of the study of literature in its historical context as well as within a new, broadly interdisciplinary context. McLuhan embedded his teaching in literary history, but also in the history of grammar, logic, rhetoric, and early theories of education as well as in the inter-relationship between literature, the arts, and the everyday culture – a fairly rare combination at the time. When around 1950 he discovered the importance of communication theory to the arts, his combination of history, contemporary poetry, art and aesthetics, and his new critical pragmatism provided his lifelong, unique fix on communication and technology. It was this combination that would lead him to traverse many of the same directions (with the exception of a formalized semiotics) as Umberto Eco: Joyce, the "open text," medievalism and the modern world, modernism, and studies in hyperreality.

Even though Eco has subsequently dissociated himself from McLuhan, in 1987 he was a natural, and early, recipient of the biannual McLuhan prize, since if McLuhan and he differed on the formalization of literary studies and semiotics, they shared strikingly similar sensibilities in other respects. It is regrettable that after receiving the McLuhan prize Eco subsequently sharply criticized McLuhan, since his criticisms of McLuhan's two major errors – first, that our historical period will be increasingly dominated by images, and second, that our new electronic community will be a global village – are really criticisms of mcluhanism, for, as I have noted before, McLuhan would have preferred to speak of a global metropolis or of a global theater, and he viewed orality and tactility as more central than vision to the modern world. However, McLuhan would not have agreed with Eco's conclusion that "a Rube Goldberg model seems to me the only metaphysical template for our electronic future" (Eco 1996, 306), for while he appreciated the wit of Rube Goldberg, his fix on that future emphasized the electric in contradistinction with the mechanical. Eco and McLuhan also differed radically in that while Eco separated his literary activities from his theoretical ones, McLuhan, rightly or wrongly, was crafting a social scientific poetry in prose to produce a post-Joycean "new science" of the history of artefacts – The New Science of Marshall McLuhan. [1]

My intention in the preceding chapters has not been, as some have alleged of my earlier works on McLuhan, to try to make him a lesser and somewhat confused Joyce, or to wish that he had been more a literary theorist or critic and less the type of "poet" he was to become, or, most particularly, not to demonize him as a journalist might with an unpopular politician. It is rather to contextualize McLuhan within the materials that had shaped him and to confront his work with the work of those from whom he borrowed heavily, since this illuminates his work, while also offering possibilities of new, different, and sometimes richer directions for exploring the inter-relation of culture, technology, and communication.

It is important to place McLuhan's indebtedness to the fine arts, literature, the lively arts, and the way their practitioners thought about these matters (e.g., Eliot's essays, Eisenstein's writings on film, Kandinsky or Klee's speculations about their work) in perspective, because the success of his project suggests that a rich potential for affinity between modernism, our contemporary cultural production of the last half of the twentieth century, and the study of communication, culture, and technology remains to be fully developed. The new schism that some schools of cultural theory have created between the cultural production represented by the so-called "fine" arts and the "lively arts" of today's everyday culture suppresses a rich source of insight, particularly of the rather intimate connections between them (e.g., John Cage and Frank Zappa's respective interests in Joyce), an insight which McLuhan certainly considered essential in his poetic.

McLuhan fails to appreciate Eco's semiotic and logical orientation, but he does succeed in developing the history of modes of communication and its technology as a branch of the history of artefacts that is more complex and challenging than Eco's history of the book. But he does so in a way that is anathema to an academic: he writes a poetic-satiric history rather than an empirical or theoretically oriented one. And it is a very special and particular history, since it constitutes for late modernity – pre-postmodernism – a pre-history of cyberculture and the era of digitalization. Like Joyce moving beyond Vico, McLuhan moves beyond Bacon and Vico to produce a poetic history of the world – a project paralleling that of H.G. Wells *The Outline of History* (1919) but pursued in terms of *techné* producing a techno-poetic, and thus an artefactual, history in which media and technology assume their role as artefacts – and all artefacts are media for Mcluhan – that is they are "symbolic words," which are therefore like poems or paintings or concerti, constituting messages in and of themselves.

In a series of articles beginning with "James Joyce, Literary Engineer" in 1988 and moving through a discussion of "The Hieroglyphs of Engined Egyptians" and "Beyond the Orality/Literacy Principle: James Joyce and the Pre-History of Cyberspace" (1992) to a book on Joyce's techno-poetics (1997) and another on reconstructing sense in the Joyce era of communication, culture and technology (1995), I have developed and contrasted McLuhan and Joyce's pre-histories of cyberculture and their visions of a digitalized future. But to understand these issues, it is important to realize that both McLuhan and Joyce were engaged in writing satiric (and parodic) poetic histories of percepts and affects, not the conceptual histories of scholars or researchers in human science. What makes this interesting is, of course, that McLuhan discovered the nature and importance of such histories by contextualizing Joyce within his own earlier work on the history of grammatico-rhetorical studies, so that McLuhan and Joyce were thus engaged in writing parallel, yet basically contrasting, types of satiric history.[2] Such histories are associated with poetic parody and the satire of learning and with a specific set of traditions of learned satire associated with Menippus, Lucian, and Varro in the classical world; Aretino, Rabelais, Erasmus, and Cervantes in the Renaissance; and Pope, Swift, and Sterne in the Enlightenment.

While the exact sources, nature, and role of these types of satiric poems and McLuhan's early interest in them are discussed in detail in Chapter 11, it is necessary to note here that there were two major sets of divisions within the development of these genres: the first division was between the more cynical satiric tradition associated with Menippus and Lucian and that of Varro, who wrote satires with closer affiliations to carnival and festive laughter; the second was between the post-Enlightenment treatment of Menippean and Varronian satire, culminating around the time of Pope's *Dunciad* and Swift's *Tale of a Tub*, and the Romantic treatment beginning with Sterne's *Tristram Shandy*. It is important to recognize these distinctions, since the difference between Joyce, on one hand, and McLuhan and Lewis on the other, is marked by Joyce's open, carnivalesque, and festive laughter and the more philosophic, Stoic, and dark laughter of Wyndham Lewis and McLuhan.

This is not mere generic pedantry, because what is at stake here is understanding the nature of McLuhan's project, which is distinct from what is widely understood about his work. McLuhan, who was well aware that Joyce – and to a lesser extent Lewis – had opened up poetic histories of artefacts as communicative modes and hence of media as artefacts, also realized that such a poetic history would not normally be accepted by either academia or the commercial world. He therefore modified the Menippean satire as practiced by Lewis to become the cynical, witty, sensational tricksterism of his own writings, which, he would repeatedly assert, dealt with percepts (and affects) not concepts; were modernist poetic prose and visual design not theoretical discourse; and were satire and poetic history – Menippean satire and post-Baconian, post-Viconian poetic history. Since such a postmodern satirist could also be a trickster, his work could have not only a fictional resemblance to genuine theoretical discourse and even to philosophy but also the philosophical import of aspects of the tradition of learned satire.

To understand how such a history works and how it explores percepts and affects associated with the history of artefacts and their place in communication, culture, and technology, let us begin by looking at the central role that "light" and its relationship with space and time play in McLuhan, Joyce, and some of their predecessors. Two and a half decades after the publication of the *Wake*, McLuhan enigmatically declared that in the new media world: "The electric light is pure information. It is a medium without a message" (McLuhan 1964, 8). Elsewhere he declared "tactility includes all the senses as white light incorporates all the colors."[3] He also develops a distinction that is central in his work from *The Gutenberg Galaxy* to *The Laws of Media* – adapted from Gregory Kepes's new art form of "landscape by light through" and from discussions by Ernst Panofsky and Otto von Simsky of the gothic Cathedral and stained glass – between the effect of "light on" and "light through" (Panofsky and von Simsky 1963). McLuhan applies these analyses by discussing the TV image as produced by "light through"[4] in contradistinction to film which is produced by the projection of light on the screen. It must be understood that McLuhan's complex play with such phrases, as they appear and reappear in works such as *The Vanishing Point*, operates stylistically to use such a phrase as one would in a poem and, therefore, the phrase is not in and of itself an analytical principle.

In the *Wake* Joyce, like McLuhan, deals with both light on and light through – fire and candlelight casting shadows, and light projecting through a shade to present to those outside a couple having sex in a bedroom. Since McLuhan associates his remarks about white light with color and also associates this theme, through Panofsky and von Simsky with the stained glass of the Gothic Cathedral, it is easy to connect McLuhan's interest in light to the conclusion of Joyce's *Wake*, where in the fourth book the coming of dawn is signaled by the light of the rising sun breaking through a stained glass triptych in a chapel at Chapelizod. This colorful sunrise is accompanied by a debate between St Patrick and an archdruid, Balkelly, one aspect of this mystical sage being meant to suggest the eighteenth-century philosopher and theosophist George Berkeley, who wrote *A New Theory of Vision* (a work which McLuhan also frequently cites, particularly with respect to his theories about tactility and the interplay of the senses in the perception of space (McLuhan 1962, 271).

While Joyce uses stained glass in a chapel, because of its particular suitability to his daylit nightworld, McLuhan's discussion of "light through" moves from stained glass and mosaics to Kepes's "new landscape" of the contemporary cityscape and the TV tube. Still for both "light through" should be related to Panofsky's discussion of "manifestatio" in *Gothic Architecture and Scholasticism*. It is important to note, however, that Joyce's discussion of stained glass dramatizes how the interior of a church (for his church is a village chapel and not a cathedral) with its stained glass windows, although relatively dark, has a luminous darkness that is vibrant with the radiance of the windows – something like a heavenly equivalent of Milton's "darkness visible." So, unlike McLuhan's sharp contrast, Joyce's distinction does not come from the opposition of "light on" to "light through," but from the interplay of the light through the windows and the reflected light it becomes in the interior of the chapel. The tactility of white light to which McLuhan refers here is not for Joyce the direct result of the white light of an electric bulb or any other source of white lights, but an effect of the dissemination of sunlight by refraction and reflection. Stained glass does not function like McLuhan's white light in relation to tactility, since it is the dynamic movement of light constantly changing and projecting through the glass into the enclosed space that creates the various colors. Just as with the spectrum, the light hitting the window is refracted, producing a multitude of color effects.[5]

There are other crucial distinctions, for the light in Joyce's dream is replete with color, and hence with qualitative differences in hue and saturation and a quantitative difference in intensity or brilliance. While McLuhan stresses the central importance of light in relation to space, time, and motion, his actual range in discussing light is less complex and less directed towards the virtuality of an illuminated world than the vision of light in Joyce's dream. As well, McLuhan's orientation toward the Gothic cathedral stresses scholasticism, while Joyce's village chapel is more oriented to the everyday world of the people. Conceptually as well, Joyce's discussion makes complex links between such diverse figures as Berkeley, Helmholtz, Goethe, Einstein, and a variety of other contemporary physicists associated with quantum theory and optics, as well as theological and occult sources.[6]

McLuhan's approach to the role of light satirically critiques certain theories about light, with which Joyce plays poetically: the problems raised when the speed of light is associated with time in the electric world; the logical, structured formalization of theories of optics associated with the spectrum, waves, and quanta; and the complex spatio-temporal theories of optics that arose within modern physics. For Joyce these, as well as occult theories of light from the Egyptian, hermetic, and classical worlds, celebrate the comedy of the "chaosmos"; for McLuhan they must be critiqued to reconstruct a medieval totality of vision. While Joyce's debate on light, color, black, and white can resolve itself in the sensuous experience of sunrise occupying space and moving through time, McLuhan's multi-sensuousity arises from the flat, two-dimensional mosaic of the medieval world. While both approaches contribute to the understanding of the emerging world of virtuality in cyberculture, Joyce's greater complexity can better encompass the centrality of digitalization in the new technology.

This again, is why McLuhan is less interested in the closing sections of the *Wake*, for immediately following the great debate on light there is a complex passage on human life, electro-mechanization, code, poetic history, and cosmos to which I called attention in my earlier book on McLuhan (Theall 1971, 216–8) and which other scholars and I have discussed in detail elsewhere[7]. In that passage Joyce manifests his interest in the bio-electro-mechanic nature of life and its relevance to how people communicate synchronically and diachronically through history. As I suggested in *The Medium Is the Rear View Mirror*: "what McLuhan tries to do is to translate Joyce's discussion into a flat, [less complex] discussion of a pseudoscientific nature. In the process, Joyce's richness and the richness of a scientific account of the senses are both lost, although superficially McLuhan's adaptation of Joyce's account to a general theory of sense interplay calls the average person's attention to complexities that are usually overlooked and that may be extremely sophisticated. While popularizing Joyce or popularizing the shifts within scientific thought as they impinge on human communications, McLuhan raises questions that are far too often overlooked by individuals working in these areas" (Theall 1971, 87). The point, however, is that, as McLuhan often reiterated, that the process partly fails, if his poetic vision does not lead the reader back to its roots in Joyce, the *symbolistes*, and the artistic avant-garde.

McLuhan, like Joyce, develops a contemporary artistic agenda about vision, motion, light, space, and time and situates it in a history. McLuhan derives his approach from Kepes, Moholy-Nagy, and Giedion, who outline their theories concerning the new language of vision, vision in motion, light, and space and time in modern art and architecture in relation to the new investigations of artistic structure and its elements carried out by the various avant-garde movements of the early twentieth century. The experiments of artistic avant-garde movements such as the Dadaists, the Bauhaus, and the Constructivists, among others, and of individuals such as Duchamp, Klee, Eisenstein, or Luis Buñuel generated exploration of the semiotics and technical effects of multidimensional spaces and times and multi-sensory involvements.

Duchamp, for example, became an early leading figure in splitting apart the presumed generic boundaries of painting and sculpture to explore the arts of motion, light, movement, gesture, and concept. This is exemplified in the long developmental process of his never-completed project, *The Large Glass*.[8] This work, the "assemblage" portion of which was probably not abandoned until 1923, was accompanied by the serial publication of his working notes, beginning with *The Box*

of 1914. These notes continued beyond 1923 through the publication
of *The Green Box* (1934) to *A l'infinitif* (1966). This interest in notes
as part of a total work is echoed in McLuhan's interest in such notes
(aided and abetted by the notes he himself collected on small 3x5 slips
in Laura Secord candy boxes) exemplified in his tetrads and his various
essais concrètes and Joyce's similar interest in notes and the gestations
of works, which the preservation of his notebooks attest to and which
he publicly underlined through the publication of *Work in Progress*
(the title under which from time to time various sections of the *Wake*
were published from 1928 on while Joyce was still working on the final
versions), and the commentaries about it which he organized (e.g., *Our
Exagmination Round his Factification for Incamination of Work in
Progress*, or Ogden's preface to *Tales Told of Shem and Shaun*). Furthermore, McLuhan and Joyce, like Duchamp, also explore similar
aspects of motion, light, movement, gesture, and concept.

The road to MIT's Media Lab and to cyberculture begins with this
poetic and artistic experimentation in the late nineteenth and early
twentieth century, quickly followed by the experimentation of artists
such as Robert Rauschenberg, one of the founders, with the engineer
Billy Kluver of EAT (experimentation in art and technology) (Davis
1973, 67–73). As Stuart Brand notes, many of the Media Lab
researchers of the 1960s and 1970s placed great importance on collaborations with artists who were involved in exploring the nature and
art of motion and in investigating new relationships between sight,
hearing, and the other senses (Brand 1987, 82–3, 86). The intertwining of art and technology, as McLuhan recognized, began among architects in the nineteenth century, parallelling the development of the
emerging electro-technology (a major theme of Giedion's *Space, Time
and Architecture*), and among visual artists in the early twentieth
century with Duchamp and the Futurists, the latter of which were a significant preoccupation of Wyndham Lewis in his early critical writings.
Michael Benedikt, speaking about the technoscientific basis for the
future development of cyberspace, notes that "modern physics and
mathematics revealed space's anatomy ... showing its inextricability
from the sinews of time and light, from the stresses of mass and gravity
and from the nature of knowing itself" (1992, 125).

It has been widely accepted that McLuhan's writings anticipated the
emergence of our contemporary perception of a digital cyberculture of
artificial realities and cyberspace. But the primary source of McLuhan's
insights in this area were first, modernist art and literature including
Joyce and Lewis; second, his historical awareness of the significance of
the emergence of print within the grammatico-rhetorical tradition; and
third, his identification, through his study of mid-nineteenth-century

literature in France, America, and England (*symbolisme*, Poe and Whitman, and Tennyson respectively) of the important impact of the rise of the electric era on mechanization. The latter two sources can be resituated in Joyce and the debates of English and continental modernism. To understand the emergence of the digital era of cyberculture – what Darren Tofts and I have dubbed the "pre-history of cyberculture"[9] – it is essential, even if difficult, to contextualize McLuhan's insights within this context, assessing his similarities and differences from those who influenced him. Joyce is the key because, as Michael Phillipson has established, Joyce is the focal point of pre-post-modernism to which McLuhan found himself fatally attracted (Phillipson 1989).

In a series of arguments with which McLuhan was fascinated, Lewis had attacked Joyce sharply in *Time and Western Man, The Art of Being Ruled*, and *The Childermass* for promoting a pre-postmodern anatomy of space in relation to time, light, mass, and the epistemological act in *Ulysses* and *Work in Progress*. McLuhan's early approval of Lewis's argument again demonstrates his ambivalence towards Joyce. Writing to Lewis in 1953 about Hugh Kenner's contribution to the special issue of *Shenandoah* on Lewis, McLuhan notes: "*Shenandoah* has arrived and I hasten to withdraw what I said about Kenner seeing eye to eye with me. His Joyce enthusiasm has carried him a long way towards the time-cult. But apart from that there is the appalling manner of writing."[10] McLuhan obviously shared Lewis's critique of Joyce as the prime exemplar of the "time cult."[11] Lewis had attacked what he called the contemporary absorption with time in contradistinction from space, attributing the evolution of such a situation to the philosophy of Bergson and Einstein's theory of relativity. He argued that this preoccupation with time extended into all the arts, fine and popular, manifesting itself in Joyce, Charles Chaplin, the Russian ballet, popular writing such as *Gentlemen Prefer Blondes*, and the like. McLuhan partly justified his ambivalent attitude towards Joyce by sharing Lewis's distrust of the "time philosophers" and their modernist enthusiasts. The twenty-page satiric response that Joyce made in the *Wake* to Lewis's charges is one segment of the *Wake* that McLuhan hardly ever cites, presumably because of his sympathy with Lewis's side of this debate.

Another major portion of the *Wake* that McLuhan hardly ever cites is the entire fourth book ("The Coming of Dawn"), already discussed in relation to the debate between St Patrick and the Archdruid, (the only other substantial omission from McLuhan's citations being the inquisition of the sleeping Yawn by the four annalists (III.3)). It is in this final book of the *Wake* that Joyce highlights his treatment of the nature of colour, light, and motion, climaxing with that section that he argued was the condemnation and defence of his work – the debate between the hermetic, philosophical Archdruid and St Patrick. This portion of the conclusion of the *Wake*, one of the first passages that Joyce began drafting in 1923, is permeated by technology, particularly technologies of cultural production, reproduction, and dissemination.[12]

This debate about light, with its implications for space, time, and perception, occurs in and is about a book whose writer, Joyce, "one ups" Duchamp by turning his claim to be a great engineer into his own assertion to Harriet Shaw Weaver that he, Joyce, was "the greatest engineer," a claim that McLuhan notes as being of major significance.[13] Yet McLuhan was also ambivalent about engineers and engineering for in respective letters to the French neo-scholastic philosopher Jacques Maritain and to the editor of the *Catholic World*, Richard Leuver, he comments that "the Prince of this World ... is a great P.R. man, a great salesman of new hardware, a great electric engineer and a great master of media"[14]

Even earlier than the remarks he made about the electric light bulb, McLuhan had used the new theories of light, space, and motion in relation to his analysis of TV as resulting from light moving through the screen rather than light being projected on the screen, for he asserts that the viewer, "is bombarded with light impulses that James Joyce called the 'Charge of the Light Brigade'" (McLuhan 1964, 313). (It is important to note that the actual text in the *Wake* says that the images formed by the electronic processes – not actually light impulses – that appear on "the bairdborad bombardment screen" (i.e., the tube of the TV, since John Logie Baird was its inventor) tend "to teleframe [a metenergic reglow of beaming Batt] and step up to the charge of a light barricade." (FW 349.7–10), for Joyce speaks more complexly and ambivalently about the electrons bombarding the screen, while the screen simultaneously acts as a barricade to trap them. McLuhan continues in the same sentence to further misquote Joyce, although not necessarily misapplying him, to suggest that Joyce says that the "Charge of the Light Brigade" (i.e., Joyce's "barricade") imbues the viewers "soulskin with sobconscious inklings" (McLuhan 1964, 313). This last phrase does not actually appear in the above-quoted passage about TV but twenty-seven pages later in the *Wake*, where Joyce actually speaks of a character's imaginary, or virtual, dream vision (not necessarily a TV image) of himself as a young son: "but he'll Shonny Bhoy be, the fleshlumpfleeter ... and all he bares sobsconscious inklings shadowed on soulskin" (FW 377.28). In this phrase Joyce includes all "imaginary visions" or virtual images, not necessarily applying the phrase as McLuhan does only to those images that occur in a TV set by a "charge of the light brigade" and further implies that those virtual visions are affective or emotional (i.e., "sobs"), subconscious hints or clues or possibly "vague notions" and possibly, through a pun ("inklings"), a kind of writing.[15]

McLuhan applies Joyce's phrase to a specific case of an "artificial reality" (TV), but not necessarily an exclusive one. This concern with artificial reality is the foundation of McLuhan's continuation of his discussion of TV in which he argues that the history of electric media as the road to TV culminated by re-establishing the world of "tactile synaesthesia" – the interplay of the senses – that Gutenberg technology had interrupted (McLuhan 1964, 17). Given this, it should hardly be surprising that McLuhan's works, side by side with Gibson's science fiction, were avidly read by early researchers in MIT's Media Lab (Brand 1987, 5, 224). These researchers were also dreaming of creating an artificial reality composed, like the tribal and collective "global village," of tactile, haptic, proprioceptive and acoustic spaces and involvement[s].

McLuhan's tetrad on the electric light presents a way of understanding the similarities and differences between his perception and Joyce's. In his explanatory marginalia associated with the enhancement aspect of this tetrad, McLuhan mischievously quips: "Without Edison we'd be watching TV by candlelight."[16] By 1980 such a statement was an absurd and comic hyperbole. As the tetrad suggests, electric light "enhances space as visual figure and turns it into ground," while it obscolesces "the non-visual" – to which McLuhan appends the marginalia, "limitation by night and day" (McLuhan and McLuhan 1988, 194). The electric light retrieves those nighttime activities that had normally been limited to daytime (e.g., night baseball), while reversing "blinding," thus displacing the seer, such as Homer or Milton, and becoming the intensely focused beam of light of the specialist. In *Understanding Media* McLuhan stresses the unique role of the electric light in being "pure information" and thus "a medium without a message" (McLuhan 1964, 8). Yet, paradoxically, since "light is information without content," it can also be said of light that it is clearly a domain where "the medium is the message, for "when the light is on there is a world of sense that disappears when the light is off" (McLuhan 1964, 129) .

Once again McLuhan links his discussion to contemporary artists, especially Kepes and André Girard, although it might better have been linked to Moholy-Nagy's seminal work on light rather than the relatively more minor figure, Girard. Moholy-Nagy, in *Vision in Motion* – one of the books, along with those of Kepes and Giedion, that had assisted McLuhan in developing his interests in phenomena such as light and motion – directly relates Joyce's writing to the world of electro-mechanization, film, and light. Moholy-Nagy's very extensive experiments in light and with photograms preceded those of Girard, but McLuhan had reservations about Moholy-Nagy, whom he considered an "irrationalist." He further charges that Moholy-Nagy, the constructivist, (like Marinetti, the futurist) "has been beguiled by a misunderstanding of the origins and causes of the profane configuration of life ... as of the 'sacral configuration' on the other." On the contrary McLuhan asserts, "it is possible that even admitting the merely mechanical operation of technology in 'sacralizing' and 'desacralizing' human life, that the entire group of irrationalists in our century would still elect the 'sacral' or auditory mode of organization of experience" because it is "the emergent mode of the electro-magnetic or electronic" (McLuhan 1962, 67). If he really believes this, then he must also admit this to be a problem with "the greatest engineer," Joyce, who speaks of the "god of all machineries" and who is involved in the sacralization of the profane. So Joyce also would join the "irrationalists" – a position quite consistent with McLuhan's theory about *Ulysses*, the *Wake* and the Black Mass.

While Joyce might agree with McLuhan's stress in some of the earlier citations and with his views on tactility, Joyce's treatment of light and its relation to sound is more complexly and ambivalently associated with the new emerging culture of communication technology that will evolve into cyberculture. In many ways Joyce's treatment would strengthen the genuine power of McLuhan's case, since it stresses the synaesthetic and "the orchestration of the senses" (the coenaesthetic), for Joyce's dreamworld is a world permeated by light and color as well as sound: "Goalball I've struck this daylit dielate night of nights, by golly!" (FW83.27) Light intertwined with sound and words delineates the path by which to work through to the coming forth by daylight, as exemplified in such passages as: "(Oiboe! Hitherzither! Almost dotty! I must dash !) to pour their peace in partial (floflo floreflorence), sweetishsad lightandgayle, twittwintwosingwoolow. Let everie sound of a pitch keep still in resonance, ... now full theorbe, now dulcifair, and when we press of pedal (sof!) pick out and vowelise your name" (FW359.36-360.6). Such passages intertwine light and sound with a medley of musical instruments (oboes, zithers, dulcimers, large lutes (i.e., theorbo, pianos), vocalisations, the telegraph, and Morse code, McLuhan's resonant interval, and allusions and relations of the resonant interval to sounds responding to different vowels with hints of the florescence and the "lightinggayle" nature of light organs, (a device for projecting colours in patterns just as a normal organ plays notes). Joyce's writing here responds to the world of modernist and radical modernist art subsequent to 1850, insisting on an increasing inter-relationship between light, sound, and communication. It also relates the resonant interval, which McLuhan associates with the acoustic, to the optical and visual. Joyce regards the complex of intersensory experience as grounded in the very nature of people's experience of their world: "the sound sense sympol in a weedwayedwold of the firethere the sun in his halo cast. Onmen" (FW 612.28-30). But in so doing Joyce establishes a secularly sacralized "chaosmos" in contradistinction to McLuhan's hyper-rational, neo-Thomistic theology.

Speaking of these passages might seem far from the problem of McLuhan and of mcluhanisms, but when they are reinserted into the context of McLuhan as the prophet of cyberspace and virtual reality, they are crucial for understanding in depth how McLuhan's insight and intelligence was actually a focus for a wide transmission of the implications of modernist art and literature. But they are also important to understanding how aspects of Joyce's thought, while given credit, are somewhat intentionally blunted in his transmission. To return momentarily to the debate of the Archdruid and the Saint, it should be apparent that it is is relevant to McLuhan's project, for it includes many key motifs (often ones related to Joyce and his contemporaries) that McLuhan raises throughout his writings, from *Explorations* (1953–7) and *The Gutenberg Galaxy* (1962) to *The Laws of Media* (post- 1980). This debate centres around playful allusions to (among others) Newton, Einstein, space, time, relativity physics, quantum mechanics, the complementarity principle, Helmholtz's optics, theories of color, the visual, and auditory imagination (i.e., visual and acoustic space), tactility, and communication. Joyce's conclusion even includes an exploration of the effects of the spectrum in relation to the impact of colours on the three sets of receptors (green, blue, and red) in the eye. This debate in the *Wake* is presented with allusions that situate it as an event being covered by audio-visual media, including both news and film coverage oriented toward entertaining the audience with the equivalent of a sporting event. So before it even begins it is situated in a medley of motifs associated with communication, media, and popular culture: conversation with its gossip and rumour; the televising or filming of a spectacle – "Shoot!" (FW 610.33); "Rhythm and Color at Park Mooting. Peredos Last in the Grand Natural. Velivision victor" (FW 610.34-5); journalism and theatrics – "Dubs newstage oldtime turftussle" (FW 610.35-6); animated comics blended with Caesar's "Veni, vidi, vici!" and an allusion to the Widger family associated with racing – "Winny Willy Widger" (FW610.36).

Joyce plays with the very same patterns that permeate McLuhan's various works from the 1950s until his death. While McLuhan, as he himself insists, appears to have borrowed extensively from Joyce and to have attributed to Joyce some sort of authoritative stature, McLuhan's treatment of the material, unlike Joyce's, is not embedded in a complex or ambivalent chaosmos. The concept of chaos as such in McLuhan's early work is almost always associated with his interpretation in *The Gutenberg Galaxy* of Pope's prophecy of the triumph of chaos's reign in *The Dunciad Variorum* (1742), a triumph which he attributes to association with the triumph of sensory and perceptual fragmentation and mass consciousness as a result of print culture.[17] Joyce's "chaosmos," on the other hand, is associated with quantum theory, the uncertainty principle, Gödel's theorem and what has become in the second half of the century, chaos, and complexity theory.[18] Nevertheless McLuhan's playing with Joycean and other modernist treatments of percepts and affects is partly why he is able to occupy a key position in and make a significant poetic contribution as a sophisticated populist poet to cyberculture. Yet his radically conservative orientation shuts out the possibility of his accepting the relevance of chaos and complexification to radical modernism and its aftermath, modernity's wake, although he develops many of his major insights through Joyce, modernist visual and audio-visual arts, and aspects of French symbolism.

In the second issue of *Explorations* an article on *Finnegans Wake* suggested that: "Throughout the *Wake* run thematic references to Swift and Sterne as extreme representatives of the timeless neoclassical synthesis achieved by Jonson and Pope. What Pope did in *The Dunciad* was to combine 'the stem poise for a swift pounce', working on the principle that 'samething rivisible in nightim, may be involted into the zeroic couplet.' Pope's *Essay on Man*, for example, is an attempt to provide a comic portrait of man's mind in act – a dynamic map in which the contours are changing and shifting from a series of fixed points. Joyce's interest, like Pope's, is in providing dynamic models for the changes taking place within the sensibility of man in the contemporary world" (Theall 1954, 68).

In other words, if Joyce's approach is to be followed, Pope and Joyce are looking at the "chaosmos" and constructing "map[s] of the soul's groupography" from opposite moments of a historical span; yet if Pope's couplet is "zeroic" and his vision "involted," he is playing with a world of orderly chaos – Wimsatt's world of hateful contraries (Wimsatt 1965). But if, as McLuhan argued in *The Gutenberg Galaxy*, Pope's *Dunciad* foresees a world confronted by the Newtonian and Cartesian worldview, a world where literacy assumes a monarchical primacy as descending into Chaos, Night, and darkness, Joyce's *Wake,* "coming forth by day," foresees the post-Cartesian realization that, as the chaos comes to be realized as a "chaosmos," the night becomes a "daylit dielate" moving towards the awakening into day – for one of Joyce's favorite phrase was 'Wait till Finnegan Wakes!'

That such a conception of a "chaosmos" was foundational in modernist art is confirmed by such works as M.C. Escher's 1950 lithograph, "Order and Chaos" and further confirmed by Deleuze and Guattari's discussion of modern artists and writers in relation to chaos and Klee's *Twittering Machine* (1980, 310–12). In *The Vanishing Point* McLuhan and Parker present a probe structured around a juxtaposition of Klee's *The Twittering Machine* and e.e.cummings's poem "Chanson Innocent" ("An alphabetic ballet of words in rite order – a dramatic order of language as jester," McLuhan and Parker 1968, 187). McLuhan quips that Klee's painting is a "preview of the TV aerial" – "an electric configuration patterned to pick up non-visual energy" (ibid.) So Klee's work demonstrates that abstract art signals the end of visual space and *The Twittering Machine* becomes "a type" of *sensus communis*. McLuhan's awareness that the Einsteinian speed of the electric age, which generates acoustic space and, in so doing retrieves "the non-measurable void/ the resonant interval," seems also to imply that a work such as *The Twittering Machine* is an interplay of order and chaos, which is precisely what Deleuze and Guattari's in a section of *A Thousand Plateaus* ("On the Refrain" (*ritournelle*) discussion of "The Twittering Machine") confirm when they suggest: "Sometimes chaos is an immense black hole in which one endeavors to fix a fragile point as a center. Sometimes one organizes around that point a calm and stable "pace" (rather than form): the black hole has become a home. Sometimes one grafts onto that pace a breakaway from the black hole. Paul Klee presented these three aspects and their interlinkage in a most profound way. He calls the black hole a 'gray point' for pictorial reasons" (Deleuze and Guarttari 1980, 312).[19]

That McLuhan clearly recognized the affiliation of an interest in Klee and an interest in Joyce is clear from his having reviewed Carola Giedion-Welcker's *Paul Klee* in 1953 and in his having corresponded in the 1950s with this close friend of Joyce's. He also associates Cummings's writing with modernism in *The Gutenberg Galaxy*, where bringing together work of Cummings, Gertrude Stein, Pound, Eliot, and Joyce he suggests that writing such as Stein's "with its lack of punctuation and other visual aids, is a carefully devised strategy to get the passive visual reader into participant, oral action ... *Vers libre* is for the ear as much as for the eye" (McLuhan 1962, 83). In *Understanding Media* he makes Cummings central to his discussion of the typewriter as medium – "The poet at the typewriter can do Nijinsky leaps or Chaplinlike shuffles and wiggles," (McLuhan 1964, 260–1), while in concluding the discussion in the *Galaxy* he notes that in the *Wake* Joyce sets up ten thunder words (each of which occurs at a different place in the first two-thirds of the *Wake*), exactly like an ancient manuscript.

The failure of so much commentary on McLuhan, pro and con, hot or cold – both "the heat and the light" – has been the avoidance of a genuine confrontation with both his contemporary literary, artistic aspects and with his historical interest in literature and the arts in relation to education in language, the avoidance of which he lamented in his correspondence. Nowhere is the failure of commentary clearer than in the misunderstandings that attribute a more major and central significance of the work of Innis to the foundation of his project than that of Joyce and the modernists which, as we have seen, he continually stresses. It is abundantly clear that the basic sources for McLuhan's history of communication, culture and technology – of artefacts as media – are Joyce, Vico, Bacon, and the history of the arts of language and of the learning of these arts (the history of the trivium). Among these influences as his work continually reiterates and as his posthumous *Laws of Media* confirm, the primary source was Joyce and particularly Joyce's *Wake*, which first led him along with many students in the English speaking world into their initial encounters with *The New Science* of Giambattista Vico. The very dominance of this work in *The Laws of Media* confirms its importance, which is well attested elsewhere by McLuhan.

He became most fascinated by Joyce in the late 1940s during his association with Hugh Kenner. When I met him in the early 1950s his interest in the *Wake* was increasing at the very time when the new contemporary interests in communication impacted upon him most forcefully – the cybernetic and the anthropological. The *Wake* provided a particularly interesting focus for bringing together in focus all of McLuhan's interests – contemporary literature and art; the history of the trivium; his fascination with medieval universalism; his recent work in mass media and popular culture; and his love of playing with language. But it went further than that, for Joyce had hinted that he was writing a history of the world and his history of the world was the history of a "masterbuilder" – a history in which for McLuhan, rightly or wrongly, language and technology coalesced. Joyce provided for him the keys for poeticizing the insights of Giedion, Lewis Mumford and Buckminster Fuller. By the time the works of Innis became central to his project, he was able to read Innis critically through the work of Joyce, through Vico, and through the critiques of Lewis. The perspective from which he was utilizing, critiquing, and supplementing Innis's work has not usually been understood owing to the lack of awareness of the complex historical, artistic, literary, and philosophical ground in which McLuhan's perceptions were rooted and of how he worked as poet and grammarian with percepts and affects, as he himself insisted, rather than as a theorist with concepts. Yet by becoming a pre-post-modern, intellectual, journalistic poet, he was to encourage various sets of mcluhanite advocates, who were not prepared for the depth and complexity of his insights, nor able to appreciate his perverse genius, to critique his problems, or to practice his historically and humane rhetoric-grammatical probing.

11 McLuhan as Modern Satirist

It was great fun listening to Marshall expound on Al Capp's *Li'l Abner* and on *Pogo*, two strips he loved, apparently because they were basically satiric. He would come in, stretch out on our couch, and pontificate about the vagaries and vitalities of Al Capp and others. Usually he would stay for lunch. Marshall started to tease my wife, Joan, a tall, black Irish beauty who liked to go barefoot at home, by calling her Moonbeam McSwine – the curvacious barefoot anti-heroine who always tempted Li'l Abner away from Daisy May. Joan, having been educated for four years by Ursuline nuns in a small girls college in the U. S., was a bit ambiguous in her response, finally settling for a laugh. On another occasion Marshall told her she was one of his muses. Since she understood the role of the goddess to inspire poetry and drama, she was enchanted with the idea and flattered because she so admired Marshall.

Marshall has been criticized for his fascination with such comics, since Capp is now assessed as reactionary and Walt Kelly as an old liberal; but it must be remembered that for the immediate post–World War Two reader they represented a type of social critique. "Capp is the only robust satirical force in American life," McLuhan declared in 1951, further suggesting that "You like Capp? Then you'll like *Finnegans Wake*" (McLuhan 1951, 62–3). In what might be an intimation of the McLuhan to come – the non-moralistic, post-*Bride* McLuhan whom Wolfe praises, McLuhan in *The Bride* notes that: "Capp looks at the disordered world around him not as a social reformer who imagines that much good would result from a few changes in external features of business and political administration; he sees these situations refracted through the deeply willed deceptions every person practices upon himself. The criticism which is embedded in his highly parabolic entertainment, therefore, has a complexity which is the mark of wisdom. He moves in a world of many dimensions, each of which includes and reflects upon the other" (McLuhan 1951, 64). But, prior to anything else, reading the comics, particularly *Li'l Abner*, with McLuhan was both fun and intellectual play. The latter quality arose from McLuhan's view of the strip as parabolic, multi-dimensional, and complex.

Marshall's wit permeated *The Mechanical Bride*, the publication of which in 1951 marked a critical turning point in his intellectual direction. Although not visibly affected by the relatively disappointing reception of the *Bride*, in the early 1950s Marshall developed two new directions in his intellectual life that both broadened his approach and transformed its foundations. The first of these directions, discussed earlier, was the broadening of his grammatical-rhetorical interest in popular culture in the *Bride* to an interest in communication, culture, and media as technology. His increasing interest in these areas was particularly facilitated by his meeting with Ted Carpenter, which was the beginning of a life-long friendship. Carpenter's anthropological interests, stemming from Sapir, Boas, Whorf, and others, were in art, language, and the then-current culture and personality school. The ground for recognizing the importance of communication and technology had been prepared by McLuhan's rapid recognition of the significance that Shannon and Weaver's work and Wiener's cybernetics would have on the intellectual world and the necessity of criticizing that approach from the perspective of traditional grammatico-rhetorical theories of communication.

The second, and equally fundamental, direction was towards a new mode of analysis and interpretation. By his own claim, McLuhan was a satirist – and if not in the *Bride*, in all his subsequent writings, a very particular type of satirist. His approach rests on Wyndham Lewis's theoretical orientation towards art, laughter, satire, and modernism. It was Lewis's writings that partly shaped McLuhan's interest in mass and mechanized culture and in the 1950s shifted his satiric form from the liberal moralistic stance of the *Bride* to the mask of the disinterested observer in *Explorations*, his major books, and his *essais concrètes* (*The Medium Is the Massage* and *War and Peace in the Global Village*). In *Men Without Art*, Lewis, revising an earlier pamphlet of his, "Satire and Fiction," had announced that all great art is satire and that the greatest satire is non-moral (Lewis 1934). After the publication of the *Bride* in 1951, McLuhan obviously embraced completely Lewis's idea that great art must be satire and that the greatest satire is not moral, by which he meant that the satirist does not *overtly* reveal his attitude towards the target of the satire.

McLuhan's interest in the comics as disinterested satire obviously predisposed him to adopt Lewis's position, especially after the *Bride*, a witty but rather critical and moralistic satire, had not received the acclaim McLuhan anticipated. McLuhan's satiric approach developed more fully after embracing Lewis's conception. Thus Lewis, from whom McLuhan apparently obtained the concept of the "global village," also provided him with more fundamental stylistic, structural, and philosophic components for his work.

In the first half of the 1950s, during our close association, Marshall was intensively studying, reading, and discussing Lewis's writings (as well as those of Pound and Joyce). The image from Edgar Allen Poe's *The Descent into the Maelstrom* – the quiet eye at the center of the whirlpool – which McLuhan used to delineate his activity as the *Bride*'s author even then reflected Lewis's conception of the role of the vorticist artist as a still point in a turning world. Just like Lewis in *Blast*, McLuhan was always fascinated by this image of the vortex. This can be seen in many passages in his writing, such as the one with which he concludes *The Medium Is the Massage,* where he notes that Poe's vortical image, through which the mariner saved himself by "understanding the action of the whirlpool," illustrates the stance that his contemporaries must adapt as "a possible stratagem for understanding our predicament, our electrically-configured whirl" (McLuhan and Fiore 1967, 150).

The term vortex comes to McLuhan from Lewis and Pound, who used it as the title of their artistic movement in the second decade of this century. Vorticism had to do with nodes of energy concentrated about images. Lewis's avant-garde, folio-sized magazine *Blast* provided the manifestos and an outlet for vorticist work. *Blast* presented declarations about the Vorticist movement not merely in the texts it included but in its style of headline and advertisement. The very nature of print (i.e., newsprint) became part of the artistic effect of Lewis's manifestos, which announced the vorticist view of the artist as enemy and the function of the arts as satire. The very name of his early journal – *Blast* – indicates that Lewis saw satire as cold, clear, and aggressive – a bombarding of the target – related not to mirth but to an intense and even painful sense of the absurd (Powe 1984, 115–16). This is directly related to his vorticist orientation with its cold and unromantic attitude toward the machine: "In a VORTICIST UNIVERSE we don't get excited at what we have invented./ We hunt machines. They are our favorite game / We invent them and then we hunt them down./ This is a great Vorticist age, a great still age of artists" (Lewis 1914, 48).[2] The techniques used in *Blast* were seen as weapons or, in McLuhanesque terms, a counter-environment, to be used to make the audience aware of the environment. Lewis defined the new type of artist-critic that he exemplified as an intellectualist-moralist. The intellectualist-moralist, unlike the moralists and politicians Lewis condemns, adopts the stance of disinterested observer.

When one reflects on it a moment, the phrase "intellectualist-moralist" could equally well describe McLuhan's marriage of Nietzsche and Catholicism, which provides a fascinating index to modern technoculture with its apparent social anarchy due to multicultural standards of behaviour while the multinational economy is hierarchically controlled. Both poles have contributed to the heated criticism McLuhan generates in a context where the intellectual is condemned as elitist and the Church as paternalistic. While Lewis's conception of the intellectualist-moralist is that of the artist as satirist and as society's early warning system, using anarchistic laughter to probe his world, McLuhan adopts this idea to a poetic conception of the satirical essay, which he apparently had begun exploring in *The Mechanical Bride*. As he developed this genre (culminating in the *essais concrètes*), he also adapted Lewis's particular brand of cynical satire, which was a direct function of his vorticist stance.

McLuhan recognized that an artist-satirist, like Lewis or Joyce, had to adopt the role of the poet as engineer, although McLuhan is closer to Lewis, who articulated one of the strongest defences of what was to become McLuhan's concern with satire, laughter, and the comic. "The root of the Comic is to be sought in the sensations resulting from the observations of a *thing* behaving like a person," Lewis declares in "The Meaning of the Wild Body" (Lewis 1927B, 158). He recognizes that this means all people are comic, since they are all *things* or physical bodies behaving as persons. Laughter arises from people relieving their emotions after contemplating themselves as mechanical puppets. (McLuhan's later interest in robotism is another way of articulating Lewis's "mechanical puppets" and contributed to his way of understanding technologies as "extensions of man" and, of course, woman, since "the mechanical bride" was feminine (McLuhan and Powers 1989, 66–7). Lewis catalogues the attributes of such laughter in the essay on 'Inferior Religions' in *The Wild Body*:

1. Laughter is the Wild Body's song of triumph.
2. Laughter is the climax in the tragedy of seeing, hearing and smelling self-consciously.
3. Laughter is the bark of delight of a gregarious animal at the proximity of its kind.

4. Laughter is an independent, tremendously important , and lurid emotion.
5. Laughter is the representative of tragedy, when tragedy is away.
6. Laughter is the emotion of tragic delight.
7. Laughter is the female of tragedy.
8. Laughter is the strong elastic fish caught in Styx, springing and flapping about until it dies.
9. Laughter is the sudden handshake of mystic violence and the anarchist.
10. Laughter is the mind sneezing.
11. Laughter is the one obvious commotion that is not complex, or in expression dynamic.
12. Laughter does not progress. It is primitive, hard and unchangeable.

(Lewis 1927B, 158)

Lewis links laughter here with aggression, passion, and anarchy, and with machine-like assemblages and the act of recognition of those assemblages. This is directly linked to the remarks previously cited from *Blast* 1 concerning the vorticist's hunting down machines. McLuhan easily associated the extensions of the machine into electric technology through paintings such as Paul Klee's *The Twittering Machine*, about which he notes in haikku-like style:

"Preview of the TV aerial, electric configuration
patterned to pick up non-visual energy."

– (McLuhan and Parker 1968, 189).

Generations accustomed to the cinema and to the composition of the television image find this a natural mode for thinking about the arts in a world where mechanization has taken command and where its effects have been exponentially multiplied through electricity. McLuhan insightfully transferred Lewis's treatment of the machine to technology in general and to artefacts as *techné*, certainly within the purview of Lewis's original association of machines and bureaucracy.

Some McLuhanites resist associating McLuhan with a primary commitment to the poetic, but much of the apparent obscurity in his work is illuminated by the degree to which he situated his work in an ambivalent poetic context. My intent here is to define the strengths and weaknesses of McLuhan's unique role and to clarify his own claims that his work is that of a satirist-artist and that only those readers immersed in French *symbolisme*, its English aftermath, James Joyce, and Wyndham Lewis can clearly understand his work. The strongest and most direct claim is made in a letter to Michael Hornyansky, a Canadian writer and English professor, in which he declares that "Most of my writing is Menippean satire, presenting the actual surface of the world we live in as a ludicrous image."³ McLuhan reiterates this again in the late 1970s in an interview by an old friend, Louis Forsdale, where he further suggested that he had once again become interested in the critical study of Menippean satire and was working on its history, primarily to assist his son, Eric, whom he had encouraged to write a thesis on Laurence Sterne's *Tristram Shandy* as Menippean satire (McLuhan 1978).

While initially an analysis of McLuhan's view of himself as satirist, particularly as some kind of Menippean satirist, and the relation of this to the foundations of his work having literary roots may seem somewhat technical and esoteric, it will actually deepen our understanding of the man and his work. It is particularly significant to note that this type of satire has undergone further transformations in film and multimedia, especially in relation to computer poetry and art.

Menippean satire had become a "hot" topic among literary theorists in the 1970s and remained so into the 1980s, fuelled by the French and English translations of Mikhail Bakhtin's writings on *The Poetics of Dostoevsky* (1965), and Julia Kristeva's "Word, Dialogue and Novel" (1979, originally published in Σημειωτιχή in 1969). To the best of my personal knowledge McLuhan's first major interest in Menippean satire dates much further back to the early 1950s during a period in which he was my mentor and I was collaborating with him, although he had already been pre-disposed to such an interest by his study of Thomas Nashe, in which he had come to realize the importance of Lucian in both the tradition of transmitting patristic eloquence and as an influence on the satires of major Renaissance writers such as Rabelais, Erasmus, More, and Nashe (McLuhan 1943). It is significant that in the Forsdale interview McLuhan suggested that *he has renewed* his interest in Menippean satire, confirming his early awareness of this genre as having a particular significance for him.

A short digression is necessary to explain this genre (a full examination of its complex history would require a much lengthier discussion). There were various major strands of Menippean satire but for our current discussion it is necessary to mention only two: the first, represented by fragments of Varro's satires, Rabelais, Pope, or Joyce's *Finnegans Wake*, emerges from the world of carnival, in which the Irish wake participates; the second strand, as represented in Lucian's *Satires* rises from the philosophical tradition of the Cynics, Menippus being the name of a Cynic philosopher who is reputed to have first written such satires, as well as sbeing seen in satirists such as Wyndham Lewis.

The Varronian strain is marked by the sensuous, bodily humour of the carnival and the fair, a mode of revolution (though controlled revolution) against authority, a world of misrule. The Cynic strain, although incorporating many of the comic strategies of the more carnivalesque form, is more philosophic, more detached, and usually more bitter. Naturally, since all genres evolve through history, its contemporary transformations have their own unique characteristics. Either of these modes of learned satire are adaptable to the emerging twentieth-century technoculture, which has developed its own, somewhat perverse, form of an all-pervasive, media-produced world of carnival. Either of these satiric genres is complex enough to encompass the complexities of the emerging technoculture and it would be incorrect to limit their rhetorical and poetic richness to some simple formulae in which the Menippean or Varronian is defined as only cynical, hyperbolic, and non-moral.

Although to my knowledge McLuhan did not publicly claim that he was a Menippean satirist until the mid 1970s, as early as 1971, in *The Medium Is the Rear View Mirror*, I had alluded briefly to the likelihood that McLuhan had been influenced by the Menippean satirists: "as the title *War and Peace in the Global Village* betrays, [he] is trying to write academic epic. But the particular mixing of genre as he carries it out is not that of the Menippean satirists whom he loves and who excelled in this mode (though ironically enough *The Gutenberg Galaxy* refers again and again to those individuals – Rabelais, Erasmus, Pope, Swift, and Joyce). What their visions were that McLuhan's are not, are satiric visions of the intellectual world of their time. If McLuhan writes satire, he deliberately conceals it behind a facade for the purpose of making it commercially viable and he conceals it so well that few of his critics have accused him of writing it at all" (Theall 1971, 92). Earlier in the book I had noted that McLuhan in part "makes Joyce more accessible by translating from the Menippean satire of *Finnegans Wake* into [his] essay" (Ibid., 26). It would have been more accurate to suggest that he turned Joyce from the carnivalesque mode (often described as Varronian) into the more cynical satiric mode of Lewis, for one contemporary type of continuation of this mode of Menippean satire in the twentieth century is exemplified in Lewis's writing – both in his novels, *The Apes of God* and *The Human Age*, and in his satiric essays.

To explain the importance of these connections let me digress first to discuss my personal involvement with Marshall as a mentor. In 1951 Marshall and I began a series of discussions sparked off by my having to present a seminar paper on Pope's satire, emphasizing *The Dunciad*, for a graduate course in eighteenth-century literature. In my reading I had discovered that in the prose parts of *The Dunciad Variorum* Pope had situated his poem in a particular comic tradition of the epic, which he identified, somewhat wittily, as the Little Epic and which he associated with the learned satire of Varro, Lucian, the Middle Ages, and the Renaissance. In so doing, Pope alluded to John Dryden's late seventeenth-century "Discourse on the Origin and Progress of Satire" in which Dryden had discussed Varronian satire (a term used occasionally as an alternate to Menippean satire, and also sometimes used to indicate the more intensely and purely carnivalesque works in the genre). For Dryden and Pope (and for McLuhan) Varronian or Menippean satire had been produced by writers such as Lucian, Apuleius, Erasmus, Rabelais, Cervantes, and Burton (in his *Anatomy of Melancholy*). Subsequently, McLuhan held that Pope, Swift, Sterne, Lewis, and Joyce also exemplified the form.[4]

My reading led me to argue that the entirety of *The Dunciad* as it was published (not just the poetic text) constituted Pope's poem, and that that poem was embedded in an even broader program which involved a number of other works attributed to the Scriblerus Club (Theall 1961, 11–16). In the process of this research I became interested in the problems of epic and satire and in why Pope had made significant changes from his 1728 *Dunciad Variorum*, expanding it from three books to four in the 1742 *Dunciad Variorum*. Three significant strands of McLuhan's later thought either arose from or were revived and intensified by these apparently esoteric questions of literary history: his concern with and practice of Menippean satire; his interest in the little epic (or epyllion); and his concern with the role of Rosicrucianism, Masonry, and other occult groups in intellectual debates in the seventeenth and eighteenth centuries. While these concerns may seem rather academic and pedantic in the face of the pseudo-academic journalism that the aftermath of McLuhan's project has encouraged, claims in McLuhan's correspondence and/or conversations clearly suggest that these three areas at least were central and germane to his future discussions of media.

Besides, next to Lewis, Pope played a particularly important role in McLuhan's having developed a history of media and other artefacts. This was the case because Pope's satire was an important element in the published version of his work, which was both a satire about books and mechanization and the conscious program of a group of artists – the Scriblerus Club. That there was a particular interest in this satiric genre at Toronto in the mid-1950s is shown by the fact that one of the major international books of literary theory from Toronto in those years, *The Anatomy of Criticism* (1957), written by McLuhan's Toronto colleague Northrop Frye, not only discussed Menippean satire with respect to many of the same themes and individuals already mentioned but also, as noted earlier in a discussion of Derrida and McLuhan, emphasized its intellectuality and encyclopedism and even claimed that Burton's "anatomy" form was the greatest Menippean satire in English before Swift and associated it by implication with the title of Frye's own study of literary theory (Frye 1957, 309–12). The still broader significance to the literary historical world of *The Dunciad* as a learned satire is attested to by Aubrey Williams's mid-1950s study, which McLuhan singles out for particular praise in *The Gutenberg Galaxy* (Aubrey Williams 1955, passim).

The *Gutenberg Galaxy* demonstrates McLuhan's interest in this area of satire in two ways: first, the *Galaxy* itself, in the shadow of Frye's *Anatomy*, can be regarded as an anatomy of the phonetic alphabet and print culture; and, secondly, McLuhan uses Pope's *Dunciad* climactically in the conclusion of his book. Joyce's *Wake* is an awakening from the night world of Cartesianism, Romanticism, and mechanization. The dulling effect of his era as it came of age in the Enlightenment caused Pope to announce in *The Dunciad* the impending triumph of darkness and disorder in the rapidly emerging world of mechanization and mass culture:

In vain, in vain – the all-composing hour
Resistless falls: The Muse obeys the Pow'r.
She comes! she comes! the sable throne behold
Of *Night* primeval, and of *Chaos* old!

– *The Dunciad* IV. 627–30

The Dunciad was obviously the appropriate end-point, as *King Lear* had been the appropriate opening, for according to McLuhan the interplay and integration of the senses dramatized in *Lear* and endorsed by Pope is negated by those movements dissociating and specializing the senses, which will result in the coming of darkness prophesied in Pope's poem. Pope's satire on the new emerging mass culture and in particular the impact of mass publication and other accompanying effects of mechanization provided a specific signpost towards McLuhan's eventual discovery of the "road to *Finnegans Wake*" as the end, not of the book as such but of the "Gutenberg Galaxy" that had produced the print-dominated world.[5]

The importance for McLuhan's work of the neo-Augustan moment in the eighteenth century becomes clearer when it is linked to his detailed examination of the history of modes of communication in *The Galaxy*, the work that began his career as a major figure in the study of culture, communication, and technology . That history, like the supplementary politico-economic history of his colleague Harold Innis, involves more key historical moments than those concerning orality-literacy-postliteracy or speech, script, print, and the age of electricity.

Other key moments, such as the medieval culture of high scholasticism, which provides the image of medieval universalism that McLuhan yearns for, are of special relevance for him in momentarily reintegrating the tactile with the oral and written, as evidenced in rituals, disputation, oral reading of manuscripts, Gregorian chant, and the Gothic cathedral. The eighteenth century is another complex moment of transition in that history – the moment when the mechanization of print takes command and produces the beginnings of a mass culture. *The Dunciad*, which uses the carnivalesque mode and parody of ritual to prophesize the last phase of Gutenberg culture, stands on the brink of the next phase of the complete interiorization into the romanticism heralded in the subjective grotesque of Sterne's *Tristram Shandy*.[6] In writings contemporary with his coming of age, McLuhan can identify – and in fact, in T.S. Eliot's "dissociation of sensibility," probably discovered – the phenomenon he seems to argue that Pope and Swift were prophesizing and satirizing.

McLuhan adopts the mask of the detached observer as a way of dealing with the dissociation and fragmentation brought about as electrification comes of age: "I employ the greatest boon of literate culture; the power to act without reaction – the sort of specialization by dissociation that has been the driving force behind Western civilization" (McLuhan 1969B, 158). Civilized detachment becomes the obvious antidote to moral compunction. It is this same mask that is attributed by Mikhail Bakhtin, the theorist who has most extensively discussed the Menippean genre, to post-Sterne era writers influenced by the Menippean and the carnivalesque. Bakhtin's description of the mask fits well with McLuhan's satiric stance, derived as it was from Lewis and cultivated within the wake of romanticism, for the romantic strain of the carnivalesque that Bakhtin identified as being launched by Sterne is the mode in which laughter is reduced "to cold humour, irony, sarcasm" as it ceases "to be joyful and triumphant hilarity" (Bakhtin 1965, 38–9). This could easily be used to distinguish Joyce, with his joy and hilarity, from Lewis and McLuhan, whose laughter is more problematic and ambivalent. Bakhtin's observations about Sterne, in fact, readily relate to Lewis's puppets or McLuhan's robots for "in romanticism the accent is placed on the puppet as the victim of alien inhuman force, which rules over men by turning them into marionettes ... only in Romanticism do we find a peculiar grotesque theme of the tragic doll." And it is the Romantic grotesque form of the Menippean carnivalesque mask that "is torn away from oneness of the folk carnival concept. It ... acquires other meanings alien to its primitive nature; now the mask hides something, keeps a secret deceives ... A terrible vacuum, a nothingness lurks behind it" (Bakhtin 1965, 40).

This certainly describes the world of Wyndham Lewis, the enemy and tyro, blasting and bombardiering his contemporary targets. The master puppeteer of *The Wild Body* manipulating his marionettes and mechanical dolls in *The Apes of God* and *The Human Age* clearly reveals the epitome of this carnivalesque and grotesque satire whose ultimate site becomes the ambivalent Hell of the Magnetic city (Lewis 1928, 1955) or the vacuous drawing rooms and ball rooms of Bloomsbury – a satire which focuses on a supposedly vacuous flux in the new time world of increasing electro-mechanization. It also describes McLuhan in his writings as a Menippean essayist with his mask of the detached observer and his deliberate ambivalence and obscurity behind which "hides something." To encompass his complex analysis of contemporary technoculture McLuhan, like Lewis, developed a contemporary transformation of the cynical tradition of Menippean satire in order to expose the follies of a world that was abandoning the solidity of space for the abstractness of space-time, while embracing the speed and motion of the electrocosmos and undermining the fundamental foundation of traditional theology and philosophy.

The puppet world that McLuhan shares with Lewis permeates his work, since it is implicit in the cyborgian notion of technologies as extensions of the human person. It shows up in his final posthumous work in the concept of robotism, which he counterpoises against the concept of angelism. This also relates to his interest in the gnostic aspect of Pope's satiric program, which culminated in *The Dunciad*, as well as in Lewis. McLuhan was well aware of the parallels between Pope and Lewis. In 1952, with his encouragement I wrote a paper developing an elaborate parallel between Lewis's *Apes of God* and *The Dunciad*. This structural relationship can readily be established through Lewis's extensive allusions to Pope in the *Apes* and by the fact that Lewis in his *Apes*, like Pope in *The Dunciad Variorum* (1742), uses a parodic version of the Eleusinian mysteries for the structural organization of his book.[7] But it goes further since Lewis's satire of what he calls in the *Apes* the free-masonry of the arts (i.e., the Bloomsbury insiders, such as the Sitwells and Woolfs, controlling taste and the fashionable fascination with such hermetic occultists as Aleister Crowley) parallels Pope's taking advantage of the recent condemnation of Freemasonry by the Roman Church (1738) to satirize the esoteric and occult control of culture by the booksellers, the publishers, the clergy, and academia as duncical apes of humanistic culture. McLuhan, at least in the 1950s and well beyond, tended to take Pope and Lewis's use of a gnostic association with the mysteries (and through the overtones in their treatment, of secret rites) more literally – not necessarily as always suggesting some sort of conspiracy of secret societies but at

least as a critique of the importance of the implicit gnosticism in mainline social and political life, which he discusses in *The Global Village*
as angelism.

McLuhan's ambivalent play with terms like angelism and robotism
to re-visit the problem of gnosticism is characteristic of his particular
cynical, Menippean style. The term robotism, with (in McLuhan's way
of using it) its paradoxical, perhaps oxymoronic, qualities was both a
technique for shock, perhaps even hyperbole, and for developing a particular mode of restrained witty laughter. Angelism is rigid; robotism is
flexible. But note also the description of robotism as being the Oriental living dead of Suzuki's Zen. Dissociating robotism from meaning
the "mechanically rigid behavior" that Karel Čapek coined for his play
R.U.R, (which, incidentally, was first produced in 1923 not 1938 as
The Global Village suggests), it is asserted that "robotism means the
supression of the conscious 'observer-self' or conscience, so as to
remove all fear and circumspection, all encumbrances to ideal performance" (McLuhan 1989, 67). To be fully understood such statements,
admittedly paradoxical, need to be situated within McLuhan's explanation of the cultural difference between a Canadian and an American,
for "The calculated ambivalence of the Canadian is a most efficient
way of maintaining a low profile as a receptive ground for other
people's fantasies" (McLuhan 1989, 149). This explanation then
becomes a key to his project and how he related to the various major
figures that he himself specified to be of major importance to his work.

As a "new critic" in the 1940s, McLuhan developed his esthetic of
irony, ambiguity, ambivalence, and tradition within the critical movement explicating modern poetry that included such works as William
Empson's *Seven Types of Ambiguity*, Cleanth Brooks *Modern Poetry
and the Tradition*, and William K. Wimsatt, Jr.'s *Hateful Contraries*.
His practice of ambivalence, originally developed within that movement, permeates his writing subsequent to *The Mechanical Bride*.
Early playful oppositions such as "hot" and "cool" clearly manifest
that ambivalence, just as angelism and robotism do. There is a deeper
aspect to this kind of ambivalence as it tends toward ambiguity, since
it is a way of suggesting an uncertainty about every position – or,
rather, it enables the writer to set forth both sides of an argument,
adopting neither and often implying yet a third or fourth, which themselves may remain ambiguous in value. Such is the real depth behind
the problem of McLuhan's terms orality and literacy, tactility itself,
and finally, the syncretistic integration of synaesthesia, coenaesthesia,
and the extension of the nervous system. McLuhan does not, for
example, unequivocally favour right-brain activity over left, although
he clearly sees the limitations of left-brain activity unchecked by the

operation of the right-brain. But what is "third" for his right and left brain is clearly his conception of a *sensus communis*, since such a sense would have to encompass both spheres and would then be extended cyborgically through technologies. With such an approach McLuhan, as has been argued earlier, is setting forth an exploration of percepts and affects – the province of the poet, in McLuhan's case of the Menippean poet-essayist, who is cynically presenting the abyss or vacuum – to which McLuhan's solution is not escape into tradition or flight into fantasized futures but living through the present in the faith that transcends understanding and the guiding light of history and tradition. Clearly such a position enables him to be a provider of insights to all brands of McLuhanism, to be a seer, like other poets, and yet to be a symptom of the essential cynicism of life in a cyberfied society in which it is only too easy to feel dominated by the "alien inhuman force, which rules over men by turning them into marionettes." McLuhan quite appropriately suggests he will never be a McLuhanite, because all McLuhanisms as they interpret him or apply him must, because of his technique and his intellectual position, simultaneously misunderstand him.

McLuhan learned from Lewis, particularly from *The Childermass*, the art of utilizing some of Joyce's complexity by playing with Joyce and, as one poet stealing from another, he converted that complexity to his own project. This occurred in at least four ways: first, in "jocying" phrases while developing his own headline-like, aphoristic formulae by taking any verbal fomulae and converting it into phrases such as the famous medium is the message and its various tranformations; second, in taking Joycean and other poetic phrases and weaving them into the fabric of his work by playing their context off against his; third, in utilizing Joyce's own structures but playing with them to make them the "seim anew" – a technique widely exemplified in *War and Peace in the Global Village*; and fourth, adapting Joyce's own structural guides, especially Vico, but also Bruno, Nicholas of Cusa, Dante, and the complexities of the Homeric tradition and its commentaries to his often different purposes. The crux of the difference between the Lewis influenced McLuhan and Joyce is then crucial to explore – a difference McLuhan himself identified as in the crucial areas of laughter, and the carnivalesque.

Possibly Lewis' prime difference from Joyce, as McLuhan discovered, has to do with the distinction of a variety of different modes of carnivalesque satire – which was implicit in Dryden's essay on satire but has since been much more sharply delineated by Mikhail Bakhtin. Since the later eighteenth century the Menippean type of satire had shifted from the ambivalence of the earthy, everyday raucous, sensual, irreverent carnivalesque laughter to the reduced or dampened ironic and ambiguous laughter of the romantic and post-romantic grotesque in which the carnival – although still present in a purely literary way – is muffled and minimalized. Lewis's and McLuhan's practices can be more precisely identified and understood by the realization that their muffling of that laughter is the result of its being a problematized, primarily agressive laughter – the laughter that Freud associates with the joke and which clearly predominates in the reasons for McLuhan's fondness for jokes.[9] McLuhan clearly associates the joke with grievance: "Well, I was mentioning just a moment ago that behind every joke is a grievance. And without the grievance, there'd be no joke. So the hidden ground – the joke is the figure, under the figure is a grievance. When the grievance peeps through the joke slightly, then you have fun. If it's just pure grievance, well, then, there's no laughing" (McLuhan 1978). The same motif with respect to the joke and grievance also appears in *From Cliché to Archetype*: "It is inevitable that the funny man be 'a man with a grievance,' as Steve Allen reminds us in *The Funny Men* . The mere names of Twain and Leacock and Chaplin serve to recall their bitterness. Social anger and sensitivity sharpen the awareness of the funny man so that his 'jokes' are stabs or probes into the cultural matrix that plagues him. Conversely, anyone can determine an area of social irritation and disturbance by simply checking the areas from which jokes are currently emerging. The probes or jokes generated in one area are frequently transferred for service to new areas. The 'Polack' or Italian jokes are at present current in Canada as 'Newfie jokes'" (McLuhan and Watson 1970, 132–3).

Setting aside whether the work of Twain, Leacock, and Chaplin really deals largely, if not exclusively, with grievances, McLuhan's remark suggests two interesting issues. The first is an association of Twain's, and particularly Chaplin's, type of humor, with the evolution of mechanization and electro-mechanization; the second, that McLuhan ultimately sees no laughter or humour without some grievance, mitigated only by the fact that it is "peeping" through the joke. Linking this latter point to the machinic humour of Chaplin illuminates how McLuhan's technoculture reflections are necessarily satiric. It is interesting, therefore, to confront a world in which one of its most widely diffused critiques is, by the author's own claims and by its very presence, satiric, poetic, and purposefully ambiguous. More and more claims are now being based on McLuhan as theorist rather than McLuhan as a satiric observer of signs and symptoms, percepts and affects (the latter exemplified by researchers such as Joshua Meyrowitz, who takes selected McLuhanesque percepts and develops them into a theory in *No Sense of Place*, or by Carolyn Marvin's and James

Benniger's use of McLuhan's historical percepts for developing specific theoretical history and the former exemplified by attempts to construct a continuing theory of communication from McLuhan as the disciple of Innis). It was Marshall who insisted that he was not primarily a theorist, but a satirist; that his major association was not primarily with Innis and the history of political science but with Lewis, Joyce, and the history of literature and art. He may be condemned for not more vociferously putting the record straight during his lifetime, but he certainly left all the traces for investigators willing to act like the detectives of Poe, Doyle, and Chandler, whom McLuhan loved to read and discuss.

12 Conclusion:
Rehabilitating the Arts
and the Artist

To Marshall's best graduate students in the early 1950s he was a genius and a superb mentor – not a teacher in the conventional sense, since his mind acted with rapidity in a playful and sometimes even perverse way. Insight after insight poured out and all of us received a fascinating initiation into the richness, excitement, and importance of twentieth-century art and literature, and the importance of understanding it within the richness of intellectual and literary history and the history of various periods' understandings of expressions and communication. As a teacher of undergraduates Marshall, although frequently enigmatic and allusive, inspired and stimulated, even if for less committed students he did not impart specific information in a form they grasped or did not lead them to understand Renaissance, Romantic, or Modern literature.

Ted Carpenter viewed Marshall as a shaman, trickster, and natural mystic who had already moved over to the world of mystery and initiation which Ted, as an anthropologist, studied. This identifies a major aspect of the vibrant intellectual dominated by intuition and feeling who was to become the technocultural guru of the last half of the twentieth century. Such an individual could somewhat selfishly absorb people, as Marshall did with a large number of formal collaborators – e.g., Harley Parker, Wilfrid Watson, Tony Schwartz, John Culkin – and students or associates of his centre. And, of course, if they began to differ from his point of view, he could turn against people with whom he worked, as I learned personally when he tried in the early 1960s to have me banned from any graduate teaching in my prime area of specialization, since over time we had developed different orientations toward the mainline of modernism (Yeats, Pound, Eliot, Lewis, and Joyce) and my directions in the teaching of literary theory and the history of literary theory had become increasingly influenced by linguistics and semiotics. Yet this was the selfishness of a certain type of penetrating intelligence rather than the maliciousness of a small-minded man. Marshall was always fun and exciting in the period I was his student and then colleague (1950–65).

But there was a daimon in Marshall – a daimon which contributed to his being the shamanic seer that he was and simultaneously to his becoming a dramatic symptom of the intellectual, scholarly, and mass mediatized and commodified world emerging in the 1960s. It was this McLuhan that Tom Wolfe and Ted Carpenter have described in different yet complementary ways who, under the tutelage of the public relations spin-doctors Howard Gossage and Gerald Feigen became the myth of McLuhanism. Quite likely he was already on the way to assuming that role before he met them in 1965, having published *Understanding Media* in 1964, for the way he was lured and used by the Wolfes and the Gossages was already part of his ambitions – ambitions recorded in his letters and remembered by me from personal conversations when he dwelled on the lure of power and influence.

In this book I have tried to establish McLuhan as an important intellectual and prophet while also demonstrating that his greatness is that of the inventor's intuition or the artist's power of insight into percepts, affects, and the world of feeling and sensibility. Like most complex, intelligent innovators, while McLuhan was capable of great insights and proved to be right in many areas, he could also be obtuse and misleading. Before summarizing his achievements and significance and briefly raising queries about his inadequacies, I first want to explain McLuhan as symptomatic of a disease of the contemporary infoworld. Like any period of turbulence over the basis of culture and communication and the impact of new technologies, such as the early Renaissance, the contemporary world offered prophets the opportunity to connect with the world of commercial and political power. But by the mid-twentieth century it was well established that the route to that power for those not financially powerful themselves was controlled by the PR and advertising promoters and the "media monopoly." The packaging of intellectual insights became as important for international success as the content, for here as elsewhere McLuhan's adage "the medium is the message" applied.

After the failure of *The Mechanical Bride* to receive major attention (in fact, it attracted the negative attention of many in media because of what it revealed and what it criticized), McLuhan was somewhat embittered and gradually realized that a strategy had to be evolved to allow him to pursue his critical analysis and his artistic practice while also providing a means to achieve the impact he sought. The strategy he developed involved a mixture of poetic rhetoric, prophecy, and obscurity integrated with the very strategies of the journalistic and advertising world – topicality, shock value, telegraphic headline style, use of page layout, and a wide variety of other mechanisms he had explored in the *Bride*. His most radical experiments with such strategies in the 1950s – equivalent to combinations of concrete poems and emblem literature – had been *Counterblast* and the final issue of *Explorations* ("Verbi-voco-visual"). These strategies allowed him to preserve what he felt to be the power of the contemporary poetic and artistic vision, since the very techniques of those arts themselves, which in a variety of ways encompassed his strategies, permitted McLuhan to "put on" his audience, while simultaneously playing up to them. It was this strategy that Gossage and company realized, when properly promoted, would sell McLuhan and his message to a huge public.

So McLuhan became not only the symbolic symptom of the intellectual as media producer and journalist but also the symptom of a "public sphere" in which the values of the intellectual and academic world, particularly those of literature, the traditional liberal arts, and the arts themselves, would be debunked by the media producers, publishers, and journalists who had become not only the gatekeepers of wide dissemination of cultural productions but also the generators of productions that themselves would occupy much of the space of the intellectual world, and particularly of that area of the academic world normally associated with the humanities and softer social sciences.

Simultaneously, as McLuhan realized from reading his expatriate Canadian compatriot Kenneth Galbraith, the multinational corporate world had become the power behind the media monopoly. McLuhan's project then worked not only because its quirkiness appealed to the anti-establishment youth of the 1960s and to the avant-garde art movements – particularly in New York, Montreal, and the Pacific coast – who saw in McLuhan's work a contemporary "apologia" for poetry, art, multi-media, and the popular arts, but because its observational, cynical stance also had an intrinsic value for the corporate world, since it essentially counselled detached non-involvement. Moreover, the "drop-out" of *Take Today* (1972), with its fideistic, Catholic conservatism, attracted audiences from Catholicism and the evangelical right. McLuhan, with his interest in bringing the university to the board room and the corporate world to the university, essentially pre-figured the current commercial-industrial-university alliances that, oddly enough, still skew the bias of funding within the universities to those specialist activities that many of McLuhan's aphorisms and epigrams deplored.

Promoting a cynical, skeptical detachment ethically hedged and defended by a Christian abandonment of this world for the other world, McLuhan unintentionally also foreshadows the flight of many individuals from the public sector into the emotionally manipulated, inner faith of evangelism (whether Protestant, Muslim, Catholic, orthodox Judaism, or some other extreme religious group) which has subsequently become a dominant factor in the contemporary world. The sharp divisions within such a forceful and intelligent individual – anarchist modernism vs. Catholic hierarchicalism, intellectuality vs. quietistic skepticism, yearnings for corporate power vs. bohemian dismissal – all reflect and reinforce the turning from the public to the private (since McLuhan, by his own admission a private individualist, did not welcome, although he recognized that he could not prevent, the new tribal collectivism). This is why McLuhan persistently dismissed the relevance of the critically oriented, liberal public intellectuals of the 1950s and 1960s such as Paul Goodman or C. Wright Mills. But the point is that this is not simply a flight from personal social responsibility on his part, as critics from the left in the 1970s, such as Raymond Williams or James Carey, seemed to imply. It is rather a symptomatic response to an emerging era of cynicism that McLuhan's very analyses predict and his personality personifies.

In credit to McLuhan, it must be said, at least for the years I knew him well, that he believed in his complex vision of the world, both its anarchistic and fideistic, patristic and neo-Thomistic aspects. Those who have more recently implied that he was willing to jeopardize his Catholic faith by a primary commitment to professionalism would, considering his self-image as presented in his letters and his lifelong association with Catholic institutions of higher learning (St Louis University, Assumption University, St Michael's, and Fordham) ultimately be doing him wrong. His is the dilemma of many people in the premillennial world who fear the rapidity of change and the loss of the values of the pre-electric world. His strongest defence, which he will not receive from those who wish to use him as a theorist or guru of one kind or another, is that he genuinely believed his work would contribute to a skepticism about science, social science, and critical theory as panacea for a society confronting a potential loss of the human, whether to the overly abstract or the overtly mechanistic. His belief, inherited from the closing of the nineteenth century, was on one hand in the predictive and adaptive power of art and literature and, on the other, in faith in the intellectual traditions, revelations, liturgy, and sacraments of the Roman Catholic Church.

The McLuhan that his letters and the implicit messages in his writings present is one who believes that the arts are an early warning system but, because world power is entrenched, the only mode through which he can communicate is that of the covert, perhaps subversive, satirist through writings that are obscure, ambiguous, paradoxical, and capable of a multiplicities of meanings. That, of course, produces McLuhan the seer since to the extent that through that ambivalent satire he can predict the future, while covertly attacking those who made it possible and did not look to the artists and poets for an alternate way, he has, like many of our intellectuals in media as well as the university, preserved his own integrity and sense of responsibility. To become a seer he did not have to be, nor did he believe in being, some type of mystic, for his fascination with the patristic traditions of theological exegesis, especially with Thomism, had opened up to him the concept of "natural prophecy" – a concept which dominates his project from the early days of *Explorations*.[1] This understanding of the process of natural prophecy actually permitted him to participate in the growing project of the futurlogists with whom he is often associated. Possibly it enabled him to think of the breaking down and recombining characteristics of the arts ("breakdown as breakthrough," as he put it in *The Dew Line* (1969), or Coleridge's reconciliation of opposites) as predictive, associating the traditional function of the poet as prophet with the poem (as conceived by the new criticism with which McLuhan had early been affiliated) as a paradox, reconciling opposites.[2]

That central concern with paradox stretches from the earliest stages of McLuhan's writing into the period of his major works – from the 1940s with his doctoral thesis on the trivium, patristic exegesis and Thomas Nashe and his introduction to Hugh Kenner's *Paradox in Chesterton* through his major works, particularly *From Cliché to Archetype*, to the implicit play of paradox in the posthumously published discussion of the four major rhetorical figures (metaphor, synechdoche, metonymy, and irony) in *The Laws of Media*. His seer-like and prophetic qualities are central in their affinity with paradox, which is at the very heart of theology, and the history of religious poetry, particularly, in McLuhan's case, Gerard Manley Hopkins, John Donne, and the British metaphysical poets, while he can further claim that paradox in the twentieth century is globalized through the new fascination among modernist artists for the tribal and for "the Oriental" (the East). It is not just serendipitous that paradox also occupies a major role in post-cybernetic thought about communications and epistemology in works such as Gregory Bateson's *Steps to an Ecology of*

Mind, since it provides a way in which McLuhan tries to engage and attempts to subvert cybernetics.

In McLuhan's 1948 introduction to Hugh Kenner's book on the Catholic essayist, G.K. Chesterton, whom he specifically identifies as a "metaphysical moralist," McLuhan had implicitly, perhaps semi-consciously, announced his lifelong project, which was to transform Chesterton's strategic use of paradox into a genuine poetic instrument for creating worlds of discovery. My earlier interpretation of the schizoid conflict between McLuhan's fideistic belief and his fascination with modernist anarchy is confirmed by his remarks on Chesterton, where he articulates this conflict – the division between an established religious synthesis and the modernist anarchic power of the paradoxical and the poetic – as the struggle that confronts the contemporary "Thomist" who is "sustained by" what he believes to be *the* achieved intellectual synthesis – the abstract synthesis of knowledge inherited from Thomism – yet who in quest of renewing that synthesis for his own era must nevertheless "plunge... into the heart of chaos" (McLuhan 1947, xvi).

In McLuhan's Chesterton introduction, his pantheon are romantic and early modernist poets and artists who in contradistinction to their predecessors did not "represent an already achieved psychological unity," but who having the function to "discover order" are rather to be regarded as "pioneer[s]" (McLuhan 1948, xvi). Exemplary of such artists for him in 1948 were Blake, Wordsworth, Baudelaire, Rimbaud, Picasso, and Rouault, on whom society placed a "disproportionate burden" as a result of "the failure of philosophy" (Ibid.). By this point McLuhan, particularly through his study of Bacon and the intellectual background of Thomas Nashe in the Stoics as well as Alexandria and the Church Fathers, had intuited the role that he had to play to lead to his being a seer and a prophet – a master of grammatico-rhetorical paradox oriented towards the creation of a poetic world. Yet another way in which he stands as a symptom of a contemporary dis-ease is that, in spite of his genuine and deep appreciation of literature and the arts, for his public he becomes the primary replacement if not the sole medium through which the ecological aspect of the contemporary poet's and artist's creativity in "discover[ing] order" is disseminated.

Paradoxically and partly unintentionally, McLuhan's work effectively diminishes, if not totally discourages, direct contact with what even he would insist were the richer materials that provided him with his insight and with his strategies for disseminating themand, further, leads those who came to regard him as a theorist (or a philosopher) to relegate to a very minor role the importance of his technique of studying poets and exploring the world poetically in order to understand communication and contemporary technoculture. McLuhan always insisted that modernist poets and artists and their successors possessed a unique intellectual insight into culture, communication, and technology. His oft-repeated view in his writing and interviews that he works with percepts and affects fits well with Gilles Deleuze and Félix Guattari's distinction between the artist and the philosopher and scientist in *What is Philosophy?* where they explain their understanding that the scientist deals with "functives," the philosopher with "concepts," and the artist with "percepts" and "affects" (Deleuze and Guattari 1994, 163–99).

In a letter to Ezra Pound, McLuhan provides his own description of the type of prose social satiric poet he is: "I am an intellectual thug who has been slowly accumulating a private arsenal with every intention of using it. In a mindless age every insight takes on the character of a lethal weapon. Every man of good will is the enemy of society. Lewis saw that years ago. His 'America and Cosmic Man' was an h-bomb let off in the desert. Impact nil. We resent or ignore such intellectual bombs ... Lewis clears the air of fug."[3]

McLuhan was acutely aware of the growing dilemma of the intellectual – a role his Oxbridge education, his study of Thomism, and his early admiration of Chesterton would have made personally attractive. It is interesting to look back from the end of the century at some of McLuhan's various remarks about the intellectual in *The Gutenberg Galaxy* and *Understanding Media*. In one, McLuhan, in describing the dilemma, also outlines the solution that he – perhaps cynically – pursued in his own work. Speaking about some remarks of the classical eighteenth-century father of capitalist economics Adam Smith that had been cited by Cambridge's Raymond Williams, McLuhan argues: "in this passage Smith does seem to sense that the new role of the intellectual is to tap the collective consciousness of 'the vast multitudes that labour.' That is to say the intellectual is no longer to direct individual perception and judgment but to explore and to communicate the massive unconsciousness of collective man. The intellectual is newly cast in the role of a primitive *seer*, *vates*, or hero incongruously peddling his discoveries in a commercial market" (McLuhan 1962, 269). According to McLuhan, acceptance of this world begins with Blake and the Romantics embracing the dilemma Pope had faced up to in *The Dunciad*.

As an intellectual thug McLuhan pursues the role of "the primitive seer" who is "peddling his discoveries in a commercial market," while also trying to function as a satirist such as Wyndham Lewis. In *The Galaxy*, explaining the roots of the dilemma, he takes us still further back into the history of the century, not only to Lewis's satiric and polemical writing but to Julien Benda's *The Treason of the Intellectuals* (1927) which had clarified "the new situation in which the intellectual suddenly holds the whip hand in society," since the previously alienated intellectuals blocked from power are now becoming "the flunkies of power, as the atomic physicist at the present moment is the flunky of the war lords" (McLuhan 1962, 83–4). In the 1950s and early 1960s, before becoming involved with Wolfe and the PR people, McLuhan appears to have shared the view of his colleague Harold Innis, who prophesized the distortion and corruption of the university if professors were not restricted from consulting for the private sector and government, in what must now unfortunately seem an outdated, old-fashioned and mistaken warning.[4]

McLuhan's ambivalence on another crucial issue involving the twentieth-century intellectual is reflected in his discussion of European intellectuals, particularly the avant-garde and modernist artists, whose artistic activities he embraced but whose enthusiasm for the re-emergence of the tribal collective concerned him: "Since Henri Bergson and the Bauhaus group of artists, to say nothing of Jung and Freud, the nonliterate and even antiliterate values of tribal man have in general received enthusiastic study and promotion. For many European artists and intellectuals, jazz became one of the rallying points in their quest for the integral Romantic Image. The uncritical enthusiasm of the European intellectual for tribal culture appears in the exclamation of the architect Le Corbusier on first seeing Manhattan: 'It is hot-jazz in stone' (McLuhan 1964, 106). In various places he cites similar interests on the part of Laszlo Moholy-Nagy, Sergei Eisenstein, and T.S. Eliot, among a number of others. In his graduate teaching in the 1950s McLuhan frequently introduced modernism by having his students read T.E. Hulme's *Speculations*, which grounded contemporary art in some of the moments in the past dominated by greater collectivity – Egypt and Byzantium in contradistinction to Greece and Rome, and in aboriginal art, which Hulme regarded as "primitive," "tribal" art.

Another point concerning the critique of the intellectual working in a university on which McLuhan anticipates Tom Wolfe is his seeing himself as an "intellectual thug" in his role as an academic. In the same 1951 letter to Pound quoted earlier, he describes the plight of the academic in terms which parallel Wolfe's anti-academic description almost fifteen years later in his essay on McLuhan. The underpaid, overworked university teachers are described by McLuhan as "people of lowly origins" and "no cultural background": "They take a dim view of themselves as persons out of touch with the extrovert drives of their world. They have no tradition which would enable them to be critics of their own world. They have a temperament which prefers a quiet, simple life, but no insights into anything at all. They distrust any of their number who has ideas."[5] He continues to note that they distrust any conversation because it leads to revealing their own "vacuous plight." Fifteen years later in Wolfe, *The Pump House Gang*, introducing McLuhan and discussing the trap from which he was finally extricating himself, condescendingly described in a snobbish, arrogant (and by then somewhat outdated) vignette the plight of the downtrodden, defensive, poorly paid academic with a drab life and no capability to better it.

McLuhan was consciously pursuing a goal he had been imbued with in the 1930s by his mother, Elsie, a working actress presenting one woman shows, who had strong ambitions for her son. McLuhan's ultimately achieving the power, prestige, media attention, and star status which he did does not preclude the importance or insightfulness of his writing, most of which was well developed by the mid-1960s, before he began his brief meteoric assent into being the "man of the hour." But it is important to be aware that within the university McLuhan sought to develop the same life style that marked celebrities of media such as Tom Wolfe. It was remarkable that in doing so for a brief period he carried with him the support of such conflicting groups as avant-garde artists in film, music, dance and multi-media; student rebels, particularly the flower children of "the sixties"; the world of big business particularly the media; and the counter-currents within the universities interested in more integrative, interdisciplinary approach to research and teaching.

It has been argued that his influence collapsed for well over a decade because of his intentional demonization within academia by James Carey, John Fekete, Raymond Williams, and, most particularly, my *The Medium Is the Rear View Mirror: Understanding McLuhan*, which his agent and advisors consciously tried to suppress.[6] However, such an argument is specious, first, since my book was generally regarded to be extremely positive, even though critical of a mentor whom I greatly admire even today; and, second, since the writings of Carey, Fekete, and myself had a very small audience compared to McLuhan's audience. Moreover Raymond Williams, like Fekete, primarily spoke to the New Left, who had reservations about McLuhan from the 1960s and the publication of *Understanding Media*. In addition books by Arthur Kroker and Dennis Duffy and collections of essays certainly provided a balanced commentary from within and outside academia.

McLuhan had been the "target" of conventional academia long before the 1970s: he had early offended the American communications community by what they considered his arrogant disregard for founding figures such as Wilbur Schramm; he shared with the New Critics, only more intensely, the unearned and unjustified contempt of those literary scholars oriented toward historical and bibliographical studies; his unconventional history and "poetic" theorizing, joined to a sublime lack of scholarly accuracy, led to attacks from many conventional historians and philosophers; his conservative political analyses and unwillingness to take a stance on the multinational corporate world ultimately alienated the "new left" and their successors; his strong commitment to a relatively conservative Catholicism led to his being anathema to many of the "liberal left" – yet he managed to achieve the power and notoriety that he did. Within academia he has influenced work being done by such writers as James Benniger, Carolyn Marvin, Elizabeth Eisenstein, Jeremy Meyrowitz, Walter Ong, and Neil Postman. The myth of demonization, except perhaps as I have suggested earlier when it alludes to that daimon within Marshall, does not account for his "perceived" decline, even if such conscious demonizing activities really existed, individually and not as a conspiracy, on the part of those accused of carrying them on. (In any case, an accusation such as demonization is incorrect when applied to legitimate intellectual discussion and debate, which was certainly the spirit of all of the works cited.) Yet in a sense a certain paranoia always accompanied McLuhan's rise to recognition, for he and his collaborators seemed not only to anticipate opposition but to see within it the possibility of achieving some way of strengthening their position. In the world of intellectual ascendancy, a ten-year run as an international star reopened a decade later by *Wired* for at least another ten-year run, hardly suggests a successful or serious suppression.

What happened was that during the 1970s McLuhan, like others, eventually settled into the role of an important figure and maintained a presence within the university as well as outside it. But the ongoing "McLuhanism," as special promotion of a continuing ascendancy for a unique figure, is asserting a special type of dogmatic claim that is implicit in McLuhan's work but only a minor aspect of it. As his remarks on Thomism suggest, McLuhan obviously sought and achieved intellectual synthesis for the twentieth century, and this certainly appears to be a sub-text of *The Laws of Media*. But paradoxically, and therefore characteristic of the entire grammatico-rhetorical project which McLuhan pursued from his Cambridge doctoral thesis to *The Laws of Media*, his was a project that addressed a Joycean or Deleuzean chaosmos in which McLuhan tried to traverse the rhizomatic labyrinth that lay between the solidity of his faith and his hope in a patristic, neo-Thomistic intellectual synthesis and the anarchistic world of chance and complexity underlying the insights of radical

modernism and their theorization in postmodernism and poststructuralism. What saves McLuhan is his poetic direction, his being a prose
poet-manqué, because that was his primary game: teasing people into
believing his percepts to be theoretical concepts, and persuading even
himself into believing his poetics could provide an intellectual synthesis by going forth into the chaosmos and encountering it on its own
terms.

Given such a mission and the intellectual ability McLuhan had and
given that within those parameters he also had to succeed to a situation of "power," it is not surprising that he was enmeshed in an
ongoing creative movement that was paradoxical and poetic. Yet given
his own expressed needs for moorings in a well-defined structure of
belief, it is not surprising that the very individual who most influenced
him – the figure who provided the working title "The Road to
Finnegans Wake" for his first successful and most fundamental book
The Gutenberg Galaxy – had to remain for McLuhan a "cynical
satirist" and a demonic figure celebrating an "intellectual Black Mass."

By the early 1960s, when he began writing his major works,
McLuhan had completed his main project and few major fundamentals
were added to it subsequently. His major creative career probably
ranged from *The Mechanical Bride* to Expo67, and might perhaps be
more tightly defined as ranging from the birth of *Explorations* to the
Gossage managed "McLuhan 65" in San Francisco, since his works
after that largely re-visit and redefine, adding important insights of a
more specific nature to the basic vision he had developed primarily in
the 1950s. *The Laws of Media* refines the tetrad, but refines it within
the parameters set forth in the major writings of the 1960s and his
early thesis on Nashe. While in the 1970s he developed some awareness of French theory (which in many aspects he had anticipated, particularly through the assistance of Joyce and *symbolisme*), and while he
finally had the patience to read DeSaussure, the major themes of his
posthumous works all existed in his work in the 1940s and 1950s. This
is important, because if McLuhan prophetically anticipates the emergence of cyberculture, it reveals that the foundation for his intuition of
a pre-history of digitalization and cyberculture were implicit in the
modernism, particularly Joyce's, which McLuhan loved and which he
practiced in an uneasy alliance with his faith.

The Virtual McLuhan, by contextualizing his works and his overall
achievement within his complex personality and its relation with specific historical moments, indicates that what he must have considered
his most fundamental contributions are the ones most likely to be lost.
First and foremost is his realization that the adaptation of a grammatico-rhetorical, allegorical, and poetic method for dealing with

media and other new artefactual technologies was critical to providing people with the ability to discover a still point of observation and a complex, paradoxical interpretation by which to avoid the maelstrom of change in a postelectric world. Second is his recognition that in order to achieve this end there had to be a renewed awareness of the importance of the historical and contemporary study of poetry and the traditional and the lively arts as a foundation for the process of inter-pretation and understanding. Third is his view that if there were to be a new science of technocultural artefacts (the media and other artefacts from which McLuhan constructs his tetrads), it must be grounded in an interpretive-based history joined with the pre-enlightenment histo-riography and exegesis represented by Francis Bacon and Vico. Fourth is his emphasis that any understanding of culture and technology, including media, must be based on a solid understanding of the tradi-tions and subjects that had formed the basis of the university from the twelfth to the seventeenth century and had been gradually abandoned by the modern universities that McLuhan severely criticized, for while McLuhan criticized the universities, he firmly supported the tradition of liberal studies. Fifth, the Christian intellectual in the posthuman technocultural world must assume the role of satirist and critical soci-ological journalist, since observation is necessary to the detached understanding that would become vital in a world where people had to confront themselves as robotized cyborgs inhabiting an imperfect body in a fallen world. Sixth, that new world must be understood through its arts, artists, and poets – even if they were grounded in ambivalent and arcane knowledge– was crucial. It is paradoxical, which is appro-priate with McLuhan, that the pursuit of such a program provided him with poetic insight into the emergence of global digitalization and cyberculture – a task in which the insights of the poets and artists was the vital key.

When McLuhan is not studied in the context of a knowledge of those whose works and achievements influenced him, his work can become a crib to gain a misleading "quick fix" on the potential mael-strom of exponential technological change. It is only as an allegorical exegete of the poets and artists, particularly Joyce, that McLuhan becomes one of the pre-historians of digiculture. McLuhan himself in his more ingenuous moments would have been the first person to stress that Joyce, poets, and artists were the seers he, informed and protected by the grand traditions of classical and patristic allegorical exegesis, had followed. And as a learned satiric poet, he shaped that vision into his own insightful and poetic vision.

Awareness that his project was poetic, imaginative, and visionary should serve not only to permit his works to provide stronger insights into culture, technology, and communication by freeing them from the demands of the theoretic, prosaic, or scientific but also to allow a more judicious ongoing assessment of his more persistent historical importance for the latter half of the twentieth century. As we have repeatedly discovered, this is the role for which he said he wanted to be recognized. Yet he was enmeshed or "excruciated, in honour bound to the cross of [his] own cruelfiction !" (FW 192.18–19). Just like Joyce's con-man poet Shem in the *Wake*, he wooed the immediate success of his role as the media guru by writing an ambivalent, satiric work that, because of his very schizoid desire, lies concealed beneath its more superficial, pragmatic surface of rhetorical devices for discussing the media revolution. Yet the source and the conclusion of the *Galaxy* reveal the power of the synthesis – the chaosmotic anarchism of Joyce and the quietistic Catholicism of Alexander Pope, the bridge and the paradox between *Finnegans Wake* and *The Dunciad*.

Biographical Notes and *The Medium Is the Rear View Mirror*

As Marshall McLuhan's first doctoral student, who in the Spring of 1997 included him as one of the three dedicatees of my book *James Joyce's Techno-Poetics*, I had never intended writing any account of my relations with him on and off over thirty years until the appearance of a recent "official" biography that made it apparent that not only might I be a victim of a selective writing of history but that important aspects of the McLuhan story might remain untold – aspects which would actually contribute to his genuine status, while providing a balanced critical insight into his intellectual program.

The following remarks from Terrence Gordon's biography, *Marshall McLuhan: Escape Into Understanding*, occur on pages 253–4:

At home, the "daily charade of malice" McLuhan had come to count on continued. His former student Donald Theall, teaching at McGill University, had drafted a book on McLuhan and wrote, sending the manuscript, to ask permission to quote from his work. Disappointed that one of his students had understood him so poorly, McLuhan wrote: "My approach to the media is never from a point of view but is in fact a 'swarming.' Since this is an inexhaustible process, it has to be arbitrary ... As for the book in general, Don, I think you take me too 'seriously.' It is really more fun to join the quest for discoveries than to try to classify and evaluate the processes in which I am involved. You are, in a sense, trying to translate me into an academic fixture. Perhaps that is what I mean by 'serious.' On page 222 you refer to my retaining Joyce as my major authority. Please consider that there can be no 'author-

ity' where the game is discovery ... What I *have* found is an enormous enjoyment and thrill in experiencing the events that are on every hand. It seems to me
that this steady enjoyment of these events is a sufficient value system, as it
asserts the joy of mere existence. Naturally it does not rule out the possibility
of moral judgments, in particular, existential situations, you know that I am not
averse to these in private."

Writing separately to Theall's publisher, McLuhan pointed out the
quantity of Theall's quoted material exceeded his original estimate by
ten times, adding that "any reader would sense from the outset of the
book that the author is 'snarky' and 'snide.' McLuhan has been classified and be-clowned as well as be-nighted. Even where Don doesn't
[*sic*] mean well, he doesn't understand me anyway." McLuhan denied
permission to quote, but Theall's publisher decided that the quotations were within the bounds of fair use for a work and proceeded.
Theall agreed to some revisions when his editor echoed McLuhan's
sentiments about a snide tone in the work, but the impression of a
"be-clowned" McLuhan remained in the final version, titled *The
Medium Is the Rear View Mirror*. Responding when the publisher sent
him a complimentary copy, McLuhan said: "I found the book very
dull and confused."

Having often had to decide what to quote from documents, I appreciate Gordon's problem in dealing with one long letter Marshall
drafted but never sent to me (the original, on letterhead but
unsigned, is in the National Archives of Canada) as well as a series
of shorter letters between Robin Strachan, the editor of McGill-
Queen's University Press (my publisher) and Marshall and his publishers. Yet that selective quoting, coupled with many omissions,
distort what actually occurred and has led me to give a fuller – and
I believe more adequate – account of the matter, and then to contextualize this further with the story of how I met and worked with
Marshall and of subsequent problems which regretfully occurred in
the relationship.

As the preface to my 1971 book on Marshall indicates, I had never
planned to write a book – I was urged into it by friends and by the then
dean of Arts and Science at McGill who told Robin Strachan about my
ongoing interest in Marshall and his career. Robin then urged me to let
him see some preliminary chapters and after reading them urged me to
complete a book and publish it. I did so, because I thought that Marshall's meteoric rise to prominence in the mid 1960s could well lead to
what I thought to be some of the most important aspects of his work
being lost in the media hype and debate.

I warned Robin that Marshall might well have problems with the book, since he did not readily take to disagreement from former students or associates and that he and I, while remaining in touch, had had a relative falling out in the late 1950s over a number of intellectual disagreements centering partly on my doctoral thesis, which Marshall had directed. Robin suggested that, in order to avoid any acrimony, Marshall be allowed to see the manuscript before publication. With considerable uneasiness, which I communicated to Robin, I agreed, primarily because I genuinely respected Marshall and was grateful to him as a mentor and partly because I respected Robin, who was a genuine Oxbridge gentleman as well as a gentle man.

When the manuscript was ready for publication, Robin asked me if I would send it to Marshall. I suggested that it would be better if he were to do it, and rather than mail it, he decided to take the manuscript to Toronto, give it to Marshall, and meet with him later to discuss his reaction. Robin told me that he gave the manuscript to Marshall and when he returned the next day to meet with Marshall, he seemed genuinely interested and pleased but, naturally, had some points with which he disagreed. Robin said that Marshall showed him the draft of a letter (that of 6 August 1970) which he was going to send me, but which (as the absence of a signature in the original copy on his letterhead in the National Archives of Canada confirms) was never sent. Robin and Marshall met again the next day and Marshall's mood had completely changed – he castigated me and the work and suggested that I was probably in violation of the fair use regulations under the Copyright Act. At some point, either then or shortly after Robin's return to Montreal, there was the threat of legal action against McGill-Queen's University Press, against McGill and Queen's Universities, and against myself based on the issue of "fair use." This was followed up by further correspondence which now suggested that my work was "snide" and "snarky" and that I had gone well beyond the "danger point" in quoting from Marshall's work.

But before going further, let's look more closely at the draft of that letter I never received, from which Terrence Gordon quotes small bits. Rather than contributing further to the selective quotation, I cite the whole letter to show, while exhibiting differences, that Marshall still demonstrates a collegial spirit of friendship as the last paragraph suggests:

University of Toronto
Toronto 5, Canada

CENTRE FOR CULTURE AND TECHNOLOGY

Marshall McLuhan, Director
August 6, 1970

Professor Donald Theall,
Department of English,
McGill University,
Montreal, Quebec.

Dear Don:

Have you by any chance read Jacques Lusseyran's *And There Was Light* (Heinemann, London, 1964, and Little-Brown, Boston)? Apropos page 112 of Lusseyran, the paragraph beginning: "From my own experience ...." includes my entire media approach, both privately and corporately. I think you ignore it in your book. I call it SI/SC, referring to sensory input and sensory completion. The sensory completion, or the actual experience of anything never corresponds to the event or input., i.e. there is no *matching*, but only *making* in human experience. This relates, of course, to Aristotle's *poesis* and *mimesis*, and his phrase: "It is the process by which all men learn."

I think you will see why the Kenneth Johnstone piece has some relevance here. My approach to the media is never from a point of view, but is in fact a "swarming". Since this is an inexhaustible process, it has to be arbitrary. There is no one position from which to approach any mediurn. It would be quite easy for me to rewrite every page in ten different styles and patterns. One other basic theme besides SI/SC, Don, is acoustic space, which you by-pass. It too is the world of the unvisualizable. It is like the world of the pun whose centre is everywhere and whose meaning or definition is nowhere. It is the world of the electronic simultaneity which turns the planet into a sound-light show where involvement is unavoidable and where detachment becomes a superhuman feat.

I am sending the Krugman report, not as a proof of anything, but his kinds of discovery will interest you. His formula at the end of pages 17-18 is useful in reminding us that under conditions of electric software it is the sender who is sent, and not the "message." Perhaps that is where the phrase originated "he really sends me." As you know, I study slang as indications of altered sensibility. As for the book in general, Don., I think you take me too "seriously." It is really more fun to join the quest for discoveries than to try to classify and evaluate the processes in which I am involved. You are, in a sense, trying to translate me into an academic fixture. Perhaps that is what I mean by "serious." On page 222 you refer to my retaining Joyce as my major authority. Please consider that there can be no "authority" where the game is discovery. You do tend to overlook the fact that my books are intended as fun books. Certainly I have no system or theory that I would not scrap instantly in favour of better means of discovery. I was staggered by your page 259 where you suggest that I lack a full understanding of the drama of human relations. I hasten to confess this state as entirely applicable to me. I have been *amazed* at the range of the current drama and perhaps have been mesmerized rather than *illuminated*. There is a phrase of Aristotle's: *Causae ad invicem causae sunt.* This is the drama that I am involved in, and it is very difficult to find a beginning, middle, or end except in the most arbitrary way. What I have found is an enormous enjoyment and thrill in experiencing the events that are on every hand. It seems to me that this steady enjoyment of these events is a sufficient value system insofar as it asserts the joy of mere existence. Naturally it does not rule out the possibility of moral judgements, in particular, existential situations, and you know that I am not averse to these in private. But we have surely suffered an enormous deluge of this sort of thing in public, which is directly proportional to lack of awareness of what's really going on.

Don, I have just recalled another misunderstanding that underlies your treatment of linearity vs. discontinuity in my stuff. You mention it apropos Paul Klee – the bounding line in art is sculptural and textural. Abstract lineality is non-visual. It can be seen, but its mode is audile, tactile, kinetic. This was one of Wyndham Lewis' hang-ups. He tended to confuse the bounding line of abstract and primitive art with visual values of continuity and connectedness. This is a major hang-up in all the confusion between television and movie form, for example. TV is "non visual" as Joyce understood from careful analysis. This is not the place to go into a discussion of the visual modalities of eye structure and the contrasting sensory qualities of colour vs. black and white. Colour TV is a new medium, having very small relation to black and white. In the years since you have been in Montreal, I have done a great deal of work on sensory study. Notice page 34 of Lusseyran where he mentions blindness as "dope" and "inner tripping." TV is like that. It is a "blind" medium, fostering inner trips and hallucination-the "eye of Siva" etc.

What I have encountered over the years is the very small degree of human appetite for the knowledge of forms and causes. People prefer their opinions and classifications rather than the exploratory work. It may be merely a matter of limited energy.

Classification makes some people feel secure. It seems to relieve them of any further need for study.

Thanks for making so epical an effort to present me. Hope to have a chat with you to clarify many matters which simply cannot be done in writing.

P.S. Check spelling of "Morganstern" on page 159. I happened on it, but did not make any attempt at a proof reading job. Is it "Morgenstern"?

[unsigned original in National Archives of Canada]

It is interesting to note that at this point Marshall suggests I take him too seriously, but later in the a subsequent letter to Robin (11 August 1970) after consultation with "his advisors" (in the National Archives there is an undated handwritten document concerning my manuscript from one of his advisors, obviously based on an erroneous interpretation of "fair use" which recommends refusal of permission to quote from his works) he suggests that I "beclowned" him, which hardly suggests an approach which took him too seriously, and asserts that he will "not grant permission for publication of this material as requested."[1]

This letter to Robin is interesting, since it was apparently written subsequent to advice from "his advisors" (presumably his literary agent Matie Molinari and perhaps others in his family) who advised him that apart from the amount of quotation – "well beyond the danger point" – there was the potential damaging "effect of the use upon the potential market for or value of the copyrighted words," which will have an "effect upon the distribution and objects of the original work." In the 11 August letter McLuhan claimed that I had quoted 8,000 to 9,000 words of his in a text of 60,000 to 70,000 words. According to Strachan (letter dated 25 August 1970), this actually represented my using 7,353 words from textual material of his that consisted of over 800,000 words (less than 1% of his material) (see figure 1). Nevertheless, Marshall wrote to all of his publishers asking that they refuse permission for us to quote and proceeded to threaten legal action against the press, the universities, and myself.[2]

The subsequent events involved the presidents of five Canadian universities and Northrop Frye, who by then was an internationally recognized literary theorist at the University of Toronto. The principals of Queen's and McGill had to back their newly launched press in its effort to publish the work. In Ontario, Claude Bissell and Carleton Williams, the presidents of the University of Toronto and University of Western Ontario respectively, and other personal friends of Marshall and Strachan intervened with Marshall, while Ronald Baker, the president of the University of Prince Edward Island, provided an additional assessment of the work. As a result of lengthy negotiations, the agent and the McLuhans realized the futility of a suit and decided that they would not block publication of the book. An agreement was reached that the manuscript would be submitted to Northrop Frye and that he would

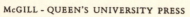

McGILL - QUEEN'S UNIVERSITY PRESS

3458 REDPATH STREET, MONTREAL 109, QUEBEC, CANADA TELEPHONE (514) 392-4421

M324/C

25 August 1970

Dr. Marshall McLuhan
Centre for Culture and Technology
University of Toronto
Toronto 5, Ontario

Dear Marshall:

THE MEDIUM IS THE REAR VIEW MIRROR

We have had five days without mail in or out but I hope
that this letter will reach you quickly.

Our word count shows that there are in the book 102,000
words (including the bibliography which you have not
seen) and that 7,573 of your own words are spread
throughout the work (i.e. 7.4%). Expert opinion
indicates that neither the total wordage nor the wordage
taken from each individual work is excessive in a
scholarly critical work of this kind under the rule of
'fair use' (as it is termed in the U.S.A.) or 'fair
dealing' (as it is termed in Canada). Under the rule of
'fair dealing' acknowledgement of the source of quotation
is made, of course, but 'permission' to quote is not
required.

Title	Total Wordage	Wordage Used	%
Gutenberg Galaxy	120,000	699	0.5
Counterblast	41,000	807	1.96
Culture is Our Business	51,000	859	1.68
The McLuhan Dew Line	---	106	---
McNamara: Literary Criticism	96,000	46	.04
The Mechanical Bride	75,000	806	1.07
The Medium is the Massage	10,000	441	4.40
Stearn: McLuhan: Hot & Cool	120,000	423	0.35
Understanding Media	133,000	1,620	1.21
Through the Vanishing Point	56,000	790	1.41
War and Peace in the Global Village	45,000	476	1.05
Look	---	217	---
Unspecified	---	280	---

...2

Dr. Marshall McLuhan   25 August 1970

- 2 -

Since receiving your letter of August 11 we have been
carefully through the manuscript with an eye to your
views about the general tone of the book and our own
anxiety to avoid the use of expressions that might appear
to be 'snide'. Don has agreed to accept a number of
changes of expression which we feel do not harm the
critical integrity of his work.

There is really nothing that I can add to my letter of
August 14 beyond saying that since we met one additional
outside reader's report has come in from an exceptionally
qualified scholar who comments that the publication of
this book should enhance your reputation. I do hope that
on further consideration you will feel able to agree with
this view (and that of another outside reader) because I
am most anxious that publication should take place
without hard feelings on the part of anyone concerned.

With all good wishes,

Yours sincerely,

Robin

Robin H. Strachan
Director

RHS/ma

make recommendations concerning any possibly offensive comments in it and that I would have the right to accept or reject them, providing I explained and negotiated my reasons with Frye.

Frye suggested changes of wording in two short phrases and one footnote. The two phrases, which I agreed could be misinterpreted, I changed, the footnote I defended on the ground that the notion of the artist as "confidence man" and the motif of the "confidence man" in view of McLuhan's interests in Melville and in a recently published book on the confidence game were justifiable – in fact illuminating, given the Platonic rhetorically oriented tradition of the poet as liar (for I had argued in my book that McLuhan was a prose poet manqué).[3] On this basis the book was published. Although I was saddened by the knowledge that Marshall would try to suppress a fair and quite good assessment of his work because he did not agree with it and that he would see a threat in open academic debate, I still continued to have some contact with him.

Marshall later corresponded with me and sent me an offprint of an article by his son Eric, one of my former students. In the late 1950s he, his mother, and Corinne visited our new house in Pickering; I met with him at Expo 67 in Montreal; and on at least two other occasions after 1971. Moreover, in a letter to Claude Bissell published in *The Letters of Marshall McLuhan*, he used as an example for the Communication Program he wished to start in Toronto the new undergraduate and graduate programs in communication that I had founded while chair of English at McGill University. "McGill already has a PhD in communications under the auspices of the English Department. They have some specific programs for the MA, but only projects and dissertations for the PhD. You see, most American universities have a PhD in communication which is almost entirely slanted toward hardware expertise. Hundreds of their students want to come up here and would be thrilled to have a course available in the language area, minus the hardware."[4]

The general assessment of my book was reflected in a review that his friend and faculty colleague in the original Culture and Communication seminars, D.C. Williams, a past president of the University of Western Ontario, wrote: "If it be true, and I think it is, that no student can be wholly objective about his teacher, it must still be said that Theall's objectivity, combined with the intimacy of his insight which long association with McLuhan has given him, has produced a work of notable and unique distinction."[5] Robin told me, which I cannot verify, but believe to be true since Robin was a friend of Claude Bissell, that Claude had suggested to Marshall that it might well be the most supportive book to be written about him.

Terence Gordon never contacted me or interviewed me, so he had no way of ascertaining whether or not I had received the letter from which he misleadingly quotes, nor did he have any way of knowing how I might comment on the situation he was partially describing. I was never part, as he suggests, of the "charade of malice" against McLuhan in the 1970s, since there was no intentional malice in my book and as astute a literary analyst as Northrop Frye found only two possibly questionable phrases in a book of sixty to seventy thousand words. To give some context to my personal relationship with McLuhan in its better and worse moments, I provide a brief sketch of the history of our relationship and of my involvement with his work over the thirty years from when I first met him until his death and then more briefly with his family and their approved disciples in the twenty years since his death.

I first encountered Marshall McLuhan in the summer of 1950. I had learned about him from professors of mine at Yale – Cleanth Brooks and William K. Wimsatt, Jr – who, knowing I was going to do graduate work at the University of Toronto, told me of a young literary historian and critic whose work had impressed them and who they thought had great promise. At this time Marshall had not yet published his first book, *The Mechanical Bride*, which was to appear in 1951, but he had written a series of essays for little magazines associated with the New Criticism, some of which were later republished in *The Literary Criticism of Marshall McLuhan*. I had planned to stay only one year in Canada, but Marshall became the main factor in my decision to do my graduate work at the University of Toronto. He was brilliant, energetic, a workaholic, widely read, and well versed in the movements of modernism.

From 1950 to 1954 Marshall and I were virtually always together whenever we did not have commitments. Most days he would have lunch with my wife, Joan, and me in our apartment at 16 St Joseph Street; we would shop together for books and for food, visit in his office and his home (the latter less frequently because of the number of young children around the house, which tended to distract Marshall's thought processes). Our meetings tended to be intellectually stimulating, devoted to such diverse subjects as literary history, the new technologies, advertising, modernist art and literature, James Joyce, Thomistic philosophy, and Catholic theology – but this is just a selection of the range of subjects on which Marshall's roving, encyclopedic mind would touch. Together we organized various reading groups: Elizabethan, Jacobean, and Restoration plays; discussions of articles from Aquinas; a reading group on *Finnegans Wake* that included Marshall, me, my wife, a reporter from Canadian Press, and a young stock broker (now president of a major firm). Marshall and I also frequently read and discussed passages from the *Wake* when we were together.

For a young graduate student, twenty-one years old when I met him in the summer of 1950 (a month after my marriage and my graduation from Yale), the association with Marshall was wonderful. I was only too happy to expose myself to his continuous monologues on all subjects and to assist him in whatever ways I could. Marshall craved collaboration and, following Hugh Kenner, I became his next collaborator, helping him with his edition on Tennyson and editing the Introduction, as he acknowledges in the foot-notes. This was not paid research work (the moneys in Canada for that did not exist in those days). I was working with him on a book on the epyllion and he urged me to write an essay on Wyndham Lewis (never published) to complement his contribution to the 1953 Lewis issue of *Shenandoah*. Earlier he had encouraged me in getting an essay on T.S. Eliot's *Coriolan* poems published in *Accent* (1951). I even assisted him in the early drafting of the proposal for the Ford Foundation seminar.

There were ideas that I brought to him that contributed to the development of his interests in those days. In 1949 I had reviewed Norbert Wiener's *Cybernetics* for the *Yale Scientific Magazine* and I introduced him to ideas concerning the new science of communication and control in the human and the machine from which part of the shift of his interest to communications and later to Innis arose. In 1951, when I was finishing my Master's thesis on T.S. Eliot's theories of communication, Marshall was just beginning to read Innis. Having encountered Gregory Bateson's earlier works in Ted Carpenter's graduate anthropology course in culture and communication, I was asked to review Bateson's new work with Jurgen Reusch, *Communication: The Social Matrix of Psychiatry* for *The Canadian Forum* and, realizing its importance, brought Bateson to Marshall's attention (his notes are on the end pages of the copy I had loaned him, still in my library). Marshall welcomed collaboration and interchange, but eventually he had a falling out with most of his collaborators.

In those days, however, our friendship was close and when *The Mechanical Bride* came out Marshall gave Joan and me an inscribed copy: "To Joan and Don From the Mechanical Bridegroom, Marshall." In September 1951 our first child, Thomas Dominic Theall, was baptised at St Basil's Church on the St Michael's College campus by the Very Reverend Lawrence K. Shook. Marshall and Corinne were his godparents. I could go on at length about the richness of this period, about often going (sometimes accompanied by my wife) to morning Mass with Marshall, who went daily, for while much has been written about this period, what I have to add would probably fill a small book. Marshall was not only a teacher and a thesis director but a guide in my studies in general. During that period, under his stimulation, I worked on the Scriblerus papers and *The Dunciad*, discovering the importance of Menippean satire to Pope and Pope's circle, Dryden's discussion of its theory in his essay on satire, and like. As I tried to understand what Pope meant by "little epic" and delved into some of its importance as the epyllion in literary history, Marshall discovered that the epyllion appeared throughout literature and was a special kind of form. He and I began drafting separate chapters of a book on the epyllion. (Much of the manuscript now resides in the National Archives of Canada and some parts of it are still it in my own files on that project and one on Pope's *Dunciad*. Some of this work on *The Dunciad* was later to surface in *The Gutenberg Galaxy* (1964) and I had applied it even earlier to the Scriblerians in a paper presented to ACUTE (the Asssociation of Canadian University Teachers of English) in the late 1950s, elaborating the concept of the Menippean as a learned satire.

A spin-off of the Swift-Pope research came about from my fascination with the use of masonry and the Eleusinian mysteries in *The Dunciad*. Marshall, somewhat prone to conspiracy theories, extended this into full-scale research on secret societies and their continuing impact on history and on modernist literature. He developed a theory about cults and their operation that is reflected in his published correspondence of 1952 to 1954. The preoccupation persisted and appears again in a letter to Walter Ong in 1962. It was a strange period; for a short time it effected my wife and me (since we, responding to Marshall's powerful convictions, also tended to see cult activity everywhere), although we began to exorcise it by comic interludes about cults with fellow graduate students – John Deck, Pat Bruckmann, Archie Malloch, and others. My eventual drift from Marshall's strength of commitment to this theory was perhaps the first "problem" that arose between Marshall and me. But it paralleled a second problem, as under Marshall's tutelage and my own readings I became more knowledgeable and independent. The liberal environment in which I had been brought up in high school and at Yale began to assert itself and I found many of Marshall's more conservative preoccupations a little stultifying. However, I rather prudently restrained myself from comment most of the time – my wife was quite a bit more outspoken on these issues.

I had initially been somewhat mistaken about the strength of Marshall's liberal views, based on an article he had written in 1951 on Henry Luce and the *Time-Life-Fortune* trio, which he published in Gershorn Legman's journal *Neurotica*. In conversation with me he defended Legman's publishing in the same issue the then-infamous article on "Letters to the Editor" (a series of replies to an ad requesting contact with partners interested in sado-masochism). (And, of course, *The Mechanical Bride* was essentially a critique of the "mass media and advertising," although a very witty and complex one.) Shortly afterward he was to begin rejecting such liberal stances as irrelevant and interfering with objectivity. While often sharply critical of the Catholic clergy and their lack of understanding of the lay people who worked for them, McLuhan always expressed a fundamental loyalty to their symbolic status, which led to his later position condoning various forms of censorship.

I was one of the persons who urged Marshall to meet Ted Carpenter and subsequently arranged an evening in our apartment to let Carpenter and McLuhan get to know one another better. I had taken a graduate course with Ted in my first year at Toronto and been very impressed with him and his work on the Inuit and their language, and with the potentialities of the newly developing study of language and culture from which ethnolinguistics emerged. Ted was to become a brilliant editor of *Explorations* and taught me a great deal about writing when he edited my first contribution to that journal, "Here Comes Everybody," an early essay on Joyce's *Finnegans Wake*, which Marshall told me later had been highly praised in a letter sent to him by the Swiss art critic and historian, Carola Giedion-Welcker.

During this period, Marshall seemed and apparently did hold me in high regard as indicated by his remarks in a letter to Walter Ong in the Spring of 1953. Marshall said: "Extremely able chap here finishing PHD on Communication theory in Joyce, Yeats, Lewis, Pound, Eliot. Catholic. Yale BA. He will teach at St. Mike's and work in our Culture and Communication project."[6] I became the first academic secretary of the Culture and Communication project, while finishing my doctorate and teaching twelve hours a week – including over 200 students in a survey course of Neo-Augustan and Romantic literature and a third year honours course in Spenser and Milton. I also worked intensively on the organization of the library for the Culture and Communication project, keeping minutes and records of the seminars and pursuing research in relation to the seminar.

The Culture and Communication seminar was exciting and the launching of *Explorations* – which I did not fully appreciate initially – was to become a vital and exciting and important event. But during this period, I was losing touch with what Marshall expected in the thesis. Since it was briefly alluded to in Philip Marchand's biography of McLuhan I believe that I should briefly amplify on this aspect of our relationship. I had originally proposed a thesis on Yeats, Pound, Eliot, and Joyce and their views of poetry and communication. This was obviously overly ambitious, but Marshall was fascinated and at that time he would never have inhibited a graduate student's ambitions. He agreed to direct the thesis. Later, as the thesis was nearing completion, Marshall wanted me to add Wyndham Lewis and, if I thought that was too much, to drop Yeats – whose works and related critical material I had already read and worked through. While I agreed that as the research on the thesis developed, Wyndham Lewis as a counterpoint to Joyce, Eliot, and Pound was quite important to understanding this period of modernism, the project of including Lewis, particularly at this stage, was too demanding. I did not feel comfortable with Lewis's radically conservative stance, and also probably did not at that time fully appreciate the complexity of his position. Marshall appeared to agree; but I realize now from reading his correspondence that he saw Lewis as the essential balance, providing the perspective of a space mind in contrast to the Joycean cult of the time mind. See, for example, his comments in his correspondence with Lewis criticizing Hugh Kenner's contribution to the Lewis issue of *Shenandoah*, that Kenner's "Joyce enthusiasm" had "carried him a long way towards the time cult." McLuhan notes that "I hasten to withdraw what I said about Kenner seeing eye to eye with me."[7] The primary difficulties that I had with Marshall concerning the thesis, I later realized, were partly involved with his concern about my treatment of Joyce's position in which I argued in favour of Joyce's having clearly rejected Catholicism, secularized the sacred, and developed a poetic which, while including a calculated "ambiviolence," also played the ambiguities of the symbolists against the logical by-play of a multiplicity of recognizable meanings to achieve a new poetic language.

I should have realized much earlier that the history of the problems that Marshall had had with those with whom he had collaborated, such as Hugh Kenner, did not bode well for a student who had an even closer relationship with him. Corinne tended to see his students or collaborators as stealing from Marshall, and frequently alluded to this when we visited. So while Marshall consciously promoted a working atmosphere of collaboration, interchange, and openness, he was simultaneously being encouraged to take an extremely protective stance with respect to those with whom he worked and to guard his claims over any insights arising from the relationship The situation with Kenner became serious enough that Marshall eventually began circulating charges of plagiarism against him. As Philip Marchand explains in his biography, Cleanth Brooks sent a letter to warn Marshall that he was doing himself no good in pursuing these accusations and reminding him that Kenner had warmly recognized Marshall's contributions in

the dedication of his first book (on Ezra Pound). Some of this posses-
siveness about communal intellectual property was perhaps defensible
in terms of the difficult financial times which faculty at St Mike's were
experiencing at that time. As well however, as Ted Carpenter and
others have observed, if you gave Marshall an idea, the next day he
would often re-present the idea to you as his own – something which
Ted took as a matter of course in the spirit of team work and collaboration.

As the multiple pressures of teaching, the seminar, and the thesis
accumulated, I realized that with a family of two small children I had
to get my degree. I also became aware that Marshall's constantly
calling with new ideas and insights and suggestions for new directions
would lead to an interminable writing of the thesis. Furthermore,
during this time I developed a number of serious health problems
resulting from overwork, so that I had to literally "hide out" and complete the thesis. This, coupled with my rejection of the idea that I
include Lewis in my thesis, and with the growing awareness on my part
that I had serious intellectual and ideological differences with Marshall
in spite of my many, many intellectual agreements with and much
admiration for him, led to my occasionally expressing some differing
point of view, which ultimately was not well received. The subsequent
frictions never led to a complete break in relations, but the warmth of
interchange was never the same.

Philip Marchand in his biography tells part of the story of my thesis,
suggesting that Marshall did not like it. Marshall never expressed that
directly to me before the defence, but I was aware that difficulties had
developed. Prior to the defence, it became apparent to the Department
of English that, unlike most directors, while he would not block the
thesis, he would not be too supportive of it either. When the defence
took place I found myself in a rather strange situation. The head of the
Graduate English Department, Professor A.S.P.Woodhouse, who generally looked down on research in contemporary literature and also did
not have the easiest relationship with McLuhan, along with other
members of the department, such as Frye, were extremely friendly and
supportive in the defence, while Marshall was extremely remote and
even critical, although not actually hostile. The defence went quite
well, and in spite of Marshall's dissatisfaction, he was reasonable and
fair in his questions. The only acrimony came from two professors –
Norman Endicott and Douglas Grant – who were not very friendly
with Marshall nor very positive about the subject matter. Woodhouse
expressed his admiration for and his belief in the long-range importance of the thesis, which he felt could be a new direction in criticism.
The evening after the defence, as head of the Graduate Department,

Woodhouse called me and apologized for the currents of unpleasant-
ness and praised the thesis, which had received very considerable
approval from the members of the examining committee after my
departure. In the final analysis, in spite of his reservations, Marshall
was fair and generous, congratulated me, and celebrated that night at
our party.

The defence was in the fall of 1954. In June of 1954 I had resigned
as secretary of the seminar, since I felt I could not carry this task along
with the demands of my first years of teaching. During the subsequent
period of my teaching Marshall and I were colleagues, he the senior
professor and, at the beginning I the most junior lecturer. In 1957,
however, an assistant professor at the age of twenty-eight, I was admitted to the Graduate Faculty of the English Department, teaching alter-
nately an eighteenth century or satire course and a course in literary
theory. By this time I had become interested in linguistics and was
closely associated with Richard Robinson, a sinologist, and John
Wevers, a Near Eastern scholar. During this period the three of us organized a program for teaching English to a group of students and other
émigrées from Hungary, wrote a series of texts in English as a second
language, and produced a series of TV programs on English as a second
language for the Canadian Broadcasting Corporation (CBC), which
received an honourable mention in the annual U.S. Educational Television awards for 1962. Dick Robinson and I, who tended to incline
toward the British school of linguistics of J.R. Firth and later M.A.K.
Halliday, on a few occasions discussed linguistics and structuralism
with Marshall, which at that time he flatly rejected, along with all
other formal linguistics (although twenty years later he was to read
Saussure). These discussions were friendly but heated, and Marshall
was convinced that I was wasting my time studying linguistics and
structuralism.

I became an associate professor in 1960. During this period I had
become more independent and in classes and to colleagues I expressed
views about literary theory, communication theory, and modern literature that were sometimes at variance with Marshall. At some point, I
expressed a desire to do some teaching in my own field of modern literature at the graduate level. Marshall went to Father Shook, then
president of St Michael's College as well as chair of its English Department, and insisted that I was not qualified to teach moderns. The
college department then took his views to the Graduate English
Department but, once again, Woodhouse intervened and I was able to
teach modern literary theory, participate in graduate committees on
modern subjects, and direct theses in the modern area.

In 1960 Marshall, who had been the college's representative on President Claude Bissell's Presidential Committee on Policy and Planning, resigned from that post. (At the time I was not aware that he was not in good health, but subsequent biographies show that he was not.) The then-president of the college, Father John Kelly, appointed me, much to my surprise, to replace Marshall. I became embroiled in college and university politics, being virtually a de facto executive assistant to Father Kelly and helping to fashion many of the statutes providing a university structure for St Michael's, to which it was entitled by charter, since it was trying to clarify its status as one of the constituent universities of the federation of the University of Toronto. Marshall warned me, probably correctly, that politics was a waste of time, but I had a fatal fascination coupled to a feeling of responsibility.

During the period from 1960 to 1964 Marshall and I grew more distant and he continued to register his belief that I lacked the qualifications to work in modern literature. In 1960 Fred Rainsberry of the CBC, to whom I had been acting as an educational advisor, commissioned me to provide a more easily accessible version of Marshall's report on his media experiments that had been commissioned by the National Association of Educational Broadcasters (NAEB), and which was a very early harbinger of what was to become *Understanding Media*. The plan was that I try to make the document comprehensible to people working in educational programming for the CBC. When the project came to Marshall's attention, he told me that the whole point of his work was that it was cryptic and to explain his work destroyed it.

The final problem arose in 1963 when the issue of appointing the first lay chair of the St Michael's English department arose. I had been in the department for the longest time of any lay member other than Marshall, I had become a full professor and was about to serve a two year term as chair of the Joint Departments of English of the University of Toronto, but Marshall's objections made it impossible for me to become chair at St Mike's, even though Marshall did not wish to assume the post himself. Consequently, I felt that it would be better for me, and for the college, if I were to try to obtain a professorship elsewhere, particularly since my interest in developing a communication program was unlikely to be realized at the University of Toronto. I obtained an appointment at the newly created York University and they granted me $25,000 to create an experimental seminar in communication, art, and technology. The group we assembled to conduct the seminar included Patrick Watson (TV), Ray Moriyama (architect), Arnold Rockman (artist and sociologist), Leslie Mezei (computer scientist), Mark Slade and Terry Ryan (National Film Board of Canada), Michael Kay (a linguist), Baron Brainerd (mathematician), and Murray

Fraser (geneticist), as well as other faculty from York. At the end of that year, McGill University invited me to become chair of its English Department, assuring me that I would be free to try to develop a communication program, if I could persuade the Department of English and the Faculty of Arts and Graduate Studies.

My first year in Montreal I was awarded a grant by the National Film Board of Canada and three other government departments, supplemented by aid from CMHC and Eastman Kodak, to direct a detailed research project on the multi-media and environmental exhibits at Expo67. Marshall's meteoric rise after the publication of *Understanding Media* made him an important backdrop figure for the Canadian theme pavilions at Expo67 and, as I was on the site almost daily, I met him on occasion at receptions and the like. Our encounters were amiable, though fleeting, but I had the sense Marshall was not quite himself – I even thought he might be ill. Nevertheless, he was enjoying immensely being lionized and he still projected the superb histrionic qualities that had shaped his teaching. I did not see Marshall again after that until after his major brain surgery and the incidents concerning my book outlined above.

My book about him, *The Medium Is the Rear View Mirror: Understanding McLuhan*, came to be because Montreal in the late 1960s vibrated with McLuhan. During that period I met Jacques Languirand, designer of the Man and His World pavilions at Expo67, who later wrote a book inspired by McLuhan (Languirand 1972). Later Jacques and I taught a bilingual course at McGill in film and media studies. While teaching summer programs in a McGill-NFB film education program I frequently spoke about McLuhan, his work, its values, and its limitations. I had become concerned with some of the directions Marshall was taking, especially since Montreal of the late 1960s had moved me further toward a radical left liberal position and my work in communication had made me more aware of the problems that McLuhan's enigmatic, cryptic style was generating. Some of his more direct proposals favoured censorship of books directed towards the sexual education of children and flippantly suggested a news blackout to cool Vietnam, while his media theories seemed generally to be moving toward media control – the latter having always been a motif in his work.

The story of the book and its aftermath has already been told. I met with Marshall a few times after that – once in Hamilton where Joan and I met him and Corinne for a short visit in their motel suite . The meeting was stiff, since Corinne, had been angered by my book. Marshall chatted pleasantly with Joan and expressed approval that she was pursuing an MA in film and communication at McGill. He was also quite warm and amiable in his conversation with me. Afterwards, Marshall and I exchanged letters. He had written to me on occasions during the 1970s sending me offprints, thanking me for entertaining a friend of his in Montreal and the like.

It seems likely that by the latter part of the 1970s the University of Toronto's School of Graduate Studies was already trying to close down the Centre for Culture and Technology. Marshall's papers had been offered (presumably for sale) to the University of Toronto, which had expressed no interest in them. Some of his family, friends, and advisors felt that it might be best if Marshall and his papers moved to the United States. Bruce Powers, a warm, congenial late collaborator and long time friend of McLuhan's, worked out a plan by which, through a grant from a foundation in the U.S., McLuhan (and Eric) would take a position at Niagara University with a substantial salary and the university would acquire his papers – and perhaps, although I am not sure, his library. When Powers approached the Toronto Graduate School to verify that he would not be offending the university by acquiring the papers for Niagara University, the dean's office reiterated that the University of Toronto was not interested in them. Eric, probably realizing that his father would not really wish to move to the United States, asked me to meet with Powers and help him to explain to Powers the possible ramifications of the McLuhan papers leaving Canada. I met with Eric and Powers at the Park Plaza Hotel's pub on Bloor Street and explained what I thought would be the outburst in the media and the cultural and academic communities in Canada if these cultural properties were to leave the country. Subsequently, the arrangement did not come to fruition and ultimately the papers were sold to the National Archives of Canada. One cannot blame the McLuhans for thinking of leaving Canada, since the University of Toronto's Graduate Faculty was treating one of Canada's great figures of the twentieth century miserably. This situation was compounded a few years later when the Graduate Faculty closed the Centre unilaterally without the knowledge of its then-president, James Ham (who had been an early participant in McLuhan's first seminars in the 1950s and an adviser on his research for the NAEB). Fortunately the Centre was later reopened and celebrated its thirtieth anniversary in 1998.

In late 1979 I returned to Ontario to become the third president of Trent University. I was away from Canada when Marshall died on 31 December 1980. My contacts with McLuhaniana from the early 1980s until 1995 involved the writing of two encyclopedia articles on McLuhan, a review of his *Letters* for the *Canadian Journal of Communication*, an article arising out of a UNESCO sponsored Paris seminar on him, and the provision of some material to William Toye for the notes of the Oxford edition of McLuhan's *Letters*.

After retiring as president of Trent in 1987, I returned to academic work, primarily on literary and communication theory and modernist and post-modernist literature and art, particularly Joyce. I was guest editor of the *Canadian Journal of Communication*'s issue on McLuhan for the twenty-fifth anniversary of the publication of *Understanding Media*, sponsored by Teleglobe and released on the occasion of the 1989 McLuhan awards in Montreal, at which Joan and I had a brief social encounter with Corinne. My issue on *McLuhan* included contributions by Eric McLuhan, Philip Marchand, and William Kuhns to complement articles by Paul Heyer, Liss Jeffreys, and my wife and me.

An invitation in 1996 from Sylvere Lotringer of Columbia to speak about McLuhan at a conference on French Theory in North America (Columbia/NYU, Nov. 1997) and participation in Lance Strate's Fordham conference on McLuhan (March 1998) has led me to realize that a reconsideration of McLuhan's work from someone who was as close to him as I was during a crucial formative period is important in developing the true nature of his significance, while also providing a more personal portrait of this unique man with his strengths and weaknesses

Introduction

Edmund Carpenter, with Marshall McLuhan, co-founded the Culture and Communication seminars at the University of Toronto in 1953. As McLuhan's associate he became founding editor of the early, prestigious interdisciplinary journal *Explorations*, with McLuhan as his co-editor. At that time Carpenter was in his early thirties and teaching anthropology at the University of Toronto, where he was regarded as an impressive instructor by his graduate students. Subsequently he taught anthropology at the University of California (Santa Cruz), Harvard, and the New School.

It has been said that Edmund Carpenter defies labels as much as his books defy categories. Anthropologist, film maker, teacher, writer – he has worked in many media and lived in many cultures, including the Canadian Arctic, Siberia, Southeast Asia, Borneo, and New Guinea. As is apparent in *The Virtual Marshall McLuhan* and in Philip Marchand's biography of McLuhan, he was one of McLuhan's closest friends for over thirty years and had a significant impact on his work. He still pursues research into anthropology, archeology, and art.

He is the author of *Eskimo* (1959) (text by Edmund Carpenter, sketches and paintings by Frederick Varley, and sketches and photographs of Robert Flaherty's collection of Eskimo carvings), which was a special ninth and final issue of the original *Explorations*, and editor with McLuhan of *Explorations in Communication* (1960). His works include, among others, *They Became What They Beheld* (1970); *Eskimo Realities* (1973); *Oh What a Blow That Phantom Gave Me* (1973); *Materials for the Study of Social Symbolism in Ancient &*

Tribal Art: A Record of Tradition and Continuity Based on the Researches and Writings of Carl Schuster (edited and written by Edmund Carpenter; assisted by Lorraine Spiess, 1986-1988); and *Patterns That Connect: Social Symbolism in Ancient and Tribal Art.* Carl Schuster and Edmund Carpenter, (1996)

D.F.T.

That Not-So-Silent Sea

EDMUND CARPENTER

We were the first that ever burst
Into that silent sea.

Samuel Taylor Coleridge

Robert Fulford kindly sent me a copy of *Canadian Notes & Queries*, 45, containing his article on *Explorations*. *Explorations* was a journal I founded, named, edited, marketed, mailed, partly financed, then tried (unsuccessfully) to bury.

About the time I received his article, an announcement arrived saying *Explorations* would resume publication. I also learned of a book being written about it.

Why this interest in a journal now scarcely remembered? Fulford doesn't say. Instead, he offers an inside view of the skunk works. Earlier accounts are much like his. All share two features: their authors never consulted me and what they wrote was mostly wrong.

The problem is understandable. *Explorations*, 1953-59, was "casually" edited. One redeeming quality was unpredictability. This worried university administrators, terrified one of the co-editors, and delighted some readers.

The first issue had a printing of 1,000, while issues 2 to 7 ran to 2,000 each, all of which sold quickly. Issue 8 had a run of 3,000, but sold poorly. Issue 9 was a University of Toronto Press book sent to subscribers with *"Explorations"* printed on the cover. That book enjoyed several printings and a revised edition, totalling about 15,000 copies.

Explorations in Communication (1960), an anthology from the journal, went through numerous printings, plus many translations. Over the years it sold extremely well, mostly as a textbook in the U.S. It still pays royalties, though only minuscule, primarily for reprint rights.

Fulford's account understandably ignores articles missing from *Explorations*, though several potential articles were often more interesting than printed ones. I asked Eliot, Lewis, cummings, and others how the typewriter influenced their styles. Most answered. I was particularly interested in what Pound might say, for his typed correspondence was like no other:

> "For catholik schools/ instead of
> that empty ass in the Fattycan calling fer
> peace/ he might THINK to a basis /
> attack destruction of ALL contemplative
> life/ television/ so that NO one shall ever
> again look at anything long enough
> to get any idea how come.

"BUT we NEED (anbloodyHOW)   more communication/   less sleep as switches an bitches."

Pound's response, from St. Elizabeth's hospital, killed that article:
"15 Feb

NO
You most cert may NOT have my permission to quote my private correspondence
            UNTIL you make some effort to get me out of
bughousz
            and show interest in something more basic than Gussie Moran's tennis pants
            AND Brazil is 30 years ahead of you   anyhow
                    goRRellup yu

why dont yu go to Montreal?"

I wrote to Russian linguists, asking for articles on the effect of electronic media, especially TV, on Marxist theory & practice. Sounds crazy to imagine getting a serious reply, but I knew one scholar there who understood the question. Moreover, that scholar once stood up to Stalin and, with Western help, miraculously survived. I imagined him slipping his essay quietly past authority (which guards only its past), the way DeGaulle shipped transistor radios to Legionnaires "to relieve barracks boredom" and then, at the crucial moment, bypassed their officers and spoke directly to them: *Soldats de France ...*" Or the way

Chinese & Soviet authorities recently shut down press & TV but over-looked FAX, BBC, CNN. I wanted to know if, or how, anyone thought Marxism, so clearly a product of print, could possibly survive an electronic storm. So I wrote & wrote, suffered Soviet & RCMP visitors, and in the end got only Party Line. I printed these depressing Soviet articles only because the 'fifties belonged to McCarthy, even in Canada, and any dialogue seemed better than no dialogue.

Then there was a series of articles "authored" by one of the co-editors, Tom Easterbrook. Tom was a bit of a hypochondriac, always in doctors' waiting-rooms. On one occasion, he picked up *Medical Economics* or *Your Doctor* or something and realized that, in an article on enzymes, if "entrepreneur" replaced "enzyme", that article would delight economists. Off the new article went to Karl Deutsch, MIT economist & editor. Deutsch was about to publish it when Tom confessed. Deutsch was furious. Tom did many more "transmutations," but never let me publish one.

I also remember a class assignment on magazine biases. One student, who worked nights as a printer, chose the *New Yorker* magazine's unillustrated reviews of contemporary art. Using the same typeface as the *New Yorker*, and the same jagged column-divider, he reset three reviews, switching artists, names, and paintings' titles. He laid this new type over the old, photographed entire pages, complete with ads, then sent sets to prominent critics & academics, asking specific questions. Of those who answered (and most did), none spotted the substitutions and all agreed with the reviews. Wanted to run these re-writes & responses, but the *New Yorker* objected.

What I solicited & what I received were sometimes worlds apart. But because I'd begged, I printed. Some real clunkers got in or superb manuscripts missed deadlines and ended up elsewhere, even nowhere, including a wonderful one, "The Vertical and the Horizontal in Art and Science," by Lancelot Law Whyte.

So it went. Much that belonged was missing; much that appeared didn't belong. Focus & thrust got blurred. Still, something must have gotten through. Readers who "found" the journal included Eric Havelock, Edmund Leach, Susan Sontag, Jacques Derrida, Claude Lévi-Strauss, Roland Barthes. Most were then unknown. Several were students. Not all applauded. Ezra Pound warned: *"Explorations* sign Toronto sinking to level of Paris." But orders exceeded printings.

FOCUS

Explorations focused on media biases.[1] This concern rested on the belief that certain media favor, while others do not, certain ideas &

values, or more simply: each medium is a unique soil. That soil doesn't guarantee which plants will grow there, but it influences which plants blossom or wilt there.

The first "group approach" to this subject, at least the first known to me, was organized around 1947 by the U.S. State Department to train Foreign Service officers. George Trager headed a team consisting of Edward Hall, Henry Lee Smith, and, as consultant, Ray Birdwhistel. They studied & taught language in the broadest sense, including body language. Among their assigned readings were essays by Benjamin Lee Whorf and Dorothy Lee. To make these essays readily accessible, they reprinted several in 1952.

Whorf, a brilliant, independent scholar, wrote his first paper on spatial metaphors, his last on parallels between Hopi metaphysics & language. In between, he published several articles suggesting a deterministic relationship between language & thought. Everything he wrote was fascinating, though I found only his first & last essays convincing. But the word was out, the subject in, and much speculation followed.[2]

DOROTHY LEE

About this same time, Dorothy Lee, unaware of Whorf's work, published a series of papers on language, value & perception. These were far more sophisticated than Whorf's efforts and a major influence on & in *Explorations*.

Lee was born Dorothy Demetracopulos in 1905 in Constantinople where her father, a Greek Evangelical pastor, served as his country's ambassador. She won a scholarship to Vassar (her brother Raphael Demos won one to Harvard; he later became Royce Professor of Philosophy). For a time, Dorothy lived at the home of Alfred North Whitehead.

In 1931, she took a PHD in anthropology at Berkeley, writing her dissertation on the language of the Wintu, a paleo-Indian tribe. She then married Otis Lee, who shortly afterwards became chairman of the Department of Philosophy at Vassar. When Otis Lee had left Cody, Wyoming, to accept a scholarship at Harvard, the high school band had played as the train pulled out. At Oxford, as a Rhodes Scholar, he founded a chamber-music group. At Freiberg, the Lees watched helplessly as student thugs drove a Jewish professor from his classroom. They saw both sides of existentialism: for Heidegger, Nazism; for them, freedom.

Otis Lee died suddenly in 1948. Just before he died, he had asked Dorothy how various tribesmen might answer certain philosophical questions. After she'd finished dinner and helped four children with schoolwork, she wiped the kitchen table clean and sat down to answer those questions. The result was a series of remarkable essays on languages that lacked or minimized temporal tenses, adjectives, metaphors, first-person singular, as well as all equivalents to our verbs "to bell & "to become"; languages that blurred the distinction between nouns & verbs, that conjugated & declined from plural to singular, but also possessed forms alien to Standard Indo-European languages.[3]

As that silent dialog faded, Dorothy gradually gave up writing. She preferred one-to-one dialog. Print got in the way. She loved the subject of anthropology, but not the profession. She worried when students followed her uncritically, losing their autonomy. She resigned from Harvard and in her last years moved about the country, teaching in home economics at Iowa State, in art at Immaculate Heart, wherever she found dialog. I write about her here because she was *Explorations* most influential force.

Whorf died in 1941, so his influence on *Explorations* was only indirect. Lee's, however, was direct. Six essays by her, as well as four commentaries on those essays, appeared in successive issues. Letters from her filled several folders. She met with our group repeatedly, first in Louisville at a conference organized by Ray Birdwhistel. Also in attendance were Edward Hall, George Trager, Henry Lee Smith, Margaret Mead, Larry Frank, Robert Armstrong, and others whose contributions constituted about a fifth of *Explorations*.

COMMUNICATIONS SEMINAR

When I speak of "our group" I refer to members of a Toronto communications seminar funded by the Ford Foundation, 1952–53: Tom Easterbrook, Economics; Marshall McLuhan, English, Jacqueline Tyrwhitt, Town Planning; Carl Williams, Psychology; and myself, Anthropology.

The seminar started with great enthusiasm, but instantly got nowhere. I proposed a journal. Claude Bissell, who was then vice president of the university, agreed and obtained Ford Foundation approval. The result was a humanistic journal, appearing at a time when social sciences modeled themselves after physical sciences, complete with claims of "objectivity," in the manner of *Time* reporters.

The humanistic approach ultimately led to friction within the seminar, but not at first. Tom Easterbrook took Harold Innis as mentor. Marshall McLuhan saw poetry as the sap of life. Jacqueline Tyrwhitt regarded architecture as a holy pursuit. I thought of anthropology as art availing itself of scientific findings. Carl Williams, however, sought to refine psychology to an objective science. It was for this reason he was invited to join the group. We felt we needed his bias to balance ours, and also to get Ford funding.

Carl provided the first breakthrough. He used the phrase "auditory space" in describing an experiment by E.A. Bott. The experiment itself was more roadblock than bridge. But the phrase was electrifying. Marshall changed it to "acoustic space" and quoted Symbolist poetry. Jackie mentioned the Indian city of Fatehpur Sikri. Tom saw parallels in medieval Europe. I talked about Eskimos.

Earlier I'd wondered if Plato's & Aristotle's "hierarchy of senses" enjoyed counterparts in tribal societies. Did each culture possess a unique sensory profile? Why was sight so often muted in tribal art & dance? Was non-representational art direct sensory programming?"

Acoustic space" offered a clue. If the ear's "grammar" could pattern space, could other sensory codes explain silent music, invisible art, motionless dance? Were the senses themselves primary media? Was hard-edged art tactile patterning?

Carl sent a paper on "auditory space" to *Explorations*, minus all seminar dialog. So Marshall & I put it in. A mistake. Two articles, one on the mechanics of auditory space, the other on acoustic "patterning," might have been more diplomatic. But we needed some input from Carl, and clearly it wouldn't come without help.

The same problem arose in an experiment about media biases. For several years I'd supplemented my teaching salary by free-lancing in TV, radio, print. I did what all free-lancers do: I tried recycling the same material in several media. It rarely works. No medium is wholly neutral. Certain ideas lend themselves kindly, others do not, to specific media. If all media were alike, we'd need only one.

To test this, I prepared a single script for simultaneous presentation as lecture, TV, radio, & print, plus a single examination for the four audiences. I tried not to slant the script toward any one medium. This probably doomed the experiment from the start. Ideally, I should have chosen a subject already available in several media, e.g., *The Caine Mutiny*, then popular as book, play, film, & TV. But the mechanics of an ideal experiment weren't feasible.

A much better test was run several years later by a former student of mine. He asked two audiences to view the governor general's funeral on TV: one in color, the other in black & white. Both audiences answered the same factual questions, then wrote essays. Black & white answers were far more accurate and essays nearly five times longer. However, those who saw it in color expressed greater enjoyment with the show and warmer feelings toward the deceased.

But to return to the first experiment. I asked the whole seminar to get involved. Carl scored the answers, which was great, but then published a paper on the experiment which compared media in terms of general effectiveness. I felt this missed the whole point — that different media offered different paths to different realities. I objected.

There was also a difference over money. The Ford grant provided for released faculty time. A colleague's illness canceled my free time. I asked that the funds be applied to *Explorations*. The university, having spent them, demurred. The head of Anthropology, as always, supported the administration. So did Carl. I suggested the Ford Foundation be consulted. The funds went to *Explorations*.

Finally, Carl insisted that his name be removed from the masthead of *Explorations*. The immediate reason was my acceptance of an article by G. Legman on censored ballads, an article now regarded as a definitive reference. Readers today might be puzzled by its reception in 1956. The printer took it to the head of the press. He in turn took it to the president, a former dean of law. President Smith phoned me, using words far more earthy than anything in Legman's article. I offered to delete whatever he blue-penciled. He lived next door to the museum where I worked. I was soon on his doorstep. A maid took the galleys, leaving the door slightly ajar. It was very cold. I wore a raincoat left over from the Marine Corps. I waited & waited. Finally an arm extended the galleys. There were no deletions.

MARSHALL MCLUHAN

I mention these differences only because Fulford raises them. He also speaks of differences between Marshall & me. Not so. We got along famously, almost daily, whenever & wherever possible; spent our time in one another's kitchen; shared all readings, all confidences; hung out in jazz clubs; walked the streets. Life with Marshall was pure theatre. I recall one afternoon in the museum coffee shop. It was pouring outside. A stranger appeared & announced: "Just the two I want to see." He unrolled a great scroll. It showed a crudely drawn giant hurling boulders at a mountain village labeled "Mechanization." "Aha," said Marshall, "Toronto's William Blake with a low I.Q." The man rolled up the scroll and, pointing a finger at Marshall, ordered him to put out his cigar, "that product of mechanization." Marshall took a long draw, then slowly blew out the smoke. "That cigar," he said, "was hand-rolled along the thigh of a Tahitian maiden."

In thirty-two years of friendship, I recall only two differences between us, both minor. One concerned a bungling designer who interfered with the printing of *Explorations* 7, wasting money. I asked Mar-

243 That Not-So-Silent Sea

shall why he tolerated him. "Every man," he said, "needs a dog." A harsh judgement, harshest on himself.

The second incident concerned *Explorations* 8, which I didn't edit. That was pure McLuhan, his first involvement. *The Toronto Telegram* ran full-page Sunday ads, but these had a reverse effect. The large, costly printing scarcely moved. Marshall stashed the printing at home while gone for the summer. We were obligated to print one more issue. With funds exhausted, revenue zero, no accounting, I wrote to him. I still have his reply:

"Gee whiz Ted, what a breath of fresh hair. Let us up periscope and see if the concrete is hardening. Yep, it's hardening up and down the budget valley. Now don't go into a feminine flap. If I didn't think you could raise $50,000 in half an hour any time you set your mind to it, I'd do it for you."

I raised the money, though nothing like that, and not in half an hour. The crisis passed. Still, I wanted out. I wrote a book entitled *Eskimo*, printed *"Explorations"* on enough copies to fill paid subscriptions, and hoped I'd buried *Explorations* forever. Marshall, however, wanted it to go on.

Now some things everybody can do: drive a car, serve in the military, work in a factory, edit a magazine. But Marshall wasn't like everybody else. He wasn't even like anybody else. One thing he could never do was edit a magazine. His plan was to provide the ideas, then let the rest take care of itself. *Explorations* became an unread supplement in an alumni quarterly.

I was no longer involved and, in a curious way, I gradually became uninvolved with the earlier issues. I'd made a selection from them, written an introduction, then taken this anthology to Oxford Press. It was rejected. I mentioned this to Marshall. He offered to show the manuscript to a friend, just appointed editor of Beacon Press. Beacon accepted the book, the only change being the addition of Marshall as co-editor. It sold well, in American & foreign editions. The Japanese edition dropped my name, inside & out.

It was also dropped whenever the journal was mentioned in the press, confirming my conviction that hack journalists shun primary sources. The reason was simple: hype focuses. Those who hyped Marshall, starting with Gossage & Feigen, a PR firm, ignored the community of contributors who generated these ideas. Instead, they assigned everything to one guru. This wasn't Marshall's doing, though he didn't object.

One idea commonly associated with "McLuhanism" is the contrast between linear & non-linear codifications of reality. Yet the study itself belongs wholly to Dorothy Lee. She borrowed the term "linear," she tells us, from the physical sciences.[4] In *Explorations*, she contrasted pre-literate & literate pattern-making & pattern-perceiving. In another issue of that journal, Harold Innis treated media as history-shapers. I linked Lee & Innis and proposed print as the final force in the development of linear codes. Marshall, with his unfailing genius for coining phrases, spoke of "Typographic Man."

THE RIGHT PHRASE

Phrases. Marshall found them, coined them, modified them, then used them in unpredictable ways. When he was young, he read that the best way to enlarge a vocabulary was to use a new word each day in various contexts. He and Tom Easterbrook were then working on a farm. The farmer, Tom said, was bewildered.

An easy way to find the source of many of Marshall's phrases is to examine the back pages of the books in his library. As he read, he jotted down phrases & ideas, by page, in the rear. "Global village," properly noted, appears in a Wyndham Lewis book. Marshall liberated that phrase. It will probably (and properly) enter Bartlett's *Familiar Quotations* under "McLuhan." A more accurate phrase, as Marshall later realized, was "global theatre." But this proved unappealing to journalists who considered themselves neutral reporters, not theatrical producers.

"The medium is the message," came from Ashley Montagu's lecture, "The Method is the Message," which Marshall & I attended. Marshall improved the wording and extended the concept. "The medium is the massage" came from Sam Zacks. Marshall had been asked to explain his earlier phrase, to which Sam, who favored steam baths & massages, replied: "You mean, like a massage?" At which point, message became massage, mass-age, mess-age.

So it went, an Andy Warhol factory. Everything from classics to comics got recycled. With input from 360, Marshall distilled, shaped, burnished, orchestrated. He had an astonishing capacity to summarize, then christen ideas with unforgettable headlines. I recall a formal lecture by Suzanne Langer. The chair called for questions. Marshall was instantly on his feet. Without preamble, he summarized Langer point by point, in modified nursery rhymes, ending with Little Jack Horner and then, with his thumb in his mouth, left the room. The chair apologized. It was surely the best commentary Langer ever received.

I also recall an afternoon when Marshall flipped through Vincent Massey's 1951 call for High Kulcha in Canada. He laughed & laughed, then scribbled a response modeled after Wyndham Lewis' *BLAST*,

1914. I immediately set it in type on a museum labeling machine. *COUNTERBLAST*, 1954, privately printed, appeared a few days later. If anyone wants to know what an hour with Marshall McLuhan could be like, read that review.

Words, words, spoken, written, in earnest, in jest. He warned the expressway-loving Premier of Ontario: "Mere concern with efficient traffic flow is a cloacal obsession that sends the city down the drain." When he learned that Harold Innis was baptized "Herald" after *The Family Herald*, and as a child had excelled at wringing turkey necks, he remarked: "Hark, the Herald Innis wrings." Images poured forth, day & night, as late as 3 a.m. I sometimes took the receiver off the hook before going to bed.

Writers commonly speak of Marshall's original ideas. He had none. Be grateful. They would have been right off the wall. His genius lay in perceiving, not creating. He accepted the world as he found it and simply described what he saw, free of the haze he believed obstructed all others.

He also had no small talk. He might mention small matters, but when he did, his unflinching directness transformed that subject, no matter how humble. Once we saw a turd in the center of the broad steps forming the grand entrance to the Royal Ontario Museum. "Human," he said. The bizarre scene this (correct) judgement required would have escaped all conventional minds.

MATCHING

Marshall possessed what Lévi-Strauss called "the dithyrambic gift of synthesis, the almost monstrous faculty to perceive as similar what other men have conceived as different." He treated academic boundaries as barriers; professionalism as constipation; ignorance as asset. His approach resembled Operations Research, a World War Two program where biologists & psychologists worked on problems ordinarily assigned to engineers & physicists.

He loved to apply one discipline's insights to another discipline's data. Stopping a colleague on campus, he'd announce his latest "breakthrough," in ten thousand words, nonstop. These onslaughts could wreck anybody's day. Each contained enough truth to put in jeopardy one's dearest convictions. Worse, each contained enough contradictions & comedy to put in jeopardy the university itself.

The magic of joining opposites delighted him. Every cliché became a reversed cliché, borrowed or coined: life imitates art (Wilde); invention is the mother of necessity (Veblen); an idea that outlives its uselessness (McLuhan); in the land of the blind a one-eyed man is a hunted criminal (McLuhan). Scientific laws, he argued, worked equally well in reverse.

Everything, absolutely everything, went into this mix. Marshall skimmed several books a day, jotting notes. These became the next article. John Brockman, a devotee, tried the same thing. He asked a dozen academics to list the books most influential to them. He then bought a copy of each. Over a long weekend on Cape Cod, he skimmed the lot, briefly summarizing what he regarded as key concepts. These notes became the text for *The Late John Brockman*, a book differing from Marshall's writings solely in quality.

Marshall's files were a pirate's wardroom, loot from Seven Seas, previous owners forgotten. As Pound wrote to him: "11yr/ writing will become a lot livelier when yu start looking for credits rather than debts / not matter much where a man GOT what, but what he did with it (or without it) AFTER he got it."

What, then, did Marshall do with all this loot? Using a format borrowed from Pound, he combined seemingly disparate elements into "mosaics." When you interface the right images, each illuminates the other, like a blade on a grindstone. Sparks fly. His ultimate model was the front page of the daily press with its discontinuous, randomly juxtaposed items. His more immediate model, as he repeatedly stated, came from Pound.

The capacity to link seemingly unrelated concepts is also, of course, at the heart of science. Jacob Bronowski compares it to the blind man discovering that the inside & outside of a cup hang together, or to the Sherpa who recognizes the mountain he sees in a neighboring valley as the opposite side of the mountain where he grew up. Marshall's early efforts at mixing & matching proved wonderfully productive. I was reminded of this by today's *Wall Street Journal* which lists, *in separate articles*, recent newspaper & department store bankruptcies, catastrophic in number. Forty years ago Marshall equated department stores (all products under one roof) and newspapers (all news in one paper), and predicted TV would render both obsolete.

Later, as his health deteriorated, he mixed & matched randomly, with diminished results. He even patented a set of cards, each printed with a riddle or aphorism. Executives were invited to shuffle the deck, draw a card, then apply that riddle or aphorism to a current problem, say a strike or bankruptcy.

Was there a grand scheme behind all this? A grand man, yes, but more? A contribution to science? Most scientists believe that reality is not in appearances but in the underlying laws that govern appearances. Toward the end of his life, Marshall announced his discovery of four underlying "laws" that govern media. He invited skeptics to disprove them. No one stepped forward. All four were basic notions long accepted, each with a considerable literature behind it. He simply liberated, described, then juxtaposed those concepts to form a tetrad. He applied this tetrad to a variety of phenomena, in the manner of a parlor game. Like dousing, it sometimes worked.

LABELS

Critics called Marshall this or that, then responded to their own labels. But no label fit. If he reminded me of anyone (and he didn't), it would have been a 19th century tinker, at some crossroads in rural America, who produced endless inventions, some practical, most not, using materials at hand and unfamiliar methods.

Post-literate & pre-literate materials, both at hand, also provided alien methods. Marshall's interest in myths & oracles extended to the methods that produced them. He borrowed from poets, shamans, tricksters, magicians, as well as from scientists. He regarded Symbolism as in no way incompatible with radical scientific thinking. He felt no conflict between reason & belief. He accepted evidence rural priests would question.

Like Ananda Coomaraswamy, he saw miracles as "things that can be done even today by those who know how, and therefore present no intrinsic problem"; on the other hand, the question whether such and such a miracle was actually performed on a given occasion seems to me unimportant compared with the transparent meanings of miracles (this takes us back to symbolism).

Symbolism presupposes real analogies on different levels of reference. Hence also symbols and their references are inseparable — the symbols are the language of revelation, not a language to be constructed at will in the sense of 'let this be understood to refer to this' (that may be signification, but not symbolism).

I was reminded of all this recently in Washington, at the unveiling of Bill Reid's monumental sculpture, *Black Canoe*. Here, in an overloaded canoe, the principal characters of Haida mythology play out their ancient roles. Each also enacts its Washington bestiary. At the bow, a huge bear, moving bare-assed backwards into the future, faces an aggressive eagle; beaver paddles ignoring both; wolf grasps eagle's wing; etc. In the center sits a serene Haida chief who closely resembles the sculptor. Bill compared the work to a family drive on a rainy Sunday with the car windows closed.

Sit Marshall in a small tub, fill that tub with improbable media characters, especially those up to no good, then set them all adrift into that not-so-silent sea, or (in fact) sit him in an East Side pub with Walt

Kelly, crowd the air with characters from politics & literature, comics & classics, Plato to Pogo. Add songs, drinks, cigars.

Rainmaker, sorcerer, trickster, juggler, poet, punster, magician, scientist. It was no accident he teamed up with an ethnologist. The main difference between us was that he'd long ago crossed over to the other side. What I studied, he lived. Forget art imitates life/life imitates art; for him, life was art/art was life. The world he lived in was not Toronto, 1950. I didn't need to go to the Arctic to find an informant from another world.

When I left Toronto, he had his college buy my library on European magic & witchcraft. I had assembled it to study what I regarded as pathology. His interests went way beyond my prejudices.

Had Marshall labeled himself poet, artist, composer, few would have objected. But he insisted his "mosaics" were "scientific." This at a time when social scientists took themselves very, very seriously.

Today it's hard to imagine how seriously. In 1950, a prominent physician acknowledged in wistful seriousness an introduction to an anthropologist: "Ah, yes! You are an anthropologist — one of the only group of men who might be trusted with power to rule!" Americans, their wealth & optimism vastly increased by the Second War, dedicated both to science, not least to social science. Marshall knew he could never sell himself to the world, nor his services to its leaders, as poet or trickster. So he put on a lab coat.

Later he called *The Gutenberg Galaxy* "a footnote to the observations of Harold Innis." Still later he suggested parallels with St Thomas Aquinas. Thomists at St. Michael's remained unconvinced.

HAROLD INNIS

I remain unconvinced of his allegiance to Innis. I was present at several of their few meetings, arranged by Tom Easterbrook. Marshall talked on & on, at one point drifting into politics. Innis detested dictators, monopolies, censorship, racism. He was firmly committed to an open society. Marshall was just as firmly committed to a closed society. He thought Blacks, Jews, Protestants, would all be happier elsewhere. He defended Franco's suppression of Protestants. Innis said nothing.

Other differences divided them. Marshall loved America's "cornucopia of surrealism." He thought Canadians were missing out on a good thing. Innis feared its impact on Canadian identity. William Lyon Mackenzie King, he wrote, "found Canada a nation and left it a colony in relation to U.S. – particularly as a result of radio."

Innis, with only a short time to live, drew up a document to be read after his death. It proposed guidelines for faculty serving as consultants to government & business: unpaid advisors who traveled by coach. He was particularly worried about who his successor might be, so he included faculty evaluations, with recommendations. When this document was opened, it was quickly suppressed.

Innis's successor was Vincent Bladen, author of a textbook on economics. A student took a copy from the Reserve Reading Room to the toilet, defecated between its covers, then returned it to its shelf. The librarian who discovered this went directly to the head librarian: "Dr MacDonald, I thought it was a cookie."

Bladen's knowledge of anthropology was, as far as I knew, nil. Yet he got himself elected president, Society for Applied Anthropology. He wanted to sell anthropology to businessmen, especially advertisers. He asked that a junior member of his staff be granted, without examination, a PHD in anthropology. I objected. The proposal was abandoned after it reached the graduate committee. But ill-feeling followed.

One form it took was a review by an English critic of *Explorations 1:* "excessive scientism," "flagrant lack of elementary caution," "hysterical outburst." The review had been commissioned by one of Bladen's coterie. Soon a second English critic assumed the burden. Along with several other journalists, Frank Kermode set himself up as interpreter & judge of these ideas and, over the years, made a good thing out of it for himself. His criticism reminded me of a dog who nips at your heels, then wags when you face him. He commissioned & edited Jonathan Miller's *McLuhan*, a book without merit. Sir Frank continues to provide commentaries, but has yet to contribute to the dialog.

Innis was never Marshall's mentor, not really. Marshall followed no one. Only poetry & scripture escaped correction. Nor would Innis ever have become Marshall's defender. Mixing & matching, OK, but huckstering? Innis remained, even after his death, a symbol of integrity. Identifying with this icon helped deflect criticism.

The gap between them was wide, the difference, say, between Frost & Pound. Harold Innis was a social model. He personified reason, justice, democracy. When he spoke, he seemed to speak for society. Marshall spoke for himself. He suppressed nothing, least of all contradictions. He loved books; he loved the media replacing them. He was totally unique; he announced the end of individualism. He promoted his public image; he loathed that public image.

One day we were swapping "Greatest Invention" jokes: "Not the lever, not the wheel, but the thermos bottle." "The thermos bottle? That just keeps liquid hot or cold." "Yeah, but how do it know?" Etc. I told him of an elderly farm woman who quietly proposed "Screens, to keep out flies." To which Marshall replied, with equal gravity, "the electric shaver": for ten years he'd avoided looking in a mirror.

Differences between McLuhan & Innis were unbridgeable, though their writings covered much the same ground and employed much the same style. Innis's last books, *Empire and Communication*, 1950; *The Bias of Communication*, 1951; and *Changing Concepts of Time*, published posthumously in 1952, were written in haste, under pressure. Each week he checked out a bagful of books and took them home by streetcar. His distilled notes, on cards, read like telegrams to Tasmania. Each morning he added those cards to several stacks on his office floor. Card by card, stacks became books. These books aren't easy to read. I once assigned them at Harvard, but even the best students stumbled. Everything you want is there, but impossible to grasp until you independently reach those same conclusions.

Marshall reached his own conclusions. He took examples from Innis, the best of course.[5] What Marshall did with them was something else.

The same problem arises when we compare tribal & modern art. Did Picasso sit at the feet of tribal artists? We know he collected their art. We know bits from it appear in his art. But Picasso's art is not out of Africa.

This business of who-took-what-from-whom misses the point. In one of his last essays, Eric Havelock, who left Toronto in 1947, suggested that the so-called Toronto School of Communications started with a phrase he used in a lecture possibly attended by Innis. From Innis this went to McLuhan and from there to the world. Nonsense. This wasn't a torch race. It was a light show.

Let's start with Toronto, where it all began. Even into the 1950s, the city remained a depressing place: its architecture, food, meanness, what Marshall called, "The cringing, flunkey spirit of Canadian culture, its servant-quarter snobbishness resentments ignorance penury." Not a joyous place at all. Leopold Infeld described it as perhaps the finest city in which to die, especially on Sunday afternoon when "the transition between life and death would be continuous, painless and scarcely noticeable."

Then, suddenly, refugees appeared, different hued, many tongued, talented, hungry, including BBC directors looking for work, Hollywood writers fleeing McCarthy. In 1950, CBC-Radio spun off a competitor, CBC-TV. Magnetic tape broke recording monopolies. LPs filled the air with African drums, Medieval music, Black humor, anything. Little mags appeared & disappeared: the Mellons backed one, the Ford Foundation several, the CIA at least one. A vendor just off campus stocked many, even one from Brazil. Others were available by mail or under the counter. A small bookstore on Yonge specialized in serious writings.

A cauldron of diversity. An open market. Even the university showed signs of life. Its elders still suffered from mildewed respectability, its faculty union still smelled of moth-balls, but returning servicemen made every class an adult class. Where Northrop Frye could legitimately ask, "How do you teach Milton to a class in heat?" now classes included students who had been to Hell & back.

All this was also happening elsewhere in North America, but with one difference: from Toronto, you could see it happening. It was like living on an island, studying the mainland. You saw the whole show. Its main event was the electronic revolution. The local blackout highlighted that distant glow.

There was never a "Toronto School of Communications." It was simply a bunch of islanders watching the greatest show on earth. A table in the museum coffee shop served as meetingplace. There, at four o'clock, McLuhan & Tyrwhitt & I gathered, along with Don Theall & John Irving, a few students, occasionally Easterbrook, rarely Innis, plus Dorothy Lee, Sigfried Giedeon, Ashley Montagu, Karl Polyani, Roy Campbell, a dozen other visitors, and talked until the place closed.

Toronto had other oases, all unofficial. Two I knew well. TV producers, film directors, editors, cameramen, talked media far into the night at the home of the Hungarian cartoonist George Feyer. Artists, scholars, composers, architects, gathered almost nightly at the art-filled apartment of Sam & Ayala Zacks. Dialogue became Toronto's real academy. I recall walking north on Avenue Road with Ashley Montagu. Deep snow slowed us. As we struggled along, he told me the tale of the Elephant Man. Fifteen years later, in New York, I urged an editor to call him. A tale told on Avenue Road entered Western memory.

Jackie Tywritt knew how to translate thought into reality. Never thanked, never credited, she helped change Toronto. One incident in particular comes to mind. Years earlier, the city had granted leases to private citizens for beach properties on Toronto Island. Those leases were about to expire. Developers had friends. The matter was to be settled by referendum.

Jackie assigned this project to a Town planning class. Each student illustrated his proposal with a maquette. Maquettes are perfect for TV. Days before the referendum, Jackie & class broadcast a one-hour TV show. TV was then new and potentially very persuasive. I recall in particular an attractive Chinese girl eloquently explaining her elegant model. Each student recommended public ownership. Developers were expected to win. Opinion shifted.[6]

You could do that sort of thing in the 'fifties. For one brief moment, media were open, democratic. I recall another instance, this one personal. I discovered that the ancient Serpent Mound near Peterborough, though on government land, had been sub-divided. Trees had been cut. Bulldozzers stood ready. Officials ignored me. So I mounted a one-man media crusade. Officialdom closed ranks. On the last day I gambled. I was never certain, but I suspected a $3,000 bribe, at a low level. Higher-ups, I knew, feared the charge of cover-up. I called the provincial minister of Education. The moment I got through, I warned: "Destroy that mound and I'll wipe your fucking ass across every headline in this province." It worked, instantly. The place is now a park. I believe a plaque there honors those same officials.

I mention these two incidents to illustrate changes in media access. Today (in the U.S. at least), private citizens, unless they possess immense wealth, have little access to media. This wasn't true of Toronto in the 'fifties. Media were then open, competing, democratic. A remarkable moment. It didn't last. Power & profit got their act together. From open market, media went to closed networks.

Before the nets closed, one could explore, speculate. It was McLuhan's gift or genius to tap this rich dialog, then summarize it in the manner of headlines. He loved headlines, collected them: *Berra's Big Bat Banishes Bums, Undercovermen Undercover Underworld Underwear, LaGuardia Gives Last Ball for Charity*. Headlines & ads captured real life. Skip content. Skim books, alternate pages only, distill four hundred pages to four sentences. His plan: weave insights, headlines, ads, lyrics, jokes, puns, into an all-media Baedeker, Joycean style.

THE GUTENBERG GALAXY & UNDERSTANDING MEDIA

In 1959 I moved to Northridge, California, where the State was starting a new campus. When I arrived, it was an orange grove. Today it has over forty thousand students. The anthropology department combined appointments in conventional fields (ethnology, archeology, linguistics, physical anthropology) with appointments in performing arts. Dorothy Lee left Harvard to join us and stayed six years. Other *Explorations* contributors came, as well as a jazz cellist, animator, multiscreen innovator, African author & drummer, folklorist, etc. All fit comfortably into the anthropology curriculum. A fabulous faculty! The administrators backed us all the way, including equipment & funding for a wide range of experiments, especially in film.

Marshall & I stayed in contact through letters, several a week, exchanging ideas & anecdotes. Free-lancing had given me some contact with media, but here we were testing & playing, right at the edge. We worked closely with Charles Eames, who was then perfecting the multi-screen film. When U.S. military bases closed, we acquired U2 140mm cameras & editors which we used for animation; filmed on & through smoke; married a slide projector & movie projector; painted & scratched 70mm film; mixed animation & shadow plays; etc., etc. — experiments Hollywood lacked time & patience to attempt. Several innovations gained wide acceptance. Several films took international awards.

Marshall followed this with great interest, providing sharp insights. I was writing from southern California, surely the first post-literate society. Students came from homes without books, privacy, conversation. Some reached university having never heard a completed sentence. When they first encountered an idea, any idea, it had the effect of religious conversion. This was a land awaiting the Coming of the Word. That Word arrived, a few years later, via Marshall.

On my first trip back to Toronto, I found him at St Michael's College, sitting at a long table. Spread out before him were scores of books: Innis, Mumford, etc. Books by contributors to *Explorations* were stacked behind each issue. Out of this came *The Gutenberg Galaxy*, Marshall's best book. It was also, in certain ways, his last.

Understanding Media had a more complex origin. In 1959, the National Association of Educational Broadcasters (NAEB), commissioned Marshall to develop a media syllabus for eleventh-graders, funded under Title VII, an education act administered by the Pentagon. From this came a mimeographed *Report on Project in Understanding Media*. Excerpts were ridiculed on the floor of the House of Representatives, then printed in the *Congressional Record*. The syllabus was put aside.

Marshall suggested we turn it into a book. We modified & enlarged the text, exchanging chapters by mail. I still have them. They fill a box. We'd collaborated before, on articles, but this was a book. My approach was conventional, cautious, pedestrian. His approach was that of the poet who, in the words of Laura Riding, attempts "to make language do more than express: to make it work: to redistribute intelligence by means of the word."

For Marshall, effect mattered most, preferably as satire. Exaggeration provided thrust & flavor. I admired his style, stood in awe of it. But it was his, not mine. I gradually withdrew. The final version of *Understanding Media* mixed both our contributions. This partly explains its uneven tone. Before it was printed, its editor asked me to supply the sources of most of the quotations.

Editing Marshall, no matter how sympathetically, turned bang into whimper. Even self-editing didn't help: [6.27.62] "Am trying to translate some of my own mosaic into lineal form, but not doing too well."

His later books were all collaborations, all edited, all hash. He was at his best in conversation. Next best: informal letters. Over the years, he sent me hundreds & hundreds, mostly scribbled. Those I saved fill two boxes. Here's one:

"On p. 265 of Leonard Duhl's *The Urban Condition*: Naomi Rothwell found there 'were few complaints about privacy if the barracks were cold.' Man! Consider that in relation to the fact that Northern Europe seemed to have literate characteristics before literacy. Coolth = fragmentation, psychic and social?

"Theme of Duhl about unhappy slum dwellers when transferred to fine new housing. Consider. Slum is tactile, olfactory, discontinuous, asymmetrical, non-lineal, ie. synesthetic, deep involvement. New planned housing is visually intense, non-tactile etc, fragmented etc. No wonder they feel isolated, desolate.

"Note modern intellectual 'goes slumming' when he wants synesthetic involvement. High-brow art is slum-tactual. *Mad* magazine is a high-brow slum."

Editing can stretch this, slow it down, but in no way improve it.

The Gutenberg Galaxy, Marshall's best book, suffered least from editing. Everything else got mauled, including a *Playboy* interview, often cited as the one instance when Marshall was understandable. First attempted by Jean Shepherd in 1967, the interview was successfully concluded by Gerald Stearn in 1969. I wasn't present, but I was told that Marshall's monologs left Stearn stunned. He solved this problem by excerpting phrases & ideas from Marshall's sources & writings, as well as from writings about him, translated these into conventional prose, then organized the whole as questions & answers. The result satisfied the many.

MARKETING MARSHALL

In 1965 I was invited to join Marshall at the offices of a PR firm in San Francisco. Gossage & Feigen held forth in a former firehouse. What I witnessed there is today so commonplace, so accepted, it dates me to say how much it disturbed me.[7] Howard "Luck" Gossage and Gerald Feigen pioneered in creating news for clients. News costs little to invent, nothing to broadcast. A network of journalists cooperated.

Gossage invented the icon T-shirt, backed *Ramparts* magazine, converted a ski resort into a year-round operation, mixed marketing & news, design & promotion, PR & journalism, etc., etc. The pump house became an "in" scene, heady with power, the ultimate in Innis' "fact faking factories." Journalistic ethics weren't high on the agenda.

Some day a biographer may detail the personal tragedies that followed. In the meantime, we have Tom Wolfe's "The Pump House Gang." Tom was there. His account left out a lot.

One omission that comes to mind concerned planted news. A secretary quietly interrupted the conference by placing in front of Gossage an open copy of *Time* and next to it Gossage's copy for one of its articles. He compared the two, smiled, then exhibited them. They were almost identical.

The conference disturbed me. I left several days early. One of my sons and a friend of his were with me. We headed for the Sierras. No gear, but we found old tarps in a dumpster, bought food at a country store, located a mountain stream. As I crumbled paper for a fire, I noticed a column in a San Francisco paper. It contained a planted plug. I recognized the source. Other examples appeared in the same paper, as well as in a copy of *Time* I was burning. No question, Gossage & Feigen were effective, frighteningly so in clear mountain air.

Having seen possibilities in *Understanding Media*, they offered Marshall their services, plus a $6,000 budget. Their plan: convert him into an internationally recognized media guru, then peddle him as a business consultant, fees to be established. Their success in this endeavor is now history. Immediately following this conference, a hurricane of McLuhan interviews, reviews, articles, books, cartoons, TV & radio shows, etc., etc., swept through the media. Promotional methods previously reserved for products & stars, especially rock stars, were now used on behalf of an academic, all stops out.

Marshall undertook a whirlwind tour as lecturer, consultant, guru. He advised executives on every conceivable subject. While stopping over with me in California, he received a call from the mayor of Los Angeles who sought guidance on riot prevention. Watts was burning.

Fame couldn't have come at a worse time. He was far from well. After finishing his NAEB report, he suffered a seizure so severe the last rites were administered. Blackouts followed. In San Francisco, he blanked-out for ten minutes; in San Diego, for nearly half an hour, unable to recognize me. The conference sponsor refused to pay him. It was a foretaste of what was to come.

The most diverse editors begged him for manuscripts. He might dictate several in one day. Each condensed yesterday's readings. Some got printed; most didn't. A publisher who bought two magazines, one on politics, another on food, told me she found a McLuhan article in the dead files of each. "I imagine every editor in North America has one."

Journalists compared Marshall to Newton & Einstein. Though he himself was a master at dissecting hype, he now became its victim. He impatiently awaited the Nobel Prize, in what field I never asked. In the end, the same journalists who hyped him, chopped him. Once credited with every 20th century insight, he was now denied any. Behind this shift lay a pattern. Power & profit & minions appropriated those ideas that served them, ridiculed the rest, then cut off the dialog.

NEW GAME, NEW PLAYERS

For me, the most interesting aspect of all this was the role of journalists. Many became instant authorities. PR releases, slightly modified, carried different by-lines. Journalists drew from journalists. Errors (repeated, expanded, preserved) entered public memory.

The ball was now in another court. All ideas acquired a single player.[8] Previous players were banned to the bleachers.[9] This created problems:

First: Credit. Marshall might protest, "I got it from nobody," but in fact, he got everything from somebody. He just never remembered. It was strange, especially in later years. Describe a new discovery to him, or tell him a joke, and the next day he'd phone: "Big breakthough ... " and back it all came. Explorations became revelations. He confided in me that God had made him an instrument to convey messages to mankind. Not as weird as it sounds with his use of images, religious commitment, prophet role. But, though he didn't remember, others did.

In the end, this didn't matter. Innis, one of his main sources, was dead, so that was no problem. But even if he had lived, this shy, quiet scholar was hardly one to envy Marshall's public image. Lee was equally private, so much so she discouraged Mary McCarthy from writing a profile on her for the *New Yorker*. On receiving a letter from a stranger who read about her in the press, she protested: "I'm not a news item." Edward Hall, from whom Marshall took "extensions of man," noted that he, himself, picked up the idea from Buckminister Fuller and added: "We all get things from each other." Louis Mumford was upset, so were others, but for most, like myself, acknowledgement was never a serious problem.

How those ideas were used was another matter. I think it safe to say that all of Marshall's sources were personally committed to social betterment. We wanted to harness the new media to human ends or at least prevent their misuse. Marshall declared "his" discoveries to be neutral, and offered them for sale. During the outcry against the Vietnam war (and its apologist, Humbert Humphrey), newspapers nationally showed Marshall at a head table, between Humphrey and a general. He cared less how ideas were used: study the world, don't shape it. True, in the 'seventies he opposed construction of a freeway, but that freeway threatened the tranquility of his neighborhood and opposition to it put him back in the news.

Finally, the real problem was more basic: did Marshall's methods produce the insights with which he is widely credited, or did his "anti-book" style simply popularize those insights? George Steiner, after accepting Marshall's rhetoric on its own terms, passed judgement on his findings: accepting some, dismissing others. Those that Final Word Steiner accepted were all the work of others, restated by Marshall.

Did Marshall's methods produce any valid insights? Of course. But not the ones for which he's best known. Those were obtained by others, employing conventional, historical, literate, Western methods.

Let me offer an analogy. Suppose a publicity-conscious explorer, say another Stefansson, announced that his arctic maps were made like Eskimo maps, from direct sensory experience. Some details prove wrong, but overall his maps are the best available. Then it's noticed that his maps are actually composites of pre-existing maps made by others using conventional means: compass, aerial photography, hard work, etc. Which method do we then choose: Eskimo or modern?

Ethnologists constantly face this problem: our methods or theirs? Must we think like a shaman to understand a shaman? It helps to try. It brings us closer to the subject. But when we analyse that subject, we use Western methods. Ethnologists who identify completely with tribesmen, who "pass over" (some have), stop writing.

Can we present that subject in its own format? It helps to try. A book written in a style and designed in a format compatible with its subject may draw readers closer to that subject. Marshall's presentation of post-literacy in anti-book format was highly successful; his use of non-literate methods for historical analyses, far less so.

This point might be considered by those seeking to revive the "McLuhan Method" as a means of discovery. That method may work for art & poetry, but not, apparently, for historical analyses. It served McLuhan mainly as rhetoric. Can it serve lesser minds? or is this effort at revival just job-making: welfare with dignity?

FORDHAM

Back in Northridge, the combination of anthropology & art proved immensely popular with students. (It should be duplicated everywhere.) Unfortunately for the future of the department, a disproportionate number of majors backed civil rights and opposed the Vietnam war. One day, with teargas drifting across the campus and students charging the administration building, I overheard the president say,

"Here come the anthropologists," and I knew it was time to move on. Twelve of us scattered.

I was about to begin work at the Nationalmusset, Copenhagen, when Marshall asked me to join him at Fordham. Thanks to Gossage's obedient journalists, he was now internationally famous, the world's first celebrity scholar. He was also very ill. A brain tumor was removed. Warmth & brilliance faded. I recall a moment backstage before he faced an audience of executives. He called for "the book." "The book" was *A Thousand and One Jokes for All Occasions*. Several were chosen at random and read to him. He laughed at each, though all were awful. In the end that didn't matter: he mixed up punch lines, leaving his audience thoroughly perplexed. One listener asked for help in unraveling what he assumed was a deliberate riddle. Others dismissed the speaker as fraudulent or mad.

Yet even in the worst scenes, there could be wit. During a totally incomprehensible lecture, a student noisily gathered his books and left. As he stalked out, Marshall called after him, "Out, out, bright light."

I also recall an absolutely superb lecture Marshall gave at this time to a group of advertisers. Relaxed, witty, thoroughly enjoying himself, he enchanted them. He said they no longer needed products: images were enough. They loved it. No longer salesmen: they were now recognized as creators. Eight years of Ronald Reagan made that observation cliché. But it wasn't cliché in 1967.[10]

Harper's Bazaar commissioned Marshall to write a special McLuhan issue. He was about to undergo surgery. The fee was large & needed. Not a word had been written, not a photograph assembled. On Friday, the publisher warned me: if an acceptable manuscript wasn't in his hands by 9 a.m. Monday, the contract was cancelled. It arrived on time and appeared under Marshall's name. Three years later it appeared as a book, *They Became What They Beheld*, under my name.

The Fordham effort collapsed. Marshall returned to Toronto. I returned to California, this time to UC, Santa Cruz. Then I moved to New Guinea where I worked for the local government. From this came *Oh, What a Blow that Phantom Gave Me* on the impact of alien media on tribal peoples.

In 1970, I began teaching at the New School for Social Research in New York. Over the next few years, Marshall & I met irregularly in Toronto & New York. The exuberant, witty rainmaker was now a wary, irritable jukebox reciting old phrases in random order. Sarcasm provided protection. One evening in New York, he arrived first for dinner. When Kurt Vonnegut walked in, Marshall asked, "Who's that?" "Vonnegut." "Can't stand his work!" This in a loud voice.

Then, "Who's that?" "Warhol." "He even looks like a peasant!" Sittings were rearranged.

Insults kept critics at bay. Businessmen, OK, but no academics, all hopeless. In Toronto, he surrounded himself with dysfunctionals: sycophants, intellectual basketcases, celebrity parasites, cult followers, the worst. They reminded me of Jackie Tywhitt's description of Mahatma Gandhi's entourage.

It was so different when we first met, at his home in a great old house, once St. Mike's infirmary. He stood before the fireplace, Corinne beside him, the fire bright, the two of them tall, extremely handsome, she regal, he witty, punning, quoting jazz lyrics, classics, Yeats, headlines, slang, ads, a Joycean display, then singing, not McCormack, but full & fun.

About a year before he died, a stroke left him permanently silent. I immediately went to see him. He stood before the fireplace, next to Corinne, looking much the same as when we'd first met, but now no words came & his hands flew about in frustration. Corinne took them & held them before her: "Tell me, Marshall. I can understand you. I can tell Ted." She looked into his eyes & he smiled & they both laughed, holding hands, and this was communication even more dazzling than that first day.

He spent his last summer with us on Long Island, on a farm by the sea. He walked, waded, rode horseback. But he could not speak. Only during Mass did words & songs & gestures return, however feebly. Then it all seemed to come together and his face relaxed.

The rest must have been Hell. One afternoon, we were sitting with Tom Wolfe. The conversation began with jokes. Marshall laughed at every one. But then the talk veered to Shaker furniture at hand and the notion that in simplicity lay function & beauty, as well as spiritual & social amelioration. Marshall desperately tried to speak. His face became contorted; his hands froze in mid-air. He stood up with a cry of anguish. Then he shrugged, gave us an embarrassed grin, and went off by himself.

I was called early one morning to be told he'd died in his sleep. My first reaction was to arrange for a band of pipers to pipe him over, and they were there, playing *Amazing Grace*, their drums encased in black. And if there'd been time, I would have had a New Orleans funeral band playing *The Saints Go Marching In*, for all that belonged to the best years, the ones that mattered.

After the funeral, Tom Easterbrook & I talked & talked. He said, "When I saw the casket coming down the aisle, I knew it was all over." We spoke of earlier times, good times. He'd been Marshall's closest friend, for over fifty years, since school days. Then Tom spoke bitterly of the exploiters, his children in particular who, he said, isolated him from old friends, promoted celebrity contacts, and exploited him even when ill. If that's true, in fairness it should be added that no one sought fame more eagerly than Marshall. He never walked over others to achieve it, but he let others walk over him. And they did. His public presence wasn't easy to admire. Yet privately he remained, to the very end, a proud man, a lovely man, an endearing friend.

I finished Marchand's book, *Marshall McLuhan*, feeling saddened, depressed. In spite of errors & omissions, he caught the man, at least as he knew him: wounded, down, fighting off the dogs.[11] But his account bore no resemblance to the earlier man I knew & loved. The difference reminded me of two events. Years ago, walking north through Central Park, I saw coming toward me, like a silent jet, the most handsome, graceful, powerful man I'd ever seen. Pure energy. He stared me right in the eye as he shot past. Muhammad Ali. Last year, in a hotel lobby in Islamabad, I saw him again: listless, witless, flabby. Strangers lifted his arms into boxing position and posed themselves for pictures while throwing mock punches at his jaw.He was then led to the water fountain and his head pressed down to drink. I thought of Marshall.

THE MESSAGE

I returned to the study of traditional culture. In 1949 I'd publicly debated this subject with Northrop Frye, arguing that Frazer & Frobenius, Jung & Campbell, were blinded by racism. Then, in the late 'fifties, I met a remarkable scholar. Carl Schuster sought to trace a memory link from yesterday back to paleolithic times. He simply appeared at my back door in desert California. I had just returned from Siberia. He asked about Magdalenian specimens I'd studied there. We became friends. I was with him when he died, ten years later. I promised to finish his work. I thought it would take a year or two. It took seventeen. I moved to Basel where I worked at the Museum fur Völkerkunde. At one point, I sent a bit of it to Frye, who expressed continuing interest. When I finished the whole, I asked him whether I should send it to his office or home. The question mattered, for each set contains 12 massive books weighing 97 pounds. He suggested his home, but died before it was shipped.

Printing was limited to 600 sets, all sent free of charge to academic libraries & scholars throughout the world. A seedbed to be cultivated, weeded, extended. No reviews, no hype, no consumers. Contributors only. I learned the hard way with *Explorations*.

ENOUGH, ENOUGH

Enough has already been written about these events to fill several shelves in a dozen libraries, plus bulging files in a hundred newspaper morgues. My account, by comparison, is brief, not complete, of course, yet it brings us close to events as I knew them forty years ago, played out among friends now gone, in a city changed beyond recognition.

Notes

PRELUDE

1 It should be noted that colour film was available for photography by 1907 and that colour movies had been made much earlier than 1930, but they only became prevalent during the early 1930s. During World War Two the Pathé News was still shot in black and white.

2 Patrick Watson first started making such observations in the mid-1960s on occasions such as his participation in an experimental seminar at York University in which we were co-particpants (1965–66). An example of one such statement can be found in the interview with Watson on the *Understanding McLuhan* CD ROM.

3 A working definition of McLuhan's probes might be the use of verbal and/or other semiotic devices, including clichés, in witty, comic, or other poetico-rhetorical ways to illuminate the deeper ambivalent meanings of acts, objects, events, and social and technological phenomena for the purpose of obtaining and relaying information about them.

4 Edmund Carpenter, "The New Languages," in Carpenter and McLuhan (1957, 162); it originally appeared as an article in *Explorations*.

5 McLuhan cites as support an article that originally appeared in *Explorations*, "The Efffect of the Printed Book on Language in the Sixteenth Century," reprinted in Carpenter and McLuhan (1960:125–35).

6 This is illustrated by the "Probes" section of the CD ROM *Understanding McLuhan*, though it should be noted that the programming of this disc makes it much more difficult to use than similar CD ROMs devoted to material on a single author, such as the Past Master series or discs of

texts, such as that accompanying the Modern Language Association's TACT publication.

7 HMM to John Polanyi (4 Jan 1974), (McLuhan 1987, 487).

INTRODUCTION

1 Laura Secord is a well-known Canadian chocolate manufacturer and retailer.

2 Schizoid is used here in the sense of Deleuze and Guattari's usage in *Anti-Oedipus* and *A Thousand Plateaus*; McLuhan adopted the concept of the split man from Wyndham Lewis: see, for example, "The Split Man," Part 5, in Lewis 1930, 143–73.

3 Tom Nairn, in an essay, "mcLuhanism: the myth of our time," picked up on the role McLuhanism was coming to play as myth: "It is more important to see the sense of the whole process than deprecate it. That is, to see that McLuhan's odd way of expressing himself and the social form his ideas have assumed amount to a kind of contemporary *mythmaking* ... Myth was once the natural way of making sense of the world, in spite of its limitations and conservatism; in the twentieth century it has become a way of imposing such conservative limits on thought, a strategy of evasion as well as a way of grasping reality" (Rosenthal 1968,141). Nairn argues that McLuhan is the first mythmaker of the dilemma of the "loss of language and meaning," paralleling Beckett, Godard, and other creators. His argument says that McLuhan, at an intermediate stage between poetry and theory, half expresses and half theorizes about this common, fundamental problem (144).

4 McLuhan was quite familiar with Gilbert Seldes and his *The Seven Lively Arts*. Seldes gave a TV script-writing course at the University of Toronto which I attended in the early 1950s.

5 See Appendix B by Ted Carpenter.

6 It must be noted that part of the problem of Pound's adoption of Italian fascism was a function of his recording the downsides of the loss of Jeffersonian democracy in the USA. While this does not justify his ideological position, it still indicates that before World War II he was hypersensitive to currents, particularly in American as well as European society, that were to generate the major post-war conflicts of the next half century.

7 For a discussion of the term "articles" used to describe essays that are collages of images, headlines, and print, see Theall 1971, 239–42.

8 Raymond Williams said "paradoxically, if the book works it to some extent annihilates itself," (Stearn 1967, 186–94. Originally published as "A Structure of Insights," *University of Toronto Quarterly*, April 1964).

9 Shannon and Weaver 1949; Deutsch 1952; Reusch and Bateson 1951. (It should be noted that Bateson participated in conferences sponsored by the Josiah Macy Jr. Foundation with McCulloch, Wiener, Pitts, Hutchison, and others.) My copy of *Communication* still has McLuhan's annotations on the inside back cover.

10 It is important to note that the original seminar around which the seminal journal *Explorations* was published was entitled a seminar in culture and communication, since the emphasis on the title culture and technology begins in McLuhan only in the 1960s.

11 It was later printed as a book, *Explorations*, by Something Else Press (1967). Parts of it were also reprinted, along with his agenda for media study, in McLuhan 1967, 106–10, 146–57.

12 For details see Marchand 1989, 128. See also see Ted Carpenter's remarks in Appendix B.

13 See Hulme 1949, with which McLuhan usually commenced his graduate courses in modern literature in the 1950s, and supplement I, "The Problem of Meaning in Primitive Languages" by Bronislaw Malinowski in Ogden and Richards 1947, 296–336.

14 Kroker 1984. See especially "Tracking Technology I: The Catholic Legacy," 61–70. Kroker's remarks on McLuhan's quietism, however, fail to note the influence of Montaigne and Pascal and the problem of his strong emphasis on his simple faith, in spite of his claims to Thomism. See also McLuhan 1954A.

CHAPTER ONE

1 Robert Anton Wilson, author of the controversial science fiction books *Schroedinger's Cat Trilogy* and *Masks of the Illuminati*, commentator of Joyce, new age guru, friend and co-spirit of Timothy Leary, considers *The Bride* to be McLuhan's most important and lasting contribution.

2 His continued presence in the counter-cultural perspective of cultural studies was also due in part to Arthur and Marilouise Kroker, authors of books and CD-ROMs on the cyberage. Arthur wrote one of the earliest major studies on McLuhan in relation to his compatriots George Grant and Harold Innis and he and Marilouise founded and edited *The Canadian Journal of Social and Political Thought* and established the digiculture-oriented on-line web site and journal *C-Theory*, where they continue to promote McLuhan as the prophet of digital delerium. Bob Dobbs of *Flipside* (the alternative music magazine) has continued to keep McLuhan a living presence in New Age culture. Assessments by such cyberculture critics as Mark Dery and Gary Wolfe, while contributing to the revival, have also provided a balanced, critical assessment of McLuhan's canonization.

3 The term coenaesthetic comes from C.K. Ogden and I.A. Richards 1923. It is more normally referred to as an "orchestration of the arts"; see, for example Eisenstein 1949.

4 Sapir and Whorf came to my attention through an anthropology course in language, culture, and personality taught by Ted Carpenter in 1950–51 and I then brought them to Marshall's attention.

5 For corroboration of the importance of Sapir and Whorf in the original proposal, see Marchand 1989, 117, 119 and Appendix B. The actual application to the Ford Foundation for the grant that established the seminars referred to the media as "new languages."

6 A passage from Archibald MacLeish often quoted by new critics in the 1940s and 1950s. McLuhan was even more fond of quoting Mallarmé's riposte to Degas that poetry is composed of words not ideas. Re: "news that stays news," Ezra Pound had provided the aphorism: "Literature is news that STAYS news" in *The ABC of Reading*, n.d., 29.

7 Deleuze and Guattari 1991, particularly chapter 7, "Percept, Affect and Concept," and the conclusion.

8 The various numbers quoted here were developed by searching the data bases of *The Gutenberg Galaxy* and *Understanding Media* provided on the Voyager CD-ROM. I prepared my own database of *From Cliché to Archetype*. I used computerized notes for *The Laws of Media*. For *The Global Village* I used the index. There could be minor discrepancies, but I am certain that the range of differences is correct.

9 Fekete 1977. See especially part 3, "Marshall McLuhan," 135–93.

10 Some have suggested that an analysis such as Fekete's suggests the wish that McLuhan had continued to develop as a literary critic, but it actually values those aspects of McLuhan that have been the source of his influence on Baudrillard, Kroker, and Virilio. Fekete 1982. For Baudrillard and Virilio, see Gary Genosko's seminars mentioned in the later chapter on McLuhan and French Theory.

11 Of the thirteen articles in *Explorations 1*, six can be classed as anthropology or sociology; five as art, literature, or popular culture; one as psychology; and one as medical (Hans Selye's article on stress). Of the ten articles in *Explorations 2*, four could be classed as anthropology or sociology; four as literature, art, or popular culture; and two as psychology. In the third issue there is one posthumous article by Innis and some discussion of Innis by members of the seminar; of the other thirteen items, seven could be classed as anthropology or sociology; four as art, literature, or popular culture; and two as pyschology. In *Explorations 4* over 60 per cent of the articles are in the art, literature, or popular culture category. In *Explorations 8: Verbi-Voco-Visual*, which McLuhan edited on his own, over 80 per cent of the content is oriented toward the arts.

12 In 1951–52, while working closely with McLuhan, I was taking a graduate course in Neo-Augustan literature with Douglas Grant at the University of Toronto. When I began realizing the importance of Pope's remarks
about the "little epic" and about specific writers and writings in the
satiric tradition, McLuhan and I began discussing the potential significance of this for modern works like those of Joyce and Lewis. From that
came our shared and ongoing interest in the Alexandrian literary forms,
especially the briefer seriocomic epic and in the tradition of Menippean
(or as Dryden preferred, Varronian) satire. For a particular application to
the eighteenth-century satiric program of Swift, Pope, and others, see
Theall 1961.

13 Eric McLuhan 1997. The reduction of all Menippean satire to cynical
satire may have been Marshall McLuhan's view as well since it has a
certain affinity with his satire; but the complex traditions of Menippean
and Varronian satire strongly demonstrate that this is not true of the
genre as a whole, even when cynic satire is related to the origin of such
satire among the Cynics. For a more thorough assessment of *The Role of
Thunder* see Downing 1998 and the discussion of Menippean and Varronian satire in chapter 11.

14 For a note discussing McLuhan's interest in the figure of the "con man,"
see Theall (1971, 18n).

15 Telecosm (or telecosmos) refers to post-electric extended global telecommunication, including the earthly global metropolis with its internet and
communication network in space.

16 For an extended discussion of figure and ground, see McLuhan and
McLuhan (1988, 5), where McLuhan suggests that, "The study of
ground on its own terms is virtually impossible; by definition it is at any
moment environmental and subliminal ... The ground of any technology
or artefact is both the situation that gives rise to it and the whole environment (medium) of services and disservices that brings it into play."

17 See *Playboy* interview, "Marshall McLuhan: A Candid Conversation
With the High Priest of Popcult and Metaphysician of Media," *Canadian
Journal of Communication* 14 (December 1989): 101–37.

18 I may well have been the first to do this – see Theall 1986, 79–88.

19 For a brief account of the university at this time and its relation to
McLuhan, see Theall (1971, 245–51), Appendix 4, "The Influence of the
Canadian University Milieu on McLuhan: A Speculative Note."

CHAPTER TWO

1 McLuhan 1987, HMM to William Kuhns (6 December 1971), 448.
2 Ibid., HMM to Edward S. Morgan (16 May 1959), 254–5.
3 Ibid., HMM to Claude Bissell (23 March 1971), 429.

4   Ibid., HMM to William Kuhns (6 December 1971), 448.

5   Ibid., HMM to Ezra Pound (5 January 1951), 218.

6   Ibid., Quoted by William Toye, 131.

7   Ibid., HMM to Claude Bissell (23 March 1971), 429.

8   Ibid., HMM to Harold Innis (14 March 1951), 223.

9   Ibid., HMM to the Editor of the *Toronto Star* (4? July 1978), 539.

10 Ibid., HMM to Jacqueline Tyrhwitt (23 December 1960), 278.

11 Ibid., HMM to Ann Landers (17 December 1969), 393.

12 Ibid., HMM to Felix Giovanelli. (10 May 1946), 183.

13 Ibid., HMM to Walter J. Ong, S.J. (21 January 1953), 234.

14 With respect to Proust's contributions, see (Deleuze 1972, especially 148–50).

15 McLuhan 1987. HMM to Jane Bret (3 January 1973), 459. William Toye's note describes Jane Bret as "a teacher and writer of North Dallas,Texas [who] wrote a piece on liturgy and the media which attracted McLuhan's attention" 459.

16 Ibid., HMM to Harold Adams Innis (14 March 1951), 221.

17 Bateson (1972, 135–6). My copy of Reusch and Bateson, *Communications: The Social Matrix of Psychiatry* (1951) has a series of handwritten notes by McLuhan, which he made while he was reading it. We discussed Bateson's work frequently during the period from 1950 to 1953.

18 "Miraculously founded / Still more miraculously re-formed." McLuhan 1987, HMM to Wilfred Watson (December 15, 1967), 347. An E-mail correspondence with Professor Gregory Downing brought to my attention the error in the Latin quoted by McLuhan in the text. He suggested also the following more forceful translation: "Wonderfully you built [the dignity of the human essence}, and more wonderfully you reformed/ restored/ fixed/ redeemed [it]."

The words are said at the opening of the Offertory of the Mass when the Priest is preparing the chalice at the right of the altar. The text in Latin, with a translation from the missal follow, since they are relevant to the point that McLuhan is making to Wilfred Watson:

P. Deus, qui humanae substantiae dignitatem mirabiliter condidisti, et mirabilius reformasti:da nobis per hujus aquae et vini mysterium, ejus divinitatis esse consortes, que humanitatis nostrae fieri dignatus est particeps, Jesus Christus Filius tuus Dominus noster: Qui tecum vivit et regnat in

D: O God, + who established the nature of man in wondrous dignity, and still more admirably restored it, grant that by the mystery of this water and wine, may we come to share in His Diviity, who humbled himself to share in our humanity, Jesus Christ, Your Son, our Lord: who lives and reigns with You in the unity of

unitate Spiritus Sancti Deus:	the holy Spirit, one God
per omnia saecula saeculorum	forever and ever. Amen.
Amen.	

19 Ibid., HMM to Wyndham Lewis (11 July 1955), 248.

20 Ibid., HMM to Ezra Pound (16 July 1952), 232.

21 Ibid., HMM to Bernard Muller-Thym (5 May 1960), 270.

22 Ibid., The reference to media ecology programs restricting the use of TV is from a letter to Clare Booth Luce (29 August 1977), 534.

23 Ibid., HMM to Robert J. Leuver (30 July 1969), 385.

24 Ibid., HMM to Barbara Ward (9 February 1973), 466.

25 Ibid., HMM to Michael Hornyansky (3 February 1976), 517.

26 Ibid., HMM to Jacques Maritain (6 May 1969), 370.

27 Ibid., HMM to Robert J. Leuver (30 July 1969), 385.

28 Ibid., HMM to Jacques Maritain (6 May 1969), 370.

29 Ibid., HMM to Jonathan Miller (8 January 1965), 316.

30 Ibid., HMM to Lawrence D. Conklin. (2 February1973) ,465.

31 Ibid., HMM to Ernest Sirluck (3 February 1971) ,423.

32 Ibid., *Life* Interview (26 February 1966), 176.

33 Ibid., HMM to Prince Bernhard of the Netherlands (14 May 1969), 372.

34 Ibid., See notes on this subject, 235. This will be discussed further in the chapter on McLuhan and the cults.

35 Ibid., HMM to William Jovanovich (1 December 1966), 339.

36 Ibid., HMM to J.G. Keogh (6 July 1970), 413.

37 Ibid., HMM to Bernard Muller-Thym (5 May 1960), 271. The phrase "university of being" refers to Muller-Thymes' study *The Establishment of the University of Being in the Doctrine of Meister Eckhart of Hochheim.*

38 In this statement I include my own early work *The Medium is the Rear View Mirror: Understanding McLuhan*, for at the height of McLuhan's international reputation as the guru of communication, it seemed important to stress disproportionately certain characteristics of McLuhan's work which were aspects of the surface of his satire, such as his pseudo-technological determinism, his apparent claims as a theorist, and his complicity with the world of big business. While I believe the main thrust of my work to be correct, it does take the stance of examining McLuhan as a social theorist in a way that was consistent with his reputation but not with the importance with which he viewed his role as an artist and satirist.

CHAPTER THREE

1 HMM to William Kuhns (6 December 1971), McLuhan 1987, 448.

2 McLuhan discusses the labyrinth of cognition and its relation to Daedalus, Stephen Dedalus, and Mallarmé's *Le Démon de l'Analogie* in *From Cliché to Archetype*, 148.

3 The second phrase refers to the subtitle of the companion posthumous volume to the *Laws of Media The Global Village* (1989), co-authored with Bruce Powers.

4 McLuhan and McLuhan (1988, x, 3, 95, 117, *127ff, 227ff*). Italic numbers indicate the major entries.

5 W.K. Wimsatt (1965). "Zeroic couplet" appears in Joyce (1939 284.10).

6 Ezra Pound shows how an ideogram that puts together "abbreviated pictures" of

ROSE   CHERRY

IRON RUST   FLAMINGO

allowed the Chinese to make a general picture of the idea of "red" (Pound n.d. 22). This led to the popular critical phrase among Pound critics, "The rose in the steel dust."

7 NAEB is the National Association of Educational Broadcasters (U.S.). The book is available from University Microfilm Inc. (UMI) in Ann Arbor, Michigan.

8 McLuhan and McLuhan (1988, 158–9). McLuhan cites Tony Schwartz's *The Responsive Chord* (1973), where Schwartz points out that in reassembling bits of information the brain utilizes the eye in the same way it has always used the ear.

9 McLuhan's term for what is retrieved. See Chapter 6 for an extended discussion of the possible import of "occult" for McLuhan.

10 Theall (1997, 177–9). For the relevance of Duns Scotus in contemporary modernism and post-modernism, see Deleuze (1994, 35–40).

11 McLuhan (1943, 128, 186n, 216ff, 218n, 250, 271n, 347–9). See also McLuhan (1991, 7–27), a posthumously published article which is "an expanded version of a paper written for the M.L.A. meeting of 1942."

12 Modernist cultural producers (both in the traditional and technologically produced spheres) tended to speak of media convergence in terms of the orchestration of the arts (e.g., Serge Eisenstein). The authoritative father of the New Criticism, I.A. Richards, and his semanticist collaborator, C.K. Ogden, use the term "coenaesthetic" for this emerging movement towards convergence. In a recent book I have partly explored this phenomenon in relation to contemporary poetics, specifically discussing McLuhan's role in chapter 5, "Beyond Media" (Theall 1971, 91–108). See also my article "Beyond the Orality/Literacy Principle: James Joyce and the Pre-History of Cyberspace" (Theall 1992).

13 It should be noted that I am using *techné* in the original Aristotlean sense where it should be translated as art. *Techné* (Gk. "art," "skill," "craft," "cunning of hand," "technique," "a handiwork," a "trade," "a system or method of making or doing something"). The general meaning of *techné*, especially as found in Aristotle, refers to anything deliberately created by humans, in contrast to anything not humanly created (which

is a product of *physis* or nature). A less general meaning refers to a hand-iwork, a craft, a technique, or a skill, which includes any skill in (a) *making* things (sculpture, shoes, poems, vases); (b) *doing* things, (c) in *acting*, (d) *dancing*, and (e) *singing*. Throughout his work McLuhan plays on the association of *techné* with technic, technique, technology, etc., associating them with the arts through the Aristotlean and Greek use of *techné* both for any of the arts and for a wide variety of ways of making and doing which were humanly created. (Adapted from Angeles, 1981, 289–90.)

14 Reprinted in *Elizabethan Critical Essays*, ed. G. Gregory Smith (London: oxford University Press, 1959), I:156.

15 "The famous portrait of a "Nude Descending a Staircase," with its resemblance to an artichoke doing a strip tease, is a cleansing bit of fun intended to free the human robot from his dreamlike fetters. And so with Wyndham Lewis's *The Apes of God*, Picasso's *Doll Women*, and *Finnegans Wake* by James Joyce – the latter especially being a great intel-lectual effort aimed at rinsing the Augean stables of speech and society with geysers of laughter" (McLuhan 1951, 100–1).

16 CNS (central nervous system) as a contemporary scientific account of the operations of the *sensus communis* held to process all sensory informa-tion in classical, medieval, and early Renaissance discussions.

17 For angelism see Fowlie (1946). The term cyborg was coined in 1960 by the space scientist Clyne (Dery 1996, 227). McLuhan's use of the term angelize can be confirmed: "What is very little understood about the elec-tronic age is that it angelizes man, it disembodies him, it turns him into software" (McLuhan 1971). McLuhan suggests that he has adopted his interpretation of roboticism from Ruth Benedict's *The Chrysanthemum and the Sword* (McLuhan 1989, 67). For "chu," see ibid., 69.

CHAPTER FOUR

1 HMM to Tom Wolfe (22 November 1965), McLuhan 1987, 330. The letter is written with relation to the earlier version of Wolfe's article in *New York*, the Sunday magazine section of the New York *World Journal Tribune*. This version is reprinted in Stearn (1967, 15–34). The earlier version is not as directly equivocal about the EngLit and other aspects of McLuhan as the version published in *The Pump House Gang* (1969).

2 HMM to Prince Bernhard of The Netherlands (14 May 1969), McLuhan 1987, 372.

3 Wyndham Lewis uses the term "time-mind" throughout *Time and Western Man* to describe modern artists, writers, and philosophers who stress the new discoveries about the nature of time in Einstein and in Bergson's philosophy.

4 HMM to John W. Mole, O.M.I. (18 April 1969), McLuhan 1987, 369.
5 HMM to Tom Wolfe (25 October 1965), McLuhan 1987, 326.

CHAPTER FIVE

1 This is further recognized and documented in the publication of McLuhan's unpublished essay on Francis Bacon in the first volume of *McLuhan Studies* (McLuhan 1991, 7–25). It is also confirmed by innumerable references in McLuhan's thesis, *The Place of Thomas Nashe in the Learning of His Time*.
2 See chapter 11 for a detailed discussion of McLuhan's conscious relationship to Menippean and Varronian satire
3 See McLuhan (1943, 70n). See also Lanham (1991, 57–9).
4 See Lewis (1915, 91). The note in *Cliché to Archetype*, 214, is incorrect in saying it is in *Blast No. 1*.
5 See T.S. Eliot's essay on "Baudelaire" in Eliot 1932, 331–45.
6 It should be noted that the page numbering of *Explorations 8* begins only after McLuhan's own contribution, which occupies well over 50 per cent of the pages in the journal.
7 For further remarks on Pythagoreanism, see 107 and 107n12.

CHAPTER SIX

1 For an indication of the interest of Pope and Swift in Masonry and Rosicrucianism, see Patricia Bruckmann, "Fancy's Maze," PhD Thesis (1961), and her subsequent study of the Scriblerus Club, *A Matter of Correspondence* (1997).
2 See McLuhan (1987 235n1) and letters to Ezra Pound and Walter Ong, 231, 233, 235–7,283. See also Marchand (1989,102–5), and Gordon (1997, 157–8); but it should be noted that Gordon is totally incorrect in believing that this issue only occupied McLuhan for a year. It surfaces by implication even in his posthumous work in his extended discussions of angelism, since that is one aspect of what he considered to be the core of gnosticism. Marchand's version is certainly correct in that McLuhan never abandoned his "thesis about a Masonic conspiracy" and that his lifelong belief was that his Toronto colleague Northrop Frye was a Mason and derived his eminence as a literary critic from this. Gordon should have noted that in a letter to Ong dated February 1962, the year *The Gutenberg Galaxy* was published, McLuhan suggested "The real animus against the book will be felt in Gnostic and Masonic quarters, who will rightly find the rug pulled out from under their matter-spirit bias" (McLuhan 1987, 283). McLuhan's biographers, with the exception of William Toye's biographical materi-

als in the *Letters*, are always very muted in speaking about this interest in the gnostic and the occult.

3 In the 1950s McLuhan read with interest and excitement Eric Voeglins *The New Science of Politics: An Introduction* (1952), which I frequently discussed with him. His interest in Voegelin continued well into the 1970s, particularly influencing a book such as his *War and Peace in the Global Village* (1968).

4 With respect to the term *essai concrète* see my study of McLuhan (1971), especially chapter 11.

5 This was a commonplace of Renaissance thought throughout Western Europe. See, for example, Sidney's "An Apologia for Poetrie," (Sidney 1595, 148–207).

6 See also Valéry (1977).

7 Jung's writings on alchemy, esoteric religion and mysticism are well-known. It should be noted , though, as early as 1917 Herbert Silberer's *Hidden Symbolism of Alchemy and the Occult Arts* – originally entitled *Problems of Mysticism and its Symbolism* – dealt with a wide variety of such topics from a psychoanalytic point of view.

12 Yates, 1972. Yates' various works were originally published between 1964 and 1972 in book form. McLuhan certainly read *Giordano Bruno and the Hermetic Tradition* when it first came out in 1964 and her *The Art of Memory* when it came out in 1966. Much of the same material was available earlier in other forms. I am using Yates primarily, however, not to suggest a link between Yates and McLuhan but to establish the prevalence of knowledge about such movements among Renaissance scholars.

13 McLuhan 1962, 255–263. Note especially his headline callng attention to the ":parody of the Eucharist."

14 See particularly Yates 1983, chapters 8, 9 and 13, and Yates 1969.

15 Joyce 1957, 251. In *Finnegans Wake*, Shem, the figure who resembles Joyce and is a poet, is described as an "alshemist." See also my article "James Joyce – Literary Engineer" (Theall 1988, 111–26).

16 McLuhan and Fiore 1968. Throughout the volume quotes from Joyce appear as marginalia commenting on the text.

17 The term poetic theology is a deliberate attempt to suggest that McLuhan sees a natural theology as a poetic theology.

18 Because of the brevity of this chapter it will not be possible to explore all the ramifications of the many symbols and images in McLuhan's writings that have occult, gnostic, or hermetic roots. It is worth noting that the labyrinth of cognition as an archetype of the initiatory process in the intellectual life is developed from Joyce, the symbolists, and other contemporaries and filled out with information from such writers as Gertrude Levy (*The Gates of Horn*), Jane Harrison, Robert Graves, the eighteenth-

century cleric Bishop Warburton, Clement of Alexandria, and esotericists such as A.E. Waite. Obviously Joyce's Dedalus in *The Portrait of the Artist as a Young Man* and *Ulysses* and Mallarmé's writings on the ancient gods, the labyrinth, and poetic creation are important exemplars of this motif, which can be applied to the ear, to the function of the creative process, to auditory and tactile media, etc.

19 The term phatic communion probably enters McLuhan's critical discourse from the writing of the anthropologist Bronislaw Malinowski. See Supplement I "The Problem of Meaning in Primitive Languages" by Malinowski in Ogden and Richards (1947, 315). Phatic communion (coined in 1923): "of, relating to, or being speech used for social or emotive purposes rather than for communicating information." For a discussion of phatic communion by a media professional and former assistant of McLuhan at the Coach House, see Dobbs (1992).

For McLuhan's familiarity with the term "phatic communion," see McLuhan and Watson (1970, 198) in a discussion of "the happening" as a form of theatre. Malinowski's more general importance to McLuhan is clear in a letter written to Ong in May 1946 (McLuhan 1987, 187) where he speaks of "the application of Thomistic principles to the area of Freud, Fraser and Malinowski." See also McLuhan and Watson (1970, 141) and McLuhan and Powers (1989, 40).

20 See references to Gilson in McLuhan 1943, 94n, 115–16, 138–9, 156n, 242, 278, 296–7, 346.

21 Lewis 1932. See, for example, the description of Lord Osmund on p.322: "whereas his expertness and his method entitle him in the great freemasonry of Apehood, to the title grand-master of all branches of Ape-work whatever." There are frequent references with respect to initiation rituals. For example, on p. 241 Dan is described as a postulant. The whole of "Lord Osmund's Lenten Party" is shaped on an initiation ritual reflected in the costumes which Horace and others wear.

22 Joyce's work has been widely discussed in terms of its alchemical, cabalistic and hermetic aspects. McLuhan borrowed so extensively from Joyce that this borrowing is in itself a major subject. For extensive discussions of Joyce and McLuhan and their relation to modern communication technology, see Theall (1971); also chapter 5 of Theall (1995).

23 McLuhan 1964, 350ff. With respect to the whole discussion of electricity and apocalypse in McLuhan and others, see Carey (1981, 172–5); also Carey and Quirk (1970).

24 HMM to Walter Ong, S.J. (31 May 1953), 237; and (14 October 1954), 244. In the first letter he specifically mentions Eric Voeglin and suggests the importance to Dominicans Bruno, Savonarola, and Campanella of gnostic techniques of *gnosis* via the passions. In the second letter to Ong he discusses the issue in the context of a discussion of Madam Blavatsky's

Isis Unveiled (1886) – Madame Blavatsky was corresponding secretary of the Theosophical Society of New York City – and Robert Graves' *The White Goddess*. (1948). Also see HMM to Ezra Pound (3 December 1952), 233, and (28 February 1953), 235. My thanks to William Toye, editor at Oxford University Press, who oversaw the publication of the McLuhan letters and first called these letters to my attention prior to their publication.

25 For a discussion of the epiphany in Joyce, see McLuhan (1962B).

26 See Joyce (1958, 103–4, 223). On 104 Stanislaus comments on the "Circe" section of *Ulysses*, which works out analogies between the creative imagination in the intellect and the "sexual instincts in the body ... with a fantastic horror of which I know no equal in literature, painting or music." See also Joyce (1966, 101–6).

CHAPTER SEVEN

1 Macksey and Donato (1970) is a collection of papers and discussion from a conference held at Johns Hopkins University in October 1966. de Man was not a participant.

2 McLuhan 1987. HMM to Marshall Fishwick, (31 July 1974), 505.

3 Ibid., HMM to Marshall Fishwick (August 1, 1974), 506.

4 The final point about the sublime and the interior landscape is explained in McLuhan's essay "Tennyson and Picturesque Poetry" in McLuhan 1969, 135–55). In addition to the question of the evolution of the interior landscape from the picturesque tradition, McLuhan's writings on Tennyson also involved questions of the initiatory, and hence the gnostic, of Manicheanism, and of the predominance of the epyllion or little epic in contemporary literature. See Introduction to Alfred Lord Tennyson, *Selected Poetry* (McLuhan 1956, x, xiii, xxiv).

5 McLuhan 1951. As Greg Wilmott points out in *McLuhan or Modernism in Reverse* (1996), his ongoing commitment to this goal is attested by his reading on the vinyl record produced by CBS in 1967, paralleling the book publication of *The Medium Is the Massage*.

6 Gordon 1997, 332. It should be noted, however, that Ogden inspired a very different linguistic tradition – the British school emanating from Firth and Halliday – than did Saussure. It should also be noted that McLuhan not only did not read Saussure until the mid-1970s, but that in the late 1950s he had clearly rejected structuralism and would not consider reading de Saussure.

7 The term Mennippean satire became more widely recognized in literary criticism after the publication of Mikhail Bakhtin's *Rabelais and his World* (1965), and *Problems of Dostoevsky's Poetics* (1929) (The entire 1963 text had been published in a "faulty" English translation in 1973);

276 Notes to pages 132–49

and in Julia Kristeva's *Desire in Language: A Semiotic Approach to Literature and Art* (1980) (originally published in France in 1979). The term was familiar in North American criticism in the 1950s as evidenced by its appearance in Northrop Frye's *Anatomy of Criticism* (1957) to which Derrida refers in *La Carte Postale*.

8 For an elaboration of this phrase, see Barker 1995, 14.

CHAPTER EIGHT

1 McLuhan 1987, HMM to Claude Bissell (23 March 1971), 429.
2 McLuhan 1987, HMM to Harold Adams Innis (March 14, 1951), 223.
3 Ibid., 222.
4 It should be noted that Carpenter's major academic contributions subsequent to the McLuhan association are concerned with social symbolism in ancient and tribal art. They include the magnificent twelve volume *Materials for the Study of Social Symbolism in Ancient and Tribal Art* , based on the research and writings of Carl Schuster and written by Edmund Carpenter (1986); and Carl Schuster and Edmund Carpenter, *Patterns That Connect* (1996). Earlier he published major works on Eskimo language, culture, and art and on the media. *O What a Blow that Phantom Gave Me!* (1972, 186–9) brilliantly relates native arts and story-telling to the way the media "swallow cultures" by being "invisible environments which surround and destroy old environments."
5 Williams 1964; reprinted in Stearn 1967 186–9. Shortly after, Williams turned against McLuhan, attacking him for what he considered to be his technological determinism.
6 Dasenbrock 1984, 41; see also Wees, 1972.
7 Williams, 1955. For an explanation of Williams' alienation from the Culture and Communication seminar, see E.S. Carpenter in Appendix B.
8 McLuhan 1987, HMM to P. Wyndham Lewis (18 December 1954), 245.
9 McLuhan quotes T.S. Eliot: "What I call the 'auditory imagination' is the feeling for syllable and rhythm, penetrating far below the conscious level of thought and feeling, invigorating every word; sinking to the most primitive and forgotten, returning to the origin and bringing something back, seeking the beginning and the end" (Eliot 1933, 118–19).
10 The use of Joyce texts in relation to the theme of war and peace is intriguing in that shortly after the publication of this *essai concrète* (in 1971) Jacques Derrida made his derisive comment about McLuhan's work at the Université de Montréal; a decade later Derrida would independently visit the same topic of Joyce and war as part of a lecture at the Centre George Pompidou in Paris. For Derrida's remark on McLuhan see Derrida 1982, 329, for the lecture on Joyce see Derrida 1984, 148–159.

11 James Carey has spoken of McLuhan's view of the electric apocalypse with propriety, if not with a full understanding of its literary and artistic roots, or its significance for Baudrillard's account of the "ecstasy of communication" (Carey and Quirk 1988).

CHAPTER NINE

1 For the story of McLuhan's reservations concerning my thesis, mentioned in Marchand 1989, 232; and in my 1971 book on McLuhan, and selectively and hence incorrectly analysed in Gordon 1997, see Appendix A.

2 Nevertheless, the symbolistes (Baudelaire, Laforgue, Rimbaud, Mallarmé, and Valéry), Eliot, and particularly Pound and Lewis were his key influences, along with his studies in the history of the trivium and of medieval and Renaissance humanism (including Thomistic scholasticism, which, in the spirit of some of his philosophical colleagues at the Pontifical Institute of Medieval Studies in Toronto, he interpreted as being humanistic but without being fully aware of its neo-Platonic and occasionally Scotistic aspects). (See Gilson 1948, especially Part 2, chapter 7). References to the grand figures of Anglo-American high modernism and the French *symbolistes* appear in all of his works from his early criticism and his first book (1951) until his last posthumously published The Global Village (1989). Gilson.

3 McLuhan 1987, HMM to Felix Giovanelli (May 10, 1946), 183.

4 For a discussion of learned Menippean (or Varronian) satire as "cynical," see McLuhan 1997, chapter 1. Eric co-authored *The Laws of Media* and other books with his father. His view of Menippean satire as cynical satire does not take into account many of the major traditions involved, nor does it examine the contemporary discussions of the genre by Mikhail Bakhtin, Julia Kristeva, and Northrop Frye. For a more detailed discussion see chapter 11 and Appendix A of this book. For a critique of McLuhan's *Thunders*, see Downing 1998.

5 Regarding Johannes Duns Scotus, see Theall 1997, 177–9.

6 See particularly the Conclusion of my 1997; see also Theall 1992.

7 James Joyce to Harriet Shaw Weaver (16 November 1924), Joyce 1957, 222. Ellmann quotes the Swiss sculptor August Suter in his 1982, 543, and Budgen quotes Suter when Joyce described his enterprise: "I am boring through a mountain from two sides. The question is, how to meet in the middle" (Budgeon, 1948, 24).

8 In the Introduction to *Alfred Lord Tennyson: Selected Poetry* (1956) McLuhan first discussed the little epic or epyllion in relation to the history of literature and the work of Pound, Joyce, and Eliot. On page xvii, note 20 indicates that this was material related to a study that he and I were in the process of working on. At that point he had written the

sections on Greece and Chaucer and I had written the sections on Rome, particularly Ovid and the Neo-Augustan writings of Pope, Swift, and Sterne. The major work up to that point on the "little epic" was Marjorie Crump's (1931).

9 With respect to the relation of the term cliché to printing, see McLuhan and Watson, 1970, 55.

10 This chapter complements a major article of mine, "Beyond the Orality/Literacy Dichotomy: James Joyce and the Pre-History of Cyberspace," and also relevant chapters of my books *Beyond the Word: Reconstructing Sense in the Joyce Era of Technology, Culture, and Communication* (1995) and *James Joyce's Techno-poetics* (1997).

11 Their insights are still crucial for understanding cyberculture and illustrate how they, along with some science fiction and utopian and dystopian writing should provide major guides for developing an appropriate practico-theoretical understanding of the poetics of cyberspace.

12 The centerpiece of *War and Peace in the Global Village* (1968) presents Joyce's ten thunders, which McLuhan argued presented the history of media, a thesis extensively developed in Eric McLuhan's 1997. McLuhan's thunders end in III.1 of the *Wake* at page 424, which precedes both the inquisition of Yawn (III.3) and the rise of the sun at Dawn (IV), both of which Joyce, in the notebooks, associates with aspects of the tele-electronic era: telegraph, telephone, wireless, and telepresence. The thunders, while involving various developments of media, are telling the tale of the history of the world. If, as McLuhan suggests, major elements of the tenth thunder involve mud and turd, it is interesting to note that they immediately precede the "extermination of the name of God" (Baudrillard's phrase in *Symbolic Exchange and Death*) by Shaun, preceding the thunder voice : "making act of oblivion ... which he picksticked into his lettruce invrention" and at the conclusion of the thunder voice: "Thor's for you" (FW 424.23). There is a final eleventh serio-comic thunder when the debate between Patrick and the Archdruid ends with a turd being dropped. McLuhan's over-stressing the thunders leaves major and key portions of III.3 (the climax) and IV (the conclusion) unaccounted for. An alternative, chimerical, account of the thunders has been provided by Dobbs 1995.

It should be noted that Joyce regarded the *Wake* as a history of the world, somewhat in the Wellsian sense, and that what the McLuhans discuss as media is what Joyce considered that aspect of his world history that is the history of science and technology – a major aspect for his project to be paralleled by the religious history, political history, and cultural history of everday life. All of which is embedded in the biological machine of the human person – Humphrey, Anna, Shem, Shaun, and Izzy.

13 McLuhan 1987, HMM to Jacqueline Tyrwhitt (Dec. 23, 1960), 278, shows his own awareness of the difference between "global metropolis"

and "global village." The former is multicultural and nomadic; the latter tends towards totality and integration. Note also that in the *Wake* Joyce plays with Dublin as a city of the sun – the Egyptian Heliopolis, the utopian *City of the Sun* by Tommaso Campanella (1568–1639) – but also as a city dominated by political power. (Timothy Healy was the politician and friend of Charles Stewart Parnell who eventually betrayed him, and in the *Wake* Joyce speaks of the "Heliopolitan constabulary," playing on the Royal Irish Constabulary.)

14 See my article "Beyond the Orality/Literacy Principle: James Joyce and the Pre-history of Cyberspace," Theall 1992.

15 This quotation is taken from the posthumously published McLuhan and Powers, 1989, 103. *The Global Village* was edited and rewritten from McLuhan's working notes, which had to date at the latest from the late 1970s, since he died in 1980.

16 Michael Joyce and Eco 1996 exemplify exceptions to this in their discussions of hypertext and the book. For a critique of McLuhan's approach to the book in the same volume, see James J. O'Donnell "The Pragmatics of the New: Trithemius, McLuhan, Cassiodorus," 37–62.

17 "Joyce, Mallarme and the Press," in McLuhan 1969, 5–21; and "James Joyce Trivial and Quadrivial," in McLuhan 1969, 23–47.

18 McLuhan 1987, HMM to the editors of *Life* (March 1, 1966), 334.

19 Dr Robert Jacobson, a virtual reality researcher, formerly associate director of the Human Interface Technology Lab at the University of Washington, pointed this out to me. It should also be noted that Michael Heim, author of *Electric Language* (1997) and *The Metaphysics of Virtual Reality* (1993), has recently associated virtual reality and synaesthesia.

20 McLuhan, *Gutenberg Galaxy* 1962, 83. I have been unable to locate the Joyce quote, which McLuhan does not foot-note.

21 There is a potential for double entendre in the chorus of "Phil the Fluter's Ball":

> With the toot of the flute,
> And the twiddle of the fiddle, O'
> Hopping in the middle, like a herrin' on a griddle, O'
> Up, down, hands arown'
> Crossin' to the wall,
> Oh, hadn't we gaiety at Phil the Fluter's Ball!

(U12:997–8). See Bowen 1975, 220.

CHAPTER TEN

1 "That the early gentile peoples, by a demonstrated necessity of nature, were the poets who spoke in poetic characters. This discovery, which is the master key of this Science." Vico, 1948, 19. McLuhan, prophesizing a new tribalism, naturally crafts new poetic characters.

2 McLuhan, 1953, 24–8. McLuhan is relating Joyce to material that he developed in his doctoral thesis, *The Place of Thomas Nashe in the Learning of His Time.*

3 McLuhan and Parker, 1968, 55. He goes on to suggest that the acoustic scientist von Békésy "illustrates multidimensional auditory space with two dimensional Persian paintings."

4 For examples, see Kepes, 1956; for the Gothic cathedral, see Panofsky's remarks on *manifestatio* in 1963, 44ff, 58ff.

5 It is interesting to note that McLuhan does not mention the spectrum in his discussions about light in the *Galaxy* or *Understanding Media* or in most of his other major works, including *The Vanishing Point.*

6 For a full discussion of the importance of light and the debate on light in Joyce's work, see Theall 1997, 169–83.

7 See Weir 1989.

8 "The *Large Glass* is an illuminated manuscript consisting of 476 documents; the illumination consists of almost every work that Duchamp did" (Adcock, 1983, 28).

9 See the early introduction of the idea of a pre-history of cyberspace in my article "Beyond the Orality/Literacy Dichotomy; James Joyce and the Pre-history of Cyberspace" (1992). This theme is further developed in *Beyond the Word* (1995), particularly in the conclusion. Darren Tofts' *Memory Trade: The Pre-History of Cyberculture* (1997) also develops this idea.

10 McLuhan, 1987, HMM to Wyndham Lewis (Oct 16/53), 240.

11 Lewis 1927, 91–131; Lewis also analyses Joyce critically in the first volume of *The Human Age, The Childermass* 1928, esp. 174–8.

12 For a detailed analysis of this aspect of Book 4, see Theall 1997, chapter 13, "The Relativities of Light, Colour and Sensory Perception," 169–83. In this debate, when he plays with the new math, the new physics, and other contemporary sciences, particularly optics and theories of colour, it should be noted that many of these references and other references to technologies and technoculture arose in later elaborations of the earliest drafts, often composed in the 1930s. Hayman 1990; in a personal communication, William Cadbury first brought to my attention that technological, technocultural, and scientific references seemed to be part of the later stages in the elaboration of the *Wake*; see also McLuhan 1969, 44–7.

13 Joyce 1957, James Joyce to Harriet Shaw Weaver (postcard, 16 April 1927), 251. See also Theall 1988.

14 McLuhan and Watson 1970, 62–3; McLuhan 1987, HMMs to Jacques Maritain (6 May 1969), 370. (In the 1950s and early 1960s Maritain was regarded as one of the leading French neo-scholastic philosophers); and McLuhan 1987, HMM to Richard Leuver, C.M.F., editor *U.S. Catholic* (30 July 1969), 387.

15 The passage McLuhan quotes actually occurs twenty-seven pages later than the previous one about the Light Brigade in a context which refers not to television, but to the hearse, the coffin and the death of the hero in which the hero as a younger man (or perhaps as reincarnated in one of his sons) is imagined as being an Irish postman delivering the night mail, carrying his flashlight "and all he bares sobsconscious inklings shadowed on soulskin" (FW377.28); according to the 10th Webster dictionary, the meanings of inkling are "1: a slight indication or suggestion: hint, clue 2: a slight knowledge or vague notion."

16 It should be noted that McLuhan used marginalia extensively, primarily from Joyce, throughout *War and Peace in the Global Village*. The idea of using marginalia in this way appears to have originated in Joyce's use of left and right side marginalia and foot-notes in the "Triv and Quad" section of *Finnegans Wake*. There is also extensive marginalia in *The Laws of Media* McLuhan and McLuhan) 1988.

17 See, for example, the concluding sections of McLuhan 1962, on Pope.

18 This and a number of related subjects are discussed in my book, 1997, which includes topics such as Menippean satire and the satire of learning; electro-mechanization and the Electro-Mechano-Chemical Body, the machinic and the mimetic, mathematics, the new techno-culture of space-time, dynamic mechanics of Quanta and the Chaosmos, light, colour, and sensory perception. For further observations on chaos and complexity theory in Joyce, see Thomas Rice, *Joyce, Chaos and Complexity*, 1997.

19 It is noteworthy that earlier in the same work they had associated Cumming's atypical language with a singularity that is a kind of "composed chaos" – what Joyce calls a "chaosmos."

CHAPTER ELEVEN

1 "Satire and Fiction" appeared in 1930 as an appendage to the publication of Lewis's *Apes of God* (1932).

2 For a discussion of Vorticism see the articles by Reed Way Dasenbrock and by William Wees in *Blast 3* (1984).

3 McLuhan 1987, HMM to Michael Hornyansky (3 February 1976), 517.

4 In his interview with Louis Forsdale, noting the significant value of recently published discussion of Menippean satire and the carnivalesque in Bakhtin's *Problems in Dostoevsky's Poetics*, McLuhan observes that: "Menippean satire includes ... the dialogues of Lucian; ... Petronius, the world of funny stories including *The Thousand and One Nights* . These are all Menippean satires, and they come on down through the Boccaccio's *Decameron*." He goes on to speak of such satires as "the world of funny stories," comparing them to the Marx Brothers.

5 For a discussion of the Scriblerian satiric program particularly with reference to these issues, see Theall, 1955, 207–17; for a relating of the Scriblerian program to Varronian satire and Joyce, see Theall, 1997, 21–9.

6 Eric McLuhan's book on Menippean satire was encouraged by his father, after Marshall's first suggestion that he work on Sterne's *Tristram Shandy* did not work out. The book arose from Eric's thesis and while *The Role of Thunder in Finnegan's Wake* does not discuss Frye, Bakhtin, or Julia Kristeva's work in this area, the first chapter of the thesis does to some extent discuss Frye and Bakhtin, although it does not discuss Kristeva, even in a discussion of the "academic" literature about Menippean satire. Naturally Marshall McLuhan, writing in the late 1950s and 1960s before the major impact of Bakhtin and long before that of Kristeva, did not mention them. Eric McLuhan is right in suggesting in his thesis that Frye's denominating his *Anatomy of Criticism* as Menippean satire was somewhat odd. I would venture, knowing Frye, that it was a sophisticated piece of academic wit. I discussed the history of Menippean satire with relation to Pope in a seminar paper in 1951–52, published in 1960. As noted in the text, I indicated its importance to Marshall's writing in *The Medium is the Rear View Mirror* (1971).

7 The role of the mysteries in Pope is well illustrated in the book of his literary editor and annotator, Bishop Warburton, *The Divine Legation of Moses*. This book intrigued McLuhan not only – Jacques Derrida devotes a section to it in his *Grammatology*. For brief allusions to Warburton in relation to the history of communication theory, see Heyer, 1988, 14, 35.

8 A term McLuhan possibly borrowed from Wallace Fowlie's 1953 study, *Rimbaud's Illuminations: A Study in Angelism* that McLuhan and I read when it first came out. The term derives from Jacques Maritain, "Letter to Cocteau." This French Catholic neo-Thomistic philosopher had close associations with the Pontifical Institute of Medieval Studies in the University of St Michael's College in Toronto where McLuhan taught for nearly thirty years. Ironically, in *The Global Village* McLuhan partially inverts Maritain's concept, making the intuitive, which he associates with the right hemisphere of the brain, the characteristic of robotism, as contrasted to angelism, in which the rationalism of the left hemisphere of the brain is dominant. Nevertheless, it is what he regarded as the abstract aspect of the gnostic – its disembodiment – that leads him to use the term in contradistinction to the robotism of the world of electronic media.

9 It is significant to remember here the story that Ted Carpenter recounts about the publication of Legman's article in *Explorations.*, see Appendix B.

CHAPTER TWELVE

1 Marshall and I read together the sections in St Thomas Aquinas on "natural prophecy" with which he became thoroughly familiar.
2 cf. the importance of the concept of paradox or of hateful contraries and the concept of reconciliation of opposites in the writings of Cleanth Brooks and William K. Wimsatt, Jr., whose *Literary Criticism: A Short History* was one of the first major works to make use of McLuhan's Cambridge doctoral thesis on the grammatico-rhetorical background of Nashe; George Williamson *The Senecan Amble* (1951) and Aubrey Williams *Pope's "Dunciad"* (1955) also used material from McLuhan's thesis.
3 McLuhan 1987, HMM To Ezra Pound (22 June 1951), 227.
4 Innis, 1951, 82–6. For Innis's general concerns about the commercial-industrial dominance of the university see "Appendix II: Adult Education and Universities"; further observations can be found in his posthumously published notes *The Idea File* (1980), especially Appendix A; for a discussion of Innis and the university, see Theall 1981, 1–13.
5 McLuhan 1987, HMM to Ezra Pound, (22 June 1951), 227.
6 See Appendix A.

APPENDIX A

1 National Archives of Canada, HMM to Robin Strachan (11 August 1970).
2 National Archives of Canada: HMM to McGraw Hill Book Company (August 11, 1970); Mildred Hird to HMM (September 2, 1970); HMM to Mrs.M. Hird (October 2, 1970); Mildred Hird to Robin Strachan (October 8, 1970)
3 For McLuhan's own view that paradox and casuistry affirm art as lie, see *From Cliché to Archetype*, 162 and the section entitled "Casuistry (Art as Lie), 29ff.
4 McLuhan 1987, HMM to Claude Bissell (May 10, 1973), 476.
5 D.C. Williams, review of *The Medium Is the Rear View Mirror: Understanding McLuhan, University of Toronto Quarterly* (Summer 1972): 413.
6 McLuhan 1987, HMM to Walter J. Ong. S.J. (31 May 1953), 238.
7 McLuhan 1987, HMM to Wyndham Lewis (16 October 1953), 240. See an earlier letter to Lewis in which McLuhan had expressed his approval of Kenner (14 July 1953), 238.

APPENDIX B

1 *Explorations* published articles on stress, as well as on self-concepts, particularly in non-literate societies. Today, these subjects might seem far removed from any study of media biases. But 1992 isn't 1952. The Pentagon had just then published a remarkable report on American troops captured in Korea. Many had collaborated. Some had committed treason. The Pentagon charged brainwashing. From this came Dr Ewen Cameron's de/re-programming "research" at Allan Memorial Institute, Montreal; *The Manchurian Candidate*; and much more.

   Explorations explored an alternative explanation. The United States was the first literate nation. In previous wars, its troops were nearly all literate, some highly literate. Literacy, it was argued, promoted inner dialogue, privacy, individualism, independence from environment, and much more. Literate troops rarely collaborated. Bound, gagged, in solitary confinement, they wove civilian clothing, counterfeited money, forged passports, escaped. Robinson Crusoes. Few switched allegiance.

   American troops in Korea were post-literate, with quite a different self-identity. The electronic brainwashing Cameron attempted had already been achieved by electronic media. Now that Dr Cameron's work has been disclosed and discredited, perhaps we can get back to exploring this alternative explanation.

2 Whorf's collected essays appeared posthumously as *Language, Thought, and Reality*, edited by John B. Carroll, 1956. His work is often referred to as the Sapir-Whorf theory. This misleads: Sapir's contribution was minimal. He certainly encouraged and endorsed Whorf and passages about relations between language and thought appear in several of his writings. But he never addressed himself directly to this subject and appears not to have recognized aspectual verbs as timeless.

   Whorf's critics focus entirely on his deterministic view of the relationship between language and culture. His two key essays, on spatial metaphors and Hopi metaphysics, are rarely addressed, perhaps because they ignore determinism. The latter, "Language, Mind and Reality," appeared in *The Theosophist*, Madras. Whorf addressed this audience not as a convert to their philosophy but because he felt they might be better prepared to receive and sympathetically understand the unconventional, mystical formulations which he wished to communicate – because such an audience would be ready to ascend, with him, to a state beyond mind itself in order to look at the world-mind as expressed in the phenomena of language. "Science, the quest for truth," he wrote, "is a sort of divine madness like love."

   Whorf and Sapir died before this subject gained wide interest. Dorothy Lee, however, was alive. Critics who wrote about Whorf's writings ignored hers, perhaps because she might have answered. She was by far the most brilliant scholar I ever knew.

In Canada, the *Canadian Forum* published an essay on Whorf by me (33:387, 1953). That same year, Lister Sinclair did a highly successful radio broadcast on language and culture, principally about Whorf's work, while I did several radio and TV shows on Lee's work.

3 Most of these essays can be found in Dorothy Lee, *Freedom and Culture*, 1959. A posthumous collection, *Valuing the Self*, 1976, contains talks to educational groups. Her last "publication," an interview on dignity ("Are There Universal Values?", *Penney's Forum*, JC Penney Company newsletter, Spring/Summer, 1972) was pure Dorothy: she knew what she wanted to say and to whom she wanted to say it. Many of her early studies on California Indian languages are listed in the bibliography of the *Handbook of North American Indians*, vol. 8, 1978.

4 Although Lee went uncredited, the influence of her study of lineal and non-lineal codifications of reality is easily demonstrated. Prior to 1950, the word "linear" was restricted primarily to the physical sciences and, even there, rarely used. Since then, thanks to McLuhan and his promoters, the word has entered common speech with the meaning Lee first gave it. If this and other ideas had never been promoted by McLuhan, it remains unknown if they would ever have surfaced publicly or what other ideas might have appeared instead. Lee, like other unwilling contributors to "McLuhanism," by choice addressed small audiences. She feared that, when one-way communication replaced human dialogue, the message changed.

5 For example, Innis: "As early as 1831 Lamartine would write: ' *Le livre arrive trop tard; le seul livre possible des aujourd'hui c'est un Journal*'"; McLuhan: "About 1830 Lamartine pointed to the newspaper as the end of book culture: 'The book arrives too late.'"

6 Anyone who opposes power, pays. Jackie's teaching contract wasn't renewed. She stayed on with the Communications Seminar another year, then joined Harvard's faculty. In fairness, I must add that this sort of thing didn't characterize the university as a whole. It was a fine university. But departments varied greatly. Jackie's and mine were at the bottom.

7 Earlier this year, here in New York, a new magazine was planned that would detail stories behind the news: why this news, not that; why this slant, not that. The masthead listed more Pulitzer Prize winners than the entire Ivy League employs. A survey indicated high reader-interest. But of six potential sponsors, five expressed fear of retaliation against their companies. The magazine never went beyond mock-up.

8 Let me illustrate. An encyclopedia editor commissioned me to write an entry on McLuhan. He returned my copy with the request that I credit Marshall with additional contributions, starting with the multi-screen

film. I replied that the multi-screen, with French antecedents, was pioneered by Charles Eames in the 'thirties, transferred to film by Archer Goodwin in the 'fifties, and introduced into Canada by Christopher Chapman in the 'sixties. Marshall commented on the finished product. The editor disagreed, paid me, inserted his additions, and left the entry unsigned.

9   A typical example is the case in hand. In responding to Fulford's article about *Explorations*, I'm forced to comment on Carl Williams' contribution, which was minimal, and to focus almost entirely on Marshall's, which was crucial, but no more so than that of several others. Thus, even when I try to correct this imbalance, a journalist defines the subject. A serious account of *Explorations* would cover different ground.

10 That year (1967), Clifford Solway's CBC-TV film, *Mr. Reagan, Mr. Kennedy*, included a political analyst describing an ideal candidate: wealthy, ambitious, handsome, devoid of any commitment. This ideal (actually real) candidate was hidden in the Bahamas, out of sight, out of sound, until after the election. In the meantime, TV and radio ads filled screen and air. He won in every precinct.

11 Let me correct one minor error. Marchand tells how, during a graphic lecture on Polynesian sex, I called after a coed who was stalking out, "The ship doesn't leave for two days." Alas, it's an old story. When I was a student, it was attibuted to Ernest Hooton of Harvard, but was probably already old then. A better story, perhaps also apocryphal, concerned Hooton's dislike of coeds who knit in class. "Miss X, are you aware that knitting is symbolic masturbation?" To which Miss X is alleged to have replied: "Each in his own way, Professor Hooton."

Bibliography

Adcock, Craig E. 1983. *Marcel Duchamp's Notes from the "Large Glass": An N-Dimensional Analysis*. Ann Arbor: UMI Research Press.

Angeles, Peter. 1981. *Dictionary of Philosophy*. New York: Barnes and Noble.

Aquinas, Saint Thomas. 1259–64. *On the Truth of the Catholic Faith: (Summa Contra Gentiles)*. Trans. Anton C. Pegis (1), James Anderson (2), Vernon J. Bourke (3), Charles J. O'Neil (4). Garden City: Hanover House 1954–56

– 1949. *On Being and Essence*. Trans. Armand Maurer. St. Louis: B. Herder.

– 1945. *Basic Writings of Saint Thomas Aquinas*, Ed., trans. Anton C. Pegis. 2 vols. New York: Random House

Bakhtin, Mikhail. 1929. *Problems of Dostoevsky's Poetics*. Ed., trans. Caryl Emerson. Introduction Wayne C. Booth. Minneapolis: University of Minnesota Press 1994

– 1965. *Rabelais and His World*. Trans. Helene Iswolsky. Cambridge: MIT Press 1968

Barker, Stephen. 1995. "Nietzsche/Derrida, Blanchot/Beckett: Fragmentary Progressions of the Unnamable." *Postmodern Culture* 6, no. 1 (September). *pmc@jefferson.village.virginia.edu*

Bateson, Gregory. 1972. *Steps to an Ecology of Mind*. New York: Ballantine

Baudrillard, Jean. 1976. *Symbolic Exchange and Death*. London: Sage Publications Ltd 1995

– 1983. *Simulations*. Trans. Paul Foss, Paul Patton and Philip Beitchman. New York: Semiotext(e), Inc.

– 1987. *The Ecstasy of Communication*. Trans. Bernard & Caroline Schutze. Ed. Slyvere Lotringer. New York: Semiotext(e) 1988

– 1996. *The Perfect Crime (Crime Parfait, 1995)*. Trans. Chris Turner. New York: Verso

Benda, Julien. 1927. *The Betrayal of the Intellectuals (La trahison des clercs)*. Trans. Richard Aldington. Boston: Beacon Press, 1955

Benjamin, Walter. 1968. *Illuminations*. Ed. Hannah Arendt, trans. Harry Zohn. New York: Harcourt Brace and World.

Benedict, Ruth. 1946. *The Chrysanthemum and the Sword: Patterns of Japanese Culture*. Boston: Houghton Mifflin Co.

Benedikt, Michael, Ed. 1992. *Cyberspace: First Steps*. Cambridge, Mass.: MIT Press

Berman, Morris. 1981. *The Re-enchantment of the World*. Toronto: Bantam Books, 1984

Blake, William. 1927. *Poetry and Prose of William Blake*. Ed. Geoffrey Keynes. London: The Nonesuch Press, 1948

Blavatsky, H.P. 1886. *Isis Unveiled: A Master-Key to the Mysteries of Ancient and Modern Science and Theology*. Vol. 1, Science, vol. 2, Theology. New York: J.W. Bouton

Borges, Jorge Luis. 1964. *Other Inquisitions:1937–1952*. Trans. Ruth R. Sims. New York: Simon and Schuster 1968

Bowen, Zack H. 1975. *Musical Allusions in the Works of James Joyce*. Dublin: Gill and MacMillan

Brand, Stuart. 1987. *The Media Lab*. New York: Viking

Brooks, Cleanth, and W. K. Wimsatt, Jr. 1957. *Literary Criticism: A Short History*. New York: Knopf

Bruckmann, Patricia. 1961. "Fancy's Maze." PhD dissertation, University of Toronto

– 1997. *A Mattter of Correspondence: A Study of the Scriblerus Club*. Montreal: McGill-Queen's University Press

Budgen, Frank. 1948. *James Joyce*. In *James Joyce: Two Decades of Criticism*, Ed. Seon Given. New York: Vanguard Press, Inc.

Carey, James W. 1975. "Canadian Comunication Theory: Extensions and Interpretations of Harold Innis." In *Studies in Canadian Communications*. Eds. G.J. Robinson and D.F. Theall. Montreal: McGill Graduate Program in Communications

– 1981. "McLuhan and Mumford: The Roots of Modern Media Analysis." *Journal of Communication* 31 (Summer): 172–5

– 1989. *Communication as Culture: Essays on Media and Society* Boston: Unwin Myman

Carey, James W. and John J. Quirk. 1988. "The Mythos of the Electronic Revolution." *In James Carey, Communication as Culture: Essays on Media and Society*, 113–41. Boston: Unwin Hyman

Carpenter, Edmund S. 1959. *Eskimo* (sketches and paintings by Frederick Varley; sketches and photographs of Robert Flaherty's collection of Eskimo carvings) (*Explorations* 9). Toronto: University of Toronto Press

– 1973. *Eskimo Realities*. New York: Holt, Rinehart and Winston

- 1972. *Oh, What a Blow that Phantom Gave Me!*. New York: Holt, Rinehart and Winston
- 1986. *Materials for the Study of Social Symbolism in Ancient and Tribal Art*. New York: Rock Foundation
- 1992. "Remembering Explorations." *Canadian Notes and Queries*. 46 (Spring): 3–14
- Ed. 1953. *Explorations: Studies in Culture and Communication*. Number 1 (December)
- 1954. *Explorations: Studies in Culture and Communication*. Explorations Two (April)
- 1954. *Explorations: Studies in Culture and Communication*. Explorations Three (August)
- 1955. *Explorations: Studies in Culture and Communication*. Explorations Four (February)
- 1955. *Explorations: Studies in Culture and Communication*. Explorations Five (June)

Carpenter, Edmund, and Marshall McLuhan. 1957. Eds., *Explorations 8: "Verbi – Voco – Visual"* (October)
- 1960. *Explorations in Communication: An Anthology*. Fourth printing, Boston: Beacon Press 1968

Corbusier, Le [Charles-Édouard]. 1953. *Oeuvre complète 1946–1952*. 7th ed. Zürich: Les Éditions d'Architecture 1976

Crump, M. Marjorie. 1931. *The Epyllion from Theocritus to Ovid*. Oxford: Blackwell

Dasenbrock, Reed Way. 1984. "Vorticism among the Isms." In *Blast 3*. Ed. Seamus Cooney, co-eds. Bradford Morrow, Bernard Latourcade and Hugh Kenner. 40–6 Santa Barbara, Calif.: Black Sparrow Press

Davis, Douglas. 1973. *Art and The Future: A History/Prophecy of the Collaboration between Science, Technology and Art*. New York: Praeger

Deleuze, Gilles. 1964. *Proust and Signs*. Trans. Richard Howard. New York: George Braziller Inc. 1972
- 1969. *The Logic of Sense*. Ed. Constantin V. Boundas, trans. Mark Lester with Charles Stivale. New York: Columbia University Press 1990

Deleuze, Giles, and Félix Guattari. 1972. *Anti-Oedipus: Capitalism and Schizophrenia*. Trans. Robert Hurley et al. New York: Viking Press 1977
- 1980. *A Thousand Plateaus*. Trans. Brian Massumi. Minneapolis: University of Minnesota Press 1987
- 1991. *What Is Philosophy?* Trans. Hugh Tomlinson and Gregory Burchell. New York: Columbia University Press 1994

Derrida, Jacques. 1972. *Margins of Philosophy*. Trans. Alan Bass. Chicago: University of Chicago Press 1982
- 1980. *The Postal Card: From Socrates to Freud and Beyond*. Trans. Alan Bates. Chicago: University of Chicago Press 1987

– 1984. "Two Words for Joyce." In *Post-Structuralist Joyce: Essays from the French*. Ed. Derrik Attridge and Daniel Ferrer. London: Cambridge University Press, 148–59

Deutsh, Karl W. 1952. "On Communication Models in the Social Sciences." *Public Opinion Quarterly* 16, no.3 (Fall): 356–80

Dobbs, Robert. 1992. *Phatic Communion with Bob Dobbs*. Toronto: Perfect Pitch Editions

– 1995. "Bob Dobbs Explains *Finnegans Wake* Via the Ten Thunders." *Flipside* 98 (October/November): 64–74

Downing, Gregory M. 1998. Review of *The Role of Thunder in "Finnegans Wake"* by Eric McLuhan. *James Joyce Quarterly* 35, no. 2–3 (winter and spring): 535–8

Duchamp, Marcel. 1934. *La Mariée mise à par ses célibataires, méme. The Bride Stripped Bare by Her Bachelors, Even: A Typographic Version by Richard Hamilton of Marcel Duchamp's Green Box*. Trans George Heard Hamilton. New York: George Wittenborn, 1960.

Eco, Umberto. 1996. "Afterword." In *The Future of the Book*, ed. Geoffrey Nunberg, 295–306. Berkeley: University of California Press.

Eisenstein, Elizabeth. 1979. *The Printing Press as an Agent of Change*. Cambridge: Cambridge University Press.

Eisenstein, Sergei. 1949. *Film Form*. Ed. and trans. Jay Leda. New York: Meridian 1957

Eliot, T.S. 1932. "Baudelaire." In *Selected Essays 1917–1932*, 335–45. New York: Harcourt, Brace and Company

– 1933. *The Use of Poetry and the Use of Criticism: Studies in the Relation of Criticism to Poetry in England*. London: Faber and Faber

– 1944. *Selected Essays*. London: Faber and Faber

Ellmann, Richard. 1959. *James Joyce*. Oxford: Oxford University Press 1982

Fekete, John. 1977. *The Critical Twilight*. New York: Routledge and Kegan Paul

– 1982. "Massage in the Mass Age: Remembering the McLuhan Matrix." *Canadian Journal of Political and Social Theory* 63 (March): 50–67

Fowlie, Wallace. 1946. *Rimbaud's Illuminations: A Study in Angelism*. New York: New Directions

Frye, Northrop. 1957. *Anatomy of Criticism*. Princeton: Princeton University Press

Genosko, Gary. 1999. *McLuhan and Baudrillard: The Masters of Implosion*. London, New York: Routledge

Gibson, William. 1984. *Neuromancer*. New York: Ace

Giedion, Sigfried. 1948. *Mechanization Takes Command: A Contribution to Anonymous History*. New York: W.W. Norton & Company 1975

Gilbert, Stuart, ed. 1957. *Letters of James Joyce*. New York: The Viking Press

Gilson, Étienne. 1948. *The Christian Philosophy of St. Thomas Aquinas*. Trans. L.K. Shook. London: Gollancz 1957

Gordon, Terrence. 1997. *Marshall McLuhan: Escape into Understanding.* Toronto: Stoddart

Gossage, Howard Luck. 1967. "you can see why the mighty would be curious." In *McLuhan Hot & Cool: A Critical Symposium*, ed. Gerald Emanuel Stearn, 3–14. New York: The Dial Press

Graves, Robert. 1948. *The White Goddess: A Historical Grammar of Poetic Myth*. New York: Creative Age Press

Harrison, Jane Ellen. 1955. *Prolegomena to the Study of Greek Religion*. New York: Meridian Books

Hayman, David. 1956. *Joyce et Mallarmé*. Paris: Lettres moderne

– 1990. *The "Wake" in Transition*. Ithaca: Cornell University Press

Heim, Michael. 1993. *The Metaphysics of Virtual Reality*. Oxford: Oxford University Press

– 1997. *Electric Language: A Philosophical Study of Word Processing*. New Haven: Yale University Press

Henderson, Linda Dalrymple. 1988. *Duchamp in Context: Science and Technology in the "Large Glass" and Related Works*. Princeton: Princeton University Press

Heyer, Paul. 1988. *Communications and History: Theories of Media, Knowledge and Civilization*. New York: Greenwood Press

Hulme, T.E. 1949. *Speculations*. London: Routledge and Kegan Paul

Innis, Harold A. 1950. *Empire and Communications*. Revised by Mary Q. Innis. Forward by Marshall McLuhan. Toronto: University of Toronto Press 1972

– 1951. *The Bias of Communication*. Introd. Marshall McLuhan. Toronto: University of Toronto Press

– 1952. *Changing Concepts of Time*. Toronto: University of Toronto Press

– 1980. *The Idea File*. Ed. William Christian. Toronto: University of Toronto Press

Joyce, James. 1922. *Ulysses: The Corrected Text*. Ed. Hans Walter Gabler et al. Middlesex: Penguin 1986

– 1939. *Finnegans Wake*. New York: Viking 1945

– 1948. *James Joyce: Two Decades of Criticism*. Ed. Sean Givens. New York: Vanguard Press, Inc.

– 1957. *Letters*. Ed. Stuart Gilbert. London: Faber and Faber

– 1966. *Letters*. Vols. 2 and 3. Ed. Richard Ellmann. New York: Viking

Joyce, Michael, and Umberto Eco. 1996. *The Future of the Book*. Berkeley: University of California Press

Joyce, Stanislaus. 1958. *My Brother's Keeper*. Ed. Richard Ellmann. New York: Faber and Faber

Kepes, Gyorgy. 1956. *The New Landscape in Art and Science*. Chicago: P. Theobald

Kristeva, Julia. 1979. *Desire in Language: A Semiotic Approach to Literature and Art*. Ed. Leon S. Roudiez, trans. Thomas Gora et al. New York: Columbia University Press 1980

Kroker, Arthur. 1984. *Technology and the Canadian Mind: Innis/McLuhan/ Grant*. Montréal: New World Perspectives

– 1993. *Spasm: Virtual Reality, Android Music and Electric Flesh*. New York: St Martin's Press

Kroker, Arthur, and Marilouise Kroker. 1996. *Hacking the Future*. Montreal: New World Perspectives

Kroker, Arthur, Marilouise Kroker, and David Cook. 1989. *Panic Encyclopedia: The Definitive Guide to the Postmodern Scene*. Montreal: New World Perspectives

Languirand, Jacques. 1972. *De McLuhan à Pythagore*. Montreal: Ferron Editeur

Lanham, Richard. 1991. *A Handlist of Rhetorical Terms*. Berkeley: University of California Press

Levinson, Paul. 1999. *digital mcluhan: a guide to the information millennium*. New York and London: Routledge

Levy, Gertrude Rachel. 1948. *The Gate of Horn*. London: Faber and Faber

Lewis, Wyndham, ed. 1914. *BLAST 1*. Santa Barbara: Black Sparrow Press 1981

– 1915. *Blast 2: Review of the Great English Vortex*. War Number (July 1915). Santa Barbara: Black Sparrow Press 1981

– 1926. *The Art of Being Ruled*. London: Chatto and Windus

– 1927A. *Time and Western Man*. London: Chatto and Windus

– 1927B. *The Complete Wild Body*. Ed. Bernard Lafourcade. Santa Barbara: Black Sparrow Press 1982

– 1928. *The Childermass* (Book 1 of *The Human Age*). London: John Calder 1965

– 1932. *The Apes of God*. New York: McBride

– 1934. *Men Without Art*. Santa Barbara: Black Sparrow Press 1987

– 1955. *The Human Age*. Book 2: *Monstre Gai*, 3–304. Book 3: *Malign Fiesta*, 305–566. London: Methuen

Lusseyran, Jacques. 1963. *And There Was Light*. Trans. Elizabeth R. Cameron. Boston: Little Brown

Macksey, Richard, and Eugenio Donato. 1970. *The Languages of Criticism and the Sciences of Man*. Baltimore: Johns Hopkins University Press

Mallarmé, Stéphane. 1945. "Le Livre, Instrument Spirituel." In *Oeuvres complétes*, ed. Henri Mondor and G. Jean Aubray, 378–82. Paris: NRF Bibilotheque de la Pleiade

Mander, Jerry. 1977. *Four Arguments for the Elimination of Television*. New York: Quill, 1978

Marchand, Philip. 1989. *Marshall McLuhan: The Medium and the Messenger*. Toronto: Random House

Marinetti, F.T. 1909. "The Foundation and Manifesto of Futurism." *La Figaro* (Paris), 20 February. In *Theories of Modern Art: A Source Book by Artists and Critics*. 1968. Ed. Herschel B. Chipp, 284–9. Los Angeles: University of California Press

McLuhan, Eric. 1997. *The Role of Thunder in Finnegans Wake*. Toronto: University of Toronto Press

McLuhan, Eric, and Frank Zingrone, eds. 1995. *Essential McLuhan*. Don Mills, Ont: House of Anansi

McLuhan, Eric, and Jacek Szklarek, eds. 1999. *The Medium and the Light: Reflections on Religion*. Toronto: Stoddart

McLuhan, Marshall. 1943. "The Place of Thomas Nash in the Learning of His Time." Ph.D. dissertation, Cambridge University

– 1948. Introduction to *Paradox in Chesterton* by Hugh Kenner. New York: Sheed & Ward

– 1951. *The Mechanical Bride: Folklore of Industrial Man*. Boston: Beacon Press 1967

– 1953. "James Joyce: Trivial and Quadrivial." *Thought* (Spring): 75–98. Reprinted in *The Interior Landscape: The Literary Criticism of Marshall McLuhan: 1943–1962*, ed. Eugene McNamara, 23–47. New York: McGraw-Hill, in association with the University of Windsor Press 1969

– 1953B. "Wyndham Lewis: His Theory of Art and Communication." *Shenandoah*. 4 (Summer–Autumn): 77–88

– 1953C. "The Later Innis." *Queen's Quarterly* 60, no. 3 (Autumn): 385–94

– 1954A. "Catholic Humanism and Modern Letters." In *Christian Humanism in Letters: The McAuley Lectures*, (series 2). West Hartford, Ct.: St. Joseph's College

– 1954B. *Counterblast 1954*. Ed. Edmund Capenter. Toronto: privately printed

– 1956. *Alfred Lord Tennyson: Selected Poetry*. Ed. Herbert Marshall McLuhan. New York: Holt, Rinehart and Winston 1966

– 1960. *Report on Project in Understanding New Media*. Prepared and published by the National Association of Educational Broadcasters, pursuant to a contract with the Office of Education, United States Depatment of Health, Education and Welfare

– 1962A. *The Gutenberg Galaxy*. Toronto: University of Toronto Press

– 1962B. "Joyce, Aquinas and the Poetic Process." In *Joyce's "Portrait": Criticisms and Critiques*, ed. Thomas E. Connolly, 249–56. New York: Appleton-Century-Crofts/Meredith Publishing Company

– 1964A. *Understanding Media: The Extensions of Man*. New York: McGraw-Hill

– 1964B. Introduction. In Harold Innis, *The Bias of Communication*, vii–xvi

– 1967. *McLuhan Hot & Cool: A Critical Symposium*. Ed. Gerald Stearn. New York: Dial Press

– 1969A. *The Interior Landscape: The Literary Criticism of Marshall*

McLuhan: 1943–1962. Ed. by Eugene McNamara. New York: McGraw-Hill in association with the University of Windsor Press

– 1969B. Interview by Eric Norden. "Marshall McLuhan: A Candid Conversation with the High Priest of Popcult and Metaphysician of the Media." *Playboy* (March 1969): 26–7, 45, 55–6, 61, 63. Reprinted in *Canadian Journal of Communication* 14, no. 4–5 (Special Issue, December 1989): 101–37

– 1969C. *Counterblast*. Toronto: McClelland and Stewart Limited

– 1969D. "Wyndham Lewis: His Theory of Art and Communication." In *The Interior Landscape: The Literary Criticism of Marshall McLuhan*, ed. Eugene McNamara, 83–94. New York: McGraw-Hill

– 1970. *Culture Is Our Business*. New York: McGraw-Hill

– 1971. "Interview with A.F. Knowles." Video tape. Toronto: York University Instructional Technology Centre

– 1978. "Interview with Louis Forsdale (17 July)." On the CD-ROM, *Understanding McLuhan*.

– 1987. *The Letters of Marshall McLuhan*. Ed. Matie Molinaro et al. Toronto: Oxford University Press

– 1991. "Francis Bacon's Patristic Inheritance." *McLuhan Studies: Explorations in Culture and Communication* 1:7–25

– 1994. *McLuhan: The Medium Is the Message*. CD-ROM. Produced by Nelson Thall and David Newfeld. Toronto: Time Again Productions

– Understanding McLuhan. 1996. CD-ROM. Southam Interactive Voyager

– 1997. *Marshall McLuhan Essays: Media Research Technology, Art, Communication*. Ed. Michel A. Moos. Amsterdam: Overseas Publishers Association

McLuhan, Marshall et al. 1967. *Verbi-Voco-Visual Explorations*. New York: Something Else Press, Inc.

McLuhan, Marshall, and Quentin Fiore. 1967. *The Medium Is the Massage*. Coordinated by Jerome Agel. New York: Random House

McLuhan, Marshall, and Quentin Fiore. 1968A. *War and Peace in the Global Village*. Coordinated by Jerome Agel. New York: Bantam Books

McLuhan, Marshall, and Harley Parker. 1968B. *Through the Vanishing Point: Space in Poetry and Painting*. New York: Harper & Row

McLuhan, Marshall, and Wilfred Watson. 1970. *From Cliché to Archetype*. New York: Viking Press

McLuhan, Marshall, and Barrington Nevitt. 1972. *Take Today: The Executive as Dropout*. Don Mills, Ontario: Longman Canada

McLuhan, Marshall, and Eric McLuhan. 1988. *Laws of Media: The New Science*. Toronto: University of Toronto Press

McLuhan, Marshall, and Bruce R. Powers. 1989. *The Global Village: Transformations in World Life and Media in the 21st Century*. New York: Oxford

Moholy-Nagy, Lazlo. 1947. *Vision in Motion*. New York: Paul Theobold

Muller-Thym, Bernard Joseph. 1939. *The Establishment of the University of Being in the Doctrine of Meister Eckhart Hochheim*. New York: Sheed and Ward for the Institute of Mediaeval Studies

Mumford, Lewis. 1922. *The Story of Utopias*. New York: Boni and Liveright

– 1926. *The Golden Day: A Study in American Experience and Culture*. New York: Liveright

– 1934. *Technics and Civilization*. New York: Harcourt, Brace

– 1952. *Art and Technics*. New York: Columbia University Press

– 1961. *The City in History: Its Origins, Its Transformations, and Its Prospects*. New York: Harcourt, Brace and World

– 1967. *The Myth of the Machine*, vol. 1, *Technics and Human Development*. New York: Harcourt Brace Jovanovich

– 1970. *The Myth of the Machine*, vol. 2, *The Pentagon of Power*. New York: Harcourt Brace Jovanovich

Nairn, Tom. 1968. "mcluhanism: the myth of our time." In *McLuhan Pro & Con*. Ed. Raymond Rosenthal, 140–52. Baltimore: Pelican 1969

Nietzsche, Friedrich. 1968. *The Will to Power*. Ed. Walter Kaufmann trans. Walter Kaufmann and R.J. Hollingdale. New York: Vintage Books

O'Donnell, James J. 1996. "The Pragmatics of the New: Trithemius, McLuhan, Cassiodorus." In *The Future of the Book*. ed. Geoffrey Nunberg, 37–62. Berkeley: University of California Press

Ogden, C.K. and I.A. Richards. 1923. *The Meaning of Meaning*. New York: Harcourt, Brace and Company 1947

Ong, Walter. 1982. *Orality and Literacy: The Technologizing of the Word*. London: Methuen

Ozenfant [Amédée]. 1931. *Foundations of Modern Art,* trans. John Rodker. New York: Dover

Panofsky, Erwin and Otto von Simsky. 1963. *Gothic Architecture and Scholasticism*. Cleveland: World Publishing

Papanek, Victor. 1957. "A Bridge in Time." *Explorations 8: Verbi-Voco-Visual*. 1–10

Patterson, Graeme. 1990. *History and Communications: Harold Innis, Marshall McLuhan, the Interpretation of History*. Toronto: University of Toronto Press

Phillipson, Michael. 1989. *In Modernity's Wake: The Ameurunculus Letters*. London: Routledge

Poe, Edgar Allan. 1841. "A Descent into the Maelstrom." *The Works of Edgar Allan Poe*, 3:141–62. New York: Standard Book Company, Ltd. 1933

Pope, Alexander. 1963. *The Poems of Alexander Pope*. Ed. John Butt. London: Methuen

Pound, Ezra. [1934] *The ABC of Reading*. Norfolk, Conn.: New Directions

Powe, Bruce. 1984. "The Hunter, Laughter and the Surgical Blade." In *Blast 3*, 115–6. Santa Barbara: Black Sparrow Press

Reusch, Karl, and Gregory Bateson. 1951. *Communication: The Social Matrix of Psychiatry*. New York: W.W. Norton

Rice, Thomas. 1997. *Joyce, Chaos and Complexity*. Urbana: University of Illinois Press

Rockman, Arnold. 1968. "McLuhanism:The Natural History of an Intellectual Fashion." *Encounter* 31:28–36

Rucker, Rudy et al., eds. 1992. *Mondo 2000 User's Guide to the New Edge*. New York: Harper Collins

Saussure, Ferdinand de. 1907. *Cours de linguistique générale. Course in general linguistics*. Ed. Charles Bally and Albert Sechehaye in collaboration with Albert Riedlinger, trans. Wade Baskin. New York: Philosophical Library 1959

Schuster, Carl, and Edmund Carpenter. 1996. *Patterns That Connect*. New York: Abrams

Seldes, Gilbert. 1924. *The Seven Lively Arts*. New York: The Sagamore Press 1957

Shannon, C.E., and W. Weaver. 1949. *The Mathematical Theory of Communication*. Urbana: University of Illinois Press; published earlier in *Bell System Technical Journal* 27 (1948) 379–623.

Sidney, Sir Philip. 1595. *An Apologia for Poetrie*. In *Elizabethan Critical Essays*, vol. 1, ed. G. Gregory Smith, 1904, 148–207. London: Oxford University Press 1939

Silberer, Herbert. 1917. *Hidden Symbolism of Alchemy and the Occult Arts*. (originally *Problems of Mysticism and Its Symbolism*). New York: Dover Publications 1971

Stearn, Gerald, ed. 1967. *McLuhan Hot and Cool*. New York: Dial Press

Theall, Donald. 1954. "Here Comes Everybody." *Explorations* 2 (April): 66–77

– 1961. "Pope's Satiric Program: The War with the Dunces." Canadian Association of University Teachers of English (CAUT), 11–16

– 1969. *A Report on Multi-Media and Environmental Exhibits at Expo '67*, National Film Board of Canada for the Departments of Trade and Commerce, Industry, and the CMHA. National Archives of Canada

– 1971. *The Medium Is the Rear View Mirror: Understanding McLuhan*. Montreal: McGill-Queens University Press

– 1981. "Communication and Knowledge in Canadian Communication Theory." *Canadian Journal of Communication* 8, no. 1 (Summer): 1–13

– 1986. "McLuhan, Telematics and the Toronto School of Communication." *Canadian Journal of Political and Social Theory* 10, no. 1–2: 79–88

– 1988. "James Joyce – Literary Engineer." *Literature and Ethics: Essays Presented to A.E. Malloch*, ed. Gary Wihl and David Williams, 111–26. Montreal: McGill-Queen's University Press

– 1989. (with Joan B. Theall) "Marshall McLuhan and James Joyce: Beyond Media." *Canadian Journal of Communication* 14, no. 4–5: 46–66

- 1992. "Beyond the Orality/Literary Dichotomy: James Joyce and the Pre-History of Cyberspace." *Postmodern Culture*. (An electronic journal of interdisciplinary criticism, available at Trent University: http://www.trentu.ca/jjoyce and Johns Hopkins University: http://muse.jhu.edu/journals/postmodern_Culture/v002/2.3theall.html

- 1995. *Beyond the Word: Reconstructing Sense in the Joyce Era of Technology, Culture, and Communication*. Toronto: University of Toronto Press

- 1997. *James Joyce's Techno-Poetics*. Toronto: University of Toronto Press

Tofts, Darren. 1997. "Fuzzy Culture." Article/Review of *Beyond the Word* by Donald F. Theall, based on E-Mail interview about the book with the author. 21*C (Scanning the Future) 25, 32–6

Tofts, Darren, and Murray McKeich. 1998. *Memory Trade: A Prehistory of Cyberculture*. North Ryde, NSW: 21*C/Interface

Valéry, Paul. 1977. "Introduction to the Method of Leonardo da Vinci." In *Paul Valéry An Anthology*, ed. James R. Lawler, 33–93. Princeton: Princeton University Press

Vico, Giambattista. 1744. *The New science of Giambatista Vico*. Trans. from the third edition by Thomas Goddard Bergin and Max Harold Fisch. Ithaca, New York: 1948

Voegelein, Eric. 1952. *The New Science of Politics: An Introduction*. Chicago: University of Chicago Press

Waite, Arthur Edward. 1911. *The Secret Tradition in Freemasonry*. New York: Rebman

Warburton, William. 1765–66. *The Divine Legation of Moses demonstrated, in nine books*. London: A. Millar and J and R. Tonson

Wees, William. 1972. *Vorticism and the English Avant-Garde*. Toronto: University of Toronto Press

- 1984. *Wyndham Lewis and Vorticism*. In *Blast 3*, ed. Seamuss Cooney et al., 47–50. Santa Barbara, Calif.: Black Sparrow Press

Weir, Lorraine. 1989. *Writing Joyce: A Semiotics of the Joyce System*. Indianapolis: Indiana University Press

Wells, H.G. 1919. *The Outline of History, Being a Plain History of Life and Mankind*. London: Newnes

Wiener, Norbert. 1948. *Cybernetics: Or Control and Communication in the Animal and the Machine*. Cambridge, Mass.: MIT Press 1961

- 1950. *The Human Use of Human Beings: Cybernetics and Society*. Boston: Houghton Mifflin Company

Williams, Aubrey. 1955. *Pope's "Dunciad"*. London: Methuen

Williams, D. Carlton. 1955. "Acoustic Space." *Explorations* 4 (February): 15–20

Williams, Raymond. 1967 "Paradoxically, if the book works it to some extent annihilates itself." In McLuhan 1967, 186–93. Originally published 1964 as "A Structure of Insights," *University of Toronto Quarterly* (April).

Williamson, George. 1951. *The Senecan Amble: A Study in Prose Form from Bacon to Collier.* London: Faber and Faber

Wilmott, Greg. 1996. *McLuhan or Modernism in Reverse.* Toronto: University of Toronto Press

Wilson, Robert Anton. 1979. *Schrödinger's Cat Trilogy.* New York: Dell Publishing, 1988

– 1981. *Masks of the Illuminati.* New York: Dell Publishing

– 1994. *Coincidance: A Head Test.* Santa Monica: New Falcon Publication

Wimsatt, William K. 1965. *Hateful Contraries: Studies in Literature and criticism.* Lexington: University of Kentucky Press

Wolfe, Tom. 1969. "What If He Is Right?." In Wolfe, *The Pump House Gang,* 105–33. New York: Bantam

Yates, Frances Amelia. 1964. *Giordano Bruno and the Hermetic Tradition.* Chicago: University of Chicago Press 1982

– 1966. *The Art of Memory.* Chicago: University of Chicago Press 1974

– 1969. *Theater of the World.* Chicago: University of Chicago Press

– 1979. *The Occult Philosophy in the Elizabethan Age.* London: Routledge and Kegan Paul 1983

– 1972. *The Rosicrucian Enlightenment.* London: Routledge and Kegan Paul 1986

Youngblood, Gene. 1970. *Expanded Cinema.* New York: E.P. Dutton & Co.

Zingrone, Frank. 1991. "Laws of Media: The Pentad and Technical Syncretism." *McLuhan Studies* 1, 109–16

Index